MERCANTILIST THEORY AND PRACTICE:
THE HISTORY OF BRITISH MERCANTILISM

MERCANTILIST THEORY AND PRACTICE:

THE HISTORY OF BRITISH MERCANTILISM

Editor
Lars Magnusson

Volume 3
The Colonial System

LONDON AND NEW YORK

First published 2008 by Pickering & Chatto (Publishers) Limited

Published 2016 by Routledge
2 Park Square, Milton Park, Abingdon, Oxon OX14 4RN
711 Third Avenue, New York, NY 10017, USA

Routledge is an imprint of the Taylor & Francis Group, an informa business

BRITISH LIBRARY CATALOGUING IN PUBLICATION DATA

Mercantilist theory and practice: the history of British mercantilism
1. Mercantile system – Great Britain – History – 17th century – Sources 2. Mercantile system – Great Britain – History – 18th century – Sources I. Magnusson,
Lars, 1952–
330.1'513'0941

ISBN-13: 978-1-85196-927-2 (set)

Typeset by Pickering & Chatto (Publishers) Limited

CONTENTS

INTRODUCTION

The judgement over what late nineteenth-century observers in Britain called the 'old colonial system' seems forever to be connected with the devastating blow Adam Smith delivered against it in the *Wealth of Nations:* 'To prohibit a great people ... from making all that they can of every part of their own produce, or from employing their stock and industry in the way that they judge most advantageous to themselves, is a manifest violation of the most sacred rights of mankind'.[1] However, Smith's condemnation was not only targeted against the 'slavery' imposed upon the subdued colonists. He also believed that empire was negative for the economic prosperity of the mother country. Hence monopoly had for Britain led to an unnatural and dangerous concentration of capital in the colonial trades, while a more happy order would have been to invest money more widely which would have led to the creation of even more wealth. The only people who according to Smith had profited and had reaped high monopoly profits were the great merchants. Adam Smith was of course not alone at this time in regarding colonies as mostly a burden to their mother country. Josiah Tucker, Dean of Gloucester and economic writer, was another public figure who already in the 1760s had aired the opinion that the costs of empire by far outweighed the benefits.[2]

However, modern scholars are not so sure. A discussion for and against the advantages of colonialism for the mother country in pecuniary terms has gone on for quite some time now and there are no clear-cut answers to be drawn. As we saw, Adam Smith was of the opinion that some interest groups had a vested concern in colonialism, while the ordinary citizen who paid taxes and invested his 'blood and treasure' in the project was on the losing side.[3] Many modern British

---

1   A. Smith, *An Inquiry into the Nature and Causes of the Wealth of Nations* (Oxford: Oxford University Press, 1976), Book IV, ch. vii, p. 583.

2   For a presentation of Tucker's views on colonies, see for example B. Semmel, *The Rise of Free Trade Imperialism. Classical Political Economy, the Empire of Free Trade and Imperialism 1750–1850* (Cambridge: Cambridge University Press, 1970), p. 20.

3   Smith, *Wealth of Nations*, p. 613.

economic historians have basically tended to agree with this analysis.[4] However, to calculate what the taxpayers might have lost and other groups gained is no easy matter. It is even more difficult to calculate the human costs in terms of lives lost in colonial wars, like the American War of Independence, which was stirring up public controversy at the time when Smith published his great book. Recently, however, a group of revisionist economic historians writing what they call 'world history' have argued that the issue of costs and benefits of empire must be looked into from a much broader perspective. Scholars such as Kenneth Pomeranz and others emphasize the important role that Asia, America and Africa played in the 'European miracle' of growth and industrialization from the middle of the eighteenth century and hence for the emergence of Britain as 'the workshop of the world'.[5] Industrialization was not merely an internal affair but had its origin in trade and capital flows which very much favoured Europe, they argue.

However, in this short introduction to seventeenth- and eighteenth-century British texts on colonies and plantations it is not necessary to involve ourselves in this discussion We have to remember that we are still situated at very beginning – in the cradle – of what later on would become the British empire. The colonial possessions we are dealing with at this time merely concern the Americas; the Caribbean islands and the present-day east coast of the United States. For contemporaries in the seventeenth and eighteenth centuries these possessions were commonly known as 'plantations'. Unfortunately the strong moral and political feelings which the colonial system has stirred up since the days of Adam Smith have meant that what contemporaries might have thought about the plantations during these early days has mostly been lost. By 1776 the East India Company was gradually taking over in India and it was even easier than before to see the connection between the private interest of merchants and the expansion of empire. Moreover, in North America a war of independence was just starting up. Adam Smith's greatest worry was over the negative political repercussions that the 'unnatural' dependence upon the colonies would bring. This was even more problematic than the economic pitfalls, he argues. Not only were revolts like the upcoming one in North America to be expected in the future, but as a consequence of the quest for colonies Britain would be also become more involved in wars with her European neighbours. Hence colonialism threatened '... to bring on the most dangerous disorders upon the whole body politick'.[6]

However, a hundred years earlier the historical context was very different. In fact, nobody at that time really raised their voice against colonies on moral

---

4   P. O'Brien, 'European Economic Development: the Contribution of the Periphery', *Economic History Review*, 2nd series, 35:1 (1982), pp. 1–18.

5   K. Pomeranz, *The Great Divergence. China, Europe and the Making of the Modern World Economy* (Princeton, NJ: Princeton University Press, 2000).

6   Smith, *Wealth of Nations*, p. 605.

grounds in the way that Smith, David Hume, Josiah Tucker and many others would do later. No one seems to have been seriously worried over the 'sacred rights' threatened by the establishment of the plantations. However, from this it is all too easy to draw the conclusion that people during the period before the middle of the eighteenth century were infested with 'materialist' presuppositions or indeed indifferent to the plight of the poor. Certainly this is the period before the rise of Scottish Enlightenment, and the more radical conclusions of John Locke's views on property were still to be drawn. However, in order to better understand an earlier generation's viewpoints on colonies and plantations we must acknowledge the context of their standpoints. By those living before the middle of the eighteenth century it was often taken for granted that the colonists were 'of them'; '... they were born with us', as Joshua Gee formulated it in 1729.[7] Basically they were regarded as subjects of their native country or, as the Bristol merchant and writer John Cary stated in 1719: 'I take this kingdom and all its plantations to be one great body'.[8] By transportation to the plantations, lower-class people of different sorts (even criminals and rouges) could find employment and were in fact given a chance to improve their lot. According to Josiah Child in 1693 those transported to New England were mainly Puritans or members of other religious sects, while Virginia and Barbados were inhabited by former vagrants and discharged soldiers.[9] These were people who would have found it difficult to find employment at home. Both sides were in fact winners in this game: England, which sent away people unable to support themselves, and the colonists, who were given a chance to carve out a new life in the territories.

* * *

Samuel Fortrey's outline, in the anti-French tract *England's Interest and Improvement* from 1673, of the British 'old' colonial system is one of the first of its kind:

> I conceive, no forein Plantation should be undertaken, or prosecuted, but in such countreys that may increase the wealth and trade of this nation, either in furnishing us, with what we are otherwise forced to purchase from strangers, or else by increasing such commodities, as are vendible abroad; which may both increase our shipping, and profitably employ our people; but otherwise, it is always carefully to be avoided, especially where the charge is greater than the profit, for we want not already a countrey sufficient to double our people, were they rightly employed; and a Prince is more

---

7   J. Gee, *The Trade and Navigation of Great Britain Considered* (1729), in L. Magnusson (ed.), *Mercantilism*, Critical Concepts in the History of Economics, 4 vols (London: Routledge, 1995), vol. 4, p. 94.

8   Quoted in E. Lipson, *The Economic History of England*, 3 vols (London: A. & C. Black, 1929–34), vol. 3, p. 155.

9   J. Child, *A New Discourse of Trade* (1693), in Magnusson (ed.), *Mercantilism*, vol. 3, pp. 106–7.

powerful that hath his strength and force united, than he that is weakly scattered in many places.[10]

According to contemporary observers the plantations could bring three kinds of services to the motherland. First, the colony could provide the mother country with all sorts of necessities and luxuries. Moreover, English consumers would have the exclusive right to what could be grown or otherwise procured in the plantations. Imports from the plantations could consist of raw materials to be worked up in English factories. Malachy Postlethwayt in 1757 was referring to such imports when he wrote: 'Whatever materials our capital manufactures we shall not be capable of raising among ourselves, we may easily do by wise encouragement in our plantations'.[11] Joshua Gee also referred to these imports in his widely-read treatise on British trade from 1729. Hence, for example, exports from the sugar plantations (e.g. Barbados and Jamaica) to England would consist of sugar and ginger and hopefully in the future also cinnamon, cloves, mace and coffee – important consumer items which England had to buy with precious money from Asia by way of Holland. Moreover, transportation from the tobacco plantations in Virginia would consist of tobacco, which could be partly resold to other countries (according to Gee such re-exportation was in general terms especially gainful and the 'surest way of enriching this Kingdom'). From Carolina – a province which 'lies in as happy a Climate as any in the World' – rice, olives, silk, indigo and many other items would be sent into England. Gee also looks ahead to a future when Carolina will provide England with hemp and flax and also raw iron.[12] The colonies in North America (Pennsylvania, New Jersey and New York) were more problematic, he thought, not being so generously equipped by nature, but they could nevertheless be a source for much-needed supplies in England such as masts, timber and tar, etc. The main problem was New England – which Josiah Child thirty years later called the 'most prejudicial Plantation in this Kingdom'. New England was, according to Child, inhabited by a more independent people '... whose Frugality, Industry and Temperance, and the happiness of whose Laws and Institutions do promise themselves long Life, with a wonderful encrease of People, Riches and Power'. However, they were sometimes apt not strictly to follow the 'Laws of this Kingdom' and they even sometimes violated the Navigation Acts through assuming 'liberty of Trading'.[13] From the point of view of the motherland the problem with New England was – according to both Child and Gee – that it really had little to offer for

10   S. Fortrey, *England's Interest and Improvement* (1673), in Magnusson (ed.), *Mercantilism*, vol. 1, p. 297.

11   M. Postlethwayt, *Britain's Commercial Interest Explained and Improved*, 2 vols (1757; New York: Augustus M. Kelley, 1968), vol. 1, p. 177

12   Gee, *The Trade and Navigation of Great Britain Considered*, p. 28.

13   Child, *A New Discourse of Trade*, pp. 122–3.

export in terms of raw materials or other 'useful' goods. In a longer perspective its inhabitants were rather to be regarded as competitors to their mother country, they believed. Not only had they already to some extent begun to establish their own manufactures in order to provide themselves with worked-up wares, but there was also the fear that they would start to sell them to their neighbours in nearby plantations, as well as to the Spanish, French and Dutch colonies. In 1757 Postlethwayt still echoed this old worry: 'The British northern plantations would also enjoy a share in the supply, not only in our own island colonies, but occasionally of foreign countries; but that should be done upon the principles of national policy, which we have before urged, in relation to the strict subserviency of colonies to their parent state'.[14]

Second, and accordingly to the Navigation Acts, the wares of the plantations were only to be transported by English vessels and must not be sold directly to foreign merchants. Such commodities were called at the time 'enumerated', and foreigners could only buy them through English ports. Much of the eighteenth-century critique against the colonial system in principle pointed to this legislation, which in effect meant that consumers from, for example, the Spanish colonies could not buy the tobacco, rice or sugar they needed directly from the British plantations in the New World. This system might have been highly profitable for some monopolizing English merchants, but it had obviously a harmful overall effect on the demand for those products. It also led to a lot of illicit trading and smuggling – practices scorned at the time but which everybody agreed were almost impossible to root out.

Third, the role of the plantations as markets for English manufactures is emphasized in contemporary texts. For example Gee recommends that 'all sorts of Cloathing, both Linnen, Silks and Woollen, wrought Iron, Brass, Copper and all sorts of Houshold Furniture' as well as food should be shipped to the British sugar plantations. Items to be shipped to the tobacco plantations should include '... almost every Thing else that may be called the Manufacture of England'.[15] Hence it was supposed that demand for manufactured products from the colonies would lead to an increase of manufactures in England and therefore to more English workers being usefully employed.[16] The colonies must be fed, clothed and housed – and who should provide for this if not English industries and handicrafts?

In much of the literature Ireland is looked upon as any other colony – its role should be to serve the parent country. However, as with New England, Ireland was seen as a potential future competitor. Josiah Child for instance felt that Irish marketing of wool, meat and corn could be pernicious to English interests,

---

14 Postlethwayt, *Britain's Commercial Interest Explained*, p. 169.
15 Gee, *The Trade and Navigation of Great Britain Considered*, p. 28.
16 Ibid., p. 49.

especially as such goods could be sold 'at cheaper rates than we can afford to the beating us out if those trades'.[17] However, opinion was divided. Many saw the advantage of wools in particular being imported to England from Ireland. Hence within a 'colonial system' it was perceived by many observers that wool sent to England in order to be worked up in the English wool industry would be extremely beneficial. Hence, as the economic historian Ephraim Lipson showed so many years ago, it was policy to prohibit imports from Ireland of cattle and corn while the wool 'export' was encouraged. Consequently, in 1699, the sale of worked-up wool manufactures from Ireland was strictly forbidden in England – and this regulation stayed in place until 1780.[18]

* * *

We have so far outlined the properties of the so-called 'old colonial system'. However, to what extent is it a more modern construction – and can we really speak about a coherent 'system'? As we saw, the question of whether there was a coherent 'mercantile system' stirred up a lot of controversy and scholarly debate during the last century. Could the same argument be used also in this context?

With regard to views explicated by leading writers taking part in the debates on foreign trade during the latter half of the seventeenth and first half of the eighteenth century, it is hard to draw any other conclusion than that we can identify a number of system-like properties. In this sense the colonial system was by no means a mere straw man constructed by Adam Smith and other enlightened thinkers in the latter half of the eighteenth century. The authors we have referred to above – and many others – took part in a discussion on whether and to what extent colonization was a good idea or not. Some of them took a rather sceptical position on this issue; for example Child often argued for a 'freer' trade (the seventeenth century often talked about 'free' trade, but this usually meant the abolishment of the exclusive monopolies of powerful trading companies, such as the Merchant Adventurers). Child's digressions on plantations are set out in a defensive tone. He defends colonization in some cases but is reluctant to do so in regard to others. Like most others at this time, he argued that the system of plantations must above all be systematically planned in order to bring benefits to the mother country. Already in the 1690s as we saw he predicted serious problems in the future with regard to the New England plantation. It is perhaps unnecessary to remind ourselves here that his worst nightmares came true some seventy years later.

However, to draw the conclusion from this – as many historians have done – that there exists a direct causal connection between the ideas of leading writers

---

17 Child, *A New Discourse of Trade*, p. 74; see also Lipson, *The Economic History of England*, vol. 3, p. 197.

18 Ibid., vol. 3, pp. 197–8.

and a fully-fledged 'system' of economic policy and action is to go too far. It is true of course that many statutes which were proposed by king and parliament during this period seem to fit neatly into such a 'system', including the Navigation Acts. However, there are at least three problems with over-emphasizing the system-like character of such policies. First, we have the difficult question of implementation. Regardless of constitutional form (absolute monarchy, republic, restoration and indeed the inauguration of constitutional rule from 1690), the seventeenth- and eighteenth-century British state was not a strong and effective state in a modern sense. Hence many of the regulations issued were not implemented properly and must be described as paper tigers which nobody really cared much about. We have already spoken of the prevalence of illicit trading which stirred up public controversy during this period. Also we have mentioned the problems which the Crown had with some of its plantations, especially in hindering colonists from selling their raw materials directly to European or neighbouring customers (like sugar from Jamaica) or its manufactured or semi-manufactured wares (New England in particular) to its neighbours within or outside the British colonies.[19]

Second, with regard to its trade and colonial policies Britain was often pursuing 'divergent and incompatible aims', as one interpreter has formulated it.[20] In general it has been pointed out that it was not unusual for different state bodies – or in fact sometimes even the same decision-making body – to pursue bits and pieces of policies that were in direct conflict with each other. As described in detail by R. W. K. Hinton and other economic historians, lucrative incomes from export and import duties were given a higher priority than the protection of industry. Hence it was the power balance between different private interests which in the end decided which kinds of duties and other regulations were introduced. Perhaps this should not surprise us after all that has been written about 'old corruption' and rent-seeking during this epoch in British political and economic history.[21]

Third, even it is possible at least to speak about some system-like features with regard to colonial policies during this period, we are certainly not obliged to draw the conclusion – which often is done – that it was founded upon some kind of well-developed doctrine of mercantilism with the favourable balance of trade as its theoretical core. The 'old colonial systems' plea for overseas supplies and markets on a monopolistic basis did not in fact need such a 'doctrine' to underpin it. Rather, the ideological foundation for a plantation system appeared

19 See R. W. K. Hinton, *The Eastland Trade and the Common Weal in the Seventeenth Century* (Cambridge: Cambridge University Press, 1959), pp. 90–1; and C. Wilson, *England's Apprenticeship, 1603–1763* (London: Longman, 1984), pp. 61–2, 172–3.

20 Lipson, *The Economic History of England*, vol. 3, p. 177.

21 See for example D. A. Walker, 'Virginia Tobacco Suring the Reign of the Early Stuarts: A Case Study of Mercantilist Theories, Practice and Results', in L. Magnusson (ed.), *Mercantilist Economics* (Boston, MA: Kluwer, 1993), pp. 143–71.

to a large extent after that, when a more simplistic version of the favourable balance of trade had already been abandoned by most economic writers and replaced by what has been described as 'theory of foreign-paid incomes' or 'labour balance' of trade.[22] The role of colonies was not in the first place to ensure that Britain would have a net surplus of monies rolling in. It was rather to guarantee that Britain on balance bought fewer worked-up products than it sold. It was this value-added that would provide employment for the poor and increase the wealth of the nation. Most of this 'old colonial system' did not disappear even after mercantilist theories had fallen out of fashion as a consequence of the onslaught of Hume, Tucker and Smith. After all, the Navigation system was only abolished in 1846 and much of the other regulative ordinances serving to provide Britain with a colonial outlet for goods and as a provider of necessities for manufactures as well as exotic goods for consumers were only gradually dismantled.

---

22   See the Introduction to Volume 1 in the present collection, pp. xxxvi–xxxvii.

[RICHARD EBURNE], A PLAINE PATH-WAY TO PLANTATIONS

[Richard Eburne], *A Plaine Path-Way to Plantations: that is, A Discourse in Generall, Concerning the Plantation of our English People in Other Countries* (London: G. P., 1624), extract, pp. 1–39. British Library, shelfmark 1483.d.8.

Richard Eburne (d. 1624) was a sermonist and writer. According to Robert Watt, Eburne also published *A Twofold Tribute of Subjects to their King and Christians to their God; in Two Sermons* (London, 1613) and *Royal Law of Equity, or a Treatise on Matt.vii.12* (London, 1616),[1] but no further details are available.

The dialogue was a popular literary style during the sixteenth and early seventeenth centuries, and was also used when economic and political topics were discussed. The essay reprinted here starts with a plea for the colonization of America dressed up in thoroughly religious and moralistic language. We have an obligation to God to colonize America, the author argues. He goes on to argue that plantations will benefit the English Crown on more 'economical' grounds. This extract covers pp. 1–39 of the original text, comprising the whole first part. Excluded are the second and third parts, which are set up as a dialogue between a farmer and a merchant, continuing the discussion on how best to establish plantations which started in the section reprinted here.

---

1   R. Watt, *Bibliotheca Britannica: or, A General Index to British and Foreign Literature*, 4 vols (Edinburgh and London: A. Constable and Company, 1824), vol. 2, p. 328b.

[RICHARD EBURNE] A PLAINE PATHWAY TO PLANTATIONS

A PLAINE
PATH-WAY
TO PLANTA-
TIONS.

The firſt Part.

The Speakers be {Reſpire, a Farmer
{Enrubie, a Merchant.

Reſpire.

 Am very glad to ſee you in health (good Maſter Enrubie) and hearing of your comming home,
I am come to ſee you, and to ſalute you.

Enrubie. I thanke you heartily for it, Neighbour *Reſpire* and am glad to ſee you and the
reſt of my good Neighbours and friends here,
to be alſo in good health I pray you ſit downe by me in this
Harbour

Reſp That I would doe willingly, but that I doubt I ſhall be trou-
bleſome to you for I ſee you are buſie in reading ſome Book, what euer
it be.

Enr. That ſhall be no trouble to me, nor let to vs For it is but
to recreate my ſelfe withall, for want of better company and ex-
erciſe.

C   Reſp. *If*

The Path-Way to Plantations.

Resp *If it be for Recreation, then I hope it is some matter of delight and speciall obseruation.*

Enr Yes indeed. It is a new and prettie Discourse of some of our new Plantations; namely, that in *N*

Resp *I maruaile what good or pleasure you should finde in such idle Bookes, fables I thinke, not worth the looking on*

Enr They are better then you yet vnderstand, I see. and therefore bee not you rash in condemning, lest you be hastie also in repenting . for, *Ad pœnitendum properat, cito qui iudicat* Hastie men (as they say) neuer lacke woe

Resp *Why? But doe you indeed find any good in reading such books, which I know of many to be but little regarded?*

Enr Yea truly . and that I doubt not but you also shall acknowledge , before you depart from hence , if you haue the leisure to stay with me but a while

Resp. *I haue lost more time then this ere now and therefore for your good companies sake, I will, God willing, see the euent and any great businesse to hasten me away at this time, I haue not, I pray you therefore tell me, what good you get by those Bookes?*

What profit may come by reading such books as concerne Plantations. Enr Besides the delight that comes by the noueltie of the contents thereof, and you know that, *Est natura hominum Nouitatis auida* we are by much nature like the *Athenians* spoke of in the 17. the *Acts* of the Apostles , desirous very much to heare Newes. I doe reape thereby vnto my selfe this threefold benefit. First, I doe thereby after a sort, as blessed *Moses* from mount *Nebo, Deut.* 34 view and behold with the eyes of my minde *those goodly Countreys,* which there God doth (offer to) *giue vnto vs and to our seed.* Secondly, Thereby I am inabled with *Ioshua* and *Caleb, Num.* 14. to stop the mouthes , and confute the malice of them , that in my hearing, like the *ten vnfaithfull spies,* shall goe about to bring vp *an euill report* vpon those good lands, and stay the murmurings of such foolish & ignorant people, as vpon euery idle hearesay, or any lazie vagrants letter, are ready to beleeue the worst & withall, thirdly, I am the better prepared to informe them and others, that are willing to know the truth and certaintie thereof

Resp. *I see there is good vse to be made of such bookes, if a man will. And therefore I shall from henceforth forbeare to thinke of them as I haue done and I shall desire you to lend me that booke of yours for a day or two, that I may reade it ouer also.*

Enr I

The first Part.

Enr I shall willingly lend you this, and one after another, two or three more that I haue of the like argument. For I wish with all my heart, that both you and all my friends were as well acquainted in them as I am.

Resp. I thanke you much for this courtesie. But seeing you make such vse & reckoning of those books, it seemes that you make more account of the actions themselues, that is, of Plantations, whereof they doe intreat, which yet I euer held, and so I know do many else, that be men of good wit and vnderstanding, to be but idle proiects and vaine attempts.

Enr Without any dislike or disparagement to any other mens wits or vnderstandings be it spoken, for mine own part I do professe, I estimate & account the Actions themselues to be very good and godly, honourable, commendable, and necessary such as it were much to be wished might be, and much to be lamented they be not, in farre better sort, *then hitherto any of them are*, followed and furthered, as which tend highly, first, to the honour and glory of Almightie God Secondly, to the Dignitie and Renowne of the Kings most excellent Maiestie. And thirdly, to the infinite good and benefit of this our Commonwealth Three things, then which none weightier or worthier, can in any Designe or Proiect be leuelled or aimed at.

Resp. You make me euen amazed, to heare of you, that so great good may be effected or expected out of those Courses, which of many are so much contemned and dispraised Wherefore for my better satisfaction therein, I pray you, let me heare of you in particular somewhat, how these notable effects might be produced, and namely first, the Glory and Honour of God.

Enr The Glory of God cannot but be much furthered thereby, were it but onely, that the *Gospel of Christ* should thereby be professed and published in such places and countries, by those alone, that shall remoue from hence to inhabite there, where before, since the beginning of the Gospel, for ought we know, or is likely, it was neuer heard, at least professed, as it is now of late come to passe, (God be praised) and we hope will be shortly in Newfound land.

Resp. Will be, say you? Me thinkes you should rather haue reckoned that among the first, because that for fiftie or threescore yeeres before euer the Summer Ilands or Virginia were heard of, our people did yeerely goe thither a fishing, and so the Name of Christ was

C 2   *there*

[margin:] Plantations themselues are Actions very commendable necessarie, &c.

[margin:] 1 By them the Church of Christ may notably bee enlarged.

there long since honoured among them

Enr   But for all that, till there be *Christians* inhabiting there, wee cannot say properly, that the Gospell of Christ is planted there, or that it is any part of Christendome. It must therefore in that respect, giue place to the other before-named, as which indeed were *Christian* before it

By the Addition of other Countries to Christendome.   Resp.   *I cannot dislike that you say. And indeed any man may see, that this must needs bee a great aduancement to the honour of God, when as the Scepter of his Sonne is extended so much farther then it was, as is from hence to those remote and vnknowne Regions Christendome will then be so much the larger. And it seemes to me it will be in a goodly order, seeing that as I vnderstand, from England to Newfoundland, and so to the Summer Ilands, and thence to Virginia, all is in one tract, no Turkish, no Heathen Countrie lying betweene. But proceed, I pray you.*

And by the Conuersion of infinite heathens to Christianitie.   *Enr.*   This is, as you see, greatly to the honour of God, but it will be much more, if when and where our people doe plant themselues in such countries where already are an infinite number of other people, all Sauages, Heathens, Infidels, Idolaters, &c   this in the Plantation may principally and speedily be laboured and intended, That by learning their languages, and teaching them ours, by training vp of their children, and by continuall and familiar conuerse and commerce with them, they may be drawne and induced, perswaded and brought to relinquish and renounce their owne Heathenismes, Idolatries, Blasphemies and Deuill-worships. And if (for that I take it cannot be denied) the Papists haue done much good that way, by spreading the Name of Christ, though but after their corrupt and superstitious manner, into so many vnknowne Nations that liued before altogether in the seruice and captiuitie of the deuill, (for *Better it is, that God bee serued a bad way, then no way at all.*) How much more good must it needs be, if the Name of the true God, *in a true and sound manner*, might there be published and spred abroad?

The Papists haue much endeuoured this way.

To which purpose, I would to God, there were among vs, vs *Protestants*, that professe and haue a better Religion then they the *Papists*, one halfe of that zeale and desire to further and disperse our good and sound Religion, as seemes to be among them for furthering and dispersing theirs.   Which not found,

The first Part.

for our zeale is coldnesse, and our forwardnesse, backwardnesse in that behalfe, in respect of theirs, I need not say, *we may feare; but rather, we may assure our selues*, that they shall *rise against vs in the day of Iudgement, and condemne vs* As they haue deserued, so let them haue the *Palme and Praise* in this point. For what other ends soeuer they proposed in their conquests and courses, questionlesse *Religion, the Christian faith*, according to their knowledge, was not the least, nor the last, since certaine it is, They neuer set foote in any Country, nor preuailed in any Coast, wherein they did not forth-with endeuour to root out *Paganisme*, and plant *Christianisme*, or leaue behinde them at least some Monuments and signes thereof.

And who can tell? (I speake this to prouoke ours the more withall) who can tell, I say, whether God hath euen therefore, as to *Iehu that rooted out Baal*, himselfe continuing to worship *Ieroboams Calues, 2 Reg 10.* 30, 31 bestowed on them a great part of that successe in warres, increase in wealth, and honour on earth, which had we stood foorth in their stead, and gone before them, as we should, and might haue done; he would more admirably, happily, and abundantly, haue conferred on vs? For he that is so kinde to his enemies, what would he haue beene to his friends?

Resp *I easily perceiue that this might redound not a little to the glorie of God, if the Conuersion of such People and Nations might be accomplished Lord, How many thousands and millions of soules might so be saued, which now run headlong into hell! It were a glorious worke, imitating notably that of the blessed Apostles, which conuerted the world so long agoe, from dead Idols to serue the liuing God. And in so holy and religious a labour, I am sorry to heare that we should not be as forward as Papists, but that to be verified twixt vs and them also in this case, which our Sauior said in another The children of this world are in their generation wiser then the children of light. But as I must needes confesse, that the worke were a worthy piece of worke, if it might be wrought, and that happy were our Land, if the children thereof might be made of God, Agents therein So me thinkes, we had need to haue some assurance of the will of God, that it should be done. For as you know better then I can tell you; If the time of their Conuersion be not come; or if God, as he hath wrapped them hitherto in vnbeliefe, so he be not pleased nor determined to release them, to call them to the knowledge of his truth, and to manifest his Son vnto them at*

all

all our labour then will be but in vaine, and our attempts not pleasing, but displeasing in his sight.

Enr That God desireth and willeth his Name, his truth and Gospell by vs to be published in those Heathen and barren lands, the inclination and readinesse alone of those people and Nations may sufficiently assure vs, who as it were prepared of God, to receiue the Gospell *from our mouthes*, if it might be but sounded vnto them, doe euen of their owne accord offer themselues to be taught, suffer their children to bee baptized and instructed by vs; and, as weary of, and halfe seeing the grossenesse of their own abominations, and the goodnes of our obseruations doe make no great difficultie to peferre our Religion before theirs, and to confesse that it is God that we, and the deuill that they doe worship

It is Gods will to call them to the knowledge of his truth.

For my owne part, I am perswaded, that God will *instantly* haue them either by vs or by others, *if we will not*, called to the knowledge of his Truth, & turned from darknes to light, & from the power of *Satan, vnto God*, that so the words of our Sauiour may be fully fulfilled, who, *Math.* 24. 14 hath foretold vs, That *the Gospell*, before the end shall come, *must be preached throughout the whole world* and *Mark* 13.10 *be published among all Nations*, which, howsoeuer most hold is long since accomplished, in that it either *now is*, or *heretofore hath beene preached to all*, or neere *all Nations of this vpper Continent*: yet I am now resolued, (let it bee my priuate errour, if I doe erre) that they will not bee fulfilled indeed, according to our Sauiours intent, vntill that vnto them also that *inhabit that other*, the vnder *Continent*, it be made manifest, which it seemeth vnto me, God doth now hasten to accomplish, in that within *our Age alone*, a great part thereof hath had the same, though corruptly, though imperfectly, brought vnto them.

And their conuersion must be before the end of the world can be.

Resp. You doe well to say, that this is your owne priuate Opinion, for no man else, I thinke, is of that minde.

Enr Not many, it may be, but yet I assure you, I am not alone. For there was but few yeeres past, a Preacher in *Dorsetshire*, of some note and name, that in a Sermon of his intituled, *The Marigold and the Sun*, now extant in Print, page 40. vpon these words of his Text, *Luk.* 1. 79 *To giue light to them that sit in darkenesse, &c.* saith thus: *This light rising first from the Iewes, as from his East or Orient, is carried ouer all the world, and hath giuen light to*

vs

The firſt Part.

vs (Engliſh) that ſate in darkeneſſe Of his *firſt riſing reade* Luke
24 47. *beginning* (ſaith our Sauiour there) *from Ieruſalem. Hence
ſprung this bleſſed light firſt, and thence , beſides his diſperſion into o-
ther parts of the World, was carried ouer all Greece, Italy, Germany,
France, and roſe to vs alſo , and is now making day to the Indians and
Antipodes For the world ſhall not end, till he haue finiſhed his Courſe,
I meane, till, as the Euangeliſt* Math 24 14. ſaith, *The Goſpell be
preached in all the world, and be a teſtimony to all nations and then
ſhal the end come* Thus he. D. *Keckerman* likewiſe, that famous pro- D.Keckar
feſſor of Arts and Learning, diuine and humane, in his *Manudu-* Dantiſcan
* Ction to Theologie ,* of late tranſlated into Engliſh by my worthy
friend Maſter T. *Vicars* Batchelour in Diuinitie, pag.94 writes
of this matter in this manner *And doubtleſſe towards the end of
the world, the true Religion ſhall be in America as God is now preparing way for it by the Engliſh and Low-Country Merchants , that ,
that of Chriſt may be fulfilled, Math. 24.14. This Goſpell of the
Kingdome ſhall be preached through the whole World, for a witneſſe
vnto all Nations, and then ſhall the end come. For God in all his works
is wont to effect a thing ſucceſſiuely, and therefore firſt he ſends to thoſe
Nations ſome light of his Eſſence and Truth by the Papiſts , and afterward will make theſe things ſhine more clearely vnto them by the
true and faithfull Miniſters of the Goſpell* Thus farre he
  So that in their opinion, as well as mine, this is a worke that
muſt be done before the end can be Wherefore ſince it is a worke,
and a moſt holy and neceſſary worke, which muſt be done, before
the day, the great day of the Lord can come, I ſee not how we can,
without ſinne (hauing any thing to doe in thoſe parts) withdraw
our ſhoulder from this burthen, or with-hold our hand from this
plough. And ſo much the more will the ſinne be, by how much it
is farre more eaſie for vs this to hold and vndergoe , then it was
for thoſe that did vndertake the like taske for vs, I meane, the
Conuerſion of our Anceſtors and predeceſſors in this land, a people as rude and vntractable, at the leaſt that way as theſe now, in
as much as they were to preach and not to ſubdue but wee may
plant as well as preach, and may ſubdue as well as teach, whereby
the Teachers ſhall need to feare no loſſe of goods or life, no priſon
nor ſword, no famine or other *perſecuting* diſtreſſe for the Go-
ſpels ſake Whoſe ſteps, if our Nation now , if our Countrimen
in their intended Plantations among thoſe Infidels would in any
                                                         meaſure

8   *The Path-Way to Plantations.*

meafure follow , how many foules might they faue aliue ? How many finners might they conuert from going aftray? How much might they ampliate the Kingdome of Chrift in earth ? aduance the name , glory, and worfhip of our , the onely true and euerla-fting God? and prepare for themfelues an abundant , or rather a fuperabundant heape of glory in heauen, according to that which is written, *Dan* 12.3 *They that be wife, ftill fhine as the firma-ment and they that turne many vnto righteoufneffe , ftall fhine as the ftarres for euer and euer?*

Refp *That thefe courfes tend to the glory of God, I plainly fee and ackowledge : But how may they be to the renowne and benefit of the Kings moft excellent Maieftie?*

2. By them the Maieftie and renowne of the Kings of England may be much aug-mented.

Enr. Thefe could not but much augment and increafe the Ma-ieftie and renowne of our dread Soueraigne , if thereby his Do-minion be extended, as it were into another world, into thofe re-mote parts of the earth, and his kingdomes be increafed into ma-ny moe in number, by the Addition and Acceffe of fo many , fo fpacious, fo goodly, fo rich, and fome fo populous Countries and Prouinces, as are by thefe Beginnings offered vnto his hands

We fee the Euidence and certaintie of this Affumption as cleare as the Sun-fhine at high Noone , in the perfon of the King of *Spaine,* whofe Predeceffours and Progenitors accepting that which others did refufe, and making better vfe of fuch Opportu-nities, then any elfe haue done, he is thereby become *Lord*, not onely of Territories , almoft innumerable, but alfo of Treafures and riches in them ineftimable

Whofe Right thereto, and to the reft of that Continent, be it what it may be, cannot, I fuppofe, in any equitie or reafon, be any fufficient Barre to any *Chriftian Prince*, why hee fhould not yet, by any lawfull and good meanes feize into his hands, and hold as in his owne right, whatfoeuer Countries and Ilands are not be-fore *actually* inhabited or poffeffed by him the *Spaniard*, or fome other Chriftian Prince or State. Of which fort , fince yet there are many, it were much to be wifhed, That his Maieftie might in time, while Opportunities ferue, take notice and Poffeffion of fome of them, whereunto thefe courfes of Plantation (being right-ly profecuted) are a fingular, if not the onely meanes.

Refp. *All this is moft apparant . but may the like be faid for your third point, The good of this land likewife?*

Enr. Yes

The first Part.

9

Enr Yes verily. Whosoeuer shall but lightly consider the estate thereof, as now it stands, shall plainly see, and will be enforced to confesse, That the prosecuting, and that in *an ample meafure*, of those worthy Attempts, is an enterprise for our Land and common good, most expedient and necessarie For,

3 By them the good of this I and may notably be procured.

First of all, whereas toward the Supportation of their Regall estate, for many and vrgent Necessities, the Kings of this Land are oft occasioned to demand and take of their Subiects, great summes of money by Subsidies, and other like wayes, which to many of the Subiects, specially the Clergie (who for the most part, to such payments, as things now stand, pay eight or ten times as much proportionably, as other Subiects doe) is somewhat hard and heauy to endure. This Burthen would be more easily borne, and could not but become much the lighter, if by the accession of more kingdoms to their crowne, store of treasures being brought into their Coffers, the same were borne by diuers other lands and Subiects, as well as of this, and the rest, yet vnder their subiection.

1. In the easier supportation of the Regall state.

Secondly, Whereas our Land, at this present, by meanes of our long continued both *Peace* and *Health*, freed from any notable, either warre or Pestilence, the two great deuourers of mankinde, to both which in former Ages it was much subiect, euen swarmeth with multitude and plentie of people, it is time, and high time, That like Stalls that are ouerfull of Bees, or Orchyards ouergrowne with young Sets, no small number of them should be transplanted into some other soile, and remoued hence into new Hiues and Homes.

2. In ridding out of the land the great and superfluous multitude thereof.

Truly it is a thing almost incredible to relate, and intolerable to behold, what a number in euery towne and citie, yea in euery parish and village, doe abound, which for want of commodious and ordinary places to dwell in, doe build vp Cotages by the high way side, and thrust their heads into euery corner, to the grieuous ouercharging of the places of their abode for the present, and to the very ruine of the whole Land within a while, if it be not looke vnto, which if they were transported into other regions, might both richly increase their owne estates, and notably ease and disburden ours.

Resp. These be motiues of some weight and likelihood but let me heare more to these, if you haue them.

3 In abating the excessiue high prices of all things to liue by.

Enr. Next, Thirdly, Whereas at this present, the prices of all
things

D

The Path-Way to Plantations.

things are growne to such an vnreasonable height, that the Common, that is, the meaner sort of people, *are euen vndone*, and doe liue, in respect of that they did for thirtie or fortie yeeres past, in great needinesse and extremitie, that there is neither hope, nor possibilitie of amending this euill, but in the diminution of the number of people in the land. Which, if men will not, by departing hence, elsewhere effect, we must expect that God, (they hauing first eaten out one another) by warre or pestilence doe it for them

    I know, that much helpe in this case might be had, if our Magistrates and great ones did take some good course (*cum effectu*) for the encrease of Tillage But neither thereof is there any (great) hope, nor therein a sufficient helpe, since it is out of all doubt, that vnlesse it be in an extraordinary fruitfull yeere, and of them now a dayes, God for our sinnes, sends but a few, our land is not able to yeeld corne and other fruit enough, for the feeding of so many as now doe lie and liue vpon it And when it which was wont to helpe feed other countries, must, as of late we haue to our cost both seene and felt, bee faine to haue helpe and food from others; how can our state bee for the commons, but wofull and ill? Likewise, if some good course might bee taken for restraint of excessiue Fines and Rents, whereby Landlords now a daies, *grinde the faces of the poore*, and draw into their own hands all the sweet and fat of the land, so that their poore Tenants are able, neither to keepe house and maintaine themselues, nor (as anciently such houses did) to relieue others, then could not the prices of all things but much abate and come downe Yet this were but an *imperfect Cure*. The true and sure remedie is, *The diminution of the people*, which reduced to such a competent number, as the land it selfe can well maintaine, would easily cause, not onely the excessiue height of Fines and Rents, but also the prices of all things else, to fall of themselues, and stay at so reasonable a Rate, that one might (which now they cannot) liue by another, in very good sort

＊ In enriching the poorer for thence removed.   4 Consider also the great riches, wealth, and good estate which such who here liue, and cannot but liue *parce & duriter*, poore and hardly, might by Transplantation, within a while rise vnto: while as they may haue otherwhere, for their bad cottages, good houses, for their little gardens, great grounds, and for their small

backsides,

The firſt Part.

backſides, large fields, paſtures, meadowes, woods, and other like plentie to liue vpon

5 The benefit that might that way accrew vnto Merchants, and all kinde of Aduenturers by Sea, is infinit For Traffique and Merchandize cannot but by meanes thereof wonderfully be bettered and increaſed And withall, which is not the leaſt point in Obſeruation, moſt commodious and delightfull muſt merchandizing and traffique needs bee, while it ſhall be exerciſed for the moſt part, betweene one and the ſame people, though diſtant in Region, yet vnited in Religion, in Nation, in Language and Dominion Which ſurely is a thing likely to proue ſo materiall and beneficiall, as may turne the greater part of our Merchants voyages that way, and free them from many of thoſe dangerous paſſages which now they are faine to make by the Straits and narrow Seas, may finde them out their rich and much-deſired commodities, and greater ſtore, and at a better hand then now they haue them otherwhere, an I vent them many a thing, which now doe ſeldome, or not at all paſſe their hands

In amending the Trade and Traffique of Merchants.

But of all other, I need ſpeake little of the Merchants good, as who can, and I am perſwaded, doe ſo well know it of themſelues, and thereupon affect the enterpriſe ſo much, that if other mens deſires and endeuours were correſpondent, it would take both ſpeedy and condigne effect.

6 The laſt benefit to our Land, but not the leaſt, is the curing of that euill Diſeaſe of this Land, which, if it be not lookt vnto, and cured the ſooner, will bee the Deſtruction of the Land, I meane, *Idleneſſe the Mother of many Miſchiefes*, which is to be cured, and may be rooted out of the Land, by this meanes, yea by this onely, and by none other, viz. by Plantation

In rooting out Idleneſſe out of this Land.

Reſp *Idleneſſe is a naughtie vice indeed, but commonly it doth hurt none but them in whom it is, and yet except that fault, many that be idle be honeſt men, and haue in them diuers good qualities and therefore me thinkes you ſte be too hardly of it, to call it* The Mother of Miſchiefes *There be worſe vices a great many in the Land, as this Drunkenneſſe and vnthriftie ſpending of their goods, which are euery where ſo common*

Eur. I perceiue by you, it is a very bad cauſe that cannot get a Proctour That which I haue ſpoken againſt Idleneſſe, is but little to that I could ſpeake, and which writers both humane and

The Path-Way to Plantations.

The fruits of Idlenesse.

dinine haue spoken of it, to whom I will referre you, lest we pro-
tract this our Conference ouer-long. But for the vices you speake
of, if they be, as you say, worse then Idlenesse; yet, as sometime
of a bad mother, there may come worse daughters; I assure you,
they and many more, as filching and stealing, robbery and couse-
nage, adultery and incest, fornication and all kinde of wanton-
nesse and vncleannesse, beggery and roguery, prophanenesse and
idolatry, and a number more, that vpon the sodaine, I cannot call
to minde, and with which this Land of ours is defiled and filled,
be none other (for the most part) then the fruits and offspring, the
brood and increase of *Idlenesse*; which alone taken away, and wee-
ded out, these all would fall away and vanish with her. For, *Sub-
lata causa, tollitur effectus*, saith the Philosopher, The cause of any
thing taken away, the effect is also taken away with it, and must
cease

*Resp. A happy worke indeed were the doing thereof. But doe you
thinke, or is there any probabilitie, that this might be done by so spee-
die and easie a meanes, as Plantation?*

Enr. Questionlesse, The best and the onely Cure thereof *by
the hand of man*, is this way, and none other. The diminution of
the people of the Land vnto a due and competent Number will
doe it. This is apparant by Experience. For, looke we backe to the
state of our Land for 40 50 or 60 yeeres agoe, before it did thus
exceed in multitude, and we shall see, that few or none of these
vices did then abound, nothing in Comparison of that they doe
now, as which haue since sprung vp out of Idlenesse, that since
that time, together with the multitude and increase of the people, is risen and increased.

*Resp. Indeed I remember well, when I was a young man, there
were no such swaggering Youths, potting Companions, and idle Gamesters as bee now in the Countrie little fornication, bastardie, quar-
relling and stabbing, and other like wicked facts, in respect of those
that be now, howsoeuer it be that the world is so much altered. But
that these euils may be amended by Plantations, yet I see not.*

Em. I will make you see it, and confesse it too. You haue
your selfe a great many of Children, if you should keepe them all
as home, and haue not wherewith to set them to worke, nothing
to employ them in (for all the worke you haue to doe ordinari-
ly, is not enough for aboue two or three of them) must they not
needs

The first Part.

needs fall to Idlenesse ? what will most of them proue but Idlers and Loyterers? Now, to preuent and auoyd this, what other remedie haue you, but either to get worke for them into your own house from other men, if you can haue it, or else perforce to place them forth of your owne house into other mens, one to this trade or occupation, another to that, where they may be set aworke, and kept from Idlenesse.

Resp. *This is true But what is this to our purpose?*

Enr Very much. For the cases are very like. Thereby you may plainly perceiue, that, as the onely way to rid Idlenesse out of your house, hauing no worke for them at home, is, to place abroad your children into other houses, as it were, into Colonies, where they may be set aworke; so the onely way to rid Idlenesse out of a whole parish, towne, countie or countrey (the same being not able to set them that are idle therein aworke And it is a thing so euident, that for the idle people of our Land, what by the great number of them, which is almost infinite, and what by the present dampe and decay of all Trades and employments, the Land is not any way able to set them aworke, that it needs no proofe, is to place abroad the Inhabitants thereof, which therein be not not can be set aworke, into other parishes, townes, counties and countries

Resp If this Course should be taken, it would touch very neere a great many of the best liuers in the Countrey, who, both themselues, and their children be as idle as any can be, and yet would be loth, hauing so good meanes here to liue by, to be remoued into Plantations abroad

Enr These might be brought from Idlenesse, and yet abide at home too. For, if the superfluous multitude of our Land were remoued, those which you speake of, would for their owne need fall to worke, and leaue Idlenesse, because that multitude remoued, they should haue none to doe their worke for them, as now they haue, while they goe to playing, potting, and other like vaine and idle courses.

The Magistrates of our Land haue of late made many good statutes and prouisions, for the beating downe of drunkennes for setting the poore and idle people to worke, and otherlike : but how little effect hath followed ? Drunkennesse encreaseth daily, and laughes the Lawes to scorne. Pouertie more & more ariseth,

The Path-Way to Plantations.

and idle people still doe multiply. Other sinnes and disorders are sometimes punished, but yet they still remaine, and, as it were, in despite of Lawes, they spread more and more abroad. The reason is, (if a man may be bold to giue the reason of it, *They strike at the boughes, but not at the Rootes.*) If there were the like good Orders taken for the rooting out and beating downe of *Idlenesse it selfe* in our Land, which can be done no other way, but by Plantations, both Idlenesse it selfe, and all the rest of the Euils beforenamed, and other like that arise out of it, would vanish away as smoake before the winde, and melt as Waxe against the Fire.

Ale houses.

Then, these blinde and filthy Ale-houses, which are none other than the *Deuils Dennes*, wherein lurke his beastly slaues day and night, which all the Iustices in the Countrey cannot now keepe downe, would sinke of themselues to the ground

Tobacco-shops.

Then, these Tobacco-shops, that now stinke all the Land ouer, would shortly cease to fume out their infernal smoakes, and come to a lower rate and reckoning by an hundred fold.

Idle Trades.

Then, the many idle Trades, which of late are risen vp in the Land, vnder colour to keepe people from idlenesse, and to set the poore on worke, such, I say, as the former Ages knew not, and our present Age needes not, as which serue to nothing, but to the increase of pride, and vanitie in the world, would quickly grow out of request.

Prisons.

Then, the Prisons, and Sheriffes Wards, would not be one halfe so full of Malefactors and Bankrupts, as now they are. And last of all, (but not the least; for, who can reckon vp all the benefits that this one Remedy would bring vnto our Land?) then

Violent deaths.

should not one halfe so many people of our Land bee cut off, by shamefull, violent, and vntimely deaths, as now there are

Resp. Your speeches are very probable but by this meanes, so many idle people of our Land, as you intimate, being remoued, the Plantations will then be pestered with them there, as much and as bad as we are here; and so, those good workes be discredited, and haply ouerthrowne thereby. It is but the remouing of euill from one place to another.

Enr. Howsoeuer, such a Remouall made, our Land (which is the poynt in question) shall be cleared and cured But of that extreme hurt to the Plantations that you fore-cast, there is no feare.

The first Part.

feare For, whereas there are in our Land at this present many
idle perfons, fome are fuch as gladly would worke, if they could
get it. They are idle, not for any delight they haue in idleneffe,
but becaufe they can get no body, nor meanes to fet them on
worke. Some are idle indeed, as may worke and will not. They
haue wherewithall to keepe themfelues from idleneffe, that is,
worke enough of their owne to doe, but, delighting in idleneffe,
and counting it a difgrace to men of their meanes, to worke and
labour in their vocation, they will haue and hyre others to doe
their worke, to be their feruants, and labourers, which they
needed not, and which other men of like quality and ability, that
are thrifty, and good Common-wealths men indeed, doe not,
nor will doe, and they themfelues the while liue idlely, fpend
their time vainely, lye at the Ale-houfe, or Tauerne, bibbing and
bowzing beaftly, fit at Cards or Tables loofely, haunt idle and
lewd company fhamefully, and giue themfelues to no good practice or exercife commendably, but runne on from ill to worfe,
to the fhame and difcredit of themfelues and their friends, and
many times to the vtter vndoing and ouerthrow of them and
theirs miferably A third fort there are, as it were a mixt kinde
of people, neither altogether idle, nor yet well and fufficiently
fet a worke. Of thefe, fome worke at a low and fmall rate, many times glad to ferue for any thing, rather than to begge, fteale,
or ftarue: and fome of them fet vp idle and pelting Trades, as it
were fhifts to liue by, for lacke of better imployment, that fo
they may haue one way or other fomewhat to liue vpon.

Of all thefe, if the firft and third fort were remoued into Plantations, where they might haue either good Liuings of their
owne to liue vpon, or good imployment by others to labour vpon, it is no doubt, but that the moft part of them, would be glad
of the exchange, and proue laborious and induftrious people, to
their owne good, and the good, not the hurt, of the Countrey into which they fhall be remoued. And then for the fecond or
middle fort, it is not much to be doubted, but that the occafions of their idleneffe taken away, as I faid but now, they alfo
will leaue to be idle, fall to doe their owne worke as they fhould,
learne to thriue and become profitable to themfelues, and this
our Countrey, wherein they remaine. and be at length as much
afhamed

afhamed to be idle and vaine henceforth, as heretofore they were to worke and labour.

If any continue their former lewd and difordered courfes, being but a few, fo many of their wonted Companions being feuered and gone from them, there is hope that a little feuerity of the Laws, which eafily reclaimeth a few, when on a multitude fometimes it can doe little good, will and may bring them alfo to a better courfe.

And thus I hope you fee, That it is not impoffible the idleneffe that is in our Land, to be notably cured and expelled · and that this may be done either onely, or at leaft no way fo foundly, readily, and fpeedily, as by Plantations And therefore, the ftate of our Land confidered, if there were no other benefit that might arife of Plantations, yet this alone, viz the rooting out and deftroying of idleneffe out of the Land, which elfe *Viper-like*, will in time root out, and deftroy the Land it felfe, wherein it is bred, were caufe all-fufficient, and reafon enough, why fuch attempts fhould be vndertaken, and by all poffible meanes furthered and haftened

Refp *I cannot but like well of all that hitherto you haue faid, touching the goodneffe and neceffity of thefe Actions But yet, mee thinkes, there may be a Queftion, Whether they be lawfull or not? For, mee thinkes, it fhould neither be lawfull for any people to forfake the Countrey wherein God hath placed them, and in which they and their Progenitors, for many generations haue remained nor to inuade and enter vpon a ftrange Countrey, of which they haue no warrant nor affurance that God is pleafed, they fhould aduenture vpon it*

Plantations be lawfull.

Enr. If any will make queftion of the lawfulneffe of fuch Actions, Nature it felfe, which hath taught the *Bees*, when their Hiue is ouer-full, to part Company, and by fwarming, *to feeke a new habitation* elfewhere, doth euidently informe vs, That it is as lawfull for men to remoue from one Countrey to another, as out of the houfe wherein they are borne, or the parifh wherein they are bred, vnto another If *humane reafon* fatisfie not, (for fome will make doubts in cafes moft cleare) there is *diuine warrant* for it that may For it was Gods expreffe commandement to *Adam*, *Gen* 1. 28. that hee fhould *fill the earth, and fubdue it*. By vertue of which *Charter*, hee and his haue euer fince had

The first Part.

had the *Priuiledge* to spread themselues from place to place, and to *haue, hold, occupie, and enioy* any Region or Countrey whatsoeuer, which they should finde either not pre-occupied by some other, or lawfully they could of others get or obtaine

Vpon which clause, wee *Englishmen* haue as good ground and warrant to enter vpon *New-found-Land*, or any other Countrey hitherto not inhabited or possessed by any Nation else, Heathen or Christian, and any other that we can lawfully, (I say lawfully) get of those that doe inhabite them, as to hold our owne natiue the English soyle

Resp *But this, though I see it to be lawfull, seemes yet to be a very strange course, the like whereof, in former Ages hath not beene vsed.*

Enr. That this course hath beene in former times both vsuall and ancient, and not as you seeme to imagine, new and strange, though I might proue by coniecture onely. For how else had it beene possible, so many, so diuers, so distant, and so great Countries to be peopled, but by remouing from one Countrey to another? or referre you to *humane Histories*, which are full of such Narrations. and of them, aboue all to the *Romane state*, which from their very first yeeres, *ab vrbe condita*, after that *Rome* it selfe was builded, fell apace to that practice, and had euer in hand, one or other *Colonie*. One of good Antiquity, and therefore not partiall, and of great Obseruation, and therefore regardable, *Tully*. doth tell vs expresly, That as other things common by nature, so Lands, so Countries, (for they also are a part of his *omnia*) haue become priuate, from time to time. *aut veteris Occupatione, aut victoria, aut lege* either by ancient vsurpation, men finding them void and vacant, or by victory in warre, or by legall condition or composition in peace. But what need I care what such say, or say not, when as holy Writ it selfe tels vs very plainely, *Gen* 10 5. That whereas after *Noahs floud*, there were no more aliue on earth, of all the posterity of *Adam*, but *Noah*, and *his sons*, and their *wiues*, eight persons in all, *Of them only were the Iles of the Gentiles diuided in their Lands, euery man after his tongue, and after their Families in their Nations*? And againe, *verse* 32 *Out of these were the Nations diuided in the earth* that is, These, as they increased, disperssed themselues, and inhabited, and replenished, first one Countrey, and then another, as wee see at this day And

    E   this,

Marginal notes: Plantations no new nor strange course but both vsuall and ancient.   Tully.   Gen 10 5.

Gen. 9. 1.

this vpon warrant of that *Grant* which *Adam* had, being renew-ed and confirmed vnto *Noah*, and his sonnes, *Gen. 9* 1. *Replete terram*, Replenish yee the earth, or fill it vp againe. Lastly, let such but looke backe and thinke, How at first wee, *the Inhabitants of this Land*, came hither. Were all *Indigenæ?* or rather *Terrigenæ?* Did they at first spring vp heere out of the earth? Are we of the Race and off-spring of *Noah*, or *his sonnes?* and therefore *per conseq* vndeniable, (as all our Histories doe accord) haue come from other-where? Why then should that seeme so insolent to vs, and in our time, which haue beene so vsuall at all times, and in all Ages?

Resp. *Ton haue, mee thinkes, well iustified this course in generall: Now, if you can as well cleare it in some particulars, I shall haply at length bee of your minde also, for the maine*

Certaine Obiections answered. 1. Obiection. Answere.

Enr. Obiect your particulars, and I doubt not whatsoeuer they be, but I shall be able reasonably to satisfie you in them.

Resp *The places, the Countries to be planted and inhabited by vs, are very farre off from hence.*

Enr. To that I say, first, If neerer places cannot bee had, better a good place, though farre off, than none at all.

Secondly, others, as the *Spaniards*, haue and doe remoue and plant farther off, by a great deale.

Thirdly, *Abraham*, *Jacob*, and other good men, haue beene content in lesse need, saue that G o d so commanded to depart farre from the places of their birth, as wee may see, *Gen.* 12 4, *Act.* 7 3. and other-where.

Fourthly, When God calls, and as with vs now, Necessitie doth so require, good men should be indifferent to dwell in one Countrey, as well as in another, accounting, as one said well, *Ubi bene, ibs patria* wheresoeuer a man is, or may be best at ease, that is, or should be to him (as) his Countrey. A very Heathen man could say:

Ovid.

Omne solum forti patria est, vt piscibus æquor

Ut volucri, vacuo quicquid in orbe patet   that is,

Vnto a valiant-minded man, each Country good is his:

As is wide world vnto the Birds, and broad Sea to the Fish.

And, another being asked, *Cuius esset Vrbis?* answered, *Orbis* as who would say, The World at large were his Seate or City

Fifthly,

The first Part.

Fifthly, *Sifter-land*, or as it is yet commonly called, *New-found-land*, which for the present seemeth to be the fittest of all other intended *Plantations*, is not very farre off. It is not with a good winde, aboue foureteene or fifteene dayes sayle As easie a voyage in manner, the Seas and passage considered, as into our next Neighbour-Countrey *Iland*, whither of late yeeres many haue out of *England*, to their and our good remoued.

Sixthly, Our Merchants, in hope of present but vncertaine gaine, doe yeerely and vsually trauaile into farther Countries a great deale : and why, then should any for his assured, certaine, and perpetuall good, thinke it intolerable or vnreasonable to make one such a iourney in his life?

Resp. *The Countries themselues are wilde and rude : No townes*, 2. Obiect. *no houses, no buildings there.*

Enr. Men must not looke still, in such a case, to come to a Answ. Land inhabited, and to finde ready to their hands, as in *Israel*, in *Canaan, great and goodly Cities, which they builded not : houses full of all manner of store, which they filled not wells digged, which they digged not : Vine-yards*, and Orchards, *which they planted not* : as *Moses* speaketh, *Deut* 6. 10. It must content them, that God prepareth them a place, a Land, wherein *they may build them Cities*, Townes, and Houses *to dwell in*, where they *may sow Land, and plant them Vine-yards* and Orchards too, *to yeeld them fruts of increase*, as the *Psalmist* writeth, *Ps*. 107. 39.

2. Thinke they it is no bodies lot but theirs? And doe they imagine, that in any Countrey wheresoeuer, where now there are Castles and Towres, Houses and Habitations of all sorts settled, there was not a time when none of these were standing? but that the ground was as bare and naked thereof, as wilde and void of Couerture, as any of our *Plantations* are. For, according to our English Prouerbe, *Rome it selfe was not built in one day.*

3 They that shall at first come there, may account it a benefit to finde the places vnbuilt, in that they may thereby chose them seates, and diuide the Countrey at their owne will : That they may enter large Territories, and take to themselues ample possessions at pleasure, for them and theirs for many Generations : That they may be freed from these extreme Fines, and ouer-tackt Rents, which make their old Neighbours and natiue friends

E 2   behind,

20

The Path-Way to Plantations.

behind, to groane, and may well make them weary of the Land it selfe : For, who can beare them?

4. And if they can be content here to build vp houses vpon the High-way-side, though there be not the fourth part of an A-cre of ground lying vnto it : or thinke themselues bountifully dealt with, if any Gentleman would giue to any of them , three or foure acres of ground, for their owne time , at a reasonable rent , (and yet few be the Land-Lords that be so liberall) so as they would build a House on it; why should they not rather goe where they may haue an hundred, fiue hundred, or a thousand Acres of ground, to them and theirs for euer, at the like rate?

Resp. *But what, and how shall men doe the whi e, for houses and dwellings, till they can build, &c?*

Enr. They may and must for a time dwell in Tents and Pauil-lions, as Souldiers doe now in the Field, Tradesmen in a Faire, and as in ancient times men of good and great account, from time to time, from place to place, many yeeres together haue done, as appeareth, *Hebr.* 11 9. The particulars whereof you may reade at leasure, *Gen* 12. 8. and 15 5. and 18 1 and 24 67. and 31 33 So dwelled all *Israel* in the Wildernesse , full for-tie yeeres, as you may finde, *Leuitie* 23 42 and *Numb.* 14 33, 34. Yea, was not G o d himselfe content to dwell in *a Tent, in the middest of Israel*, till the dayes of *Dauid*, and reigne of *Sa-lomon*, who found that fauour in his eyes, that hee might build him an House ? as it is written, 2 *Sam.* 7. 63. and *Act* 7 45. The like did the Family of the *Rechabites*, as appeareth at large, *Ierem.* 35. for the space of three hundred yeeres together, when as all *Israel* besides dwelt in houses, and in walled Townes and Cities, and sauing for the commandement of *Ionadab*, the sonne of *Rechab* their Father, so might they haue done So that it is neither vnnaturall, vnusuall, nor vnpossible to take paines this way for a time, and that a long time, if need be

Resp. *Your examples I must needs yeeld, are al good, because they be so authenticall. But yet I see not that the vse of Tents can be any thing seruiceable , for that being made , as commonly they are , but of raw cloth or canuase , besides that they are very cold , they are not able to keepe off any raine or wet an houre to an end.*

Enr Well and artificially made , they are more seruiceable then you take them to be. Reade but *Exod.* 7. and 14. and to conferre

Tents may serue for a time.

The first Part.

conferre it with *1. Sam*. 7. 2 and you shall finde, That they may be made very durable : and that to the well making of Tents, there may goe a *Couering or two* of skins, or other stuffe, so dressed and fitted, as nor wet nor cold can easily pierce them

Resp. *I see it well ? pray you proceed.*

Enr Besides these, Men may, hauing once gotten place certaine for their abode, soone erect some Cabbins and small houses, which may for a time, some yeeres if need bee, serue for habitation, and afterward when they can build better, may be conuerted to inferiour vses, as for corne, cattle, &c. Men must bee contented at first with low and plaine buildings *England* hath beene inhabited two or 3000. yeeres at least, and yet what poore, what homely houses be there many till this very day, and within your remembrance and mine, many more there were? If the Liuing be good, though the house be but bad, it is no great matter, good Husbands will say.

Resp. *The Countries themselues are scarce habitable and good and the Soile thereof but barren and bad.*

3 Obiection.

Enr Experience it selfe, the surest teacher, sheweth altogether the contrary. For, if any credit be to be giuen to those that haue set vs forth their owne knowledge, and triall thereof by the *constant testimonie of them all*, not one of those Countries intended or attempted to be be planted by vs, but is found to bee exceeding good and fruitfull In euery Countrey to bee inhabited, three things are specially to bee respected, The Temperature of the Climate, the goodnesse of the Aire, and the fatnesse of the Soile All and euery of these in those Regions (a thing seldome found in many of this vpper Continent,) in comparison of many of our Northerne parts, are in the superlatiue degree, *viz* The Soile most fat and fertile, the Aire most sweet and healthy, and the Temper most milde and daintie If those that lie neere (or vnder) the *Æquinoctiall*, seeme at first to be somewhat of the hottest, yet since they are inhabited with Naturals of many sorts, and our men by their abiding there *some yeeres together*, haue found that they can inhabit them, there is no doubt, but that that excesse of heate, whereby as *Spaine, England*, they exceed these our Northerne Climates, will by vse and time become very tolerable and kindly to men of our Constitution, as well as of others.

Answer.

E 3   Th-

The Path-Way to Plantations.

The Healthinesse of any Countrie, by plantation and inhabitation must needs be much increased. For, the ridding of grounds, casting of ditches, and watercourses, and making of fires, together with the destroying of wilde and filthy beasts, all which, and other like, doe necessarily accompany any good Plantation, further much to the clensing of the aire, cleering of fogges, and so ridding of much corruption and vnhealthinesse from the place.

Adde to these the two much-desired Commodities in all good Habitations, I meane, *Wood* and *Water*, (the former whereof so fast decaies with vs, that very want of it onely, within few yeers is like to proue exceeding hurtfull to our Land, and can bee no way repaired, but by transplanting the people) and it is out of all question, That neither *England* nor *Ireland*, nor any countrey else in this part of Christendome, can at this present compare with those, much lesse exceed them. All which considered, what need any doubt, but that *The Sunne*, as the old Prouerbe is, *doth shine there, as merrily as here?* and that a little good husbandry will make the dwelling there, as commodious as healthfull, as gainfull, and euery way as good, as any other-where.

Resp. Your words doe sound somewhat pleasing But yet I haue heard some say somewhat otherwise, as namely, Those countries are very barren and vnfruitfull.

Enr. I beleeue you; For I haue heard say too, *Euill will, will neuer say well.* Many idle wretches, when they come into such places, because they cannot haue the plenty without paines, nor finde those golden mountaines they dreamed of at home, though many things bee notable and very good, yet will cauill at, and blame euery thing

Suppose it be somewhat as they say, that is, The ground not so fruitfull as some places here in *England*, yet doth it follow therefore, it is not worth the hauing? If I be not deceiued, There bee few Countries in *Europe* that can compare with *England* for richnesse of the Soile, and fatnesse of the earth, yet we all know, they are not therefore forsaken Againe, in *England* it selfe, all places are not alike good. As there be some of excellent mold, so there be barren, heath, and hungry Soiles a great many: yet we see, people are glad to inhabit them. Be it then, that some of those parts be no better then our worser grounds, our heaths, Mendip hills, Wiltshire downes, Salisbury plaines, and other like; yet I hope
they

The first Part.

they are better then none. A great deale of such ground together, I thinke, may be as good, as a little good ground. If any man will thus consider of such complaints and murmurs, he shall see no great cause to regard them. These therefore thus satisfied, if you haue any thing else to say, say on.

Resp. *Some say also, That those Countries are so ouergrowne with wood, trees, bushes, and such like, that there is no roome for building, no ground for pasture and tillage, or at least, not without excessiue labour and charge, or intolerable and pittifull spoile of the woods and timber to no vse.*

Enr It cannot be, but that those countries, hauing either not at all, or but little as yet beene inhabited, must needs be much o-uergrowne with woods, and no small part thereof to be a very Forrest and Wildernesse, yet certaine it is, that there are (a thing very admirable, and almost beyond expectation.) there are, I say, in them to be found many goodly parts of those Countries, that are very cleare of woods, faire and goodly open champion ground, large Meadowes and Pastures many hundred, sometimes thousands of Acres together. So that besides the wood-lands there is abundantly roome, and ground enough to build and inha-bit vpon, for more people, I beleeue, then will hastily be gotten ouer to dwell there: and more ground open and cleare already rid for pasture and tillage, then yet there will be people and cattle enough had thither to such vses, the same to conuert and employ.

And therefore there needs not, either that Complaint which they make, of the excessiue store and encomberment of woods, nor, which is worse, of that present and hastie spoile, and bur-ning vp of woods on the sudden, for making of roome, that some doe talke of, and would haue to be made; and, as it is reported, haue already made by burning vp thousands of Acres together This, truly in my opinion, is a thing very wicked, and such as cannot but be displeasing to Almightie God, who abhorreth all wilfull waste and spoile of his good creatures. *Gather vp that which is left,* saith our Sauiour, *Ioh. 6. 12 that nothing be lost* and a thing that in common ciuilitie and humane policie, should not be suffered to be done, or being done, not passe vnpunished.

The spoyle of woods in those countries not sufferable.

Wee may know by our owne present want of wood here in *England*, what a pretious commoditie wood is, and be warned by our owne harmes, to make much of it, if we haue plenty there-

of,

The Path-Way to Plantations.

of, and no further nor faster to cut it downe, then present vse and good occasions from time to time shall require. We should not be so blinde as not to foresee, that if the countries come once to be inhabited, there will be so many, and so great occasions of cutting downe wood and timber trees, as will quickly cause infinite store thereof necessarily to be imployed, and so the grounds from time to time speedily enough to be made cleare and ridde for other vses.

For, first, the very building of Houses, to which adde the necessary making of fences about houses and grounds, will vse an infinit deale of Wood and Timber.

Secondly, The store that will daily and yeerely be spent in necessary vses for fire, which at the first specially, till houses bee warme and drie, and the ayre corrected, will and must be more than ordinarie, cannot but, if once any number of Inhabitants goe ouer, be exceeding great.

Thirdly, The building and making of Ships and shipping, will require and consume very much there. And such order may bee taken, that by the woods there, great spare (a thing very needfull) may be made in *England*, of our Woods here for that vse.

Fourthly, To these places may be transplanted, the making of Glasse and Iron, as well for *England*, as for the same Countries: two things, that as it is well knowne, doe deuoure (yet vpon necessary vses) wonderfull store of Wood continually.

Fiftly, The Trades of Potters for earthen vessels, and of Coupers for treen Vessels, both very necessary, specially at the first, will and must still from time to time spend vp much Wood and Timber

Sixtly, And little behinde them in expence of Wood, will be that very necessary Trade of making of Salt, considering how great vse there is and will be thereof there, for the fishing voyages, besides all other vses thereof, both there and else-where

Seuenthly, No small quantity thereof likewise may be cut vp and transported into *England*, for our Buildings, for Coupers, Ioyners, and Trunk-makers trades heere, which now at a daerer hand, wee buy and fetch out of other Countries.

Eighthly, Besides, the Woods standing are of themselues, and by industry more may be made, a great fortification for the Inhabitants against man and Beast, till the Countries be, and can be better employed and fortified.   These

The first Part.

Thefe, and other like neceffary and great vfes of wood confidered, which either muft, or may be made thereof, little reafon
or caufe is there, why, as if it could, like the waters in the riuers,
neuer be fpent while the world ftands, there fhould any fudden
and needleffe fpoile by fire or any other waftfull hauocke be made
thereof. and feuerely deferue they to be punifhed that fhall make
it, and fharply the reft to be reftrained, that none like hereafter
be made

Resp. *Thefe Countries are full of wilde Beafts, Beares, &c*

Enr 1. Some of them, as the *Summer Jlands*, haue no fuch at
all No harmfull thing in them.

4 Obiection.
Anfwere.

2 None of them, efpecially *Newfound Land*, as farre as I
heare, haue any, or at leaft, any ftore of noyfome creatures, as of
Serpents, Crocodiles, &c. as haue many parts of this Continent,
which yet long hath beene, and ftill be inhabited.

3. It is well, there are fome beafts there, wilde at leaft, if not
tame That is an argument vndeniable, that tame beafts may
there be bred and liue

4 Better wilde then none at all For of fome of them, fome
good vfe may be made for the prefent, viz for labour, for food,
and for apparell, till better prouifion can be made To which
purpofe fuch infinite ftore and varietie of beafts, birds, fifhes,
fruits, and other like commodities, as in them all are already
found, and doe abound, ought rather to prouoke people to goe
thither, affured they cannot, if they will be anything induftrious,
want neceffaries ad victum & amictum, for backe and belly, where
fuch plentie is, and to praife God that hath, as for *Adam* in Pa-
radife, before he placed him there, *Gen.* 1 fo for them, before he
bring them thither, prouided fo well, rather then the want of
fome better or other, fhould moue them like the Ifraelites againft
God, *Exod* 16. to murmur and repine, or which is worfe, who-
ly to refufe and forgoe the places.

5. Haue not other Countries, thinke you, or at leaft, haue had
the like? Is *England*? Is *Ireland*? Is *France* altogether free? was *Canaan*, euen that bleffed land, without the, yea good ftore of them?
I take it no, and that not at the firft only as one may gather, *Deut*
7.22 but alfo many ages after, there were Lions. *Iudg* 14.5. and
1 *King*. 13.24. Beares, 2. *King*. 2.24. Foxes, *Iudg*. 15 4. Hornets,

      E   *Deut.*

The Path-Way to Plantations.

Deut 7. 20. Serpents, *Esay* 30. 6. &c.

Resp. *Among other meanes in these Plantations requisit, the ha- uing thither of tame cattell, as horses, kine, and sheepe, seemeth hard to bee compassed, and yet most needfull,* and that with the very first, *to be prouided, considering those Countries, howsoeuer they abound in other, are altogether destitute and vnprouided of these. And it will be obiected, That,* besides the difficultie of Trans-portation, *our Country is not able of them to make any spare.*

What meanes for profitable cattell to be had and trans-ported.

Enr. But if I bee not deceiued, It were easie to take such a course as might at will furnish that want, and yet leaue vs farre better stored then now we are : and that is,

1. For horses, if all Transportation of them into *France* and other vicine parts beyond Sea, were restrained, that so all such as were wont to passe out of the Land that way, might now goe this

2 For Kine and Sheepe, our Land is well stored of them, or rather pestered with them, that if of the one sort, some hun-dreds, and of the other, some thousands yeerely were thither sent, our Landshould haue thereby no losse nor lacke, since it is a rule infallible in husbandrie, howsoeuer it seeme to some a *Paradox* in sense, *The more Kine, the dearer White, The more Sheepe, the dearer Cloth.* And therefore we must neuer looke to haue those two Commodities (*White* and *Cloth*) at any reasona-ble hand, till the Number of those two kinde of Cattell be, and that in a good measure too, diminished in our Land It is also a *Maxime* vndeniable *The more Cowes, the fewer Ploughes,* and *The more Milkings, the fewer Weanlings.* And therefore till those cattell (*Kine*) be diminished, and that in a good Number, wee must not looke to haue *Corne* and *Flesh* plentie, *Bread* and *Beefe* cheape in *England* againe But (alas) *Narratur fabula Sur-do.* For whose hands bee deeper in this sinne, then theirs that should redresse it?

3. If a strict course might bee taken (and for a publike good, why should not our wanton appetites be a little dieted?) that in *England*, from the third of *February*, till the first of *May*, or happely but from *Septuagesima* Sunday, till the first Sunday after *Easter*, the chiefe time for breed, no Calues whatsoeuer should be killed, but all to bee weaned and kept for store; within a yeere or

two,

The first Part.

two, without all doubt, we fhould haue Biefe better cheape in our market a great deale, then now it is, or for many yeeres paft it hath beene, and yet many hundreds, haply thoufands, of faire yeerelings to bee had for thofe our new Countries which now haue none.

Where, if any good courfe be taken, and well obferued for pre-feruation of euery kinde, I doubt not but they would fafter there increafe and fill the Countries, then the inhabitants fhould be able to make roome for them, by deftroying and killing vp thofe wilde and vntamed beafts, which now doe fo there abound.

4. It were good too, our Fifh dayes all the yeere long, were better kept. For it is certaine, *The more fifh is fpent, the more flefh is fpared*: and as both flefh and fifh will be thereby the better cheape: fo Beeues, young Bullocks will be the more fined, for the helpe and vfe of thofe which to ftore their Plantations, fhall want them.

5. Befides, *Wales*, and here of late, God be thanked, *Ireland* feeme by the great drones which yeerely they fend ouer, fo well ftored, that thence alone, though *England* helped not, Prouifion enough might be had, for more kine and young cattell of that fort, then eafily there can be Tranfportation had for.

6 Laftly. As they that write of thefe Difcoueries doe relate, There be alfo fome countries neerer to fome of our Plantations then either *England* or *Ireland*, from which if men will feeke for them, all forts of tame and profitable cattell that we can or doe want, may at a very reafonable hand be had.

If it feeme hard and ftrange to any, to *make Tranfportation of cattell*, and, that in the Countries themfelues are none naturally to be had: Let them be pleafed to vnderftand that to be no new thing: and that where now they are moft plentifull, time hath beene, None, not one was to be found: but that fuch cattell, as wel as men, (for all came out of *Noahs* Arke, *Gen.* 8.17.) were brought and conueyed from place to place. And if they will but a little enquire of elder men & times, they may learn; It is but as it were the other day fince fome countries neere vnto vs had no fheepe, other no kine, other few horfes, & that at this very inftant, *France* is willing to haue frō vs our horfes, we frō *Wales* their Burs, & frō *Ireland* their Cowes. All which doe paffe from one countrey to ano-

ther

The Path-Way to Plantations.

ther by Transportation. And therefore men must be contented, as themselues, to dwell where before they haue not done , so to get thither cattell , profitable cattell, where before they haue not beene.

5 Obiect.
Answ.

Resp *The people of those Countries are rude and barbarous*

Enr. They that like to dwell alone, may. There are countries found, and more to bee found, I doubt not, not yet inhabited and actually possessed by any people , nation , or state whatsoeuer.

2. They with whom wee haue to doe, are not so rude as some imagine, I beleeue Most, if not all of them, specially they of *Guiana*, doe shew themselues, their breeding considered, exceeding tractable , very louing and kinde to our Nation aboue any other · industrious and ingenious to learne of vs, and practise with vs most Arts and Sciences and which is most to be admired and cherished , very ready to leaue their old and blinde Idolatries, and to learne of vs the right seruice and worship of the true God. And what more can bee expected from them in so small time and meanes? or what surer probabilitie or hope would we haue , that we shall or may easily, and within short time , win them to our owne will , and frame them as we list? Verily I suppose , if all things be considered well , and rightly compared , we haue neerer home worse neighbours a great deale.

3. The *Spaniard* hath reasonably ciuilized , and better might, if he had not so much tyrannized , people farre more sauage and beastiall then any of these.

4. We ought to consider, that time was, the old *Brittons* the ancient Inhabitants of this Land , were as rude and barbarous as some of these of forraigne parts, with whom wee haue to doe. And therefore considering , *Quâ sumus Originenais* , (for wee are also their Off-spring) wee ought not to despise euen such poore and barbarous people , but pitty them , and hope, that as wee are become now, by Gods vnspeakeable mercy to vs-ward, to a farre better condition , so in time may they

6. Obiect.

Resp. *The Aduenturers are very dangerous , and lyable to losses of life and goods, to troubles manifold , so that they may well bee called Aduenturers, that will hazard themselues in them.*

Enr. Good

The firſt Part.

Enr. Good words, I pray you.

1. Many fore-caſt perils where they need not : and ſo, many times are more afraid than hurt. As *Salomon* obſerued long a-goe, *Prou.* 22 13 *The ſlothfull ſaith, A Lyon is without, I ſhall be ſlaine in the ſtreetes.*

2. Our life and ſtate is not without perils at home : and I tell you, if theſe Aduentures as you call them, be not better fol-lowed than yet they are, they will, and cannot but more and more increaſe.

3 No Aɛ̃ion of ſuch a weight and worth as theſe are, can bee without ſome perils, hurts and loſſes, which yet muſt be aduen-tured and indured in hope of a greater good, and ampler recom-pence another way.

4. Hee is not worthy to receiue ſuch benefits as theſe Ad-uentures may yeeld him, that for feare of euery inconuenience and danger, is ready to fall off, and diſclayme them *Neque mel, neque apes,* ſaith the olde Prouerbe. No Bees, (for feare of ſting-ing) no Honie.

5. Of perils and miſaduentures, ſome are meerely *Caſuall*, and not to bee auoyded, ſome are altogether *needleſſe*, and might haue beene preuented The former of theſe muſt be borne with, as a part of that common calamity, whereunto the life of man is ſubieɛ̃, and of thoſe croſſes and afflictions wherewith God doth either try his Children, as Gold in the fire, or afflict and puniſh them and others. For theſe, no man ought to bee troubled and diſmayed in theſe courſes, more than for the like in any other, nor diſlike them one iot the worſe.

Wee finde, when God would bring his owne people the chil-dren of *Iſrael* into that good Land, the Land of *Canaan*, which ſo oft & ſo ſolemnely he had promiſed to them and to their Fa-thers, he did it not without letting them paſſe, and feele ſome pe-rils by the way ; as the ſtopping at the red Sea, the purſuite of *Pharaoh*, one while the want of fleſh, another while of water in the Wilderneſſe, the terrour of fiery Serpents, and the aſſault of many and mighty enemies, with other like. Wee finde alſo, that he was much diſpleaſed with, and ſharpely ſometimes did pu-niſh thoſe of them that murmured becauſe of thoſe things, and would haue returned backe into *Egypt*, regarding not to pro-ceed, and accept that Land, that good Land, which the Lord their

God

The Path-Way to Plantations.

God had giuen to them and their feed. And may not this teach vs, That we muſt not looke to haue the hand of Gods proui-dence extended vnto vs without ſome dangers and incumbran-ces: And that the Lord is not pleaſed with thoſe that for feare of euery mis-hap and trouble, will bee diſcouraged them-ſelues, or will diſ-hearten and diſcourage others from ſuch At-tempts?

Chriſt likewiſe the Sonne of God, ſending abroad his Apo-ſtles to preach the Goſpell, is ſo farre from ſecuring them of all troubles and dangers in their indeuours thereabout, that hee fore-tells them, *He doth ſend them forth as Lambes among Wolues* That they ſhould be *hated, perſecuted, and put to death for his ſake, &c.* But were the Apoſtles by this diſmayed? Did they therefore refuſe to vndertake their charge, and proceed in the worke of the Lord? We know the contrary Notable to this purpoſe is the proteſtation of the Apoſtle Saint *Paul,* 2 *Cor* 6 4. and 11.23.

Reſp *I pray you recite the very words, for I deſire to heare what ſo great an Apoſtle hath ſaid to ſuch a purpoſe*

Enr With a good will Speaking there both of himſelfe, and the reſt of his fellow Apoſtles and Labourers in the Goſpell, thus he ſaith. *In all things we approue our ſelues as the Miniſters of God, in much patience, in afflictions, in neceſsities, in diſtreſses, in ſtripes, in priſons, in tumults, in labours By watchings, by faſtings, by puritie, by knowledge, by long ſuffering* and a little after, *By ho-nour a d diſhonour, by euill report and good report, as deceiuers, and yet true as vnknowne, and yet knowne: as chaſtened, and yet not killed as ſorrowing, and yet alway reioycing as poore, and yet making many rich. as hauing nothing, and yet poſſeſsing all things.* And in the ſame Epiſtle, Chap. 11. 23. oppoſing and conteſting againſt falſe apoſtles of thoſe times, that ſought to debaſe and diſgrace him, thus he writeth of his owne particulars. *In labours more abundant, in ſtripes aboue meaſure, in priſon more plenteouſly, in Death oft. Of the Jewes fiue times receiued I forty ſtripes ſaue one, I was thrice beaten with roddes I was once ſtone I I ſuffe-red thrice Ship-wracke. Night and day haue I beene in the deepe Sea. In iourneying I was often in perils of waters, in perils of rob-bers, in perils of mine owne Nation. in perils among the Gentiles*

The first Part.

in perils in the Citie, in perils in the Wildernesse in perils in the Sea in perils among false Brethren. In wearinesse, and painfulnesse, in watchings often, in hunger and thirst, in fastings often, in cold and nakednesse. Beside the things which are outward, I am combred daily, and haue the care of all the Churches. Who is weake, and I am not weake? who is offended, and I burne not? You haue heard abundantly of the sufferings, heare also the inuincible constancy and magnanimity of this admirable Champion of the Lord, expressed with his owne mouth, *Act* 20.22. *And now behold, I goe bound in the Spirit vnto Ierusalem, and know not what things shall come vnto mee there, saue that the Holy Ghost witnesseth in euery City, saying, that Bands and afflictions abide mee. But I passe not, (for it) at all, neither is my life deare vnto mee, so that I may fulfill my course with ioy, and the Ministration which I haue receiued of the Lord Iesu, viz. to testifie the Gospell of the grace of God* And Chap. 21 13. *I am ready not to be bound onely, but also to dye at Ierusalem, for the name of the Lord Iesu.* Hauing such Lights and Leaders for our example, shall we grudge and vtterly refuse to suffer any thing, to hazard any troubles, and to beare any crosses at all, (And it is not possible we should meet with such a measure and heape thereof, as they did by many degrees,) for the Gospels sake, and, besides all other good that may come thereof, that wee may helpe to enlarge the Kingdome of God and his *Christ* on earth? And thus much of the first sort of euill accidents and mis-haps

The other sort, which I called needlesse or wilfull, by which I meane such as men wilfully, through their owne fault doe cast themselues or others into, by their euill managing of any such businesse, by rashnesse, disorder, ouer-sight, or the like, ought not to be imputed to the Actions themselues, as which doe not necessarily draw any such after them, but to the Authors and Actors of the same. As if men meete with dangers at Sea, by setting forth at vnseasonable times, in the Winter, in foule weather, or other like: If they bee surprized by an Enemy at Sea or Land, they going without sufficient forces, both of men, and munition, for such an enterprize: If they be distressed with want of victuals, and other prouisions, when they set forth slenderly, poorely, and ill prouided, with other like.

6. These

The Path-Way to Plantations.

6. These Actions, our Plantations, I meane, properly and in their owne nature, are lyable to as few hazards and mishaps, as any such lightly can be.

For, first, Our Passage to any of the places intended, is very easie, open, and cleare, Sea-roome at will, and, if we take time and season conuenient, as nauigable and pleasant as need to be desired. Few Pyrates on those coasts, and fewer it is probable there would be, if some good course were taken for their repulse and dissipation.

2. Our Accesse and Entry is free and facile for the most part No man once offereth to forbid or hinder our landing there.

3. The people of those Countries, if any bee, ready either for loue and hope of good from vs, kindly to receiue and entertaine vs, or for feare and weakenesse of their owne accord to flye from vs, and betake themselues to more remote and inland parts of those Regions, or to submit themselues tractably to liue vnder vs

4 The Countries themselues free, for the most part, of any noysome or very dangerous either beast or Serpent : not infe-ted nor infested, as some of this Continent, which yet are, and long haue beene well inhabited, with the most dreadfull of these sorts, that the world doth yeeld

5. Wee need not make way for our selues into any one of them at all with fire and sword, as either our progenitors the *Saxons* and *Normans* did into this Land, or our later fore-fathers the *English*, into both *France* and *Ireland* So that euery thing considered, *Wee cannot well wish or expect, in these dayes to finde out, to haue and gaine any Countrey or Place for Plantation with lesse troubles, fewer losses, and smaller dangers*, if things be well hand-led, *then these we may*. Nor is it likely, if wee neglect and ouer-slip the so faire and many opportunities now offered vs, that euer we shall haue and finde the like againe.

Obiect.

Resp. *The profit is small, and little the good that is like to arise of so great labours, dangers, and expences. For whatsoeuer you, and some others talke of great riches there, and that way to bee had, wee heare of none that proue rich and wealthy there*

Answer.

Env It may be so, and there are many reasons for it.

For, first, It is not long that any haue beene in any of these Plantations, and there must be a time for euery thing. They

that

The firſt Part.

that will haue corne from the ground, muſt tarry the ripening of it It is not one yeeres worke or two, to get a good ſtate in Lands, and to get ſome ſtore of wealth about a man in the ſame likewiſe. They that goe ouer to ſuch a buſineſſe, haue many things to doe firſt, before they can haue time to gather wealth about them; as to build, to rid their grounds, to make ſenſes, to deſtroy wilde and hurtfull beaſts, to get ouer good and profitable cattell, to plant and ſow their grounds, and the like : All which be matters of great labour, time and expence We ſee in daily practice with vs, a man that is a Purchaſer, till he hath recouered his Fine, and ſtockt his Liuing, cannot be aforehand and get wealth about him nor can they there, till they haue done thoſe and other like things, which are to them, as it were, their Fine and In-come It is well if ſeuen, or ten, or twentie yeeres hence, happely in the next generation, men can attaine vnto riches. It is enough for the fathers to take in the grounds, and ſettle the lands and liuings for them and theirs againſt the time to come, though for the preſent, and for their owne time, they hardly ſtand vp, and meet with ſome difficulties.

2. Men there, can, making nothing of their grounds yet, farther then any can themſelues employ them to paſture or tillage. It is not there as in *England*, where, if a man haue little ſtocke or imployment of his owne for his grounds, yet he may let them out at a reaſonable rent, but there, more then a man can ſtocke and till himſelfe, lies ſtill, and will yeeld him nothing at all. Make it your owne caſe. If you had the beſt Liuing in this pariſh in Fee ſimple, and had little to put vpon it, nor could get any to rent it, at your hands, could you grow rich in haſte? This is their caſe.

Reſp *Your ſpeech is very reaſonable, I muſt corfeſſe but goe on, I pray you*

Enr 3 All in manner that haue gone ouer hitherto into any of theſe parts, are poore men, men of ſmall meanes, and therefore with little or nothing, it is not poſſible they ſhould in a little time attaine to any ſtore of ſome thing. And the leſſe poſſible, for that the benefit of their labours redounds for the moſt part, not to themſelues, but, as in regard of their great aduentures and expenſes, reaſon is it ſhould, to the benefit of rich men here, that haue ſent them thither.

4. Diuers of them that haue gone ouer, haue beene Bankerutps
G

The Path-Way to Plantations.

rupts and Spendshrifts, Idlers and Loyterers, who, as they thriued not in *England*, (for how should they thriue that run thriftlesse and heedlesse courses?) so will they not commonly in any Land. *Cælum non animum mutant, qui trans mare currunt* : as saith the Poet, Weeds will be weeds, where euer they grow

When men of fashion and meanes doe go ouer, that are able to set vp themselues and others, and that will be industrious to take the benefit of the time and place, then I doubt not but it will soone appeare what good may be done in those places, and that men may, if they will, easily and quickly proue rich and wealthy there Then, and not till then, if riches arise not, let men blame the places from whence it was expected they should arise.

6. The manner of proceeding in these attempts, may also be a great cause, why men attaine to riches there more slowly, then they might and should, if they were otherwise managed.

As, First, If the Plantation begin with a small number, farre too little for such a businesse. For then neither can they bee able to extend themselues farre into the Countries in a long time, and so not to finde out the goodnes, sweetnesse, and benefit thereof: nor to set vp all kinde of necessary trades and faculties among themselues, whereby they may bee able to assist and set one another a worke.

2. If they that remoue hence, goe sparely and ill prouided of cattell, corne, and other necessaries for Plantation and Habitation, which those countries afford not: impossible it is for them to make that profit, and get that increase by their Lands and Liuings there, which they might, if they were well and throughly prouided of such things at the first

7. This is the onely way which men in ancient time did finde out and obserue to get riches and wealth withall, to increase and amend their estate by, when as by multitudes of people their country was, as ours now is, so ouerland, that they could not thriue and prosper therein. Neither were they euer lightly deceiued, but the euent and computation did answer their intent and expectation: And no doubt, if the like courses bee now attempted, they may and will, if they be well carried, produce the like, or rather better and speedier effects to vs then to them. For we haue many helps for peace and warre, for shipping and nauigation, for defence and fortification, for traffique and negotiation,

for

The first Part.

for building and habitation, for religious and ciuill conuersation, for skill in many needfull arts and occupations, which they had not, to further vs withall.

8. Of all other meanes to get wealth and riches by, *Husbandry* (which of all courses of life is that, which in those places must chiefly, and most of all, be followed and employed)hath anciently and worthily euer beene accounted the chiefest, best, and surest. Wherein, though it be somewhat more chargeable, combersome, and for a time, vncomfortable, to enter into a void and desolate country, ouergrowne with woods, thickets, and other like, yet who knowes not, what great oddes and aduantage to the getting of riches and wealth there is: first, betweene the breaking vp of such grounds as were neuer yet employed, but hauing lien waste, vntoucht, and vntilled from the beginning, haue all their sweetnesse and fatnesse in them, and the tillage and vsage of poore and hungry soiles, that from time to time haue beene turned vp and worne out to the vttermost: and then betwixt the hauing of great and goodly Lands, (for there one man may easily haue as much as ten or twentie haue here) and of small and simple Tenements?

9 When *Brutus* came first into this Land, who would haue imagined it would haue proued so goodly, so plentifull, so fruitfull, so rich, so excellent and happy a Land, as we (God be praised for it) doe finde, and all the world about vs doth know it is? And who but sailing along the Coasts of any of those new Countries, or but going ashore here and there, not aboue a mile or two, happely within the Land, can imagine, or conceiue, much lesse, know and vnderstand what wealth and riches, what goodly fields and pastures, hills and valleys, mines and metals, woods and waters, what hidden treasures and sundry commodities are to be found, and had therein?

10 The name of a *Kingdome* is verie great: and what should not, or heretofore, what would not men doe, to gaine a Kingdome? By these meanes opportunitie is offered vnto our Land, to our English Nation, to get and gaine, to possesse and take, to haue and enioy, together with Plantation and Habitation for thousands, and hundred thousands thereof, more then one or two Kingdomes, great and goodly Prouinces, that

The Path-Way to Plantations.

by Gods bleſſing and prouidence towards vs , may in time bee
vnited to the Crowne , the ſimperiall Crowne of this Land.
Which by conſequence , (for what infinite ſtore of riches and
wealth, how many places of peferment and honour, for hundreds
and thouſands of particular and inferiour perſons is there contai‐
ned and comprehended within a *Kingdome?*) muſt needs bring
with euery of them ſeuerally, riches and wealth of great, and in
manner infinite valew and eſtimation

The Engliſh loſt in *France* in the time of *Henrie* the ſixth, two
ſeuerall parts of that ſpacious Countrie , that had beene Engliſh
neere about three hundred yeeres before, that is *Normandie* and

Normandie
and Aquitaine
in France loſt,
and when.

Aquitaine, in the former whereof (ſaith an Engliſh Hiſtorie,
as minding to expreſſe the greatneſſe of the loſſe by the particu‐
lars) there were (then) an hundred ſtrong townes and fortreſſes,
one Archbiſhoppricke, and ſixe Biſhopprickes , beſides ſome o‐
ther townes deſtroyed in the warres : and in the latter , foure
Archbiſhopprickes, fifteene Earledomes, two hundred ſixtie and
two Baronies , and aboue a thouſand Captainſhips and Baili‐
wicks.

Suppoſe we now the ſame had fallen out in our times , (and I
hope I may without offence make vſe of former and forraine
things) would we not, or ſhould we not (thinke you) account
it an ineſtimable loſſe and damage to the Crowne and Countrey
of *England*, worthy to be redeemed with hundred thouſands of
our mony and goods , and to be recouered (if it were poſſible)
with thouſands of the liues of our men, and no ſmall effuſion of
Chriſtian blood? If now contrariwiſe, we may in our dayes , not
loſe, but get, not hazard, but aſſuredly haue and gaine, and that
ſine ſanguine & ſudore, euen without bloud or blowes, and with‐
out any waſte or ſpoyle of our treaſure and ſtate,(I will not ſay the
ſame that we had loſt, but in ſtead thereof) ſome other Regions
and Countries , Territories and places for Habitation, as great,
and (likely in time to proue) as gord as they , might not this bee
iuſtly accounted a gaine and good , an enlargement and increaſe
to our Nation and Kingdome ineſtimable and exceeding great?

Note this

If the name of a *Kingdome* ſhall bee thought too high and ex‐
cellent, too great and glorious for Countries ſo vaſte and waſt,
ſo remote, and obſcure as thoſe of our Plantations yet are , let
them

The first Part.   37

them bee vouchſafed the name but of *Dukedomes*, as thoſe I laſt mentioned, or *Lordſhips*, as *Ireland* for a long time was, or by whatſoeuer other titles, parts or members of a kingdome, hee ſhall be pleaſed to ſtile and nominate them, *Quem penes arbi-trium eſt, & ius & norma loquendi*, as one ſaith, for ſo we haue the thing, it is no great matter for the name : yet, if there may be had, as the probabilities, poſsibilities, and opportu-nities already had and made vs, doe plainly declare there may *in one place*, a Countrey as great, at the leaſt, as that of *Norman-die*, *in another place*, as that of *Aquitaine*, in a third, twiſe as much as they both, that is, ſuch a one wherein there may be in time erected, conſtituted and made (ſpeaking ſomewhat, thought not altogether according to the former proportions) for-tie Earledomes or Counties, foure Archbiſhopprickes, ſixe and thirtie Biſhopprickes, three or foure hundred Baronies, fiue or ſixe hundred townes and fortreſſes, one or two thouſand Cap-tainſhips and Bailiwicks, ten or twelue thouſand pariſhes, and foure or fiue hundred thouſand families, ſhall it notwithſtanding be thought, that there is no wealth or riches, no place of prefer-ment, no hope of dignitie or good there to be had?

Reſp. *If there be ſuch Poſsibilities, yet before the Countries*   8 Obiect. *themſelues can be reduced to ſuch a ſtate, and ſuch diuiſions ſetled therein, as you ſpeaks of, great ſtore of treaſure and wealth muſt bee ſpent, and man y yeeres of time be ouerpaſt.*

Enr. **1.** For Expenſe, not ſo much happely, as one lin- Anſwer. gring warre, the euent whereof is moſt vncertaine muſt and will conſume.

2. The Countries themſelues will yeeld meanes and money enough, if they be well handled, to defray or repay whatſoeuer ſhall be needfull for the effecting of all theſe with aduantage

3 The hazzard and loſſe of life and limme is this way won-derfully ſaued and auoyded.

4 And for time, ſooner happely this may be thus effected, at leaſt, in ſome tolerable meaſure, then a Countrey loſt can bee recouered and quieted As we may obſerue, by the children of *Iſrael*, who ſetting vpon the Land of *Canaan*, and that with a mightie armie, not ſo few as an hundred thouſand men of warre, and with more then ordinary, euen admirable ſucceſſe, *The Lord*

The Path-Way to Plantations.

being euer with them, yet were scarcely setled therein all the daies of *Ioshua*. and neere home too, in our neighbour Countrie. The *Netherlands*, which being reuolted from the *Spaniard* long agoe, he hath not beene able in all our time, to reduce to his obedience againe.

5. And you know, a country being gotten by the sword, may be lost againe by the same. For, *Non minor est virtus, quam quærere parta tueri.* There is more adoe to keepe, then to get such a thing. Of the which there is little or no feare in the attempts that we talke of.

6. In a word, both the expectation and the expence for reduction of those Countries to such effects, will, and may be speedily and abundantly recompenced in the facilitie, libertie, and securitie of the getting, setling, and keeping of them.

Wherefore, *Rumpantur Ilia Cedro*. Let froward *Enuie* her selfe swell till she burst againe, and detracting *Malice*, or timorous *Ignorance* speake the worst they can, yet all that will not be blind, may see, and whosoeuer will vnderstand the truth, may know, that there are Riches and Preferment, much for the present, more for the times to come to be had, if men will but take them, and to be gotten and gained, if they be but laboured and searched for, in the places and precincts of our present intended Plantations.

And now I thinke good neighbour *Respire*, I haue for the satisfaction of you, or of any not peruersly minded, sufficiently iustified these Proiects and Attempts of Plantations for the *generall*, to be in themselues *honourable, needfull, gainfull* and *lawfull*; and for *the particular*, to be neither so *dangerous* or *difficult*, nor so *strange* or *vncommodious*, as at the first shew they may seeme to be.

Resp. You haue indeed, in mine opinion, spoken exceeding well to those purposes. Your latter words bring to my minde that worthy saying of Salomon, Eccl. 11. 4. if my memorie faile me not The words, I am sure, be these He that obserueth the winds shall not sow, and, he that regardeth the clouds, shall not reape. and your whole discourse makes me feare so vrge you with any more Obiections concerning these matters, as which? see by your readie, plaine, and plentifull answer to these already moued, be to little purpose, and will vanish, when they come to be sifted, as smoke before the winde. And if you can yeeld mee

the

The Summe of this first part.

The first Part.

the like satisfaction in some other points, that I conceiue very necessary
to be considered about these Actions, I shall like of them a great deale
better then euer I had thought I should; and be as readie to praise and
commend them, as I haue beene to dispraise and blame them. But therewith I will not trouble you at this present, but deferre it to another
meeting, which God willing, shall be shortly. For I shall not be in quiet,
till I haue heard the vttermost that you either can say, or I am desirous
to heare touching these matters.

Enr I am glad truly, that our little Conference hath so much
preuailed with you. And I shall be ready, and because I finde you
so tractable and reasonable, the readier, to giue you the best satisfaction I can in any thing else, whensoeuer you shall be pleased to
that end to come hither againe

The end of the first part.

BALTHASAR GERBIER, A SOMMARY
DESCRIPTION

Sir Balthasar Gerbier, *A Sommary Description, Manifesting that Greater Profits are to bee done in the Hott then in the Could Parts off the Coast off America: And how much the Poublic Good is Concerned Therein. Referring to the Annexed Advertissement, for Men Inclined to Plantations* (Rotterdam: n.p., 1660). British Library, shelfmark 1029. e.8.(4–6.).

Sir Balthazar Gerbier (1592–1663/7) was an English agent, painter of miniatures and architect. He was born in Middleburg, Zeeland, in the Netherlands, the son of a Huguenot emigrée. On his arrival in England in 1616 Gerbier became a factotum, agent and the keeper of the picture collection of the famous George Villiers, first Duke of Buckingham. After Buckingham's assassination in 1628 Gerbier became an English national, entered the service of the King and was knighted. He is probably today best known for his long and friendly cooperation with the painter Rubens, whom he met for the first time in Paris in 1627. After 1631 Gerbier became the King's agent in Brussels with the mission both to uncover plots against England and also to collect paintings and other objects of art. During the tumultuous 1640s Gerbier stayed in Paris as a political refugee and could only return to England in 1649. Trying to recover his reputation and find a new occupation he published tracts on various issues and involved himself in different projects. However, he was not very successful in his desperate attempt to find a new master or new sources of income. The 1660 pamphlet reproduced here was written at a time when Gerbier had become involved in a failed project to search for gold in Guiana on the west coast of Africa. Sir Balthazar had to flee to Amsterdam after his daughter Catherine had been murdered,[1] and to a large extent this text is a moving piece in which Gerbier gives his personal account of what has happened to him and his family. The last part of the tract is more straightforward and includes a check-list

---

1   For further information, see the entry on Gerbier in *Oxford Dictionary of National Biography* (Oxford: Oxford University Press, 2004), written by Jeremy Wood.

as well as providing practical advice – guided by Gerbier's personal experiences no doubt – for any man who seeks to become a colonizer in America.

A Sommary
DESCRIPTION,
Manifesting that greater Profits are to bee
done in the hott then in the could parts off the Coast off

AMERICA:
And how much the public good is concerned therein

Referring to the annexed

ADVERTISSEMENT,
For men inclined to Plantations.

 N Advertissement for men inclined to Plantations manifesting that greater profits are to bee donne in the hott then in the could parts off the Coast off America, (and which was printed att Rotterdam as appeares by the annexed) hath promissed this Summary Description/ and the which was conceaved fitt to bee publisht with all due and zealous respects unto his Sacred Majesti, as att so greate incomparable an example (of his most extraordinary gratious care for the publicke good) all men are obliged to bee awakened/ and to offer (according unto theire tallent whatsoever may bee off use: And should not all men doe soe? then must every one bee an open
enemy

enemp to himselfe / as also outwozthp that a Souberapne should (as to sap) fatigate himselfe in seeking and practpsing all abbantages / whereby benefits map bee pzocured unto them / which hath so mani-festlp appeared as forrayne nations have not only admired his gracious bounty in the behalffe off his Loyall subjects, butt moved some to offer likewyse certayne expedients. Whereby his service and the good off his subjects may bee much advanced.

The said beeing not onlp a manifest truth concerning fozrapne Nations in Europe, but a most remarcable one in the Inhabitants off the coast off America, who about the tpme of his Sacred Majestys, returning into England) when no Courriers noz weeklp Intelligencers could bzing that happp neewes theire) expzest theire ressentments / which man well deserve to bee taken / notice off / as lickewpse that thp had the tp-ding even in the month of Map Anno 1660. which the heabens must habe bzaught unto them.

The said wilde (in namebut not wilde in nature foz that thp are off a most milde dispofition) said that thp could not endure those men whoe doe not lobe theire Anna Cajoury (which is to sap king oz Scheeff) butt bid wilcome all such as are true unto him bzing them / refreedments off Annasses. And other fruites / as also Wilde deare, fish, and foule, befp-des all what thp could finde in those parts which thp doe inhabite.

And as thp knowe that number off them are on the Ilands of Bar-bados / S. Chzistofters / as also on the same Coast of America as at Sarename, thp (foz as much theire capacity makes them difcusse mat-ters) doe not a little wonder how such a fleave the cold clpme in Euro-rope will transpozte themfelbes to the cold parts of America, and not pzeferre the hot where it never winters / and no fire needes to bee made but to boile theire fish and Crabs / and to coste wilde deere and foule.

That then the lobe off a Chzistian (foz the abbanement of the publick good) map not bee said to bee moze could then the frozen Noztheren clp-me / noz the innocent Charibdiens repzoache unto such a one (whoe thp habe not fapled to bisitte and to impart unto him what the hot parts off America is capable off) his want off charitp. This Summarp Descrip-tion must defend / and most reasonnablp free frome desadbantagious explications on the fresh returne off a notable Equipage whited in the peare 1659. hath been sent from Amsterdam to the Coast of America, and that likewpse no men (indued with comon Sence) map habe anp just cause tot doubt of the truth that this Descripion is wel grounded / it hath seemed necessarp to hould fozth the cause of the re in fata returne of that Equipage; and top the men whoe were sent to that much moze bene-

beneficiall hot partt off America then the cold did not settle theire/ which though it should require averp ample Description hath beene thought fit to contract in as feew lynes as possible map bee/ since it is but to serve as replaye unto the particular Quæritur which map bee made conceening the cause of such returne; yet must the sapd description bee taken frome the spring off the evill/ the which proceded frome a hellish ambition off certayne Thrusties sent whith the afore said Equipage, and who before theire departure frome Texell conbyned against the cheeff Commandor and Patron off an intended Colonie to bee setled on the Coast off America. To make them selves masters, so thy could dispocesse him, or distroy his persson and his familly, that theire migst remayne no pretenders to the Land which he was to pocesse.

Which conbination beeing discovred to the soid cheefe Commandor Sir Balthazar Gerber, authorised bp speciall commission off the Lords Estates generall off the united Provinces/ and off the West-Indian Company/ obliged him (bp the prime Law of selffe preservation, to defend him selffe (as much possibly hee could against such a damnable plot/ which neiuer oughst to have beene expected frome rationals/ nor frome men to whome hee was a benefactor/ and whoe would not have beene admitted without his consent.

Yet so farre had the spirrit off Diluzion charmed them as forgetting God/ and the property off Human Soules/ thp only represented to them selves (as the Phabulous Midas) tot choake them selves with Gold and Silver/ and to ruine head long to those parts were precious things are said to bee had/ as also to meete with cheefs off famillies who might sheew them the wap to el Dorado, and Manua.

Thp thought on nothing eisse save to destrop theire cheeff Commandor/ and his famillp/ as Otto Keye the prime leader who could not so much as dissimule his murdering inclination/ when as hee vented (before his departure from Texel) That hee wold make short worke with the Commandor, and his familly; and (beeing once sett on firme ground in America) either gett a golden fleece, or a rope about his necke) that hee would theirefore copulate with one off the cheef Indian his Daughter,' and then kill him, to make him selffe master off all. So as killing and murthering was the mapn delight and scope off this worsse their Barbarian disposition/ as that off his choist fellow trustees.

In fine/ so as the evill begunne it was pursued, and never ceassed untill after the arrival of the Equipage on the Coast off America.

The Equipage did consist off a hew good Dessels/ wel provided with all necessarpes/ as Dictuals/ Amunition/ Cargazoen/ to Trafficke

A 2

with

with: materialls / Ingredients to purge mineralls Coels to worke with / and to manuer the Land ; One Rijnier Van Buren the Commissary off the Magazyn (a notable hellish monopollist) agitating (as impudently and Impprudently sayd) accordyng unto his secret instructions receaved before his departure frome Amsterdam to combyne against the sayd Commandor resolved as Wel as the others after having made use off severall stratagemes. to make an end off the sayd Commandor and off his harmlesse familly / remitting as his other fellow trustees the prosecution off the establishing off the Colonie / and all the mayne for the which the Equipage was sent untill thy should have performed theire bluddy worcke. which thy compassed in part ; as is particulaly mentionned in the afforesaid annexed advertissement ; Whereby the Quæritur concerning the reinfacta returne of the Equipagie is answeared / and may wel serve for an argument that the sayd Sir Balthazar Gerber could never have donne anny good with such men / who as thy minded but his extirpation / never suffered him after the arrivall off the Equipagie on the Coast off America to settle the intended Colonie / nor to repaire in persson n'ay not so much as to enquire after all such things where unto the Equipagie was sett forth / for thy thought to have gotten outt off him all what soever thy were to purchasse in America and were confident enouff that theire was a fleece to bee had / butt thy would putt it into theire particular sack / for thy were not Ignorant that all the world hath spoken off El Dorado , and Manva , as credible men have publisht that Don Diego d'Ordas , Capitapn to Cortez, (whoe conquered Mexico) did discover richesses in the King dome off Guaiana , as Gaspar de Sylva , and Jean Gonzales did relate Wondrous things off that continent / soo have thy beene sought by Philip d'Uren , Pedro de Lympias , Geronimo d'Ortal , Ximenes , the brother off Ximena de Guesida , Pedro d'Offima and the monck Sala whoe braught cast golden Aigles from thence

Therfore the said combinators kneew wel also / that it was sayd that when the Duke of Buckingham was attending the Prince of greate Britane att Madrid , one Don Anthonio Hennin , had (by Sir Balthazar Gerbeer, been examined / and Introduced to the sayd Duke , that the sayd Don Hennin produced the mynerall / which hee had braught frome America , and that the sayd mynerall did render a verry rich quantity off gold Thy kneew also (especially Otto Keye who had beene present att Delff when by the appointement off that Magistrat a proefe was made off the mynerall) That itt did render gold / and that it was off the
same

same which in the yeare 1656 (in a Schip called the Liesde, which brought from the coast off America.

But so greate theere uniust scope was as to mynde nought butt what might contribute to the rendring off them sole pocessors off all/ and suffer them selves to bee persuaded to make use off anny falcehoods/ whereby thy might disguise theire bluddy deßyne/ and sent horride relations to theire confident Patrons/ among whome theire is one whoe was not aßhamed to boaste to have sayd to a Souveraÿne Prince that Sir Balthazar Gerbeer did not agree with theire Trusters: which iff hee had done by yeelding to theire intent (which was to distroy him and his Innocent familÿ) had beene a most barbarous resolution in him/ and a ßhamefull sygne off weaknisse. As would at present ar= gue no leße incensibillity in him incasse hee should not (as a second Colomba) aquaint men capable off truth off the apparant good which may bee done in the hott parts off the American coast/ and wherefore this Sommary description is putt forth/ where off the particular an= notations must bee on this Prinniple/ That the profits to bee done in the hott parts off America are incomparably more then those which men inpru= dently seeke in the cold. Which to prove on certayne grounds it wilbe best first to fix on a calculation concernnig the charges which men who transporte them selves towards America must bee at/ and therefore to specify a partiular some off mony/ which some have put forth on like occasion/ As for example/ that men who had bestowed one hundred and seventy nyne pounds/ for theire necessary expences for theire trans= portation/ and the preparing off fit grounds in the cold part off America, had not (at the ende off a yeares turmoyle and Labour) advanced a bove thzee pound/ which should seeme to bee al most In= credible.

But that this trueth may plainly appeare the following calculation may serve for the manifestation off the same.

First, a man must for transportation and food for him
selffe; his Wyfe, two Servants, children, and also
for transportation off his houshold - stuffpay att the
least — ff 52 - 0 - 0
For one Child. — ff 1 - 4 - 0
For the first yeares maintenance for foode clothis and
light for him selfe, his Wyfe child and two Servants
att the least 20 Sc. per Weeke, which is per anum. — ff 52 - 0 - 0

For

For the heyer off two labourers for a yeare	ff 12 - 0 - 0
For two Kowes	ff 24 - 0 - 0
For Seedes	ff 4 - 0 - 0
For a Cart and Plowe	ff 6 - 0 - 0
For two beds, cheeres and coverleds	ff 5 - 0 - 0
For Schuvels, Spades, Axes, Hatchets, Pickakes, andother tooles (neceffary to the manvering off Lands)	ff 18 - 0 - 0
For the Building off a houffe, for the Carpenter, with a man, daily wagers and Victuals	ff 6 - 0 - 0
For the Iron worcke neceffary to the house	ff 9 - 0 - 0
For all Kinde off neceffary houfhold ftuff, as Kettels, Pots, Difshes, and Pannes	ff 12 - 0 - 0
	179 - 4 - 0

And is to be confidered / that before any profit can bee had In such a cold clime (frome Lands that muft bee prepared) two peares Wilbe fpent at the Leaft; for that thofe Lands (as Well as others) muft bee cleered frome the Woods Which thy doe beare / the roets and ftompd Wel removed.

That one man cannott cleere / prepare nor mannuer (during the tyme off a peare) more then ten Akers of ground / confifting off fix thoufand ftods.

So as a man muft Weeklp cleere / prepare and mannuer about one hundred and fifty ftods / and / confequentlp daylp fynthien ftods.

And whoe dailp shall cleere such a parcell off ground both off the Wood / roets / and ftomps / muft labour berep hard as ftlaves doe.

Pett Were it fo that in a peares tyme a man could Infalibly prepare fo much ground to make it fit for the Plowe. And that hee could reape fome benefit there on in the fecond Peare / pet muft hee frome thofe ten Akers referve two for hape / and graffe / for two horffes / and two kowes / Which fcarcelp Wilbee fedd / bp reafon off the difference off Lands neewlp made / and thofe Which are troughlp and fullp groune.

So is it neceffarp to keepe two Akers of ground for graffe for the kowes / and the two horffes /

So as off the ten Akers remaynes fix to fowe / where of three map bee fowne with Wheate; one off the three others with ftye; the two other remapning with Barlep/ Oates/ Peafe/ and Benned/ where off the ftpe (growing uppon one off the Akers) wil bee neceffarp for the

the maintenance off the familly / since an Aker off good ground (which can bee sowne with one sacke of Rye) doth noth produce above sixteen sacks / which a familly (consisting off a man / woman / two strong labourers and children) Wil neede for a yeares tyme; As lickwyse the same familly shall neede the production off the two other Akers off ground / for housekeeping / the Barly for Beare / Pease / and Beanes / for Salt Pork / and the Oates for Horses.

The groathe off the remayning three Akers breeing reserved allone for the making good off the expences and the clering off debts made;

But there cannot bee gotten frome the said three Akers above fifty foure sacks off Corne.

Which (when all is considered) cannot yeeld more then the number off people theire can sett ayrisse thereon / no advantage beeing to bee expected by transportation off Corne to other parts off the World / which needs not to send for Corne in America.

So as when all what can bee done in the could clyme off America. (Beeing put together att the best) wil argue it to bee the worst which (men whoe seeke to make a fortune) can bee pitcht uppon iu consideration off the advantages too bee made in the hott clyme off that continent.

It wilbe verry easy to all rationalls to graunt that the said hott clyme ought to bee preferred before the could / where the ground beares al the yeare long / because it never whiters theire / grapes culd all the yeare long frome the Stalke; as all other fruites. Cattel producing abondantly; no such cost necessary as cloathe clothing (and other chargeable defence) against the feercenisse off Winter season / and no such indispositian tormentig the boddyes of men as occasionned by could mists / piercing Windes / Hayles / Snowe / and hard Frosts / etc.

All which is found to bee true / and not needing other tongues to speake it / nor yens to wryte it / then those off that people inhabitting the Charibdis Eylands / as likewyse Sarenamme, and Cajana, on the Coast of the firme Land off America; where (as is mentioned in the aforesaid annexed advertissement for men inclined to Plantations there) a most profitable settlement can bee made / and by the Service of Slaves (whoe neede no cloathis against the could / nor bedding / nor anny other such chargeable accommodations as a could Clyme doth require; from which hott clyme ready returnes of precious things can bee made without the losse off two yeares tyme / as in the could clyme;

Were no such cost must bee bestowed for the buylding off houses for men / nor Stables and chargeable barring for the placing off Cattell; for as the inhabitants (called the wilde thoug verry tame good people) will

will in feew dayes make a convenient habitation for one Axe, hatchet, and some knyffs, the Cattell lives all the yeare long in the open ayre.

The Slaves neede no clothis/ and beeing once baught and payed are during all theire lyffe tyme workmen without wagers; when by one day free to themselves in the weeke thy get theire one living/and whoe doe more worke (at there ease) then two Christians can performe/ both in the manuering off the ground/ and in digging off mynes.

Noris in the hot parts of America in the beginning off Plantations much Cattel necessary for houskeeping/and the Labouring of grounds/ the greate aboundance off fruite considered: off fish/ foule/ and Wilde Deare/ which all the yeare long is to bee had theire/ Nor neede habitants furnish theire houses with such chargeable houshold stuff as thy must necessarily have in the could parts/ nor bedding/ nor Scheetes/ for that in the hot parts a Hamack (to bee had for one hatchet) is the best bedd that can bee made usse off/ both for the night/ and for a fresh repose in the day tyme/

The difference off the profits which are to bee done on the commodityes which canbee gotten frome the sayd hot parts (and those which are gotten in the could) beeing as greate as the difference off the worth off them is/ and were of anny understanding person can make the estimate/ especially such men whoe knowe what distinction theire is to bee made betweene precious things/ or of greate exteeme/ and ordinary commodityes/ As the precious to bee had in the Hott parts of America are Gould, Silver, Stonnes, of greate value, precious Woods, for all kinde of rare workes, for Dye, Collours, as Orian, Rocous for scarlet dye, and the Ultermarin, precious Balms, Armadac, Bolus, Caffia, rare Gumes as Lemnæ; sennement, which hath the Vigor off Cloves, bessydes Hony, cleere as Christal, and Wax, as theire hath beene found store off Nutmegs with Mace about them; which though some men gathered during the rayny months, (that thy whœre as unrype Aprikoks fallen yough to the ground) have taken to bee but Wilde/ yet in all appearance (by reason of theire shape/ colour/ inward baynes/ and theire taste) may (beeing full growne and parfaict rype) prove to bee right/ and of greate concernment.

The soyle (by reason off the degrees onder the which it lyith/ and the rayne which falls in the Season which in Europe is the winter/ and yet in America continuall warme dayes) beares continuall/ without Intermition/ and in such a quantity as Jean Claasen Langendijck the Commandor in Cajana (five degrees by North the Lyne Equinoctiall) doth assure/ that certayne part off his most rocky grounds which had beene

beene decreed to habe within six months tyme after (for want off conti=
nuall trimming off the same) beene as high ober groune agayne as o=
ther part off Lands wold not habe beene in six Yeares / the which
ground Sir Balthasar Gerbeere and his familly hath seene; and otherwa=
yes would habe douted off the report.

The Planters lykwise did relate that Sugar reedes habe beene found
there as thicke as a mans arme / and that theire cannot bee better
ground in the Wor0 for Sugar / Indigo / Cotton / Tobaca / and all
kinde off Seedes.

On which infalible principle all men (desirous to Improve them
selves by plantations) may take there Levells / and bee justly moved
to preferre the Hot clyme off America before the could / and that Wit=
hout scrupule off making use off Slaves by reason off an opinion enter=
tayned by some /: that it is not Christian-lycke to use rationall creatures
in that quallity off Slabery / when as the custome Was permitted in the
old Testament , the neew forbids it nott , and the Imperiall Laws suffer the use
off them ; bycause Slaves bought in severall parts off Africa (where thy
will sell them selves agayne / thoug by the death off theire masters thy
are become free) lve theire in the Slabery off the Divill , but by theire
transportation among Christians are in the first place (by education and
good example) changed as frome brutes / into rationnalls / and in the
second by a custome (which must worke upon them / except God bee
pleased to suffer his extraordinary Mercy to lay hold on theire Soules)
braught to call upon his name / by faith in Christ Jesus , for the which
theire Slabish condition proves to them a verry great blisse / since o=
therwayes thy (as experience hath manifested but to often) returning
unto theire one / will likewyse as Dogs returne to theire Vomit; besi=
des Which reason (to serve against misse and over scrupulous men) it
may well bee said that theere is a greate mistake in manny whoe doe I=
magine that the keeping off Blacks in that manner bee a casse more hard
then that off Servants whoe all theire Lyffe long live in serbitude /
and whoe doe as much worke (according unto the constitution off theire
boddies) as anny off the Blacks , called Slaves / whoe doe not as the
Holland mades Scoure and wach on the Sabath Day) yet doe not
the Holland madens faire on the delicatnesses which the hot parts of
the world doe afforde / and may bee sayd that Anthonius (at the Table
off Cleopatra) had not better ; no kings in Europe tasting te Annas , the
fruite which King Jeames (off blessed memory) sayd the Wilde worre
on worthi off /

So all men inclyned to Plantations (by the best profits to bee done
                                    B   With)

with the neceſſary husbandʒ (which in matter of Improvementſ by negotiation/ and by manuering off groundʒ is a capital point) may (iff thy pleaſe) alſo reflect on the following calculation/ Whereby it appeareʒ/ With how much leſſe charge a Planter may fit and tranſporte Sum ſelſſe to the hot parts off America, then to the could) Where off an eſtimate is ſet in the beginning off this ſommary deſcription/ viʒ.

Iff a family (conſiſting off husbond/ Wyff and Childʒen) ſhall reſolve to tranſporte it ſelſſe to America, as the Patrons of a Company Wilber contented to beare the chargeʒ/ to receave them a gayne out of the fruiteʒ of the groundʒ/ which the Planters can (by a feew thingʒ taken allong with them (befoʒe theire departure) fynde wherewith to make good thoſe chargeʒ att an eaſy ratte/ the which cannot bee done in the could parts of America, A parcell of knyveʒ (woʒth thʒee pence a peece) ſome Areʒ/ hatchetʒ/ Siʒarʒ/ Raʒerʒ; Glaſ beadeʒ/ and ould courſſe Linnen will avayle/ them/ as is mentionned in the afoʒeſayd pʒinted advertiſſement/ to get foode/ both of fleſh/ fiſh/ and foule/ and dʒincke in abondance/ as lickwyſe many thingʒ whereon thy wilmake greate pʒofitt/ Pareſʒ/ Aeyʒ/ Monckiʒ/ Hamackʒ/ and ſeverall other thingʒ/ beſydeʒ the honny/ Balmʒ/ Gummeʒ/ and Coloureʒ/ which the Indianʒ will bʒing unto them.

And as thy ſhall not pay foʒ the tranſpoʒtation of theire ſervantʒ/ ſo thy ſhall not neede to pʒovide befoʒe hand to the nurriſſement of ſuch Slaveʒ as thy would Imploy and ſhal bee delivered unto them on the place/ ſave but foʒ eight months tyme/ untill the unpʒepared ground ſhall have been made fit/ and pʒoduce farinne/ whereof bʒead is made.

Theire muſt then (in the firſt place) bee reckonned the chargeʒ foʒ the Caſſavy, which is a roote where off the Indianʒ doe make bʒead/ and is ſold by them foʒ a top of beadʒ/ oʒ a knyffe/ not woʒth ſpeaking of/ So is theire dʒincke (called parnaw) as good Bier/ Cawalw/ and the delitious dʒincke called Jamany, fiſh/ foule/ and wilde deare accoʒdingly/ and as is particularly mentionned in the affoʒe ſayd pʒinted advertiſſement.

Whereby it appeare that Whoeſoever leaveʒ the could parts of Europe, to repayre to the cold of America, betterʒ not his condition/ but that thoſe whoe doe go to the hot part makeʒ as to a Land of pʒomiſe/ and may welſerve to Chriſtians to conclude/ that it muſt bee very good beeing in Heaven, ſince there is ſuch a wel beeing on Earth.

If therefore men ſhould bee inclyned to putt a ſtock of monny to gether/ to make an Impʒovement/ wherin the publicke good oft thoſe
off

of the Christian profession is concerned / and the encreasse of Trafficke in all the Charibdien Eylands / in the which severall things are requisitte / and in some of them wanting / as the inhabittants at S. Eustaches wel knowe / and feele; besides others / who (out of certayne respects shalbe spared to publish) The undertaking might bee begunne with a fashionnable Equipagie, and fitt to transporte a number of Planters, and men to worcke in mynes, and wel skild in the extractions off myneralls · The vessels must not drawe above 9 or 10. fotre water.

The Planters must bee rationalls, and nott bee accompanyed neither with Dames that cannot live without codlings, and rose Water, nor without to see a Cock end a Beare by ting, nor with Holland Idolatrous mad weomen, that cannot live without scouring, robbing, and washing on the Sabath day, nor expect trimmings in prancking houses, with a sect of Porcelyns, But good Husiffs, that will pust theire hands to the Planting off good Sugar reedes; at the least bee as God mayd them for, faithfull helping hands to theire husbonds in the survaying off his workmen, and Slaves

They must bee persons knowen in theire Parishes to have a good repute off a temper to live according unto the Laws off God and men. for that otherwayes it is impossible to make any good establissement / especially in an unhabitted part off the World / when boistrous men shall turne more wilde then the Salvages: and (at the Damnable Example of others) harboure but murthering thoughts / as experience speakes but to many have done; and Especially those of Tabago knowe, those of other parts can tell, and those of Cajana can relate, that the cheef Commandors have been murdered, some in theire Cabin, some in the woods, some headlong throwne in the Sea, by a rebellious generation as that of Vijpars pest Europians / forsoth.

An Equipage (well manned and well provided) may take for the fittest tyme of departure the beginning of the month of march / or the latter end of it / att furthist) to arrive (in fit season) on the coast of America after the rayny months may bee past / which commonly is at the end off may.

The Equipagie must bee a company ed with a barke built at the Bragantyne fashion: fourty foote long / thirteen foot wide / and covered / a convenient Cabin a last / the barke drawing but 3 or 4 foote water / to serve on the Rivers / and may bee provydes with two brasse peeces of ordinance / the sayd Barke must bee put to gether either at the Eyland S. Vincent, or at Cajana.

The provisions of Pease / Beanes / and other graynes / or Seedes / must bee fresh / and not off a yeare old.

The

The maine provisions must bee good Beef, Pork, dryed fi∫ck, Chee∫e, Pea∫e, Beanes, Oatmeel, Barley, Meel hard pre∫t in dry fats, Rys, Store off Oyle, ∫tore of ∫trong water.

For the Cabin {
Vinnigar, whitte wyn for∫icke per∫tons, Butter, dryed Samon, Gamon off Bacon, Oeates, Neates, Tongues, Pickeld Sturgen, ro∫ted mutton, and Hens, Layd in Butter, put in greate ∫tone pots, and in Barells, the ∫ides (on the out ∫yde of the pots) filled with bay Salt, ∫alted Concombers, turky beanes, greene broume Capers, ∫alt Lemons, ∫alted Cabus, pre∫erved Gingember, Spyces, Prunes, Rea∫ins: All kinde of Routes, Seedes, and Plants, Soape Wax and ta∫low candles, Oyle for Lamps, &c.
}

**As for commodities to trafficke with the Inhabitants / ** Storre off cour∫∫e Linnen, made Shirts, woln wa∫cots, and drawers, Felt hots, gray and blacs, Shoes, and all kinde off Sarges for the Eylanders.

But for the Inhabitants off the firme Land Store off Iron Axes, Hatchets, Knyfs, with whitte bone handles, figured, ∫trong greate and micle ∫ize Hoecks, and Harpoens, Sizars, Razers, off ∫mall price, as the Knyffs not exceeding three pence, or a groathe; Beades off all colours, and off an equall ∫i∫e: No toyes off whi∫∫els, and loeking gla∫∫es, ∫ave to give away.

As for nece∫∫aries to Planters / Sugar Mills, with theire appartainances, Kettels, Ba∫ins, Leadels, and for di∫teeling off ∫trong waters, (which are as the maine pre∫ervatifs) and without which no worke to bee performed in the hott parts.

Theire mu∫t bee likwy∫e Iron plates for the baking off Ca∫auy, Iron tooles for clean∫ing off the grounds, wheel-borrowes, Shuuells, Spades, Pickakes, Bricks, to make Hovens, Pan-tyles, Boards, nayles, Bolts, Hinges, Locks, Tents.

And for defence again∫t forrayne Invasion / Mu∫quets, fire Locks, half Pijckes, and Rapiers, wit Pouder ∫hot and match.

Burding peeces / for huntsmen / and nets for fi∫hing: Some ma∫tis and ∫pannialls for hunting.

For the purging off Mineralls all nece∫∫ary tooles, as likewi∫e engredients, materialls, and Sea coales, for the furnay∫es; ∫cailes, greathe and ∫mall, to way: Paper, Pens, Inck, Sealing wafers and hard wax.

1. All Planters theire per∫∫ons, wy∫∫s, children, and ∫ervants, with theire hou∫bold ∫tuff, to bee tran∫ported free, paying only nyne pence a day for theire food, to bee bated out off the ∫ruites which thy ∫hall ge∫t out off the ground,

2. The ∫ayd Planters to bee (on the ∫ame condition) provided by the Patrons

trees off the Colonie for the tyme off eight month, untill the grounds shall have prodveed a groath off the Soedes which the Planters shall have throone theerin.

3. As much Land allotted unto Planters as thy shalbe able to manuuer; and whereoff thy sul afterwards dispose by will, deed, or Contract, as off there are.

4. All Planters shalbee free off taxations, duyes, and all kindes off rights, for the tyme off ten yeares, and afterwars pay the tenth.

5. Iff thy discover Mynes off Gold, Siluer, Christall, precious Stones, Marble, Salgem Fishing of Perles, or Corall thy shall enjoy them freely, save that after the end off fyve yeares thy shall pay the tenth.

6. Thy shall have liberty to fish, to hunt, and to cut donne wood for building, and fyring, but not re cust precious wood.

7. Thy shall have as many Slaves as thy will for fistkeen pound a peece, and pay them out off the fruite and Production off the Lands allotted unto them.

8. All men shall enjoy Liberty off Consience, so thy Live according unto the knowne Lawes· off God, and men, and therefore theire shalbe, good Divines, preaching sound Doctrine, A juditious boddy of Councill; phisicians, and Serugiens for the boddy, chets well provided with medecinall, and Surgery drugs, and Ingredients. a trumpetter to call the people to assemble/ and for other necessary Warnings.

Finally/ it wilbe very easy for Patrons of such a Plantation to Judge that thy may doe good profits for theire disbursement on such a dessine in the a foresayd hot parts of America, and that thy will have greate reason to preferre them before other ordinary wayes to profit by/ since thy well knowe what small rents Lands doe yeeld/ to what Loue an Ebbe trafficke is in this age/ and how by reason of the greate number off men (whoe professe a trade) every trades man is almost reduced to a kinde of Slavery/ for that men must worcke frome breake of day untill late in the night/ as cohabitants in streets where hard trades are practised can witnesse the same/ and are early and late a wakned by the noise/ when as all Patrons of Plantations may in the aforesayd hot parts of America frome Lands which thy neede not to buy/ nor to fyght for (but only settle people on them as thy are of a vast extent) make theire revenue the greater/ and by the woorth of what thy will produce get more then the treble/ nay the quadruple cent per Cent for the stock thy shall puyt forth.

Therefore at it is a providence to Imploy a stock of mony on severall things (as to put marchandises in different Vessels) So lords/ gentlemen/ marchants and others may fynde it to bee good husbondry to bestowe some part of what thy can lay assyde to the tryall of this most

A 3 appa-

apparant good / and thincke that a brase of hundred poundes lesse spent in sports / feastings / and other unnecessaryes (as Tulips and Cockell Shells) would incensibly serve for this well promissing dessyn / and answeare the prudence beseeming good Commenwealths men / and the care of Fathers of families / to leave an incessant growing benefit for theire posteritye / more then by other expedients thy can promisse to them selves . As likewyse not only to encrease trafficke to the people which hath setled it selffe on the Charibdes Eplands but to become a support and mayne defence to them / against Powers) whoe (as the Portugises envaded Brazill) might in tyme set upon them / and depryve them of all the expectation of theire many yeares endeavours .

FINIS.

ADVERTISSEMENT
𝕱𝖔𝖗 𝖒𝖊𝖓 𝖎𝖓𝖈𝖑𝖞𝖓𝖊𝖉 𝖙𝖔
PLANTASIONS
I N
AMERICA.

At ROTTERDAM,
Printed by Herry Goddæus, Booke Printer att the red Bridge/
In the Booke Printing. ANNO 1660.

ADVERTISSEMENT.

A Ll men whoe doe resolue to leaue theire naturall Country
to applie them selues to Plantations must haue for theire
maine Scope either the publike or theire particular interrest / which they must promote by right and most conuenient meanes / without which it otherwayes would be
impossible to compasse the same.

So men whome doe leaue a could Country transporting them selues
far from thence / to plant in as could a clyme into annother part of the
World (as that wherein they were borne and bred) cannott Improue
them selues by Plantasions / as they might well in a more hott region /
where the ground yelds fruite and growth all the yeare long / according
as credible trauellers doe report; and as they proue how much the greater
profits can be made on the Charibois Eyslands (as Tobago granada /
guardeloupe. S. Eustache / Lucie / Martinique / Christoffers / and
Barbados / etc. (seated under a warme degree) then in Virginia /
Eschebe / New Engeland / etc. So it is most certayne that the
firme Land on the coast of America (from One untill 9. and ten degrees by Nord the lyne) is to be preferred before the Eylands; for as that
coast is not subiect to Hieracans (as the Eylands are) it is most fruitfull /
and hath many convenient Riuers for Plantasions; and in seuerall parts
inhabitants (though very fiew in number) of very good nauere.

By the late Suruey which hath been made of the coast of America /
experience tells that from one untill 9. and ten degrees by Nord the
lyne / theire are Lands where on store of People could be setled / and that
the grounds are most fit for Sugar / Tobacco / Indigo / Cotton / and all
Seedes of Fruites soeuer / Store of wilde Boares Heares and Rabits
to be had theire ; as all kinde of good foules / the Seas and Riuers abounding in store of greate / fatt / and wholsome fish / besides an infinite number of Tortuses / which is a wholsome foode ; as likewyse Sea-kowes / which the natifs (called the wilde) are willing to take / and doe
serue for those that will either transporte the same to the Eylands or feede on them; as they may bee had for so small a thing as is almost incredible /
to witt a Tortus (where on 20 men may plentiously feede a whole day /
for an Irron hatchet / and 2 pennyworth off glas beads; The Sea-kow

A 2 (waying

(waping foure a ffoe hundred pound) for a couple off Axes/ and one hatchet/ with some smal beads; twinty a thirty pots of drinke (called Pernaw as good as any beare) for one kniff with a wihet bone handle/ worth two pense and halve/ wild deare/ fish/ fruite/ and foule according unto that ratie; So as besides the feeding there with number of men theire can bee a very profitable trade settled/ and driven with the afore-said Sea-Cowes/ and Toptuses; thy being salted/ and transported to the Eylands/ where for one pound of that salted fish two a three pound of Tobaco may behad; and as for a Hamac (which costs butt one hatchet worth two schillings) twenty schillings may bee gotten.

And as the Lands on the mayne continent are more fruitfull then the Eylands/ and wholsome/ so are thy of a large extent; and doe beare in certayne parts costly woods for divers workf/ and dyinge/ all kinde off excellent gummes/ as Lemnae; Balm/ Rocour (which is a Scharlat dye) and other collours/ Arindac/ Henniment-Clour/ nutmeg/ and Mace/ as theire is Honny as cleere as Christall/ and waxe; So is theire most certainly mynes of Silver/ and Gold/ where of proofes have been made/ and certayne cheefs of the Charibdiens have shuen severall patterns/ as also off severall woods/ Colours/ gummes/ and other hings off worth to be had theire/ some off these natiffs also knowing in what parts and in what Rivers precious/ Stones are to befound/ as likwyse with what nations Must bee treated for the same/ so men will (and can) live without giving offence on the subject of their Wibes and Daughters.

The severall parts which can bee inhabited by Planters and that are free (nor needing armed men to take pocession off them) have good Rivers/ some large Bayes/ affording number of Sea-kowes; so theire Strands Store of Toptuses.

Those who would plant on Rivers which end with watter fallf must have small flatt bottom boates/ as Indian Canoos; to hayle them from one water fall to the next River over Land/ to gett upp deepe into the mayne Land; carry allong store of victualls/ and drinke/ of Strang water/ feare the want there off make them loose their labour/ and hop-full expectation; as happened to severall french and others/ wo did seeke for el Dorado/ and Manva/ and sayd to have come short butt one dayes Journey of Hills that promissed wonder full Tresors; Not to be sauht in an imaginary region/ butt to bee found on that continet by Perssons whoe are suffered to apply theire best Ende abiours to the same/ and whoe are nott Crayterously (and murderously) used as Sir Balthazar Gerbeer hath been in the yeare 1660. on the 7. day off May/ when after his arriball on the aforesaid Coast of America/ and that he had gayned on the affections off certayne cheef of the Charibbis (who braught unto him severall paterns of the things before mentioned/ and

ns

as wett in his poeſſion; contracted frenſhipp with him by theire great Eye of Poimary) was by Truſties (ſend along from Holland) nott only ſett uppon/ butt alſoo the perſſons off his Wyff and Daughters; thoſe unnaturall men (worſe then Heathens poeeſt with evill Spurrits) theire horride deſſare being as then to murder an Innocent harmleſſe familia/ to the end that theire might nott remayne one a life of the family who could pretend right in thoſe parts/ in conſequence off a graunt which the ſapd Sir Balthazar Geſber (in a tyme that his Majeſty of greate Bittane no; none of his partye was in caſſe to countenance a Plantation in that part off the World where off the late Duke of Buckingham during his being att Madrid in the yeare 1623. Yott Notice.) had receaved from the Lords Eſtates generall of the unpted Provinces/ and from the Weſt-Indian Compagny.

To which bluddy beſſyne (of the murderers which coſt the life off one off the ſapd Sir Balthazar Gerbeers Daughters to witt Catharin, the ſapd murderers truſtees were (as hath been ſince diſcovered) ſecretly inſtructed/ by a particular ring-leder (even from the beginning of the voyage from Holland) to ſett uppon the Proprietary/ as the mayne grand ſcope of men who would betray theire oune fathers/ and brothers/ to attayne to the Mamon of the World.

Truth having mannifeſted the ſame on this particular caſſe/ and that thy made no ſcruple to excerciſſe any open Violence/ which thy were not aſhamed to putt in practiſe by hailing Sir Balthazar Gerbeer (and the remnant of his family) violently from the aforeſapd Coaſt/ to the ende the abetters off the pryme Truſtye might remayne as independents/ and ſend to the place a broode off theire owne Tribe; and therefore commended highly that pryme thruſtie fo; his doings; Neceſſity to preſerve theire intereſt it ſo requiring (ſayd they) and being not aſhamed to argue that theire ſapd Intereſt had been in greate dangiour in caſſe Sir Balthazar Gerbeer ſhould have ſnowmen that the king off greate Brittanne was reſtorred to his right/ fo; that ten he would have advertiſed the Engliſh nation (the beſt off all others aquainted with Plantations) off the good which was to bee done on the Coaſt of America/ and how thy might have en larged the Colonie of the Engliſh at Sarenamme.

And therefore (ſay they) theire pryme thruſty to have deſerved greate applauſe fo; al the violence committed againſt Sir Balthazar Gerbers perſſon; and they to have had greate cauſſe to drive him to a non plus/ after his returne to Amſterdam; hinder him (iff poſſibly thy could) from departing from Holland; to remaapne in poceſſion of his papers/ Originall Evidences againſt the murderers; and producing any witneſſes againſt them/ finally to remaapne maſter of his graunts/ and Octroys/ which thy forced from him by an outragious apprehenſion of his perſ-

A 3   on

ſon; with violation off their contracts; and yett pretending that the inſraction of them and the injurious proceeding againſt the ſayd Sir Balthazar Gerbers perſſon may without knowledge off the whole aſſociation/and only hammered by two or three off theire members/ in number above thirty two/ and pretending (as thoſe two or three att the moſt ſayd) only to ſatisſy theire particular curioſity with the view off his papers/ and off the grantts/ Swearing and bowing that none off all thoſe off the Company had the leaſt thought off the world ever any more to looke after Gould nor Silver on the American coaſt/nor to ſend theither/when as to the contrary/ they being no ſooner in poceſſion off all Sir Balthazar Gerbers Evidences (now of papers) which did not concerne that deſſine and as yett by them ſhoune falſly and unjuſtly detayned) Butt this immediatly cauſed the ſhip called the Concracht to be prepared/ and retayned as many of the men as might ſitt theire turne/ which thy have appointed to returne to the place from whonce Sir Balthazar Gerber and his familly was ſo violently hayled; and have ordered theire ſayd brood to ſpend a yeare or two in a generall Search throughout all thoſe Territories/ for all what is to bee gotten theire.

But how ſuch men ſo unjuſtly proceeding may ſpeede God (whoſe arme reatcheth further then the ends off this viſible world) knowith; and tyme will Manifeſt/ As this map ſerve to all thoſe that are curious to knowe ſommarily the truth of this caſſe; and to underſtand on what conditions men might ingage on ſuch a good deſſine/ and how we Planters may improve them ſelves in thoſe parts; as namly. All Planters may poceſſe gratis in propriety ſo much Land as they can mannuer, with an entire freedome to diſpoſe thereof, either by will, deed, Covenant or Contract, all Planters bee free off Cuſtomes, rights, or dutties, during the thime of ten yeares; have ſlaves for fifthien pound a peece, pay them either in reddy monny or with the commodities off thire owne plantations, taking the tyme off five yeares for the ſame. Freely enjoy all ſuch mynes off Salpeter, Irron, Copper, Silver, Gould, Chriſtal, Precious, Stonnes; Marble, as Planters may finde within theire allotted Lands; paying for them after the five yeares a certayne duty off ten in the hundred, fiſhing, hunting, and cutting off wood for building and fire free; and enjoy libertye off Conſience: be tranſported to the place within the tyme off two months, the winds being proſperous, and make choiſſe off theire habitations, either neere the Bayes or Rivers where the Sea-Cowes are in greate aboundance, or lower, towards Cap Orannie; or in the River Wiapoca: wherein ſhips (drawing deepe ten foote water) may well ride att an A.ker, as in that off Apperwake (4 degrees by North the Lyne) for that the ſayd River off Apper, wake is in its entrance (at half Ebb) fourtein foote deepe, and hath 3. 4. and 5. fadoms water untill 14. dutch leagues up the River; ſo.
hath

hath the River on the east-side is the River Apperwake, and good Lands, some 6 or 7 mystes high: WIA betweene 4 and 5 degrees (and syding on the Eyland Cajany) a goodly River, Wherein Ships (that drawe 12 foote) may enter and ryde safely; and is deepe 4. 5. a 6 fadoms. the Land (two mystes from the Sea) a most fruitfull Soilt; so is Cananama: and Tamary by Nord Cajany, towards Surenamme.

What profits such Planters (that have somewhat to bestow on axes / hatchets / glas beades / and coursse Linnen for the inhabitans / to witt / certapne Charibdiens who frequent those Rivers with theire Canoos) may doe is plainly erprest in this Advertissement.

What profit a compan may doe (without to greate charges) is likewise demonstrated / for as a quantity, off Salt taken from the Eylands may serve to salt Sea-Cowes, and Tortuses, to send to the Charribdie Eylands; as likwyse a Chargarsoen off Beeff, Porc; Oyle, Sac. strong waters, stuffs, and Linnen Coers and other. will quitt all the charges for the transportation, and settling off the Planters. so the setting men att worke on the myres / gathering of all things off profit / and making sarch through those parts / according unto the contents off this advertissement / and the secret information which the autor had long since / which as he intends it for the publike good / so may all men (desirous to improve themselves that way) bee further satisfyed on what theire Interests may require concerning the same; by making theire adresses unto him.

And see by the following Lines / what just cause the author hath had (making mention of the perfidious proceeding of men against his person and familly) to point so particularly (as he doth) att some off them / since thy have beene so malitiously Impudent as to vent a world off false hoods concerning his proceeding / and to erpound the best care he could apply for the furtherance off the designe in an ill perverse and horride sence; theire truslies having been so abominabel wicked as to potesse all the People (that was imbarcke att Tessel) that his designe was to epose them all to a Boucherie off other nations in Europe, by cause he on the occasion off a crake which the mayne mast of the prime Ship had gotten on the highe of Hirland) consulted the Captapne off the Ship where annother mast could bee had / where on the Captapne replied England / which the perfidious Truslies made use of as to argue the same to have been a plott to runne with al the Equipage into England and that after his arrivall att the Eyland Cajana 5 degrees bynord the Lyne (where one Ian Klaessen Langendijck. One of the Westdian Companies Officer theire reteaved the authors familly / and lodged the same wanting of necessarp ryue off refreshm ent Wich Denis Gringor (heere tofore Captapne off a Frensh Ship butt now a Planter

ter on Cajana) did speake with Sir Balthazar Gerber, as likewise one Ca-
pitayn Tillet did / where on (though the sayd persons theire conversa-
tion/with Sir Balthazar Gerber tended butt to advertise him of advantages
to be made in those parts/ yett The blud thirsty disguised the moxe theire
resolved firious thereon/ and trapterously abused even off the Lords
States Generall by framing an act off arrest of the persson of Sir Balthazar Gerber, where in thy alledged/that thy where authorised to proceede
as thy did/ and that by the sayd Lord States Order; and having in
that manner surpized the capacity off Soldiours (which thy had made
drunke with strong Waters/ and provided with armes and Shott)
Lead them on the 7 of May the yeare 1660 (when the Commander Langendyck was not in his Port) to breake in his House / as thy did about
dinner tyme; sett uppon the sayd Sir Balthazar Gerbers familhy/ and after
thy had nust to kill Debora his longest Daughter/ shott Catharina)
who departed this World that night/ shott Mary her Sister through
her right Legg/ and sett a pistol on the head off Sirr Balthazar, butt
fayled/ yett would have dispatcht him and the remnant off his family
had the Murderers not been prevented by the Inhabitants off Cajann,
and by the returne off the Commander Langendyke, who putt some off
the murderers in the Irrons; save one Rijniet van Buren whoe did act his
trapterous act so (according unto the secret instructions which he pretended to have had before the departure off the Equipage from Texell)
as to goyne the masters off the Ships/ and the Sea-men to haple Sir
Balthazar Gerber and his family on board/ to worke outt that designe
where by his abetters would stripp the proprietary as afore sayd of his
ryght; which being matter off fact/ hath been (by witnesses examined uppon Interrogatoires) declared uppon oath/ before the Magistrat off Amsterdam/as appeares by theire declaration and theire Citty
Seale there unto applyed; In conclusion it may be sayd that whoe
hath had to doe with such a broade may alledge the words.

I have laboured in vayne. I have spent my strenght, for nought;
and in vayne; I Isaiah. ca. 49. v. 4.

B. G. D.

These wil bode bee had (att the weekly Intelligencer at London / as
(here after) an exact description of the profits to bee done more
in the native then in te could contries of America.

A. *het Huys van den Commandeur Langendyck.*

Otto Keye *moordenaer*   Otto Keye   *den Burre Deonly*   Adolphus Rhenanus *moordenaer*

B. *Otto Key breeckt in 't huys.* C. *is Debora Gerbier die Adolphus Rhenanus ter aerde smyt, en 't rapier ontweldigt.*

AN ANSWER OF THE COMPANY OF ROYAL ADVENTURERS

An Answer of the Company of Royal Adventurers of England Trading into Africa, to the Petition and Paper of Certain Heads and Particulars thereunto Relating and Annexed, Exhibited to the Honourable House of Commons by Sir Paul Painter, Ferdinando Gorges, Henry Batson, Benjamin Skutt, and Thomas Knights, on the behalf of Themselves and Others Concerned in His Majesties Plantations in America (1667). Cambridge University Library, shelfmark Bb*.4.16(D), 3.

The circumstances behind this petition are described at the beginning of the text. The interests of the American plantations have been disturbed by the inauguration of the African Company of Royal Adventurers, the petitioners complain. Through the monopoly of the slave trade with America the interests of the American plantations have been violated. Better than most pamphlets from this age, this shows the importance of interest groups both for the formulation of state policies and for economic doctrines and beliefs during this period. It also gives an interesting hint as to how the trade in human slaves was looked upon at the end of the seventeenth century. According to this pamphlet it was necessary in order to make profits from the American plantations in the Caribbean and the present-day Unites States.

In the Cambridge University Library copy, the pagination of this text follows the page numbering, which is incorrect. The pages have been reordered here to reflect the sense and the tag-words.

A N
ANSWER
OF THE
C O M P A N Y
O F
Royal Adventurers
O F
ENGLAND
TRADING INTO
AFRICA,
TO THE

PETITION and PAPER of certain Heads and
Particulars thereunto relating and annexed, exhibited to the Honourable House of *Commons* by
Sir *Paul Painter*, *Ferdinando Gorges*, *Henry Batson*, *Benjamin Skutt*, and *Thomas Knights*, on the
behalf of Themselves and Others concerned in
His Majesties-Plantations in *America*.

Anno Dom. 1667.

(1)

To the Right Honourable the Knights, Citizens, and Burgeſſes Aſſembled in
PARLIAMENT.

The Humble Petition of Sir Paul Painter *Knight,* Ferdinando Gorges, Henry Batſon, *Gentlemen, and* Benjamin Skutt *and* Thomas Knights Merchants*, in behalf of themſelves and others concerned in His Majeſties Plantations in* America.

HUMBLT SHEWETH,

THat His Majeſties Plantations (having been the moſt conſiderable Trade of this Nation) were at firſt raiſed, and have been brought to the perfection that they now are at, and now do, and did alwaies moſt principally ſubſiſt by the labour of *Negro* Servants, and a plentiful ſupply of them.

That formerly there hath alwaies been a freedom of Trade for all His Majeſties Subjects for *Negroes* on the whole coaſt of *Guiney,* by reaſon whereof the ſaid Plantations have been plentifully ſupplied with *Negroes* of the beſt ſort, and at an indifferent rate, to the great encreaſe of the ſaid Plantations, and the advantage and profit of this Crown and Nation.

That there is of late a new erected *Company of Adventurers* Trading into *Africa,* who claiming to themſelves the
ſole

(2)

sole and only Trade for *Negroes* on the coast of *Guiney*, have totally obstructed the former free Trade of all Adventurers thither ; and having contracted with Forreiners for the supply of the *Spanish* Plantations with *Negroes*, do leave the *English* Plantations in *America*, which produce the same Commodities with the *Spanish*, either ill supplied, and at excessive prices, or not at all supplied ; by reason whereof, and of the obstruction of the freedom of Trade for *Negroes* as aforesaid, all His Majesties Plantations in *America* are at present much decayed, and unless a timely remedy be provided, will speedily be brought to inevitable destruction.

> *Your Petitioners do therefore most humbly pray Your Honours, upon consideration of the Premises, and of the Paper hereunto annexed, to provide such remedy therein as to Your Grave Wisdoms shall seem fittest,*

And Your Petitioners, as in duty bound, shall ever pray, *&c.*

Paul Painter.	*Ferdinando Gorges.*
Henry Batson.	*Benjamin Skutt.*
Thomas Knights.	

Die

(3)

Die Veneris, 15 *Nov.* 1667.

A Petition of Sir *Paul Painter* Knight, *Ferdinando Gorges* Gent. and others, on the behalf of themselves and others, concerning His Majesties Plantations in *America,* and the Paper of certain Heads and Particulars relating thereto, and annexed to the Petition, were read.

Refoved, *&c.*

THat the *faid Petition and Paper annexed be committed to the Committee of the whole Houfe appointed to take into confideration the general Ballance of Trades ; And that the Clerk of this Houfe do deliver Copies thereof to fuch perfons as fhall defire the fame on the behalf of the Royal Company, or other perfons concerned, who are to deliver in their Anfwer thereto in writing by this day feven-night ; and that the Royal Company do then caufe their Charter to be brought in.*

WILL. GOLDESBROUGH,

Cler. Dom. Com.

The

(4)

The Paper of certain Heads and Particulars annexed, and relating to the aforementioned Petition.

THE great and high Advantages which have formerly accrued unto his Majefty and his Subjects, by his Majefties Colonies in *America* , may much appear in thefe Particulars.

1. The faid Colonies have yearly imployed above Four Hundred Sayle of Ships, moft of them confiderable both of burthen and force, to the great encouragement of Navigation, and increafe of Sea-men, which have been ever reputed as the mayne Bulwark and Defence of this Nation.

2. The faid Ships for the moft part were fraughted out with Manu-ctures of *England*, (viz.) Shooes, Stockings, Serges, Broad-cloaths, Carfeys, Hatts, all forts of Wrought Iron; with great ftore of Provifions, as Beef, Butter, Flower, Peafe, &c. which gave Imployment and Bread to many Thoufands of Families here , and put a Value upon the Commodities of our own Growth and Manufacture ; which otherwife would have foon abated in their price, and been of little worth.

3. The faid Ships in return of the faid Goods and Manufactures came laden home with Sugars, Cotton, Ginger, Indigo, Tobacco, &c. all which were produced by the Induftry of the laborious Planter, with the help and former conftant fupply of *Negroes* brought to them from the Coaft of *Guiney*, &c. without which the faid Colonies muft inevitably be reduced to ruine and deftruction.

4. The Manufactury of this Nation exported, as alfo the Sugars, &c. imported, brought in a great Revenue unto his Majefties Cuftomes; which was not onely very confiderable in its felf, in refpect of other vaft Advantages which accrued thereby unto his Majefty and Subjects in general , (viz.) The moft part of the faid Sugars, &c. were from hence fhipt out again and exported into Foreign Countries , and by that means retuned back unto us laige fummes of Money or Commodities equivalent, for that upon the great Wheel of Trade of good and Staple Commodities are little inferior to, or lefs affected than ready Bullion.

An

(6)

An Accompt of divers Oöſtruċtions to the beforementioned Advantages,
occaſioned by the late erected Company of Adventurers *trading*
into Africa, *who have ſolely ingroſſed the* Guiney *Trade for* Negroes;
which muſt inevitably ruine His Majeſties ſaid Colonies in America, *unleſs timely prevented.*

1. **T**HE ſaid *Guiny* Trade for *Negroes* was formerly Free to all
Adventurers, and that without prejudice to the Gold Trade
there, which was heretofore mannaged by the *Eaſt India Company*, for
that the ſame cannot be well maintained without a great and general
Charge, as the building of Forts, ſettling continued Factories, &c.
which the Trade for *Negroes* in no wiſe requires, It being the moſt
uſual way for the ſaid Adventurers to procure their *Negroes* by Ranging
or Coaſting it along thoſe vaſt Territories, without intrenching upon,
or aſſiſtance from the ſaid Factories and Forts. By which freedom of
the ſaid Adventurers Trade the Planters were heretofore plentifully
ſupplyed with *Negroes* upon reaſonable tearms, without which they cannot ſubſiſt; And likewiſe had of courſe conſiderable Credit with the
ſaid Adventurers, whereby the ſaid Colonies have attained unto their
late perfection, without any coſt or charge to this Kingdom; And unleſs
ſuch freedom be continued, the Plantations already compleated will
ſoon decay, and thoſe that are in their Infancy never advance.

(8)

2. The faid late erected Company are of late very much funk in their Gredits amongft Merchants, Owneis of Shipping and Tradefmen, to many of whom they are very much indebted for Freight of their Ships and Goods, And being often demanded to pay the fame Debts, they have refufed, and ftill do refufe to pay the fame, declaring they have no effects in their hands to enable them fo to do; and fo by confequence their Trade following their Credit, they are, and needs muft be very un-capable to afford the faid Golonies any fuitable fupply of *Negroes*, and alfo mannage their Gold-Trade; Whereupon they have lately taken up an unknown way of granting their Licences to others of his Maje-fties good Subjects to fetch *Negroes* from *Guiny*, exacting for the fame two, three, four and five Hundred pounds a Ship; which faid Snmmes of Money fome have been inforced to give, or fit ftill, and fuffer their Plantations to come to ruine, which is the moft intollerable Grievance and Oppreffion that ever was impofed upon his Majefties Subjects planting in thefe parts, and trading to the fame.

3. They

(10)

3. They have contracted with the *Spaniards* to supply them yearly for a term of years with Thousands of *Negroes*, which the *Spaniard* imployes in planting the same Commodities in his Plantations, as are now planted in His Majesties Plantations ; which Contract the said Company hitherto have not, and for the future must not faile to perform, although his Majesties Plantations remain totally unsupplyed; whereby the *Spanish* Plantations and Commodities must of necessity flourish and rise, and his Majestie's moulder away, and come to nothing, Whereas the Free Adventurers for the *Negroes* Trade formerly never used to sell any *Negroes* to the *Spaniards* or other Foreigners whatsoever, but brought all to his Majesties Plantations, and thereby the same being plentifully and at indifferent rates supplyed with *Negroes*, have risen to be so considerable a part of the Interest and care of the Crown of *England*, as they now are.

4. They have greatly opposed the Planters in putting an unreasonable Price upon the *Negroes*, which were brought upon the said Companies Accompt, for that formerly they were sold for 12, 14, and 16 pounds Sterling a Head, or 1600 *l.* and 1800 *l.* of sugar, And now of late Five and twenty pounds a Head Sterling would have been given by his Majesties Subjects the Planters, when at the same time they sold to the *Spaniards* the Chief of their *Negroes* for Eighteen pounds Sterling a Head,

(12)

Head, intending thereby to compell the said Planters to a most unreasonable Complyance ; By which means also none but the Refuse *Negroes*
were left to be sold unto the *English* Planters , who refusing to buy the
said Refuse most of them died upon the said Companies hands ; And
the said Planters have been of late so meanly supplyed , that *Negroes* are
now sold to them at the rate of Thirty pounds Sterling, or Five thousand
pound of Sugar each *Negro* ; This usage so discontented the Planters,
that they resolved not to load upon the said Companies Ships, although
the Freight was offered by them under half the value then given to other
Ships, and the Grievances of the Planters in this particular in all probability might too much contribute to the too easie Surrender of *St.*
Christophers and *Syrinam.*

5. The Affairs of the said late erected Company are managed and
carried on in a way very grievous; for when any Disputes have arisen between them and their Masters, and Owners of Ships, or Seamen, *&c.* they
will ever be their own Judges; They have unjustly , and without any
good colour , seized and converted to their own uses here in *England* divers parcels of Merchants Goods without any legal proceedings , alledging that they will not be tryed by Juryes, *&c.* And if it happen that any Person whose Goods they have wrongfully seized seek
his remedy by his Majesties known Laws of the Land, they presently
threaten to cause the Matter to be brought before and determined by
his

(14)

his Majefty and Council; and accordingly have done it, to the end they might over-awe all Perfons at their own will and pleafure, and affright them from endeavouring to feek after the ufual, plain and appointed way of Legal proceedings for the redrefs of the Wrongs they receive from them.

6. The *Dutch Weft-India Company* had formerly a farre greater Trade to *Guiney* than the *Englifh*; but for many years paft, before the conftitution of this Company, and whilft the Trade for Gold was in the management of the Worthy the *Eaft-India Company*, and an open free Trade for *Negroes* allowed to all Adventurers, the faid *Dutch* Trade did yearly fo apparentiy decay, that One hundred pound Sterling of their Original and Principal Stock was not worth Ten pounds Sterling, Whereas fince the faid late erected Company have taken place, each One hundred pounds Sterling of the *Dutch* is now become worth near Sixty pounds Sterling, And the Concerns of the *Englifh* go as much to wrack, and will undoubtedly in a few years, as alfo his Majefties faid Colonies in *America*, unlefs feafonably prevented, be brought to nought.

7. If it fhall be objected, That this Company doth not participate of a Monopoly, becaufe their Books were laid open for all men to fubfcribe that would? It is anfwered, That their Books indeed were for fome time laid open, But not till upon good grounds it was generally
believed

(16)

believed that the moſt part of their Stocks was conſumed, And they had run themſelves upon ſo many other great Inconveniencies, That no prudent Merchant, who onely aimed at a Profit upon the Stock, without ſeeking after indireĉt Advantages from the Company in other by-wayes, would engage amongſt them.

Paul Painter.   *Ferdinando Gorges.*
Henry Batſon.   *Benjamin Skutt.*
Thomas Knights.

(5)

The Anſwer of the Royal Company to the Paper of certain Heads and Particulars annexed and relating to the afore-mentioned Petition.

THe ſaid Company do acknowledge, That his Majeſties Plantations are conſiderable for the Trade of this Nation, and ſo were, before the Eſtabliſhment of this Company : But they ſay, That the ſaid Plantations were never ſo well ſupplied during the pretended freedom of Trade for *Blacks,* as they have been by this Company,ſince they were eſtabliſhed, nor his Majeſties Revenue by Cuſtoms larger,nor the Trade for thoſe parts ever more fully ſupplied with all ſorts of Merchandiſes and Proviſions.

And

(7)

And as to the Obstructions which they object this Company have given to that Trade, They hope this Honourable House will by the Answers hereunder written receive satisfaction, and judge that the Petitioners Complaints are altogether causeless.

In Answer to their first Article, the said Company say,

THe whole Trade of *Guiney*, *Binny*, and *Angola*, was incorporated many years since by a Patent, as now it is ; and those Patentees purchased Lands of the Natives, and for their necessary security erected several Forts, Garrisons, and Factories, on the Gold Coast, and other places ; who after they applied themselves principally to the Trade of Gold, did in few years lose the greatest part of their Stock ; and the reason was, because the profit of that Trade would not defray their charge of maintaining Forts and Factories, and the hire of Ships, which brought home nothing but a Pot of Gold to defray their freight, there being at that time very little or no Trade for *Blacks* to the Plantations. About ten or twelve years since they licensed Ships at 10 *per Cent.* on the *Cargoes* : And then, the exporting of Gold out of *England* being prohibited, and the Trade of *India* being principally carried on with ready money, the *East-India* Company for their conveniency hired the Castles, Forts, and Trade of the Gold-Coast, of the said former Company, which did turn to account to them , in regard their Ships outward bound to *India* touched there without any considerable charge, landed their Goods, and carried away the Gold to *India* : But since this Company was erected, they having setled several more considerable Forts and Factories, and been at charge to maintain them, they have found, That the Trade of the Gold-Coast cannot possibly be maintained without the *Negro* Trade : And notwithstanding what the Petitioners say to the contrary, That very *Negro* Trade cannot be carried on so well as by going first to the Gold-Coast, and taking thence some of those *Negroes* for Guardians to the Leeward Coast *Negroes*.

And should not this Trade for *Negroes* be carried on by a Company, as the Petitioners confess the Gold-Coast Trade ought to be, the Traders would be subject to the Injuries, Affronts, and Losses as formerly, of which the private Traders a little before the beginning of the late *Dutch* War complained to this Honourable House against the *Dutch*, alledging their Losses alone, immediately before the erecting of this Company, to amount unto 300000 *l. Sterling*, or thereabouts ; for the prevention of which, this Company since their Trading there have constantly

B   sent

(9)

sent out Ships of force to protect their Trade for *Blacks*; and whenever that care is neglected, that Trade will be lost; for the charge of its protection cannot be maintained by private Traders.

And the said Company farther say, That they have supplied the Plantations more plentifully and cheaper, and given as much credit or more for *Negroes*, then ever the private Traders did or could give, as will appear; by which means all the Plantations have flourished more then ever they did, until the late War broke out : So that it may reasonably be concluded, That if the *Negro* Trade should be separated from the Gold-Coast Trade, and so left open, it would certainly lose the Gold-Trade, which cannot bear its own expence, and prove a great prejudice to, if not the ruine of the *American* Plantations.

To the second the said Company say,

It's too true, That the Company is indebted to several persons, occasioned by their great losses; *viz.* There was taken from them at *Goree* by *de Ruyter* the value of 100000 *l. Sterling*, at *Cormentine* 60000 *l. Sterling*, at *Sereleon* 4000 *l. Sterling*, at *Syrinam* and *S. Christophers* 20000 *l. Sterling*. But these Losses could not have sunk the Companies Credit, had the Planters and Merchants, especially those of *Barbados*, complied with their obligations, who owe the Company 90000 *l. Sterling*, of which they of *Barbados* owe 60000 *l. Sterling*, which last debt is thrice as much as the Company owes to any besides their own Members. Yet the Company do not refuse to pay their debts, but pay interest to all their Creditors, and do discharge Principal and Interest as fast as their effects come in, which are coming daily. Nor have they only enough left to pay their debts, but likewise to carry on the Gold-Trade, and furnish the Plantations yearly with as many *Negroes* as they shall have occasion for, and that at moderate rates, hoping they will pay their old debts, and be more just and punctual in their payments in future.

But yet they acknowledge, because their Effects were abroad, they were forced rather then the Plantations should want a supply of *Negroes* for this time, to give Licenses to several persons to Trade to *Guiney*, and have taken of them towards the maintenance of Forts 3 *l. per* Ton, or 10 *per Cent.* on the *Cargo*, which is less then the Company pays in proportion upon their whole Trade; which is the course that hath been taken not only by the former *Guiney* Company, but by the *East-India* Company in their late united Stock : And the Company hath hitherto been so careful to supply the Plantations, that in the time of the great

B 2   *Contagion*

(11)

Contagion (when all people fled from the City) they did difpatch nine Ships to *Guiney* purpofely to fupply them with *Negroes*, and fo have continued difpatching Ships fucceffively all the time of the late War, fo that there hath not been any want of *Negroes* in any of the Plantations.

To the third the faid Company fay,

It is true, That the Company underftanding that the *Spaniards* were Treating with the *Dutch Weſt-India* Company to furnifh them yearly with a number of *Negroes*, for preventing of that Bargain to the *Hollanders* (which muft inevitably have brought a great inconveniency upon the Plantations, by the competition with the *Hollanders* for the procuring of *Negroes*) and to bring a confiderable return in ready money into this Kingdom, and hoping thereby in time to introduce a Trade into the *Spaniſh Weſt-Indies*, did contract with them for the delivery of a certain number of *Negroes* yearly (though at a low rate, yet fuch as would have brought yearly into this Kingdom in pieces of Eight 100000 *l. Sterling*,) on purpofe to keep the Trade from the *Dutch* : But they never delivered to the *Spaniards* more then 1200 *Negroes*, nor are they obliged to deliver them any more, becaufe they have broken their Articles with the Company. And notwithftanding that Agreement, the Company furnifhed the Plantations with 6000 *Negroes* and upwards every year; which were more than they would buy of the Company, who were forced to keep many of them on their hands until they perifhed : And it feems very ftrange the Planters fhould complain of the Companies felling *Negroes* to the *Spaniards*, when as they themfelves fold many of the *Negroes* they bought of the Companies Factors to the *Spaniards* ; Nor do the *Spaniards*, as they alledge, imploy their *Negroes* to make the fame Commodities as our Plantations do furnifh : For it's well known they ufe them chiefly in their Silver-Mines, and Domeftick-Service.

To the Fourth the faid Company fay,

The Company did fupply very plentifully all the Plantations with *Negroes* ; and that there might be no caufe of Complaint, they informed themfelves immediately after the fealing of the Patent how *Negroes* had been fold the four precedent years, and found that 17 *l. per* Head or 2400 pound of Sugar was the *medium* price, and they ordered their Factors to fell them to the Planters accordingly, and gave notice thereof

to

(13)

to his Excellency the L. *Willoughby* Governor of the *Barbadoes, &c.* to be communicated to all the Plantations ; Who did publish the same by Drum and Trumpets, and caused the Companies printed Declaration to be fixed in all publick places of the Island of *Barbadoes, &c.* Copies of both which Letters are hereunto annexed. And the Company say its utterly untrue, That the Planters would have given 25 *l.* for such *Negroes* as were sold the *Spaniards*, or that none but Refuse *Negroes* were left to be sold to the Planters ; for that the Company always did order them to be sold in Lotts according to the custome of the Countrey. It may be true, they have of late (by reason of the Accidents of the War) paid 30 *l.* for *Negroes* ; and so we have in *London* given 6 *l. per* Chaldron for Coals, when before the War they were sold at 20 *s.* But it is utterly untrue, That the Planters for that pretended cause refused to load Goods on the Companies Ships ; for they have constantly refused those advantagious offers of cheap Freight on the Companies Ships from the beginning, even at that time when *Negroes* were sold them at 17 *l. per* Head. And it is a sufficient Evidence, that *Syrinam* and *St. Christophers* were very well supplyed with *Negroes*, by the great Loss the Company had in each place ; and also by Letters received from the Governor of *Syrinam*, who ownes, That the Credit they had from this Company had brought that Place to that good condition they were in before the *Dutch* possessed it.

To the fifth the said Company say,

There have never any differences arisen between the Company and any of their Masters and Owners of Ships, or Seamen, which have not been amicably ended in the same manner as the *East-India Company* determined matters of that nature: And as to that charge, That the Company have unjustly, and without any good colour, seised and converted divers parcels of Merchants Goods to their own use, the Company say, That they never did use any such unjust practice ; but they acknowledge, That the Petitioner *Skutt* having let a Ship to this Company for a Voyage to *Guiney*, and by *Charter-party* covenanting to carry no other but the Companies Goods therein, the Company upon search made in the said Ship found a parcel of Goods which were none of theirs, nor licenced by them to be carried, and thereupon they ordered them to be taken out of the said Ship, and carried into the Companies Warehouse ; and afterwards one *John Kirkham*, who it seems was Partner with the said *Skutt*, brought his Suit in the Exchequer against some of the Servants
imployed

(15)

imployed by this Company; and thereupon (true it is) that the Company did humbly represent the truth of the matter before the King and Council, praying their direction therein, conceiving if a practice of this nature should be admitted, it would be destructive to the Charter: But the King and Council made no Order therein; and afterwards the said *Kirkham* did agree to refer the matter to two of this Company, yet to this day has not made any application to have the same determined; and the Company now are and ever were ready to appear and answer any Suit he or any other shall commence against them at Law; And they say, that is absolutely false, that the Company ever said they would not be tried by Jury; which imputation being so scandalous and false, the Company hopes this Honourable House will give them reparations against the Petitioners.

To the sixth the said Company say,

It's wholly untrue what they alledge; for it is notorious that from the time of the forming of this Company, to the time of *de Ruyters* taking their Ships at *Goree*, the *Hollands West-India* Stock declined from 14 to 10 *per Cent.* and was never since valued at above 18 *per Cent.* at highest, which advance proceeded from their Capture of this Companies Estate, and not from the mal-administration of the Trade; for without reflection upon the *East-India* Company, they affirm, (and let their Books and this Companies be Judges) That this Company sent out more Goods in one year to that Coast, than the *East-India* Company did in all those five years in which they had the Trade: And which is yet more, for every shillings-worth of *English* Manufacture which that Company exported for that Trade, this Company sent a pounds-worth, and that of Manufactures of the same Species, which this Company procured to be made here, and the *East-India* Company bought from *Holland*: So as it appears, That neither the *Hollanders* Trade or Stock is so much encreased, nor ours decreased, as the Petitioners most mistakingly alledge; nor can this Company be affected with any thing but what befel them by the War, which was their misfortune, and not their crime.

To the seventh the said Company say,

The Companies Books were open when the Charter was first granted and made publick, as by the several Printed Declarations hereunto annexed doth appear, which were fixed in all parts of *England*, and in all
C the

(17)

the *American* Plantations : And no difparagement to the Petitioners, as prudent and honeft men as themfelves did fubfcribe without any of thofe indirect and by-aims as they pretend, as this Honourable Houfe will perceive when they perufe the lift of the Adventurers names hereunto annexed ; and we doubt not but they will likewife give reparations to fo many worthy perfons as by this Article are fcandaloufly abufed ; Efpecially when it fhall be confidered,

First, That the Stock which preceded this prefent Stock was never more than 17400. *l.* and though the moft part of that were laid out in erecting two Forts, and fetling Garrifons to fecure the whole Trade of the River of *Gambia* ; yet no man that knows any thing of the importance of that River, would think that a confumption of the Stock, but a moft prudent imployment of it, from whence a plentiful harveft of profit was rationally to be expected, and hath been, and may yet more abundantly be reaped ; and therefore the Merchants who engaged in the new Subfcription were not fo im. prudent as the Petitioners report them.

Secondly, That thofe Merchants who engaged in this prefent Additional Stock , were not men that aimed at indirect Advantages by it ; for *de facto* it will appear by the Books, that thofe who had the adminiftration of it , did fo faithfully and induftrioufly. manage the Trade and fo far engaged their own perfonal Credits for the Common Intereft, that before 80000 *l.* of the fubfcribed Stock was paid in, they had fent out to the value of 150000 *l.* and by a clear ballance of the Books had gained 80000 *l.*

From all which this Company doth humbly prefume to hope that the Wifedom of Parliament will difcover :

That this Trade incorporated to this Company is in its Conftitution National.

That without Forts and force by Land and Sea, it cannot be fecured to this Kingdom.

That without the Royal Authority, and a Joynt Stock, thofe Forts and Forces cannot be fupported.

That the whole Charge cannot be born , but by the United Advantage of the Trade of the whole Coaft of *Africa*.

And upon the whole, that thefe Petitioners Allegations will refolve into this, That they being poffeffed of a fufficient part of our Stock on which to manage the Trade of *Blacks* themfelves, they would have the Authority of this Houfe to follow it for their own Accounts, as they have had the advantage of the dilatory proceedings of the Courts of *Barbadoes,*

C 2

badoes,

(18)

badoes, to detain the Companie's Estate from them, wherein the Planters (our Debtors) are Judges.

One thing the said Company must needs adde, That they believe a Correspondence must needs have been between these Complainers and the *Dutch* ; for before we knew any thing of their Design, or before they had presented their Petition to this Honourable House, they had taken care to make the *Dutch* rejoyce at the Ruine of the *Royal Company*, which is expressed in the *Harlem Gazett* of the 30th. of *October*. So that we have too much cause to suspect they are under-hand set on by the *Dutch West-India Company*, who doubtless would purchase the Dissolution of this Company with a greater Summe of Money than ever was subscribed to support it.

By Order of the Company of Royal Adventurers of England *Trading into* Africa.

ELLIS LEIGHTON, Secret.

NEWS FROM NEW-ENGLAND

News from New-England (London: J. Coniers, 1676). Bodleian Library, shelfmark Pamph. C 137 (15).

While the plantations in the south of the present-day United States depended upon the transportation of black slaves from Africa, other problems faced the colonists in the northern colonies. This fascinating account provides a vivid picture of the clashes between the natives and the British colonists which occurred quite frequently (but perhaps not in such a dramatic manner as is recounted in this pamphlet). Even today there is no consensual view of how intense such clashes were, or indeed how much the native Indians suffered from the early colonization by British immigrants and traders. However, the great Indian wars, during the War of Independence and in the nineteenth century, were at this time still far in the future.

NEWS FROM

New-England,

BEING

A True and laſt Account of the preſent Bloody Wars
carried on betwixt the Infidels, Natives, and the
Engliſh Chriſtians, and Converted Indians of
New - England, declaring the many Dreadful
Battles Fought betwixt them : As alſo the many
Towns and Villages burnt by the mercileſs Hea-
thens. And alſo the true Number of all the Chri-
ſtians ſlain ſince the beginning of that War, as it
was ſent over by a Factor of *New-England* to a
Merchant in *London*.

Licenſed *Aug.* 1. *Roger L' Eſtrange.*

LONDON,

Printed for *J. Conyers* at the Sign of the *Black-Raven*
in *Duck-Lane*, 1676.

(1)

*A True and Last Accompt of the Present Bloody Wars carried
on betwixt the Infidel Natives and the English Christians
and converted* Indians *of New* England, *&c.*

THOSE Coals of Discention which had a long time lain
hid under the ashes of a secret envy; contracted by
the Heathen *Indians* of New-*England*, against the English; and Christian Natives of that Country brake out
in *June* 1675. both Armies being at a distance without doing any
thing remarkable till the 13 of *December* following; at which time
the *Massachusets* and *Plymouth* Company marching from *Seconk*, sent
out a considerable number of Scouts, who kill'd and took 55. of
the Enemy, returning with no other loss but two of our Men dis-
abled, about three days after came a perfidious *Indian* to our Army
pretending he was sent by the *Sachems* to treat of Peace, who was
indeed no other but a Spy and was no sooner conducted out of
our Camp but we had news brought us that 22 of our Strag-
ling Souldiers were Slain and divers barns and out houses, with
Mr. *Per. Bull,* dwelling house burnt by him and his Trecherous
confederates which waited for him. The next day as the *Connectick*
Army under the Conduct of Major *Treat* was Marching to Joyn
with the *Massachusets,* and *Plymouth* Company; they were assaulted
by the *Indians*, but without any loss, they taking eleaven of the
Assailants Prisoners.

The 8th. of *December,* our whole Army being united under
the Conduct of Major, *Genr: Winslaw,* went to seek out the Enemy whom we found (there then hapening a great fall of Snow) securing themselves in a dismal Swamp, so hard of access that there was
but one was for enterance which was well liv'd with Heathen
Indians, who presently went out to assault us; but we falling
in Pel-mell with them; with much difficulty gained the Swamp
where we found above 1500. Wiggwams and by night, had pos-

A 2   session

(2)

feffion of the fort; of which we were difpoffeft foon after by an
unexpected recruit of fresh *Indians*, out of an adjoyning Swamp,
but our Noble Generals infatiable defire of victory prompted
him to fuch brave actions, that we following his example to the
enemies coft made our elves abfolute Mafters of the fort again,
Although we purchafed our fuccefs at fo dear a rate that we have
fmall caufe to rejoyce at the victory; yet when we confider the
vaft difadvantage they had of us in number, whom we collected
to have 4000 fighting men, and we not much more than half fo
many, we have great reafon to blefs God we came of fo well,
our dead and wounded not a Mounting to above 220, and the
enemies by their own Confeffion to no lefs then 600, the chief
officers kild on our fide were Capt. *Davenport*, Capt. *Johnfon*,
Capt. *Marfhal*, Capt. *Gardner*, Capt. *Gallop*.

　　Captains Wounded were 4 viz. *Sealey*, Major *Waii*, and
Bradford, Leiutenants wounded were 4 viz. *Savage*, *Ting*, *Upham*
and *Warn*.

　　In this bloody Battle we gave fo bitter a Relifh of our Englifh
valour and our converted *Indians* refolutions, that they dreaded
our neighbourhood and thought themfelves unfafe till fecur'd
by fix or feaven miles diftance from our remaining Army, where
they remain'd near a month not attempting any thing confiderable till the firft of *Feb.* at which time a certain Number of them
made defperate through hunger came to *Pal kse*, a Little Town
near Providence, and attempted the houfe of one Mr. *Carpenter*,
from whom they took 20 horfes 5 head of Cattle and 150 fheep
And fet fire on a houfe at South bury wherein were two Men,
one Woman and feaven children, on the 4th, of *February* the
Chriftians received private intelligence from the Inda who had
Sculked ever fince th laft Battle in certain woods fcituat about
3 miles from *Malbury*, that they were drawn up into a body
and encamped in a well fortified fwamp where, notwithftnds
might the foe affaulted the Rear, wounded our of our men, and
we killing fo many of theirs that they thought fit to to take their
flight and leave both it and their wigwams to our if or l,
who lodging in their Rooms that night fet fire to a 5 of their
Wigwams next morning, and by this light purfued them fo clofe
that we kill'd divers of them whom age or Wounds rendred incapable

(3)

pable of keeping up with their Companions, and refolving to continue, the queft with all the celerity immaginable; they led us to another Swamp, whofe Rocky afcent propounded fo great a difficulty to attain it, as would have Staggar'd the refolution of any but a refolved Mind; but we attempted it with the like refolution and fuccefs as we did the Laft; the enemy by a fpeedy flight leaving us in full poffeffion of all they left behind them.

We Perfued them two dayes after this encounter, but then (which was on the 5th Feir.)finding our men wearied with fpeedy marches, our provifion fcarce through continual expence and no recruit, our horfes tir'd, and our felves hopelefs of overtaking them who had great advantage of us in paffing over Rocks and through Thickets, which our Foot not without much difficulty could, and our horfe were altogether Incapable to do; our Commanders after a Councel of warr, refolved to fend the *Maffabufets* and *Plymouth* Company to *Malbury* and the *Connecticks* Army to their own homes which was accordingly done. And Major Genr. *Winflow*, only with two Troops to *Bofton* leaving the foot at *Malbury* and *South-bury*, who came home on Munday following and were all difmift to their feveral habitations except Capt. *Wadworth* who was left at *Malbury* in perfuit of the Enemy, of whom he deftroyed about 70 Old Men Women and Children who wanted ftrength to follow the fugitive Army.

The Defperate heathens takeing advantage of the difmiffion of three Difbanded Companies, ftudied nothing but Maffacres outrages, and trecherous hoftillitie, which within two days after thofe faid Companies were difpers't they found opportunity to commit in a Town called *ufhaway* which they fet fire to and burnt to the Ground taking no lefs than 55 Perfons into their Mercilefs captivity, and becaufe the reader fhall underftand the Damnd antipathy they have to Religion and Piety; I would have him to notice how they endeavour to Signallive their Cruelty and grave their enrag'd Spleen chiefly on the promoters of it; for in thefe 55 captives the Minifter of the Town's relations made no lefs then 9 of them viz. Mrs Rowlofon the Minifters wife and three of his children, her fifter and feaven Children, and his fifter and four hildren. The Minifter himfelf with his fifters husbands returning from Love, a little after the engage-

ment

(4)

ment to their infinite grief found their houses burnt to the ground, and their Wives and Children taken Captive, nor was this crueltie commited, as the extent or *Nepolus Ultra* of their vengance, but rather as an earneft of their future *Bearba-ny*. For no longer than the next day after three men Going out, with the Cart were feiz'd on by thefe *Indians*, one of them killed, and the other two not to befound, the day following at *Cox ord*, they burnt one houfe and murder'd three perfons.

In fhort, their outrages are fo many and different, that I muft intreat the reader fince they will not be brought into affuent Narration, to accept them plainly and dyurnully according to the time, place, and manner as they were committed, which is the only way to avoid omiffions, and confequently to Satisfie the inquifitive, who I fuppofe would willingly hear of all the extremities have happened to the fuffering Chriftians in this New *Eng'and* War.

On the 17 of *Febr.* therefore ye muft know that the Town of *Medfi d* was begirt with a regiment of refoleut *Indian*, who affail'd it fo briskly, that maugred all the refiftance made by Capt *Jacobb*, who was then ingarrifon'd there w th a hundred Souldiers for its fecurity the enraged Heathens never defifted their defperate attemps, Battering the Walls, and powering fhowers of Arrows into the bofome of the Town, they had diftroyed above 50 of her inhabitants and burnt 30 of her houfes.

The 9*th.* of *March* following thefe bloody *Indians* march't to a confiderable Twon called *Croa on* where firft they fet fire to Major *Willards* houfe, and afterwards burnt 65 more there being Scaventy two houfes at firft, fo that there was left ftanding but fix houfes of the whole Town, the next day after two men coming from *Ma'bury* to *South'ury* were flain: and the Sabbath day enfuing, thefe deftroying *Ind'ans* came to *P'ym u h* where fixing only on a houfe of one Mr. *Clarke* they burnt, and murthered his wife and all his Children, himfelf Narrowly efcapeing their crueltie by happily at that Juncture being at a meeting.

On the fecond of *April* 1676. Major *Savage*, Captain *Mofele*, Captain *W l an T rnor*, and Captain *Whipel*, with 300 men marching from *Malb row* to *Quabury*, where they had ordered the *Conne en* Army to remain in readinefs againft their coming, whih being effected, a ordingly they joyned forces, and began

their

(5)

their march towards *Northampton*, but by the way were affaulted by the *Indians*, whom they repelled without any other damage, then only Mr. *Buckly* wounded, killing about 20 of the Enemies in a hot perfuit after them.

The tenth Ditto, about 700 Indians encompaft *Northamp'on* on all fides where they fought very refolutly for the fpace of an hour, and then fled, leaving about 25 perfons dead upon the place, the Chriftians loofing only 4. men and 1. woman, and had fome barnes burnt, on the 12*th* inftant they affaulted *Warwick* with fo unhappy a fuccefs that they burnt all the Town except four Garifon houfes which were left ftanding, fix days after Captain *Peirce* Brother to Captain *Perce of London*, with 55 men and 20 Chriftian Indians went to feek out their Enemies, the Indians whom according to their Intelligence they found rambling in an obfcure Wood, upon his approach they drew into order, and received his onfet with much difficulty, being in the end forced to retreat, but it was fo flowly that it fcarcely deferved that Name, when a frefh company of Indians came into their affiftance, bet et the Chriftians round, Killed Captain *Pierce*. and 48. of his men, befides 8. of the Chriftian Indians. The Fight continued about 5 hours, the Enemy bying the Victory very dearly, but at laft obtained it fo abfolutly that they deprived us of all means of hearing of their lofs.

At *Malbrow* on the 12*th* Ditto, were feveral houfes burnt whilft the miferable inhabitants were at a meeting, and at *Springfield* the fame Lords day, thefe devillifh Enemies of Religion feeing a man, woman, and their Children, going but towards a meeting-houfe, Slew them (as they faid) becaufe they thought they Intended to go thither.

The 28*th*, of the fame inftant *April* laft, Captain *Denifon* collecting a Regiment of 500 and 200 *Englifh* Paquet Nimerafs *Indians* marcht out of New *London* in fearch of that Grand fomenter of this Rebellion. *Anthony* the *Se ham* whom at laft near the Town call d *Providence* he recovered, and after a hot difpute wherein he kill'd 45 of the Sechems men, Took him their Commander Prifoner with feveral of his Captaines, whom they immediately put to death but were at ftrong debate whether they fhould fend him to *Bofton*, but at length they carried him to

New

(6)

New *London* and began to examine him why he did foment that war which would certainly be the diſtraction of him and all the Heathen *Indians* in the Country, to which and many other interrogatories he made no other reply but that[he was born a Prince, and if Princes came to ſpeak with him, he would anſwer them, But none of thoſe preſent being Princes, he thought himſelf oblig'd in honour to hold his Tongue] This Anſwer though it might Challenge their admiration, was not ſo prevalent as to obtain their pitty.

Notwithſtanding the Surviveing Sechems were not long in revenging his death, for on the Sixth of *May*, they burnt all *Melborow* except three Garriſon houſes, kill'd Capt. *Jaco∙ſon* and Leiutenant *Prat*, and two dayes after burnt 24 houſes in *Conktury*, kill'd ſeveral of the Inhabitants who vainly expected Capt. *Wadsworth* and Capt. *Brookſel* to their Relief; for theſe unfortunate Gentlemen were intercepted by 700 *Moors* with whom they fought for the ſpace of 4 houres till not only they two but Capt. *Sharp* and 51 Chriſtians more lay dead upon the place.

At *Woodcock* 10 miles from *Secouch* on the 16th *May* was a little Skirmage betwixt the *Moors* and Chriſtians, wherein there was of the later three ſlain and two wounded, and only two *Indians* Kild.

May 28. 1676. Capt. *Danison* and Capt. *Evry* with 50 Engliſh and about 150 Paquet *Indians* Scouting among the Woods in 8 days ſpace kill'd 25 *Indians* and took 51 priſoners, one whereof was Grand-child to *Dunhan* who was kill'd by Capt. *Peirce* in the engagement on the 26 May.

The number of Chriſtians ſlain ſince the beginning of the late Wars in New *England*, are 444. Taken Priſoner, 55.

The number of *Indians* Slain in this war is uncertain becauſe they burn their Dead, keeping their Death as a Secret from the Chriſtians knowledge, but the number mentioned herein is 910.

We have Received very late news, that the Chriſtians in New *England* have had very great Victory over the Infidel Natives.

There has been a Treaty between them, the *Indians* proffer to lay down their Armes ; but the *Engliſh* are not willing to agree to it, except they will give up their Armes, and go as far up into the Country, as the Court of *Boſton* ſhall think fit.

F I N I S.

ARTHUR DOBBS, AN ESSAY ON THE TRADE AND IMPROVEMENT OF IRELAND

Arthur Dobbs, *An Essay on the Trade and Improvement of Ireland*, 2 vols (Dublin: J. Smith and W. Bruce, 1729–31), extract, vol. 1, pp. 1–8; vol. 2, pp. 17–40. Cambridge University Library, shelfmark Hib.5.731.1.

Arthur Dobbs (1689–1765) was colonial governor and writer on trade born in Girvan in Ayrshire. His father was an army officer and sheriff stationed in Ireland. After serving as a dragoon in Scotland, Arthur Dobbs became a sheriff and landlord in Antrim, Ireland. In 1733 he was appointed by the Walpole administration as Engineer-in-Chief and Surveyor-General to Ireland. In 1742 he moved to North Carolina where he became Governor. According to his biographer Robert M. Coulhon, Dobbs seems to have been a very ambitious colonial officer: 'No governor in any of the Southern royal colonies worked as hard or manoeuvred as adroitly as Dobbs to curb legislative autonomy and maintain his own Board of Trade's influence over appointments and fiscal policy.'[1] He clearly believed in the need for effective government – both in Ireland and in America – in order to gain from the colonial possessions. At the same time he argued for more tolerance towards Catholic worshippers in Ireland and for more self-regulation for British colonists in America. His main published work is *An Essay on the Trade and Improvement of Ireland*, published in two parts, an extract of which is reproduced here. In this work he suggests a number of reforms with regard to the system of land tenure in Ireland and the improvement of trade relations with England.[2]

---

1   See Calhoun's entry on Dobbs in *Oxford Dictionary of National Biography* (Oxford: Oxford University Press, 2004).

2   For further information on Dobbs, see *Palgrave's Dictionary of Political Economy*, ed. H. Higgs, 3 vols (London and New York: Macmillan, 1894), vol. 2, p. 611.

[1]

AN
ESSAY
UPON THE
TRADE
OF
IRELAND.

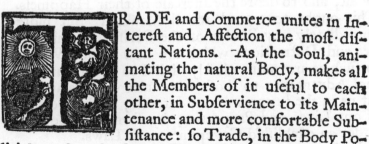

RADE and Commerce unites in Interest and Affection the most distant Nations. As the Soul, animating the natural Body, makes all the Members of it useful to each other, in Subservience to its Maintenance and more comfortable Subsistance: so Trade, in the Body Politick, makes the several Parts of it contribute to the well-being of the whole, and also to the more comfortable and agreeable Living of every Member of the munity. Every Nation, every Climate from the Equinox almost to the very Poles, may partake of the Produce of all the rest, by means of a friendly Intercourse and mutual Exchange of what each has to

A   spare,

[2]

ſpare. Thus every one may enjoy more or leſs of the Productions of different Countries, according to the Application and Induſtry he uſes to obtain them.

WHATEVER ill and miſtaken Uſe may be made of it by many in the World, it ſeems to be the Deſire of all Men, to live in Affluence and Proſperity, and to have it in their Power to do Acts of Kindneſs, Goodneſs and Mercy: Nor is it prohibited by any Precept of true Religion either natural or reveal'd. A Deſire to gratify our ſeveral Appetites and Inclinations, when we may do it without Harm to our ſelves or others, to enjoy our Friends with Pleaſure in this Life, and to leave thoſe of our Children and Friends who ſurvive us, in a Capacity of doing the ſame after us, is inherent in our Natures, and perfectly agreeable to the Ends we were made for by our good and wiſe Creator.

FROM the Pleaſure we take in our Neighbour's Proſperity, when we are not blinded by Prejudice or miſtaken Views of Intereſt; we are led to relieve them from the Inconveniencies and Apprehenſions of Want, and to deſire the Increaſe of their Happineſs. This ought to extend to all Mankind: But more immediately, by Reaſon of the Diviſions, Animoſities and Diſtractions which are now in the World, to ſuch as are more cloſely link'd to us for our mutual Advantage; to thoſe who unite with us and aſſiſt us in the ſupport of our Intereſt, in the Defence of our Lives and Properties, by forming a Society uuder an eſtabliſh'd Government and Laws.

IT is then every Man's Duty, more immediately to promote the Happineſs of the Nation wherein he lives, and by ſuch Means as are honeſt and lawful to encreaſe its Power and Wealth, that it may be the better able to defend its People from Violence, to redreſs Injuries, to puniſh Crimes, to protect the Oppreſſed, and relieve ſuch as are in Want and Diſtreſs.

[3]

trefs. This cannot be done without Induftry, and the Product of fuch Induftry will be but poor and mean, and its Ufefulnefs of very narrow Extent, if it be not improved by the well-order'd Affiftance of many Heads and Hands in contriving and executing; and if thefe Fruits of human Labour and Induftry be not difpers'd over the World by the Means of Traffick and Commerce. It ought therefore more or lefs to be the Care of every Man, according to the Station he is placed in, to promote fo general a Good to his Country, as the Trade and Commerce of it. A flourifhing Trade gives Encouragement to the Induftrious; employs the Poor; encreafes the Wealth and Power of the Nation; puts it in the Power of every prudent and induftrious Man in it, to enjoy more of the innocent Pleafures of Life, than he otherwife would, and in greater Perfection, and enables him to do more Actions of Kindnefs and Charity both in his own and foreign Nations; and by thefe Means, greatly promotes the general Happinefs of Mankind.

ISLANDS, upon a double Account, are obliged to be careful of their Commerce and Navigation, without Navigation, they are cut off from the reft of the World: And Ships and Sailors to navigate them, cannot be maintained without Trade to employ them. Without a fuperior Fleet to repel their Enemies, they are alfo liable to be attack'd by their more powerful Neighbours, and are continually expofed to the Ravages and Depredations of their Fleets.

As this is the Cafe of *Great-Britain* and *Ireland*, whofe Interefts are infeparable: It is to be hoped, that whoever endeavours to promote the Trade of any Part of them; or makes any Obfervations upon it, that may occafion its being more clofely and ufefully examin'd by others, will be favourably receiv'd by the Publick.

A 2   I HAVE

[4]

I HAVE feen but little as yet written upon the Trade and Improvements of *Ireland*; by which the Publick may come to know how our Trade ftands with *Great-Britain* and the Plantations, as alfo with the feveral foreign Countries with which we trade: And thinking it might be of fome Advantage to my Country, I have attempted to ftate our Trade with Particularity and Exactnefs, and to make fome Obfervations upon it as it now ftands; that I might afterwards upon that Foundation propofe what occurs to me, as of Advantage to *Ireland*, and that may contribute to reftore the Ballance which is now vifibly againft us.

WITH this View, whilft in the Committee of Trade, I carefully look'd over the Ledgers in the Cuftom-Houfe, and took Extracts from them for feven or eight Years, of the moft material Imports, and all the Exports; in order to form proper Calculations upon them, and to fet our Trade in a full and fair Light; that the Publick may not be impos'd upon, but that every Perfon may ufe his own Underftanding in obferving the State of the Kingdom, and contributing to its Welfare and Profperity.

To give a more general View of our Trade, I fhall firft lay down fome general Abftracts of our Exports and Imports, and fhew how the Ballance has ftood for feveral Years paft; I will afterwards confider them particularly, according to their moft material Articles, and ftate them feparately; as alfo according to the feveral Countries we trade to, as they are diftinguifh'd in the Cuftom-Houfe Books; and as I proceed make fome Obfervations on each of them.

ABSTRACTS

[5]

ABSTRACTS of Exports, Imports, and Ballance for feveral Years, each ending at *Chriftmas*.

Years.	Exports.	Imports.	Ballance.	Contra Ballance.
	l.	*l.*	*l.*	*l.*
1681	582814	433040	149774	
1695	295592	391524		95932
1696	398237	334963	62274	
1697	525004	423182	101822	
1698	996305	576863	419442	

IT is probable that our Exports, from the *Reftoration* of King *Charles* the IId, to 1688, did not exceed 600000 *l. per Ann.* which upon the Prohibition then laid upon our exporting Cattle and Sheep alive into *England*, chiefly confifted of Wooll, and the Produce of our Cattle. From that Time to the Year 1695, three Years after the Reduction of *Ireland*, we could have little or no Trade, until the Country began to be at Peace, and our Stock of Cattle and Sheep, which had been neglected and deftroy'd in thofe Confufions, were again increafed upon the wafte Lands. Hence it was that our Imports that Year, exceeded our Exports 95932 *l.* which feems to have been a confiderable Drain upon us, and much increas'd by our Imports in the Time of the Reduction of *Ireland*. But if it be confider'd that the Army employ'd here, in our favour, was paid by *England*, and the *Irifh* Army by *France*; it may be eafily conceived, that there was a conftant Influx of Money without Trade, until the Armies were

[6]

were withdrawn, and the Eſtabliſhment was paid by the Revenue of the Kingdom: It was that alone cou'd pay the Ballance of our Imports and other Draughts upon us in 1695.

It may be obſerv'd that our Exports increas'd in 1696, 1697, and 1698; but our Imports did not riſe in Proportion, which occaſion'd the Ballance in our Favour, in 1698, (being greater than ever it was in *Ireland*, except in 1715:) This Annual In-creaſe was occaſion'd by our falling into the Wool-len Manufacture; the *French Refugees*, who ſettled with us, at the ſame time laying the Foundation of the Linnen Manufacture; And it being alſo the ſuc-ceeding Year to the Peace of *Riſwyck*, *Europe* began to breath after a heavy War, and Trade to revive, which occaſioned a briſker Demand for *Iriſh* Proviſi-ons. But upon checking the Export of our Wool-len Manufacture to foreign Kingdoms, and by laying on heavy Duties upon its being Exported to *Eng-land*, in 1699 and 1700, equivalent to a Prohibiti-on; moſt of thoſe, who were imbark'd in it, were lain under a Neceſſity of removing elſewhere; and being piqued at the Difficulties they were laid under, many of the Proteſtants remov'd into *Germany*, and ſettled in the Proteſtant States there, who received them with open Arms. Several Papiſts at the ſame time remov'd into the Northern Parts of *Spain*, where they laid the Foundation of a Manufacture highly prejudicial to *England*. Many alſo of the Proteſtants who were imbark'd with Papiſts in the Woollen Manufacture, remov'd into *France*, and ſet-tled in *Roan* and other Parts. Notwithſtanding *Lewis* the XIVth had repealed the Edict of *Nantz*, and forced abroad the *French* Proteſtants into diffe-rent Parts of *Europe*, yet theſe were kindly received by him, had great Encouragement given to them, and were protected in their Religion. From theſe Beginnings they have in many Branches ſo much improv'd

[7]

prov'd the Woollen Manufactures of *France*, as not only to supply themselves, but even to vye with the *English* in Foreign Markets; and by their Correspondence, they have laid the Foundation for the running of Wooll thither both from *England* and *Ireland*, highly to the Prejudice of *Britain*; which pernicious Practice is still carry'd on, in spite of all the Care and Precautions made Use of to discountenance and prevent it. Thus a Check is put to the Sale of our Woollen Manufactures abroad, which would have given full Employment to all the industrious Poor both of *Britain*, and *Ireland*, had not our Manufacturers been forced away into *France*, *Spain* and *Germany*, where they are now so improv'd, as in great Measure to supply themselves with many Sorts they formerly had from *England*. The *French* particularly are supplanting *Britain* in many of the Markets abroad; and upon the whole, those Nations may be justly said to have depriv'd *Britain* of Millions, since that Time, instead of the Thousands *Ireland* might possibly have made: which Gain, whatever it had been, must necessarily have center'd in *England* at last. For had they then allow'd us to manufacture our Woolls, and confin'd us to the *English* Markets; it is not to be imagin'd we could have undersold the Manufacturers there, by having Provisions cheaper, considering Carriage, Commission, Freight, &c. since it is observable in our great Towns, where those Manufactures must have been carry'd on, our Provisions for several Years have been dearer than in the Manufacturing Towns and Counties in *England*.

ABSTRACTS

[8]

Abstracts continued from 1710 to 1727, ending *Lady-Day*.

Years.	Exports.			Imports.			Ballance.			Contra Ballance.		
	l.	*s.*	*d.*	*l.*	*s.*	*d.*	*l.*	*s.*	*d.*	*l.*	*s.*	*d.*
1710	712497	2	$6\frac{1}{2}$	554247	12	4	158249	10	$2\frac{1}{2}$			
1711	878237	4	$10\frac{1}{2}$	670948	13	$8\frac{1}{2}$	207288	11	2			
1712	889339	7	$\frac{1}{2}$	774420	12	$6\frac{1}{4}$	114918	14	$6\frac{1}{4}$			
1713	890437	5	$3\frac{1}{4}$	659665		$10\frac{1}{4}$	230772	4	5			
1714	1422227	7	5	1016122	13	7	406104	13	10			
1715	1529765	14	$1\frac{3}{4}$	972688	9	$11\frac{1}{2}$	557077	4	$2\frac{3}{4}$			
1716	1255083	7	10	875565	19	$11\frac{3}{4}$	379517	7	$10\frac{1}{4}$			
1717	1180012	10	4	907160	10	$10\frac{1}{4}$	272851	19	$5\frac{3}{4}$			
1718	1115304	6	$11\frac{1}{2}$	887758	16	$6\frac{3}{4}$	227545	10	$4\frac{3}{4}$			
1719	1038381	7	$1\frac{1}{2}$	891678	5	$6\frac{1}{2}$	146703	1	7			
1720	859581	5	$1\frac{3}{4}$	683364	1	$6\frac{1}{4}$	176217	3	7			
1721	986346	14	2	730558	10	$9\frac{3}{4}$	255788	3	$4\frac{1}{4}$			
1722	1074269	12	$2\frac{1}{4}$	829367	17	$2\frac{3}{4}$	244901	15				
1723	1090675	13	$5\frac{3}{4}$	920802	11	6	169873	1	$11\frac{3}{4}$			
1724	1053782	13	$11\frac{1}{2}$	819761	13	$3\frac{1}{4}$	234021	0	$8\frac{1}{4}$			
1725	1026537	6	4	889832	18	$5\frac{3}{4}$	136704	7	$10\frac{1}{4}$			
1726	1017872	15	$4\frac{3}{4}$	1030059	16	$4\frac{1}{2}$				12187	1	$0\frac{1}{4}$
Total.	18020351	14	2	14114004	5	1	3906347	9	1	12187	1	$0\frac{1}{4}$
Medium for 7 Years.	1060020	13	$7\frac{7}{8}$	830235	10	$10\frac{5}{8}$	229784	2	$9\frac{1}{4}$			
Total for the last 7 Years.	7109066	0	$7\frac{1}{2}$	5903747	9	$2\frac{1}{4}$	1205318	11	$5\frac{1}{4}$			
Medium for the last 7 Years.	1015580	17	$2\frac{1}{2}$	843392	9	$10\frac{17}{28}$	172188	7	$4\frac{1}{4}$			

[17]

THE great advantage of Trade and Commerce to a Nation arises from the variety of Employments given to the several Members of it ; by enabling them not only to supply the necessities and conveniencies of each other with what their own Country affords, but also to supply the wants of People in the most distant Regions and Climates with their produce and Labour ; and in return to receive from them all that is necessary convenient or pleasant in life which any part of the Earth can produce or whatever may be improv'd by the labour and ingenuity of Men in any Climate. This makes in effect every Nation, that is possess'd of an extended Commerce, enjoy the benefit of the best Soils and Climates ; tho perhaps, from their situation, they might otherwise be in the worst. Trade makes the People of the whole Earth as one great Family supplying each others wants. Whatever Nation can by their prudence outdo others in Trade ; so as to increase their Exports and lessen perishable Imports and so increase their Stock by the return of a considerable Ballance ; must not only be a Magazine of all commodities necessary in life, but also abound in Gold and Silver, and thus prodigiously increase their power : So that in case of War they are enabled by their amass'd Wealth, not only to defend themselves ; but to fit out Ships to protect their Trade and provide all necessaries for carrying on an advantagious War against Kingdoms of much greater extent and Numbers, where, for want of Wealth and Magazines, they can make no use of their Numbers ; for such Nations, if they can't conquer at the first attempt ; are not capable of continuing a War, but must sink under it.

C   SINCE

[18]

SINCE thefe are the advantages of Trade and Commerce, and Merchants are abfolutely neceffary to carry it on, is it not the Publick Intereft to incourage them as much as poffible? For fince the profit gain'd by the publick arifes from the particular gains of private Perfons imbark'd in Trade and Manufactures; no Perfon or Merchant will be concern'd in it, if he does not find it beneficial to him.

IT is undoubtedly then the Nations Intereft to enable the Merchant to improve his fortune by Trade; for 'tis he that fets all the Wheels in Motion. By his Correfpondence he finds out Markets for Goods: he Advances the Money and run's all rifques: whatever fums of Money he lays out unneceffarily are fo many Clogs upon Trade: 'tis his Money is the fpring of action, and keeps the whole Machine in Motion. If his Returns are quick, he will deal for lefs profit, and confequently give higher Prices for Goods at home and be able to afford them Cheaper abroad: by which means; he incourages the induftrious at home by keeping up our Markets; and always keeps a Market open abroad by being able to fell, at leaft at *Par*, with forreign Merchants.

IF this be. allow'd to be rational and true it will neceffarily follow that all Nations, who propofe to advance their Trade and Commerce, fhould prevent, as much as poffible, Merchants from mifapplying their time and Money to other purpofes and make their coming at Money as eafy as poffible that they may be contented with a fmall profit by its circulating fafter. In laying this Foundation right does the whole benefit by Trade confift: and in this; with proper Æconomy by fumptuary Laws and employment of the People of a Nation; lies the whole Myftery of Trade. To thefe three points I fhall endeavour to apply my felf, and, as far as I am capable, propofe what may be advantagious in each;

and

[19]

and afterwards consider several particular Improvements which may contribute to employ us, increase our Exports, lessen our Imports, and make us an easy and happy People.

THE principal discouragements and difficultys the Merchants of this Kingdom lie under, are owing to the height of Interest of Money; the Dutys upon Exports and Imports; and the delay and expence that attends the Methods, in this Country, of coming at their Debts.

THE benefit accruing to a Nation from the lowness of Interest, is so fully treated of by Sir *Josias Child*, that it will be very hard to add any thing upon that subject: but it is so warmly oppos'd by those who make an immediate gain by the height of Interest, and they make so considerable a Body both by their Numbers and Wealth, that I think it necessary to say something upon that subject; and the rather because it is of the utmost consequence in Trade, and therefore a matter of the greatest importance to the riches and happyness of every Country.

WHERE Interest of Money is *High*; *Land*, Provisions and all the Commodities of the Country must necessarily be cheap. As for instance: when Money was at 10 *per Cent*, And consequently Land at 10 or 12 Years purchase; would any Person improve his Lands by Building, Planting, Draining, Fencing or Soiling, and perhaps not make 5 or 6 *per Cent* for his Money; when he could purchase Land so cheap, or have such high Interest? Or would a Merchant give any tolerable price for the commodities of the Country, when he could not Trade abroad to advantage without making 15 or 16 *per Cent* Profit, considering his Risque and the high Interest he paid? For the same reason he could not sell at *Par* abroad with forreign Merchants, upon account of the excessive Freight occasion'd by high Interest; the foreign Merchants being content with less profit,

C 2   by

[20]

by procuring Money at low Intereſt and carrying their Goods at an eaſy Freight.

PROVISIONS and all Commodities at home being cheap; the Farmers and Labourers, by employing a ſmall part of their time, procur'd all the neceſſaries they requir'd and would not Work the remainder of their time. Thus all Induſtry was at a ſtand, and Indolence and Idleneſs overſpread the Country. This we had experience of, when Intereſt was ſo high in this Kingdom; then moſt Men were fond of purchaſing, or laying out their Money at Intereſt; few were inclin'd to Trade; thoſe that did, were fond of quitting a way of life that lay under ſo many difficultys and diſcouragements. The young Merchant, that had but a ſmall Stock to begin with, found it more for his advantage to act by Commiſſion for Foreigners, than pay ſuch high Intereſt as Trade could not bear; and Forreigners were tempted to lay out their Money at Intereſt here, and not only took away our Merchant's profit but alſo the very Vitals from the Kingdom.

THESE are the conſequences of high Intereſt; but let us turn the Scale, and ſee what are the effects of low Intereſt. Where Intereſt is at 3 or 4 *per Cent*, the Money-lender can't double his principal at ſimple Intereſt in leſs than 25 or 33⅓ Years, and at compound Intereſt not under 20 or 26: If he lays out his Money in Land, he has leſs; Land being better than Mortgages or common ſecurity by one, or at leaſt ½ *per Cent*. Thus, when he finds he can't live upon the Intereſt of his Money without great Æconomy, nor purchaſe Lands without greater expence; he will employ his time in ſome buſineſs or employment profitable to the Publick; and apply himſelf early to buſineſs and employ his Money in Trade, whereby he has a proſpect of ſo much greater gain; and, if he has not been bred to that buſineſs, he will lay out his Money in the Funds and joynt

Stocks

[21]

Stocks for Trade. Thus, where Intereſt is low,
thoſe who have Money muſt be equally induſtrious
with thoſe that have none, or muſt live in a low
Station and appear to have little or none.

Those who are already poſſes'd of Lands, will
find the Value of them to riſe ſo high; that inſtead of attempting to purchaſe the Lands of another
at a high price, they will incline to employ the induſtrious Poor, in purchaſing upon their own by in-
riching and improving them; which they can do at
leſs expence. Thus, as Lands riſe in Value, they will
be improv'd in goodneſs; and may, by proper induſtry, be rais'd in many places from 4 or 5, to twenty
or thirty Shillings *per* Acre. This would be an immenſe profit to a Nation, and would be in effect ad-
ding ſo much more Land to it; for the Lands of
each Kingdom may be ſaid to bear ſuch proportion
to each other, as the Produce and Numbers they
can maintain.

Thus the ſame Lands improv'd, will yield many
more proviſions and rich commodities to employ and
maintain a much greater Number of People; and yet
proviſions be kept at a reaſonable price; by which
means labour wont riſe, but Trades-men and Manufactures will be employed to advantage.

Thus Trade and Navigation would be improv'd
by the increaſe of our Exports and employment
of our People; which is the genuine ſource of a
beneficial Trade. Young Merchants, of a good
Character and Capacity, might then have Money
ſo cheap; that they could afford to Trade for 5
or 6 *per Cent* Profit; and aſſociate with others in
Trade; and at the ſame time repay the Principal
and grow rich. Building and fitting out of Ships
and freight would be cheaper than when Intereſt
was high; by Labour's being kept low from the
plenty of proviſions, and becauſe many of the Materials would be furniſh'd cheaper by the Merchant
who could deal for leſs profit.   B y

[22]

By lowness of Interest the Merchant could not only afford to sell what he imported cheaper; but also could give greater prices for our Exports, and yet undersell Merchants abroad who had not the same advantage. Thus industry would be promoted; Trade would circulate briskly; the Value of Land would rise immensely; and Merchants, when they had made considerable gain by Trade, finding no great advantage to be made by purchasing Lands at a high Value; would continue their Stock and breed up their Children in Trade and consequently would not check the Current but rather find out new Channels and look into all the sources of Trade.

TRADE has also this peculiar advantage that it is not easily overstock'd; for, as Merchants increase in Numbers, they naturally inlarge the field of Trade and make business for one another. Thus encouragement is given for new Improvements, inventions and discoveries beneficial in Trade. Fisheries and other projects where a great National gain may be made; tho small to each particular Person, would be brought to perfection; and the Carrying-Trade, which is so very beneficial, must certainly center with that Nation that has Money at lowest Interest; which by that Means is able to deal for least Profit. This is also an encouragement to build Granaries and other Ware-houses to lodge Grain &c in, when cheap; and to make benefit of the rise of Markets abroad. It will also promote the Æconomy and Frugality of a Nation, in spite of all prejudices to the contrary. I shall only mention these further advantages arising from the lowness of Interest; it compels younger Children of small fortunes, who can't maintain themselves handsomely by the Interest of their Money, to employ it in Trade or Manufactures; it also increases the Number of Merchants and industrious Persons who employ the Poor; and it lessens the Number of poor Gentlemen with their

genuine

[23]

genuine off-spring, Rakes, Sharpers, Gamesters &c.
There are many other advantages to be·had from
the lowness of Interest, but my intention is only to
point out some of the chief.

T HE next thing to be consider'd, is; whether the
benefits arising from low Interest, are to be procur'd
in this Kingdom by Laws forbidding high Interest
under·severe penalties; or whether the having plenty of Money is the only way of reducing it. Since,
People are divided in opinion upon this question; I'
will consider what may be said on either side, and
endeavour to find out·which is·the best and most
expeditious way of obtaining an end so much to be
desir'd.

O N the one side of the question it is urg'd; that
the plenty or scarcity of Money must necessarily
lower or raise the Interest of it; in proportion to
the sums wanted and Numbers demanding, and the
sums to be lent and Number of People who have
it to lend. This at first View seems to be highly
rational; for the scarcity of any commodity wanted
and the Number wanting must raise the price, in
proportion as the possession of it is necessary; and
the Reverse will happen when it is plenty, provided
the commodity be Perishable: For he who has it,
and has no use for it, wants to get rid of it least it
should perish in his hands; tho he should be a loser
in parting with it; for it would be better to·lose
part than all: But Money so far differs from many
other Commodities, that, when it is scarce, it is not
absolutely necessary but convenient; and when plenty, it is only so far to be accounted perishable, as the
gain that might have been made of it (had it been
put out to Interest) is lost, but is not·intrinsically
so in it self. We frequently see Usurers and Money-
lenders keep it by them a considerable time, in hopes
of having higher Interest or better security, even
until they lose·as much as they can propose to gain

in

[24]

in a confiderable time by the high Intereft they expect. So 'tis not abfolutely the plenty or fcarcity of Money, which raifes and lowers the Intereft; but the Circumftances and Character of the Perfons wanting, or the fecurity offer'd being good or not: This, where there is no Law, will alter the height of Intereft 2 or 3 *per Cent*; and in Countries, where there is a Law Penal to thofe that exceed a limited Intereft, a Man of good Character in bufinefs or giving good fecurity will abate the legal Intereft 1 or 2 *per Cent*.

It is plain in Kingdoms where there is no Law to limit or Reduce the Intereft of Money, if Money be fcarce, tho good fecurity be offer'd, yet Ufurers will exact a very high Intereft: And if they think the fecurity infufficent, they will exceed all bounds; and if Money be plenty, they will beat down the Intereft upon one another, to get the beft fecurity. But in Countries where penal Laws are in force to limit the Intereft, the cafe is very different, for then, tho' Money be fcarce, they muft give it at legal Intereft or otherwife attempt to evade the Law by inferting more Money in the fecurity than was really lent, under pretended Sales of Goods not eafily to be valued, or by extorting unlawful Intereft by threatning to call in the Principal. As the Lender, in both thefe cafes, would be liable to a forfeiture of the Money lent or fome other very fevere Penalty in cafe of a difcovery; and as a difcovery would be very much for the Intereft of the borrower; and no Perfon would borrow on fuch terms, but one in defperate or very diftrefs'd Circumftances; all thofe things confider'd; it is fcarce to be imagin'd that any Man in his wits would run the rifque of fo great a lofs, as that of lofing his whole Principal Money either by the Penalty of the Law, or the poverty of the borrower, for the profpect of fo fmall a gain; when he might at the fame time, by employing his Money in

[25]

in Trade, make a gain both greater and more fecure: whilft the only difficulty the borrower would be put to, would be to have no credit to borrow Money at illegal Intereft; which would be an advantage to him, and perhaps put him upon living frugally before he were quite ruin'd and reduc'd to ftarve in a Goal.

THE Confequence then of reducing Intereft by Law would be, that any Perfon of a fober Character in profitable bufinefs, or who could give good Security, might borrow Money with a View of improvement at or under the legal Intereft: And thofe who would borrow, with a View to defraud their Creditors, would find a difficulty to procure it; which would equally be of benefit to the Publick.

THUS Laws made to reduce Intereft muft take effect, where Money is fcarce; for thofe who have Money muft lend it at the legal Intereft, or run a rifque that no wife Man would venture, or muft employ their Money more to the publick advantage in Trade or Improvements; and the Extravagant, having few to fupport them, would be oblig'd to live within Bounds, and Retrench; this confequently would make Money lefs wanted, and would affift in lowering the Intereft, and procuring Money by Induftry.

IT is then highly neceffary to make Laws, to prevent exorbitant Intereft in all States. 'Tis alfo prudent, from time to time, to abate it by new Laws, tho' Money be not plenty, until it is at *Par* with other trading Nations: fince it is plain no Nation can Trade upon an equal footing with other Nations, unlefs the Merchant's gain be equal in proportion to the rifque, and he can afford to fell at *Par* with foreign Merchant's abroad. Since it is alfo obvious that the lownefs of Intereft promotes Frugality and Induftry, which confequently increafes Money, I think it is highly rational, to begin at the right end, and abate Intereft by Law; this we are fure will have

D   the

[26]

the effect: Whereas if we wait till Money grows
plenty, or the Frugal exceed the Extravagant, without making Laws to promote Frugality which will
in part execute themfelves and oblige us to be good
Æconomifts; perhaps a plenty of Money may never
happen, and Intereft confequently never be lower'd
or the Nation improv'd.

THERE are fome that allow all that has been
faid for low Intereft, and yet infift that we ought
always to follow *Britain* in lowering it, and have it
here 1 or 2 *per Cent* above the legal Intereft there:
What are the reafons that fway them to that opinion I can't eafily find out. After being convinc'd
that the lower Intereft is, the more frugal and induftrious we muft be, that Trade muft be carry'd
on to greater National and private profit, that
freight muft be cheaper, and that we fhould effectually
fhare with other Nations the carrying Trade, as alfo
in Fifheries and other Improvements; Yet afterwards
to fay it is our Intereft that *Britain* fhould have 1
or 2 *per Cent* the advantage of us, tho' they exceed
us vaftly in all other improvements and conveniencies for Trade, feems to me to be fo inconfiftent,
I could wifh to know the true reafons they found
their judgments upon.

IF the legal Intereft here being at *Par* with that
of *Britain*, were an occafion of draining our Money
from us, or obftructing our Trade, they would have
reafon for their opinion: But fince it is evident it
would have the contrary effect, and even were it
lower, would rather increafe than diminifh our Money and Trade; for we fhould be the Lenders, rather than the borrowers from thence, which muft be
allowed is always advantagious, by a conftant return
of the Intereft; this rather makes againft them than
otherwife. The only plaufible reafon I can give
for their opinion, is, that thofe who have Money
unemploy'd in Trade, would lend their Money in
Britain

[27]

Britain, and go and refide with their Debtors where their Mortgages and other Securities lay.   If this were a fufficient inducement, why don't the *Englifh*, who lend Money in *Ireland* and in the Plantations at high Intereft, go and refide with their Debtors, or the *Dutch*, when they lend their Money in *England*, go and refide in *Britain?* But the reafon is plain from what I have already faid ; when the Intereft is reduced very low, there is no incouragement to live upon the Intereft alone ; People muft then be induftrious as well as frugal, and employ themfelves in fome Bufinefs profitable to them and the Common-wealth.

THUS thofe who make Money by induftry, would be imbark'd in Trade or other bufinefs, and would not leave it to go to *England* and live upon the Intreft of their Money, where living is more expenfive : But if they gain'd more than was fufficient to carry on their Trade, they would tranfmit and lend the over-plus, if they could find no way of laying it out to advantage here, and refide here at a diftance from *London*, where they could live cheaper and at lefs expence, and follow the bufinefs they were imbark'd in.   It would alfo oblige them to breed up their Children to their own bufinefs or fome other equally beneficial ; which would induce them to refide in the Kingdom.

BUT perhaps it may be faid, that *England* being the Center of Trade and Wealth, thofe who had Money would rather go there to Trade and employ it : This reafon equally holds good for the reft of *England* againft *London*, which in great meafure runs away with the Trade, Profit and Cafh of the Kingdom : But it would be no advantage to the Country, to have Intereft 1 or 2 *per Cent* higher than in *London*, to prevent their lending Money in *London*, and going afterwards upon that to refide there.   As there are feveral Trading Towns in *Britain* very rich befides

[28]

London, as *Briftol*, *Newcaftle*, *Leverpool*, *Glafcow*, *Norwich* and other Manufacturing Towns, notwithftanding Intereft is the fame through *Britain*; fo I can't fee why *Ireland* might not have a fhare in the Trade of the World, tho' never to come into competition with *England*, fufficient to employ thofe who have Money and would be induftrious, without going to *England* to live upon the Intereft of their Patrimony, or what they had acquir'd. The improvements made in *Ireland* by reducing of Intereft, would be alfo fome inducement to take up with a retreat here if they quit bufinefs.

In our Trade, tho' we are depriv'd of the moft beneficial part of the Woollen-Manufacture, yet we have many ways left open to employ Money to advantage. We have all the improvements to be made of Land by Fencing, Draining, Planting and Tillage; we have the Linnen and Hempen-Manufactures in all their Branches, a very extenfive Trade: We may export Mettals Manufactur'd to any part of *Europe* and moft parts of *Africa*: We may undertake the Fifheries, either Herring, White Fifh, or the Whale Fifhery: We may improve our Silks and Manufactures of Cotton for our home confumption; and afterwards by proper application may get them, at leaft in mixtures with Linnen, made a Branch of our foreign Trade: We may erect Magazines and Granaries, and be a fharer in the carrying Trade of the World: So that to the induftrious a large fcope is allow'd to employ all the Money and Stock it is probable *Ireland* will ever be mafter of, without going to refide in *England*. It will only be the indolent and lazy, and not the induftrious, that will be inclin'd to leave us; and fuch Noble Families, and Men of fortune, as will always attend the Court and Circle of pleafure. Thefe we find even now do go; and it will always be fo, whether the generality of the People be rich or not: Since the Court is there, all

our

[29]

our redundant Cash not employ'd in Trade will be spent there; 'but that is no reason why we should not be in a Capacity and State of gaining more.

I f this reasoning be just, and there be not more weighty objections than do occur to me; I think no time ought to be lost in reducing Interest: And tho' it mayn't be proper to lower it at once to a *Par* with *Britain*; yet we ought not to be easy 'till it be so, but lower it with the greatest dispatch that may in prudence be thought requisite to gain the end desir'd.

T he next Clog upon Trade I shall take notice of, is, the high Duties that are paid upon most of our exports and imports. Tho' this would be less burthensome to the Merchant, if the Interest of Money were reduced; and is not so prejudicial as high Interest, which accompanys a Merchant thro' his whole Trade; this affecting him only at the time of payment: Yet it is a very great prejudice to the Publick, and discouragement to the Merchant. Money in the Merchants hand never lies idle: The moment he receives it, he considers how he may lay it out with profit either at home or abroad; in buying up our Goods to answer foreign Markets; or in taking the advantage of cheap Markets abroad for what we want to consume at home, and also to carry to other places where they may be wanted and they find the Markets are higher; either way it is a gain to the Merchant and Kingdom. Every thing therefore that draws Money from the Merchant, prevents just so much Trade. It may be objected, that the Merchant does not suffer by these Duties, because he puts a suitable price upon his Goods. To this I answer, the price of the Goods may possibly make up the private loss of the Merchant; but it never can make a recompence to the Publick for that profit which the Nation would have had, by the briskness of Trade, in the mean time between the

Merchants

[30]

Merchant's advancing Money for the Duty and his being paid for the Goods.

Duties, upon such exports as are to be encourag'd, are extremely improper and highly prejudicial to Trade, for these further reasons. They fall upon the Husband-Man or Artificer, who raises or Manufactures Goods for export, and discourage industry and labour; for they either lower our Markets at home, or raise the price of our Commodities abroad, and so prevent a ready Market and quick Return.

It would therefore be advantagious to all Nations, who have the power to do it, to take off the Duties upon exported Commodities; except the primums of Manufactures, which can be wrought up at home and give employment to the Poor; for which they have a forreign Vent: And also all high Duties inwards, which affect the Merchant and incourage Running of Goods, even the Duties upon such things as are prejudicial when consum'd at home, provided they may again be re-exported to advantage; for every thing added to the Merchants charge upon Goods, in waste and Warehouse-Room &c. is a Clog to the carrying Trade, a Trade highly beneficial to all who deal in it. It is plain no drawback will answer the End, when a high Duty is upon Goods inwards; for the Interest of the Money the Merchant paid in Duties upon importation, untill the time the Goods are re-exported, is just so much loss to him, and in so far prevents Trade.

Since all Duties inwards, besides being disadvantagious to Trade, are found to lie at last upon the Consumer; and the landed Interest, the rich and luxurious pay the greatest part: The prudenteft and best method of raising Taxes, and least expensive in Trading Countries that have many Ports to Guard, and of securing the Payment of the Duties, and preventing the frauds in Running them clandestinely, would be to take off all Port Duties, and

place

[31]

place the Taxes upon Land, Moveables and inland Excifes.

T H E Excifes fhould be fo proportion'd as to be laid partly upon neceffaries, but only in fuch a Manner as would promote induftry and Labour, in which the Poor would pay their reafonable proportion; and the remainder and greateft part be laid upon luxurious Eating, Drink, Drefs, Furniture, Equipage, Gaming, &c.

W HERE the intention is to difcourage the importation of foreign Goods prejudicial to the Publick, there to put high Licences and Excifes upon them in the Retailers or Confumers hands; and if they are entirely prohibited, then to lay the penalty upon the Confumer or wherever found. Whatever proportion fhould be thought proper to be laid upon Land would have this conveniency, that thofe who have Fortunes and don't refide in their Country, would bear a proportion of the Taxes; which is not done when all Taxes are rais'd upon the Confumer by Duties and Excifes. This method of Taxing would effectually promote Æconomy and Frugality in the rich, and Induftry in the poor; when they found the Taxes only laid upon fuch neceffaries as would oblige the Poor to apply their time to labour; and the remainder to lye upon the expenfive and idle Confumers of their Wealth and Time.

A Regulation of this kind will no doubt be extremely hard, if not Impracticable to be procur'd in a Country, where moft of the Duties are of the King's hereditary Revenue; even tho' an equivalent fhould be given to the Crown for them. However I thought it would not be improper to give the following Abftract of our Revenue at a medium of 6 Years ending Lady Day 1729: that I may fhew how much of it falls upon Trade.

Th

[32]

	l.	*s.*	*d.*
The total Revenue, at a Medium of 6 Years ending Lady Day 1729, amounts to.	540562	18	3
Charge of Collection, Light-Houses, Casualties, Premiums &c.	68655	13	5
Drawbacks, and Portage Bills to Masters of Ships.	9498	7	1¾
Drawbacks upon the additional Revenue.	4793	13	10¼
Total Charge	82947	14	5
Total of the neat produce of the Revenue at said Medium.	457615	3	10

Of which general sum paid by Merchants in part of the Hereditary Revenue. on

	l.	*s.*	*d.*
Customs Inwards	89164	16	4
Customs outwards	33325	5	9½
Imported Excise.	76790	11	9½
Prizage.	5131	8	4½
Light-House Duties, Fines, Seizures and Casualties.	4010	14	9½
Total by Merchants, towards the Hereditary Revenue.	208422	17	1

Paid

[33]

			l.	*s.*	*d.*
Brought forward			208422	17	1

			l.	*s.*	*d.*
Paid by Merchants in part of the additional Revenue on	Tobacco,		41600	1	10
	Wine,		16302	8	6
	Spirits,		12106	4	10¼
	Muslin, East India Goods, Molosses, Linnen and Yarn, Callicoe, Tea, Coffee, Cacao-Nuts, Twine and Cordage,		8615	19	4¼

	l.	*s.*	*d.*
Total, paid by Merchants, towards the additional Revenue	78624	14	7
Total upon Trade	287047	11	8

		l.	*s.*	*d.*
The Hereditary Revenue rais'd upon Land, Inland Excise and Hearth-Money at a Medium as above. by	Inland Excise,	75554	0	6
	Ale Licences,	8955	3	2
	Wine & Strong Water Licenses	3772	1	6¼
	Quit-Rents,	63552	19	11¼
	Hearth-Money,	41947	9	6¼

	l.	*s.*	*d.*
Total by Hereditary Revenue.	193781	14	9

E   Total

[34]

	l.	*s.*	*d.*
Total by Trade brought forward	287047	11	8
Total by Hereditary Revenue brought forwards	193781	14	9
By additional Excife.	59733	11	10
Total by Land, Excife and Hearth-Money,	253515	6	7
Total of the Revenue as above.	540562	18	3

THUS we fee the Duties upon Trade exceed thofe upon Land, Hearth-Money and inland Excife, by the fum of 33532 *l.* 5 *s.* 1 *d.* and that the Duties upon Trade in the whole amount to 287047 *l.* 11 *s.* 8 *d.* the greateft part of which is ready Money out of the Merchants pocket, that is feldom repaid him by thofe he deals with, till a confiderable time after; and tho' by the advanced price upon his goods, he is paid a large Intereft for his Money; yet (as I have already obferv'd) the Nation lofes the benefit he would have made in the mean time by the quick Circulation of his Money, and the employment he would have given to the induftrious Poor.

IT may be faid that the detriment is not fo great to Trade, fince in the additional, and great part of the hereditary Revenue, it is laid upon Commodities the confumption of which ought to be difcountenanc'd, as Wines, Brandies, Tobacco, *Eaft-India* goods, Silks and other foreign Goods and Manufactures, with which or as good we might be furnifh'd at home. I allow this to be true: But mayn't the Payment of the Duties be contriv'd fo as to eafe the Merchant Importer, by taking from the Retailer or Confumer; the high Duties of fuch goods as are moft liable to be run, much after the manner as now us'd by an imported account, when the Merchants do not make prompt payment, for which they are allow'd an abatement. By this method the Merchants would
have

[35]

have more Money circulating thro' their hands; it would also in some measure lessen the temptation of running of goods, when the Merchants did not pay ready Money at importation; and they could then better afford giving them Store-house room, and make a gain upon Re-exportation, when they did not advance the Duty. For their further incouragement, I could wish that no Duty remain'd upon goods Re-exported: For this would by no means lessen the Duty upon goods consumed at home, but rather increase it, by employing a greater Number of Men and Ships, when we could furnish our Neighbours by our Navigation; and no Vessel should be allowed to Export them, but of such a Burthen as might Trade with advantage to some Country beyond the *British* Isles; and also give Bond, tho they enter'd for a foreign Port, to return sufficient Vouchers, the dangers of the Seas excepted, that the goods were landed at such or some other foreign Port; which would prevent their re-landing them upon our own, or *British* Coasts.

T H E Merchants thus, not paying Duty upon Importation, ought to be accountable to the Officers of the Revenue for it, upon selling any of their goods to the Retailer or Consumer, that the Duty might not be lost. They that are allowed this priviledge, ought to be Resident and of an establish'd Character, or be oblig'd to give resident Merchants sureties for the payment of the Duties. And they might either take the Duty from the Buyer upon Sale, if he were not well known, or their Books might be Vouchers against the persons to whom sold; and they should still be liable to the Duty, if it could not be come at in the retailers or consumers hands.

T H I S would be some incouragement to the honest Merchant; the consumer would pay no more than at present for what he takes; and the Revenue would rather increase upon it than sink. The only

present

[36]

present difadvantage to the Revenue, would be the poft-poning the Duties two or three Months ; but the briskness of Trade, and the prevention of the clandeftine running of goods, would more than make amends for it. Tobacco, Brandies and Wines ought to have the Duties lower'd ; and the Retailers and Confumers of Wines and Brandies ought to be put under high Licenfes, efpecially publick Taverns, or others retailing them ; and alfo all private Houfes that take from a Whole-fale Merchant ; but not thofe who take from Taverns or Shops that pay high Licenfe. Every perfon alfo retailing Tobacco ought to pay a high Licenfe to make up the Duty taken off; and no perfon ufing Tobacco or Snuff fhould be allow'd to buy from any Whole-fale Merchant, but only from thofe who take out fuch Licenfes: And if any Whole-fale Merchant fhould fell to any perfon not Certify'd to be under Licenfe, let him be liable to a Premunire or fome other fevere penalty. Foreign Manufactures, and all other goods liable to be Run by reafon of high Duties, ought to be treated after the fame manner, in order to difcourage their confumption ; and thus the legal Duties would be regularly paid.

I muft own our prefent inland Excife upon Malt-Liquors is liable to great frauds, and attended with great expence: But if Excifes were made more general, the expence would be lefs in proportion ; and the method here propos'd of levying the Duties upon Trade, might alfo be us'd in the Excife upon Malt-Liquors, with great benefit to the publick. For if the Excife were laid upon Malt, to be paid by thofe that bought from the Malfter's, according to the proportion of Drink a Barrel of Malt would make, and that Barrel was determin'd and fold by weight, the Malfter's Books being vouchers of the Sale, and the Malt view'd in his Hands, a confiderable expence in the Salaries of Officers would be

fav'd,

[37]

fav'd, and the frauds now committed by the Retailers of Malt-Liquors would be avoided. To make the Tax payable by the Malfter, would be attended with this inconveniency ; the Tax would not fall fo much upon the confumer as upon the Farmer, and would therefore in effect be a Tax upon Land ; becaufe the Malfter would in a good meafure deduct it from the price he now gives for Corn.

I f fuch a method be thought feafible, there need be no alteration in the Taxes: And if new Taxes were at any time neceffary, they might be laid upon luxury, Drefs, Equipage and Gaming ; to be levy'd by way of Excife upon the confumer or Gamefter. Thus by lowering of Intereft, eafing the Merchant, and by that means preventing a fraudulent Trade, I would not doubt to fee our Commerce and induftry increafe ; and our prefent Revenue, without ever loading us with new Taxes, not only pay our Eftablifhment, but afford a fufficient redundancy to his Majefty to beftow upon merit and fervices perform'd to the Crown and Kingdom.

I t won't be improper here to confider the proportion our Taxes bear to thofe of *Britain*, with refpect to our Wealth and Numbers. The funds appropriated to pay the debts in *Britain*, together with the Civil and Military Lift, Fleet, *&c.* amount at prefent to about fix Millions ; and may be prefum'd to continue fo in time of peace, to reduce the debts the quicker by a larger finking fund : And when the debts in *Britain* are entirely paid, the Taxes may be leffen'd to 2500000 *l.*

T he Taxes rais'd in *Ireland* amount to 540000 *l.* and the Taxes appropriated to pay our debt, may amount to 20000 *l.* more ; in all 560000 *l.* annually.

T he Number of People in *England* in 1696, was computed by the ingenious Mr. *King* at 5500520, being fuppofed at 4$\frac{1}{16}$ to a Family ; which he computed

puted

[38]

puted gain'd by their induftry annually at a medium
7 *l.* 18 *s.* o *per* Head : So that the yearly income of
England then was about 43500000 *l.* I have already
obferv'd, that fince that time the Number of Houfes
in *England* may be prefum'd to increafe to 1600000;
and fince in *Ireland* there are computed at leaft
4.36 at a Medium to each Family; it may be reafonably fuppos'd, by the greater Wealth and Riches in
England, that there are five at a Medium to each
Family there : Thus the Numbers in *England* would
be eight Millions. And *Scotland* being added fince
1707, we may add 1500000 more; fo that there
will be 9500000 perfons in *Britain.* But fince the
Wealth of *North-Britain* is not proportional to
the Wealth of *England* ; inftead of allowing the
Yearly income of *Britain* to be 7 *l.* 18 *s.* o *per* Head,
I will even leffen Mr *King's* computation and allow
7 *l. per* Head in *England,* and 4 *l. per* Head in *Scotland* : So that the annual income of *England* will be
56 Millions, of *Scotland* 6 Millions, and of both 62
Millions. And the Taxes at prefent rais'd, not exceeding 6 Millions, don't amount to the $\frac{1}{10}$ of their
annual income; fo that if their debts were paid, and
their Taxes lower'd but to 3 Millions, they would
then pay lefs than $\frac{1}{20}$ of their annual income.

AFTER the fame manner, fuppofing the Numbers
in *Ireland* to be 1670000, and 4 *l. per* annum *per* Head
to be the income of each at a Medium, as I have
allow'd in *North-Britain*; which is fufficient, confidering the low way of living of the greateft Number of the People : Then the annual income of *Ireland* will be 6680000 *l.* and the general income of
Britain and *Ireland* 68680000 *l.* and the Taxes of
Ireland being 560000 *l,* *Ireland* at prefent pays more
than $\frac{1}{12}$ of its annual income : Which is very near
as much in proportion as *Britain* pays, notwithftanding its great debts : And fince about 360000 *l.*
more is drain'd out of the Kingdom by non-Refi-
denters,

[39]

denters, which is worfe than fo much paid in Taxes that would circulate among us; then *Ireland* pays almoft ¼ of its annual Income.

Doctor *Davenant* computed from the beft accounts he had, that the annual income of *France* before 1690 was about 84000000 *l*. It may be fuppos'd, by the Wars they had from that time to the peace of *Utrecht*, they could not increafe in Wealth and Numbers, on account of their conftant drain of Men and Money, and lofs of Territory.

Should we allow that their Trade and Peace fince that time has added to their Wealth and Numbers; and fo increas'd their annual income as much as that of *England* has been fince Mr. *King's* Eftimate, as I have computed it above, that is 12 Millions (which, confidering the difference of government, is fully as much as can be fuppos'd) Then their annual income now would be 96 Millions; and the Power and Wealth of *Britain*, including *Ireland*, would be above 7⁄6 of the Power and Wealth of *France*; and by a due incouragement of our Trade and giving proper checks to that of *France*, might in time be brought to equal it.

From thefe Obfervations *Britain* may fee that we cannot reafonably be higher taxed, unlefs we are incouraged by Trade to increafe our Numbers and give them full employment. Some are of opinion that the way to make us moft effectually add to the Power of *Britain*, would be by an equitable Union with them: That would foon increafe our Numbers to 2 Millions; and our income *per* Head to 6 *l*. fomewhat fhort of the income in *England per* Head, being at a diftance from the Capital. Then our annual income would be 12 Millions: At which time we could as eafily bear a Million to be rais'd upon us in Taxes, as we now can 560000 *l*. the ¼ of which would be enough for our Eftablifhment; and then *Britain* might have from us 500000 *l*.

to

[40]

to be employ'd in defence of them, their Colonies
and Trade, and might leſſen in proportion many of
their Taxes in time of Peace, which would be an immenſe benefit to them.

REPRESENTATION OF THE BOARD OF TRADE

Representation of the Board of Trade Relating to the Laws made, Manufactures set up, and Trade carried on, in his Majesty's Plantations in America (n.p., 1734). Edinburgh University Library, shelfmark P.486/7.

The exact author of this text is unknown, but it is signed by John Fane, seventh Earl of Westmoreland; Martin Bladen; Sir Orlando Bridgeman, second Baronet; Sir Archer Croft, second Baronet; and Paul Docminique. This is a parliamentary report which seems to have been written on behalf of House of Lords to the Commission for Trade and Plantations and addressed to parliament on 13 June 1733. It lists the different English plantations in North America and in the Caribbean, their produce and the different acts which have been set up for their governance.

REPRESENTATION of the Board of Trade relating to the Laws made, Manufactures set up, and Trade carried on, in His Majesty's Plantations in *America.*

Die Jovis, 21 Febr. 1733.

ORdered by the Lords Spiritual and Temporal in Parliament Affembled, That the Reprefentation of the Commiffioners for Trade and Plantations, laid before this Houfe the 23d of January laft, in Obedience to His Majefty's Commands, purfuant to their Lordfhips Addrefs to His Majefty of the 13th of June, 1733. for an Account of the Laws made, Manufactures fet up, and Trade carried on, in any of His Majefty's Colonies and Plantations in America, which may have affected the Trade, Navigation, and Manufactures of this Kingdom, be forthwith Printed.

Wm Cowper,
Cler' Parliamentor'

[3]

To the Right Honourable the Lords Spiritual and Temporal in Parliament assembled.

May it please Your Lordships,

IS Majesty hath been pleased by His Order dated the Fifteenth day of *June*, One thousand seven hundred and thirty three, upon Your Lordships Address of the Thirteenth of the same Month, to direct the Commissioners for Trade and Plantations to prepare, during the Recess of Parliament, and lay before your Lordships at your next Meeting, an Account of the Laws made, Manufactures set up, and Trade carried on, in any of His Majesty's Colonies and Plantations in *America*, which may have affected the Trade, Navigation, and Manufactures of this Kingdom; distinguishing when any such Manufactures were first set up, what Progress has been made therein, and what Orders or Instructions have been given to discourage the same, and when any such Trade was first carried on, and what Directions have been given, or Methods taken, to put a stop thereto.

In treating these Subjects we shall observe the Order prescribed in your Lordships Address to His Majesty, which leads us to begin with what regards the Laws of the Plantations; and that your Lordships may be fully apprized of every thing that relates to this Head, we beg leave to premise some Particulars concerning the Constitution of the several Colonies, and the Powers vested in them for the passing of Laws.

Many of the *British* Colonies in *America* are immediately under the Government of the Crown, namely, *Nova Scotia*, *New Hampshire*, the *Jerseys*, *New York*, *Virginia*, and the *Two Carolina's*, *Bermuda*, or the *Summer Islands*, *Bahama Islands*, *Jamaica*, *Barbados*, and the *Leeward Islands*.

Others are vested in Proprietors, as *Pensylvania* and *Maryland*, and not long since the *Bahamas* and the *Two Carolina's*.

There are likewise Three Charter Governments, the chief of which is the Province of the *Massachusets Bay*, commonly called *New England*, the Constitution whereof is of a mixed Nature, the Power being divided between the King and the People, in which the latter have much the greater Share; for here the People do not only choose the Assembly as in other Colonies, but the Assembly choose the Council also, and the Governor depends upon the Assembly for his annual Support, which has too frequently laid the Governors

A 2   of

[4]

of this Province under Temptations of giving up the Prerogative of the Crown, and the Intereſt of *Great Britain.*

Connecticut and *Rhode Iſland* are the other Charter Governments, or rather Corporations, where almoſt the whole Power of the Crown is delegated to the People, who make an annual Election of their Aſſembly, their Council, and their Governour likewiſe ; to the Majority of which Aſſemblies, Councils, and Governors reſpectively, being Collective Bodies, the Power of making Laws is granted, and, as their Charters are worded, they can and do make Laws even without their Governors Aſſent, and directly contrary to their Opinions, no Negative Voice being reſerved to them as Governors in the ſaid Charter : And as the ſaid Governors are annually choſen, their Office generally expires before His Majeſty's Approbation can be obtained, or any Security can be taken for the due Obſervance of the Laws of Trade and Navigation, and hold little or no Correſpondence with our Office. It is not ſurpriſing that Governors, conſtituted like theſe laſt mentioned, ſhould be guilty of many Irregularities in point of Trade, as well as in other Reſpects.

All theſe Colonies however by their ſeveral Conſtitutions have the Power of making Laws for their better Government and Support, provided they be not repugnant to the Laws of *Great Britain,* nor detrimental to their Mother Country : And theſe Laws, when they have regularly paſſed the Council and Aſſembly of any Province, and received the Governor's Aſſent, become valid in that Province, but remain repealable nevertheleſs by His Majeſty in Council upon juſt Complaint, and do not acquire a perpetual Force, unleſs they are confirmed by His Majeſty in Council.

But there are ſome Exceptions to this Rule in the Proprietary and Charter Governments ; for in the Province of *Penſylvania,* they are only obliged to deliver a Tranſcript of their Laws to the Privy Council within Five Years after they are paſſed ; and if His Majeſty does not think fit to repeal them in Six Months from the time ſuch Tranſcript is ſo delivered, it is not in the Power of the Crown to repeal them afterwards.

In the *Maſſachuſets Bay* alſo, if their Laws are not repealed within Three Years after they have been preſented to His Majeſty for His Approbation or Diſallowance, they are not repealable by the Crown after that time.

The Provinces of *Maryland, Connecticut,* and *Rhode Iſland,* not being under any Obligation by their reſpective Conſtitutions to return authentick Copies of their Laws to the Crown for Approbation or Diſallowance, or to give any Account of their Proceedings, we are very little informed of what is done in any of theſe Governments.

There is alſo this ſingularity in the Governments of *Connecticut* and *Rhode Iſland,* that there Laws are not repealable by the Crown, but the Validity of them depends upon their not being contrary, but as near as may be, agreeable, to the Laws of *England.*

All the Governors of Colonies, who act under the King's Appointment, ought within a reaſonable Time to tranſmit home authentick Copies of the ſeveral Acts by them paſſed, that they may go through a proper Examination ; but they are ſometimes negligent of their Duty in this particular, and likewiſe paſs temporary Laws of ſo ſhort Continuance, that they have their full Effect even before this Board can acquire due Notice of them. Some Attempts have been made to prevent this pernicious Practice ; but the annual Support of Government in the reſpective Colonies making it neceſſary that Laws for that purpoſe ſhould paſs from Year to Year, the Aſſemblies have
                                                                    frequently

[5]

frequently endeavoured in thofe Laws, as well as in others of longer duration, to enact proper Propofitions repugnant to the Laws or Intereft of
Great Britain, of which this Board have never. failed to exprefs their Diflike
to the Crown, when fuch Laws have fallen under their Confideration, and
many Laws have from time to time been repealed upon that Account.

But as to fuch Laws as do not directly fall within the above Rule, againft
which no Complaint is made, and where the Board are doubtful of the Effect they may have, it has always been ufual to let them lie by probationary,
being ftill under the Power of the Crown to be repealed, in cafe any Inconvenience fhould arife from them.

It has alfo been ufual, when a Law has contained many juft and neceffary
Provifions for the Benefit of the Colony where it was paffed, intermixt with
fome others liable to Objection, to let it lie by, and give notice thereupon
to the Governor of the Province, that it fhould be repealed, if he did not
within a reafonable Time procure a new Law, not liable to the fame Objections, to be fubftituted in the Place thereof : And from the conftant Difcharge
of our Duty herein it has fo happened, that upon the moft diligent Enquiry
into all the Acts paffed in the feveral *Britifh* Colonies fince the Acceffion of
His late Majefty to the Throne, there are none, that have yet come to our
Knowledge, ftill remaining unrepealed or unexpired, which are liable to Objection, excepting thofe in the following Lift ; and even againft them no Complaint
has been made to this Board till very lately, *viz.*

In the *Maffachufets Bay,* an Act paffed in the Year 1728, intituled, *An Act
for the Encouragement of making Paper.* This Manufacture, as will appear by
the following Returns that have been made to us upon the Subject of Trade
and Manufactures, has hitherto made but a fmall Progrefs, and can hardly be
faid, in a ftrict Senfe, to interfere with our own Paper, becaufe almoft all the
Paper fent to *New England* is foreign Manufacture ; but it certainly interferes
with the Profit made by our *Britifh* Merchants upon the foreign Paper fent to
this Province : However no Complaint has ever been made to Us againft this
Law.

By the Return to our circular Letter to the Governor of *New Hampfhire,*
we are informed, That *An Act* paffed many Years fince in that Province *for
Encouraging of Iron Works,* by which the Exportation of Iron Ore is prohibited ; but upon the moft diligent Enquiry no fuch Act is to be found in our Office, and we believe none fuch was ever tranfmitted to this Board ; however not
knowing whether this Act might not have paffed fince the late King's Acceffion,
we have inferted it in this Lift.

In *New York* a Law paffed in the Year 1728, intituled, *An Act to repeal
fome Parts, and to continue and enforce other Parts of the Act therein mentioned, and
for granting feveral Duties to His Majefty, for fupporting His Government in the
Colony of* New York, *from the Firft of* September, 1728, *to the Firft of* September, *which will be in the Year* 1733, wherein, amongft other Duties, one was
laid of five Ounces of Plate, or Forty Shillings in Bills of Credit, on every Negroe imported from *Africa,* and a Duty of Four Pounds on every Negroe
imported from any other Place.

The Plantations in all Times paft have laid Duties upon the Importation of
Negroes ; and as the Merchants have naturally increafed their Price in Proportion to thofe Duties, fo it is but lately that Complaints have been made upon
this Subject, unlefs when thofe Impofitions went to Excefs. But we are of opinion,
that it would be more for the Intereft of the *Englifh* Merchants, that Duties upon
Negroes fhould for the future be paid by the Purchafer rather than by the Importer ;

B

[6]

porter ; and His Majefty has, upon our Reprefentation, been pleafed to fend an Inftruction to that Effect, to all His Governors in *America*.

North Carolina hath but lately been purchafed by the Crown, and no Laws have been paffed there, fince that Purchafe, by His Majefty's Governor ; but we have lately received a Collection of the Laws of that Province, enacted during the Time of the late Proprietors, amongft which we find two Acts paffed in the Year 1715, which feem to come within the Meaning of your Lordfhips Order, *viz. An Act concerning Attornies from foreign Parts, and for giving Priority to Country Debts ;* and *An Act for raifing a publick Magazine of Ammunition upon the Tunnage of all Veffels to this Government.*

Both thefe Laws are very partial to the Inhabitants of this Province : The Firft by giving the Preference to themfelves, in the Recovery of their Debts, before the Subjects of this Kingdom ; and the Second by excufing fuch Veffels as are owned, or in Part owned, by the Inhabitants of that Country, from paying the Powder Duty thereby impofed ; otherwife we fhould have no Objection to the laft of thefe Laws, becaufe a Powder Duty has always been collected and paid in all the Colonies abroad, by Ships trading thither, without Complaint to this Office.

In *South Carolina* a Law paffed in the Year 1727, intituled, *An Act for carrying on feveral Expeditions againft the* Indians *and other Enemies,* &c. by which a Duty was revived of Ten Pounds, current Money of that Country, amounting to about 1 *l.* 8 *s.* 6 *d.* fterling, on every Negroe of above Ten Years old, if imported directly from *Africa,* and of Five Pounds *per* Head, if under Ten Years of Age, and not Sucklings ; and if imported from any other Plantations, above Ten Years old Fifty Pounds, and under Ten Years old Five Pounds, except Proof were made that they were all new Negroes, and had not been above Six Months in *America.*

Complaint was made againft this Act by the Merchants in the Year 1729, not for the Value of the Duty, but for the Manner of the Collection ; whereupon this Board propofed to His Majefty, at the requeft of the faid Merchants, that the fame fhould be made payable for the future by the Purchafer, and not by the Importer ; and it was from hence that the Inftruction already mentioned under the Head of *New York* took its Rife.

By the Charter of *Penfylvania* it has already been obferved, that the Proprietor is obliged to offer the Laws of this Province to the Crown, for Approbation or Difallowance, within Five Years after they are paffed ; and if His Majefty does not think fit to repeal them in Six Months from the Time they are fo offered, it is not in the Power of the Crown to repeal them afterwards. But fince the Year 1715, this Article of the Charter has been evaded, and the Laws of this Province have not been tranfmitted to this Board, except occafionally an Act or two ; fo that we are not enabled to lay the State of the Laws of this Province before your Lordfhips.

Maryland is a Province of which the Lord *Baltimore* is abfolute Proprietor ; and as he is not obliged by his Patent to lay the Laws paffed there before the Crown for Approbation, we know little of them, except of fuch Acts as the Merchants have Reafon to complain of, two of which are to be found in a Lift of Laws lately delivered to this Board by the Merchants, impofing Duties on the Importation of Negroes and *Irifh* Servants, which we fhall infert in another Part of this Report.

In *Bermuda* a Law paffed in 1731, intituled, *An Act to fupply the Deficiency of the feveral Funds in thefe Iflands, for finifhing the Fortifications, and for defraying the*

[7]

the other Charges of this Government. This Law lays a Duty of 3 *per Cent.* on all Goods and Merchandize not belonging to the Inhabitants, on which Account we laid the same before His Majesty for his Disallowance.

At the *Bahama's* an Act was passed in 1729, intituled, *An Act for levying divers Sums of Money for defraying the publick Charges of these Islands,* which imposes a Duty of Eighteen Pence *per* Barrel on Beer or Cyder, and Three Shillings *per* Groce, if in Bottles. There are other Duties also laid by this Act, from which the Inhabitants are exempted, and therefore we should immediately have laid the same before His Majesty for His Disallowance ; but considering the extreme Poverty of this New Colony, and the great Difficulty they are under to find out Funds to support their Government, and as these Duties are but small, we have chosen to let this Act lie by, till the Governor can get another passed for the like Purposes, not liable to the same Objections.

These are all the Laws passed since His late Majesty's Accession, that can reasonably be said to fall within your Lordships Order ; nor has any Complaint been made to us, till very lately, of any other of more ancient Date ; but upon a late Petition to His Majesty from the Merchants of *London* in behalf of themselves and others, complaining, " That as the Laws then stood in some " of the Colonies, His Majesty's Subjects residing in *Great Britain* were left " without any Remedy for the Recovery of their just Debts, or had such only " as was very partial and precarious ; as also that in several of the said Co- " lonies and Plantations greater and higher Duties and Impositions are laid " on the Ships and Goods belonging to His Majesty's Subjects residing in *Great* " *Britain,* than on the Goods and Ships of Persons inhabiting the said Colonies " and Plantations ; " We desired the said Merchants to acquaint us, whether they knew of any particular Laws against which they had reason to object : Whereupon they did deliver to us a List of Laws, wherein the said Colonies appear to have been very partial in their own Favour, in some of them exempting their Persons from Arrests, in others giving a Preference to the Inhabitants before the *British* Merchants in the Recovery of Debts, and in the enacting of Duties whereby a less Burthen is laid upon their own Effects than upon those of the *British* Merchants : But as some of the Laws in that List are already taken Notice of in this Representation, and others expired or long since repealed, we shall only enumerate to your Lordships such of them as we apprehend to be still in Force, *viz.*

An Act passed in *Virginia* in 1663, intituled, *An Act concerning foreign Debts,* by virtue of which Debts owing to Persons Non-residents are not pleadable, unless for Goods imported.

An Act passed in *Virginia* in 1664, intituled, *An Act for the Priority of Payment to the Country Creditors,* by which the Priority in the Payment of Debts is given to the Creditors who are Inhabitants of that Province.

An Act passed in *Virginia* in 1668, intituled, *Privilege of* Virginia *Owners,* by which, *Virginia* Owners are exempted from paying the Duties of Two Shillings *per* Hogshead, which the Merchants of *Great Britain* and other Owners of Ships are obliged to pay.

An Act passed in *Virginia* in 1669, intituled, *An Act for freeing* Virginia *Owners from Castle Duties,* by which, the *Virginia* Owners are also exempted from paying the Castle Duty of One Shilling and Three Pence *per* Tun, which the Merchants and others residing in this Kingdom are obliged to pay.

An Act passed in *Virginia* in 1680, intituled, *An Act for raising a publick Revenue for the better Support of the Government of this His Majesty's Colony*
of

[8]

of Virginia, by which the forgoing Privileges were confirmed to the *Virginia* Owners.

An Act paſſed in *Maryland* in 1704, intituled, *An Act confirming to the Governor of this Province the Duty of Three Pence* per *Tun upon the Burthen of Ships and Veſſels,* by which a Duty of Three Pence *per* Tun was impoſed on *Engliſh* Ships, from which the Ships of that Province are exempted.

An Act paſſed in the ſame Province in 1704, intituled, *An Act for Laying an Impoſition on ſeveral Commodities exported out of this Province,* by which Non-reſidents were obliged to pay a double Duty for Furs exported. Traders from *Great Britain* were then deemed Reſidents ; but by the Collection of Laws printed in *Maryland* it appears, that an Act was paſſed there in 1723, the Province being then under the Government of its Proprietor, intituled, *An Act repealing ſuch Part of an Act of Aſſembly,* intituled, *An Act for laying an Impoſition on ſeveral Commodities exported out of this Province, as relates to the laying an Impoſt or Duty on Furs and Skins only ; and for laying an Impoſition on Pork, Pitch, and Tar, in lieu thereof,* by which a Duty of One Shilling is laid on every Barrel of Pork, and Six Pence on every Hundred weight thereof ; One Shilling on every Barrel of Pitch, and Six Pence on every Barrel of Tar, that ſhould be imported by any but Inhabitants, in lieu of the abovementioned Duty upon Furs, and by this Act the Privileges before enjoyed by the *Britiſh* Traders are not preſerved.

By another Act paſſed in *Maryland* in 1704, intituled, *An Act for the Relief of Creditors in* England *againſt Bankrupts who have imported any Goods into this Province not accounted for,* the *Britiſh* Creditors of Bankrupts are put under ſuch Difficulties in the Recovery of their Debts, as are almoſt unſurmountable.

Another Act paſſed in the ſame Province in 1715, intituled, *An Act laying an Impoſition on Negroes, and on ſeveral Sorts of Liquors imported ; and alſo on* Iriſh *Servants, to prevent the importing too great a Number of* Iriſh *Papiſts into this Province,* by which, a Duty is laid on all Liquors imported ; and alſo a Duty of Twenty Shillings *per* Head on Negroes and *Iriſh* Servants, which Duties are not to be paid by Veſſels belonging to the Inhabitants of the ſaid Province.

It appears from the Dates in the Laws in the foregoing Liſt, that moſt of them were paſſed long ago, and might very probably be thought reaſonable at the Time when they were enacted, as Encouragements to ſuch as ſhould be diſpoſed to tranſport themſelves, and lay out their ſmall Fortunes in *America,* which we conceive to be the Reaſon why no Complaint was ever made a-gainſt them that we know of, till the abovementioned Petition from the Merchants of *London* in 1731, which having been referred by His Majeſty's Order in Council to the Conſideration of this Board, we did by our Repreſentation to the King, dated *January* the 21ſt, 1731-2. ſet forth in a very ample manner the Senſe we had of the ſeveral Matters complained of by the Merchants ; and there being many Things in that Repreſentation, which are pertinent to the preſent Enquiry, we beg Leave to tranſcribe it in this Place, and therewith to cloſe what we have to lay before your Lordſhips, in Conſequence of the firſt Head, your Order concerning the Laws of the Plantations.

To

[9]

" To the King's most Excellent Majesty.

" *May it please Your Majesty,*

" IN Obedience to Your Majesty's Order in Council of the 12th of *August*
" last, we have considered the humble Petition of several Merchants of
" the City of *London* to Your Majesty, setting forth, That as the Laws now
" stand in some of Your Majesty's Colonies and Plantations in *America*, Your
" Majesty's Subjects residing in *Great Britain* are left without any Remedy for
" recovery of their just Debts in the said Colonies, or have such Remedy only
" as is very uncertain and precarious, and that in several of the said Colonies
" greater Duties and Impositions are laid on the Ships and Goods of Your
" Majesty's Subjects residing in *Great Britain*, than upon the Ships and Goods
" of Persons who are Natives and Inhabitants of the Plantations ; which being
" great Discouragements to the Trade and Navigation of this Kingdom, the Pe-
" titioners most humbly beseech Your Majesty to take the Premisses into Your
" Royal Consideration, and grant them such Relief, as to Your Majesty in your great
" Wisdom shall seem meet.

" That we might, be the better able to offer our Opinion to Your Majesty
" upon these Points, we have discoursed with the Petitioners, who in support of
" their Complaint have laid before us some particular Cases and Facts that have
" happened in the Plantations, and have also taken Notice of several Laws now
" in Force in some of Your Majesty's Colonies in *America*, wherein they con-
" ceive great Partialities have been enacted in Favour of the Inhabitants of the
" respective Colonies where those Laws passed.

" With Respect to the Recovery of Debts due to Persons in *Great Britain*
" from those who reside in the Plantations, we conceive Suitors lie under Diffi-
" culties, both as to the Manner of making legal Proof of their Debts in Courts
" of Justice in the several Colonies, and likewise as to the Execution of the Law
" after a Verdict has been obtained in Favour of the Plaintiff.

" The first of these Grievances arises from the Expence and Difficulty of
" sending proper Persons from *Great Britain* to give personal Evidence in the
" Courts of Justice in the Plantations ; which certainly ought to be redressed,
" and in our humble Opinion, when any Person residing in this Kingdom
" shall commence a Suit in any Court of Justice throughout Your Majesty's
" Colonies in *America*, and shall transmit to his Attorney the necessary Accounts
" and Vouchers for Proof of his Debt, verified upon Oath before a proper Ma-
" gistrate, and attested in due Form by a Notary Publick, or by an Instrument
" in Writing under the Corporation Seal of the City, Borough, or Town
" Corporate where the same shall be taken, the said Affidavits ought to be re-
" ceived; and have the same Force and Validity for Proof of the said Debt,
" which the Oath of the Person deposing would have had, if he had given the
" same Evidence *vivâ voce* in the said Court.

" The Difficulty attending the Execution of the Law, after a Verdict hath
" been obtained in Favour of the Plaintiff, consists in Privileges claimed by
" some of the Colonies, particularly that of *Jamaica*, to exempt their Houses,
" Lands, and Tenements, and in some Places their Negroes also, from being
" extended for Debt ; but we conceive it to be highly reasonable that all Lands,
" Tenements, Hereditaments, and Negroes, throughout the several Colonies
" and Plantations, should be made as liable to the Payment of just Debts and
" Demands, as Lands, Tenements, and Hereditaments in *Great Britain* are,
" under the like Circumstances.

C   These

[10]

" Thefe two laft mentioned Grievances have been more than once recom-
" mended to the Governors of *Virginia* and *Jamaica* for Redrefs ; but the Af-
" femblies of thofe Colonies could never be induced to divest themfelves of
" thefe Privileges by any Act of their own ; and therefore, in our humble O-
" pinion, thefe Points may be very proper Objects for a Parliamentary
" Confideration in *Great Britain*, as they are of Importance to Your Majefty's
" Subjects trading to *America*.

" As to the Laws cited by the Petitioners, wherein they conceive the *Britifh*
" Merchants are treated with Inequality ; we beg Leave to acquaint Your Ma-
" jefty, that fome of them have never been complained of before, and are of
" very ancient ftanding, having been enacted in the Infancy of the feveral
" Colonies, when it might be neceffary to give the Inhabitants fome particular
" Encouragements, in order to increafe their Numbers, which was the Point
" moft effential to their Profperity ; but with refpect to Acts of later Date,
" fuch as have fallen under our Notice, we have never failed, upon Complaint,
" to reprefent againft thofe that have appeared to Us to be prejudicial to the
" trading Intereft of *Great Britain*, and fo foon as we fhall have throughly con-
" fidered the Nature and Tendency of the feveral Laws complained of by the
" Petitioners, we fhall lay fuch of them, as fhall be found juftly liable to Objec-
" tion, before Your Majefty for Your Difapprobation ; and in the mean Time
" we would humbly propofe, that all the Governors of Your Majefty's Colonies
" fhould be ftrictly forbid, upon Pain of Your Majefty's higheft Difpleafure, to
" give their Affent for the future to any Laws, wherein the Natives or Inhabi-
" tants of the refpective Colonies under their Government are put on a more
" advantageous Footing than thofe of *Great Britain*, and that the faid Governors
" fhould be directed to pay due Obedience to Your Majefty's Royal Inftructions,
" whereby You have been gracioufly pleafed to forbid them to pafs any Laws, by
" which the Trade or Navigation of this Kingdom may be any ways affected.

MANUFACTURES and TRADE.

WE come now, purfuant to the Method prefcribed in Your Lordfhips Addrefs to His Majefty, to take Notice of the Manufactures fet up and
and Trade carried on in any of our Colonies and Plantations in *America*, which
may have affected the Trade, Navigation, and Manufactures of this Kingdom.

The State of our Colonies being naturally fubject to frequent Variations in
their Trade, Manufactures, and other Particulars ; we thought it proper for
His Majefty's Service, and the Difcharge of our Truft, from Time to Time, to
fend certain general Queries to the feveral Governors in *America*, of which
there were feveral relating to Trade and Manufactures. Thefe circular Queries,
which were firft fent in the Year 1719, have been repeated as often as Neceffity
required, and it is from the Anfwers we have received in Return to thofe Queries
that we are enabled to lay the following Accounts before Your Lordfhips.

Nova Scotia.

With regard to *Nova Scotia*, the moft Northern *Englifh* Settlement on the
Continent of *America*, Colonel *Vetch*, who was formerly Governor of this Province, in his Anfwer to the abovementioned Queries, dated in *Auguft* 1719, informed us, that there were no Manufactures then eftablifhed in this Country,
and

[11]

and that the Trade of the Inhabitants confifted chiefly in Furs, Peltry, and Cod fifhing, in raifing fmall Quantities of Naval Stores, and in Lumber, which ftill continues to be the State of this Province with regard to Trade and Manufactures, as appears by the Returns we have received to our Queries from Colonel *Philipps*, the prefent Governor of *Nova Scotia*, dated *January* 24th, 1731-2 ; in which he acquaints us that there are no Manufactures in this Province, and that the Inhabitants trade with no foreign Plantation, except *Cape Briton*, to which Place they fend a little Corn, and a few live Cattle, which are paid for by the *French* in Money ; and that their Trade to *Europe* confifts in dry Cod cured at *Canfo*. But upon this Occafion we think it our Duty to take Notice, that we have received Complaints of the very bad Manner in which the *Canfo* Fifh is cured by the People of *New England*, which brings *Britifh* Fifh into difcredit in foreign Markets.

New Hampfhire.

Colonel *Shute* Governor of *New Hampfhire*, in his Return to our General Queries in 1719, informed us, that they had no fetled Manufactures in that Province, and that their Trade principally confifted in Lumber and Fifh.

But Mr. *Belcher*, the prefent Governor of *New Hampfhire*, in his Letter dated the Fourth Day of *December*, One thousand feven hundred and thirty one, acquainted us that the Woollen Manufacture of that Province was much lefs than formerly, the common Lands on which the Sheep ufed to feed, being now divided into particular Properties, and the People almoft wholly cloathed with Woollen Manufactures from *Great Britain* ; but that the manufacturing of Flax into different Kinds of Linen was daily increafed by a great Refort of People from *Ireland* well skilled in the Linen Manufacture.

Mr. *Belcher* has fince informed us that about Ten Years ago an Act was paffed in this Province for the Encouragement of Iron Works, by which a Grant was made of about Eight Thousand Acres of the King's Lands, as a further Encouragement to the Proprietors and Undertakers of thofe Works.

With regard to the Trade of this Province, he acquaints us that it now confifts, as it had done for many Years paft, in the Exportation of Naval Stores, Lumber, and Fifh.

Maffachufets Bay in *New England.*

In One thousand feven hundred and nineteen Colonel *Shute*, who was at that Time Governor of *Maffachufets Bay*, as well as of *New Hampfhire*, informed us that in fome Parts of this Province the Inhabitants worked up their Wooll and Flax, and made an ordinary coarfe Cloth for their own Ufe, but did not export any ; that the greateft Part both of the Woollen and Linen Clothing, which was then worn in this Province, was imported from *Great Britain*, and fometimes Linen from *Ireland*, and that, confidering the exceffive Price of Labour in *New England*, the Merchants could afford what was imported cheaper than what was made in that Province.

That there were alfo a few Hatters fet up in the *Maritime* Towns, and that the greateft Part of their Leather was manufactured by the Inhabitants.

That for many Years paft there had been Iron Works, which afforded the People Iron for fome of their Occafions, but that the Iron imported from
Great

[12]

Great Britain, was efteemed much better than their own, and was wholly ufed for the Service of their Shipping, and that the Iron Works eftablifhed in the Province could not produce a fufficient Quantity to anfwer a Twentieth Part of their Confumption.

Mr. *Belcher*, the prefent Governor of this Province, in Anfwer to the fame Queries which we fent him in *June*, One thoufand feven hundred and thirty one, acquainted us:

That there is a Refolve of the Affembly of that Province fubfifting, for allowing a Bounty of Twenty fhillings to all Perfons, and Ten fhillings more to *John Powel* the firft Undertaker, for every Piece of Duck or Canvas by them made, but he does not give us any Account of the Quantity that has been produced.

He further fays, that there were fome other Manufactures carried on in *New England*, fuch as the making Brown Holland for Womens Wear, which leffens the Importation of Callicoes, and fome other Sorts of *India* Goods into that Province.

That there are likewife fome fmall Quantities of Cloth made of Linen and Cotton, for ordinary fheeting and fhirting.

That about Three Years ago a Paper Mill was fet up, which makes to the Value of about Two hundred pounds Sterling *per Annum*. And he hath fince informed us that there hath lately been a new Paper Mill fet up at *Falmouth* in *Cafco Bay*, which at that Time had not begun to work for want of Materials.

That there are feveral Forges for making of Bar Iron, and fome Furnaces for Caft Iron, or Hollow Ware, and one Slitting Mill, the Undertaker whereof carries on the Manufacture of Nails.

As to the Woollen Manufactures of this Province, Mr. *Belcher* fays, that the Country People, who ufed formerly to make moft of their Clothing of their own Wooll, do not at prefent manufacture a Third Part of what is neceffary for their own Ufe, but are generally clothed with *Englifh* Manufactures.

We have likewife been informed by Letters of older Date, from Mr. *Belcher*, in Anfwer to our annual Queries, that there are fome few Copper Mines in this Province, but fo far diftant from Water Carriage, and the Oar fo poor, that it is not worth the digging.

Colonel *Dunbar*, Surveyor General of his Majefty's Woods in *North America*, in his Letter to us dated the Fifteenth Day of *September*, One thoufand feven hundred and thirty, takes Notice that the People of *New England* have an Advantage over thofe of *Great Britain*, in the Drawback allowed for all *India* and other Goods exported thither, which pay a Duty in *Great Britain*, but are fubject to no Duty of Importation either in this Province, or any other of the Plantations. He has likewife tranfmitted to this Board feveral Samples of Edge Tools made in *New England* : And in his Letter to our Secretary, dated the Fourth Day of *June*, One thoufand feven hundred and thirty one, he fays, they have Six Furnaces, and nineteen Forges, for making Iron in *New England*.

He alfo acquainted us in a former Letter, dated the Nineteenth Day of *Auguft*, One thoufand feven hundred and thirty, that in this Province many
Ships

[13]

Ships are built for the *French* and *Spaniards*, which are trucked with those People, by Connivance, for Rum, Molosses, Wines, and Silk. And these Informations have been in great measure confirmed by Mr. *Jeremiah Dunbar*, Deputy Surveyor of the Woods, and also by Mr. *Thomas Coram*, a Person of Reputation, who resided many Years in *New England*, to which they have added that great Quantities of Hats are made in that Province, of which the Company of *Hatters* of *London* have likewise lately complained to us, which gave Birth to an Act of Parliament that was passed in the last Sessions upon this Subject.

We were further informed by the said Mr. *Jeremiah Dunbar*, that the People of *New England* export great Quantities of Hats, of their own Manufacture, to *Spain*, *Portugal*, and our *West India Islands*; that they make all Sorts of Iron Works for Shipping, and that there are several Still Houses and Sugar Bakers established in *New England*.

But we cannot conceal from your Lordships, that it is with the greatest Difficulty we are able to procure true Informations of the Trade and Manufactures of *New England*, which will not appear extraordinary, when we acquaint your Lordships, that the Assembly of the *Massachusets Bay* had the boldness to summon the above mentioned Mr. *Jeremiah Dunbar* before them, and pass a severe Censure upon him, for having given Evidence at the Bar of the House of Commons of *Great Britain*, with respect to the Trade and Manufactures of this Province, agreeable to the Tenour of what is above mentioned under his Name.

New York.

General *Hunter*, formerly Governor of *New York*, in his Answer to our Queries in the Year One thousand seven hundred and twenty; informed us that there were no Manufactures in that Province, which deserved to be taken Notice of, and that their Trade consisted principally in Furs, Whalebone, and Oyl, Pitch, Tar, and Provisions.

Mr. *Rip Van Dam*, President of the Council in *New York*, acquainted us by his Letter dated the 29th of *October*, 1731, that there are no Manufactures established there that can affect the Manufactures of *Great Britain*: And as to the Trade and Navigation of the Province, he says, there is yearly imported into *New York*, a very large Quantity of the Woollen Manufactures of this Kingdom, for the Use of the Inhabitants, which they should be rendered uncapable to pay for, and reduced to the Necessity of making for themselves, if they were prohibited from receiving the Money, Rum, Sugar, Molosses, Cocoa, Indico, Cotton, Wooll, &c. which at that Time they imported from the foreign Sugar Colonies, in Return for Provisions, Horses, and Lumber, Productions of *New York* and *New Jersey*, of which he affirms the *British* Colonies did not take off above one half: But by an Act passed the last Sessions of Parliament, this Trade with the foreign Sugar Colonies is restrained.

New Jersey.

With Regard to *New Jersey* we have not yet received particular Returns to the Queries which we have transmitted thither upon these Subjects; but the Company of *Hatters* in *London* have informed us, that Hats are manufactured in this Province in great Quantities.

D

Pensylvania.

⌊ 14 ⌋

Penfylvania.

As to the Province of *Penfylvania*, Colonel *Hart*, who lived many Years in the Neighbourhood of this Country, when Governor of *Maryland*, acquainted us, In Anfwer to the like Queries relating to this Province in 1720, that their chief Trade lay in the Exportation of Provifions and Lumber ; and that they had no eftablifhed Manufactures, their Clothing and Utenfils for their Houfes being all imported from *Great Britain.*

And by a Letter which we received in *January*, 1731-2, from Major *Gordon* Deputy Governor of this Province, he acquainted us, that he did not know of any Trade carried on in that Province, which could be Injurious to this Kingdom; and that they do not export any Woollen or Linen Manufactures ; all that they make, which are of the coarfet Sort, being entirely for their own Confumption.

We are further informed, that in this Province are built many Brigantines and fmall Sloops, which they fell in the feveral Parts of the *Weft Indies.*

Maryland.

Colonel *Hart*, formerly Governor of *Maryland*, in Anfwer to our Quere with Regard to this Province in 1720, acquainted us, that their principal Trade was in Tobacco, which bearing a reafonable Price at that Time, the Inhabitants did not imploy themfelves in the Eftablifhment of new Manufactures, or the Promotion of fuch Branches of Commerce, as might arife from any other Productions of that Country.

And agreeable to this, the upper and lower Houfe of Affembly of this Province, in a late Addrefs to their Deputy Governor, in Anfwer to our general Queries, reprefent, that the Produce of their Tobacco, which is their chief Commodity for Trade, was alone fufficient to fupply the People with Clothing and other Necessaries from *Great Britain*, but that Neceffity had driven fome of the poorer fort of Inhabitants to make fmall Quantities of Linen and Woollen Manufactures for their own Ufe, but that no Part of them was exported.

Virginia.

In the Year 1720, we had no Returns to our general Queries from the Province of *Virginia*, but Major *Gooch*, the prefent Lieutenant Governor of this Colony, in his Letter dated the 22d of *December*, 1731, Informed us, that they carried on no Trade from thence, except that of Tobacco, nor had they any Manufacture eftablifhed amongft them, which deferved to be taken notice of, but that fome poor People provided themfelves with Clothing of a Kind of coarfe mixed Cloth made of Wooll and Cotton, and of Linfey Woolfey, where they were unable to purchafe better by their Labour in the Cultivation of Tobacco. And by a fubfequent Letter from Major *Gooch*, dated *October* 5th 1732, he informs us, that there hath been one Potters Work fet up in *Virginia* for coarfe Earthen Ware, but this is of fo little Confequence, that he believes it has occafioned little or no Diminution in the Quantity of Earthen Ware that had been commonly imported. That they have now Four Iron Works in that Colony imployed in running Pig Iron only, which is afterwards fent to *Great Britain* to be forged and manufactured.

[15]

But this Gentleman informs us, that the People of *New England*, being obliged to apply themselves to Manufactures more than other of the Plantations, who have the Benefit of a better Soil and warmer Climate, such Improvements have been lately made there in all Sorts of Mechanic Arts, that not only Scrutores, Chairs, and other Wooden Manufactures, but Hoes, Axes, and other Iron Utensils are now exported from thence to the other Plantations, which, if not prevented, may be of ill Consequence to the Trade and Manufactures of this Kingdom, which Evil may be worthy the Consideration of a *British* Parliament.

Carolina.

From the Province of *North Carolina* we have received no Returns to our general Queries, either whilst that Country was in the Hands of the Lords Proprietors, or since it hath been purchased by the Crown.

From *South Carolina* we are informed by a Letter we have received from Colonel *Johnson*, the present Governor of that Province, dated 14*th November*, 1731, that the Manufactures established there, which interfere with those of *Great Britain*, are scarce worth naming, being confined to a few Hats, Shoes, and coarse mixed Cloths made of Cotton and Wooll, for the Use of their Negroes.

Rhode Island.

The Governor of *Rhode Island*, in his Answer to our Queries, dated the 9*th* of *November*, 1731, informs us, that they have Iron Mines in this Island, but that they do not afford a fourth part of the Iron that is requisite for the Use of the Inhabitants; and he takes no Notice of any Sort of Manufacture set up there.

Connecticut.

We have had no Return to our Queries from the Governor of *Connecticut*, but we find by some Accounts in our Office, that the Productions of this Colony are Timber, Boards, all Sorts of *English* Grain, Hemp, Flax, Sheep, Cattle, Swine, Horses, Goats, and Tobacco, of which they export Horses and Lumber to the *West Indies*, and receive in Return Sugar, Salt, Molosses, and Rum. We likewise find that their Manufactures are very inconsiderable, the People being generally imployed in Tillage or Building, and in Tanning, Shoemaking, and other necessary Handycrafts, such as Taylors, Joiners, and Smiths Work, without which they could not subsist.

Having thus gone through the several Governments on the Continent of *America*, with Regard to their Trade and Manufactures, we come now to lay before your Lordships such Accounts as we have received upon the same Subjects with respect to His Majesty's *Island* Governments.

The *Bermuda* and *Bahama Islands*.

By the Returns made to us from the Governors of the *Bermuda* and *Bahama Islands*, in the Year One thousand seven hundred and thirty, we find that the only Manufactures set up in these small Governments are the building of Sloops, the making Hats of a Production called *Plat*, and a little Joyners Work; but their Sloops, especially those of *Bermuda*, make the principal Article of their Commerce, and are sold or bartered for Provisions and Negroes in the other Parts of *America*, and the *West Indies*.

Jamaica

[16]

Jamaica, Leeward Iſlands, and *Barbadoes.*

By the lateſt Returns we have received to our general Queries from his Majeſty's Sugar Colonies, *Jamaica,* the *Leeward Iſlands,* and *Barbadoes,* we do not find that they have any Manufactures (except thoſe of Sugar, Moloſſes, Rum, and Indico) upon which they have their greateſt Dependance : And theſe Colonies do likewiſe produce Cotton, Aloes, Piemento, Coffee, and ſome other Particulars of leſs Conſideration, which are Commodities that do not interfere with the Trade of *Great Britain,* but on the contrary ſome of them are of great uſe. in our Manufactures.

In the Year One thouſand ſeven hundred and twenty four, Mr. *Worſley,* then Governor of *Barbadoes,* informed us, that of Cotton they made Hammocks, a few Stockings, and Nets for Horſes.

Having thus laid before your Lordſhips the beſt Accounts we have been able to procure of the Laws, Manufactures, and Trade of the Plantations, which may have affected the Trade, Navigation, and Manufactures of this Kingdom : We come now to the latter Part of your Lordſhips Order, whereby we are directed to diſtinguiſh what Orders or Inſtructions have been given to diſcourage the ſame, and when any ſuch Trade was firſt carried on, and what Directions have been given, or Methods taken, to put a Stop thereto.

We beg Leave to obſerve to your Lordſhips, that it is impoſſible for us to aſcertain the particular Dates, when the ſeveral Branches of General Commerce, or the Domeſtick Trades and Manufactures of the ſeveral provinces enumerated in this Report, were firſt undertaken.

Some of them are founded in Neceſſity, and are undoubtedly as old as the firſt Eſtabliſhment of the reſpective Colonies, others of a more recent Date, having nothing in them inconſiſtent with the Trade and Welfare of this Kingdom; may for that Reaſon have been practiſed for a long Time, without falling under publick Notice; and with Regard to ſuch as may have deſerved the moſt early Check, for being repugnant to the Laws, or detrimental to the Trade of the Mother Country, it is not at all improbable that ſome former Governors of our Colonies, who may in general be ſaid to depend too much upon the Aſſemblies of their reſpective Provinces, for the Eſtabliſhment of their Salaries and other Appointments, may, in Breach of their Inſtructions, have given their Concurrence to Laws, or have connived for many Years at the Practice of Trades prejudicial to the Intereſt of *Great Britain,* till the Evils ariſing from them became too conſiderable to be any longer concealed.

But we beg leave to acquaint your Lordſhips in General, that there is extant in the Books of our Office a Body of Inſtructions relating to the Acts of Trade and Navigation, which were prepared by a Committee of the Lords of the Privy Council, with the Aſſiſtance of the Commiſſioners of the Cuſtoms, ſo long ago as the Year One thouſand ſix hundred and eighty ſix, in which we find mention made of former Inſtructions upon thoſe Subjects to the Governors of the Plantations, which do not appear in our Records.

But from the firſt Inſtitution of this Board to the preſent Time, it hath been a conſtant Practice for the Crown to give a Set of Inſtructions to every Governor in the Plantations relating to the Acts of Trade and Navigation, which have always been formed at this Board, with ſuch Additions

to

[17]

to thofe of One thoufand fix hundred and eighty fix, or fuch Variations from them, as the Circumftances of each Province refpectively, or the ordinary Viciffitudes incident to fubjects of this nature, may have rendered neceffary.

The Purport of the principal Articles of thefe Inftructions, which come within the meaning of your Lordfhips Order, is as follows:

That the feveral Governors of the Colonies, Provinces, and Iflands in *America*, do take Care that all the Acts relating to Trade and Navigation be duly obferved.

That all Naval Officers appointed by any Governor do give Security to the Commiffioners of the Cuftoms.

That no Ships but fuch as are built in the *Britifh* Dominions, and are owned and manned by Subjects of *Great Britain*, fhall trade in the Plantations.

That fuch Ships fhall give Security to bring the enumerated Goods to *Great Britain*, or to fome of the Plantations.

That the Governors do tranfmit Accounts of the Trade of their refpective Provinces to the Lords of His Majefty's Treafury, to this Board, and the Commiffioners of the Cuftoms.

That no foreign *European* Goods be imported into the Plantations, except fuch as are fhipped in *Great Britain*.

That no By-laws be allowed in the Plantations contrary to the Acts of Trade and Navigation.

That the Governors correfpond with the Commiffioners of the Cuftoms, and advife them of all Frauds, and of Neglects and Breaches of Duty in their fubordinate Officers.

That they endeavour to prevent the Exportation of Wooll or Woollen Manufactures from one Province of His Majefty's Territories in *America* to another.

That they endeavour to prevent Frauds in the Importation of Tobacco.

That they endeavour to prevent clandeftine Trade to the *Eaft Indies*, *Madagafcar*, &c. and to prevent the unlawful Importation of *Eaft India* Goods.

Thefe principal Inftructions are fupported by feveral others, which are diftinct. Rules contrived to enforce the Obfervation of the former; and the feveral Governors are ftrictly enjoined to put them in execution, under the Penalty of being deprived of their Offices, of forfeiting the fum of One thoufand Pounds, and of incurring the Difpleafure of the Crown. And Proprietors of Provinces are laid under the fame Injunctions upon the Penalty of forfeiting their Grants.

We beg Leave to acquaint your Lordfhips, that befides thefe general Inftructions, this Board have never failed to reprefent their Senfe of particular Grievances, and point out the beft Methods for redrefs of them, as often as we have received Complaints upon fuch Occafions, either from incorporated Bodies, or private Traders; which, from the Variety of Accidents attending Trade in the feveral Governments of *America*, have been very frequent, and have given Rife to feveral other Inftructions, particularly to thefe following, fome of which are general to all the Governors of the Plantations, and others peculiar to re-

E   fpective

[18]

fpective Provinces, as the Reafon of Things, or the Exigency of the Cafe may have required.

It is a general Inftruction to all the Governors of His Majefty's Colonies and Provinces in *America*, that they tranfmit to His Majefty, and to His Commiffioners for Trade and Plantations, from Time to Time, an Account of the Wants and Defects of their refpective Governments, what new Improvements are made therein by the Induftry of the Inhabitants or Planters, and what further Improvements may be made, or Advantages gained in Trade by the Affiftance or Interpofition of the Crown.

The following Inftructions are likewife general to all the Governors in America.

That they examine what Rates and Duties are charged upon Goods exported or imported ; that they ufe their beft Endeavours to prevent the ingroffing of Commodities, and to improve the Trade of their refpective Governments, by making fuch Orders and Regulations therein, with the Advice of His Majefty's Council, as may be moft acceptable to the Generality of the Inhabitants.

That they give due Encouragement to Merchants, and fuch as bring Trade to their refpective Governments, particularly to the Royal *African* Company and other Subjects of *Great Britain* trading to *Africa*.

That they take Care that Contracts for Negroes be duly complied with within a competent Time, according to Agreement.

That all Obftructions in the Courfe of Juftice be effectually removed, and Courts frequently held, that Traders may not receive any undue Hindrance in the Recovery of their juft Debts.

That in Time of War they ufe their beft Endeavours to hinder all Trade and Correfpondence with the *French*, whofe Strength in the *Weft Indies* gives very juft Apprehenfions of the Mifchiefs that may enfue from thence, if the utmoft Care be not taken to prevent them.

That in Times of Peace they obferve the Treaty of Neutrality concluded betwixt *Great Britain* and *France* in *November*, 1686.

That they do not pafs any Law whereby the King's Prerogative or the Property of His Subjects may be prejudiced, or the Trade or Shipping of this Kingdom be any Ways affected, until they fhall have firft tranfmitted the Draught of fuch Act to His Majefty, and have received His Royal Pleafure thereupon, unlefs there be a Claufe in the Act fufpending the Execution until His Majefty's Pleafure thereupon be known.

The Governors of all the Plantations are likewife directed to defift from their ancient Claim of the Produce of Whales of feveral Kinds, taken on the Coafts of their refpective Governments, upon Pretence that Whales are Royal Fifhes ; and that on the contrary, they give all poffible Encouragement to Fifheries upon the Coafts of the Plantations.

They are alfo inftructed not to pafs Laws whereby the Inhabitants of the Plantations may be put upon a more advantageous Footing than thofe of *Great Britain*.

Not to pafs any Law by which greater Duties or Impofitions fhall be laid on Ships or Goods belonging to the Subjects of *Great Britain*, than on thofe belonging to the Inhabitants of the Plantations, nor any Law whereby Duties fhall
be

[19]

be laid in their respective Governments upon the Product or Manufactures of *Great Britain.*

That they do not pass any Act whereby Duties upon Negroes shall be made payable by the Importer.

It is an ancient Instruction to the Governor of *Virginia*, that all Tobaccoes shipped in that Province, shall pay *Virginia* Duties.

The Governor of this Province is also directed to adhere strictly to the Terms of the Act of Navigation with Regard to the Package and shipping of Tobacco.

The Governors of *New York*, the *Massachusets Bay*, and the other *Northern* Provinces on the Continent of *America*, are directed to be aiding and assisting to His Majesty's Surveyor General of the Woods, and His Deputies, for the Security and Preservation of such Trees as shall be found proper for the Service of His Majesty's Royal Navy.

The Governors of those Provinces are also instructed to enforce the Observation of the several Acts of Parliament, of the Third and Fourth Years of Queen *Anne*, of the Eighth of His late Majesty, and the Second year of His present Majesty, for the Preservation of white Pine Trees, and for encouraging the Produce and Importation of Naval Stores into this Kingdom from those Provinces.

But having been required by the Lords of His Majesty's Privy Council, in the year One thousand seven hundred and twenty eight, to lay before them the best Informations we could procure of any Projects then carrying on, or that might have been undertaken for promoting the Silk, Linen, or Woollen Manufactures in any of His Majesty's Plantations, and to what Degree of Perfection the same might have been brought : We beg leave to close this Representation with the following Extract of our Report upon that occasion, which we conceive will fall within the meaning of your Lordships Order.

" Upon discoursing with several Persons who had been Governors of some " of His Majesty's Plantations, we found that in the Colonies of *New Eng-* " *land, New York, New Jersey, Connecticut, Rhode Island, Pensylvania,* and " in the County of *Somerset* in *Maryland*, the People have fallen into the " Manufacture of Woollen and Linen Cloth for the Use of their own " Families, but we could not learn that they have ever manufactured any " for Sale in any of the Colonies, except in a small *Indian* Town in *Pensyl-* " *vania*, where some *Palatines* have of late Years settled.

The Reasons which may be assigned why these People have begun those Manu- factures are,

" I. That the Product of these Colonies, being chiefly Stock and Grain, " the Estates of the Inhabitants depend wholly upon Farming ; and as this " could not be carried on without a certain Quantity of Sheep, their Wooll " would be entirely lost, were not their Servants imployed, in Seasons when " they had most Leisure, principally during the Winter, in manufacturing it " for the Use of their Families.

" II. That Flax and Hemp being likewise easily raised, the Inhabitants ma- " nufactured them into a Coarse sort of Cloth, Bags, Plough-traces, and Hal- " ters for their Horses, which they found to be more serviceable than those " imported from *Europe.*

" III. Those Settlements which are distant from Water Carriage, and are " remotely

[20]

" remotely fituated in the Woods, have no Opportunities of a Market for
" Grain, and therefore as they do not raife more Corn than is fufficient for
" their own Ufe, they have more time to manufacture both Wooll and Flax
" for the Service of their Families, and feem to be under a greater neceffity
" of doing it.

    " Upon further Enquiry into this Matter, we did not find that thefe People
" had the fame Temptation to go on with thofe Manufactures, during the
" Time that the Bounty upon Naval Stores fubfifted, which gave them Encou-
" ragement to direct their Labour into another Channel, and more profitably
" both for themfelves and this Kingdom; for the height of Wages, and the
" great Price of Labour in general throughout *America*, make it impracti-
" cable for the People there to manufacture Linen Cloth, for lefs than 20
" *per Cent.* more than it would coft in *England*, or Woollen Cloth for lefs
" than 50 *per Cent.* above the Price of that which is exported from hence for
" Sale: But as the fmall Quantities, which the People of *America* manufacture
" for their own Ufe, are a Diminution of the Exports from this Kingdom,
" it were to be wifhed that fome expedient might be fallen upon to divert
" their Thoughts from Undertakings of this Nature; and fo much the ra-
" ther, becaufe thefe Manufactures in Procefs of Time may be carried on
" in a greater Degree; and the moft natural Inducement which we can think
" of to engage the People of *America* to defift from thefe Purfuits, would
" be to imploy them in raifing Naval Stores, with which we might be fur-
" nifhed in Return for our own Manufactures, and much Money be faved
" by that Means, in the Balance of our Trade with the *Northern* Crowns,
" where thofe Materials are chiefly paid for in Specie.

                  All which is moft humbly fubmitted to your Lord-
                  fhips great Wifdom.

Whitehall, January 23,
   1733-4

WESTMORELAND.

M. BLADEN.

ORL° BRIDGEMAN.

AR. CROFT.

P. DOCMINIQUE.

[MALACHY POSTLETHWAYT], THE AFRICAN TRADE

[Malachy Postlethwayt], *The African Trade, the Great Pillar and Support of the British Plantation Trade in America* (London: J. Robinson, 1745). British Library, shelfmark 601.i.6.(1.).

Malachy Postlethwayt (*c.* 1707–67) was a writer on economic issues and a speculator. Very little personal information is available on him, but in his time he was a prolific, productive and highly read author. Postlethwayt seems to have been involved in a project for the manufacturing of lead somewhere in the north of England. The project eventually failed, most probably due to Postlethwayt's ignorance of smelting and refining, according to Peter Groenewegen.[1] He is mainly known for his encyclopaedic *The Universal Dictionary of Trade and Commerce*, 2 vols (London: John and Paul Knapton, 1751–5). At the time dictionaries of this kind were popular, and Postlethwayt's work is a translation of the best known of these, Jaques Savary des Brulons's *Dictionnaire universel de commerce*. Postlethwayt's most important works are *Britain's Commercial Interest Explained and Improv'd* (London: D. Browne, A. Millar, J. Whiston, B. White and W. Sandby, 1757) and *Great Britain's True System* (London: A. Millar, J. Whiston, B. White and W. Sandby, 1757). Postlethwayt regarded agricultural improvements in Britain combined with plantations as the main pillar of Britain's future wealth.[2]

It is likely that Postlethwayt was at one time a paid agent for the Royal African Company, and he certainly wrote at least three pamphlets defending the Company against critical opponents. The text reprinted here was published anonymously on the occasion of a general discussion in both parliaments in 1745, and it is clearly written by somebody standing close to the Royal African Company, probably Postlethwayt. It consists of a plea for extending British trade with Africa as well as for taking up new colonies there, in order to compete with

1 See Groenewegen's article on Postlethwayt in *Oxford Dictionary of National Biography* (Oxford: Oxford University Press, 2004).

2 For further information on Postlethwayt, see *Palgrave's Dictionary of Political Economy*, ed. H. Higgs, 3 vols (London and New York: Macmillan, 1894), vol. 3, p. 176.

the French and their plantations. It is also a plea for creating more favourable working conditions – privileges that is to say – for the Royal African Company, which the author argues should be treated equally with the East India Company.

THE
AFRICAN TRADE,
THE GREAT
PILLAR and SUPPORT
OF THE
British PLANTATION TRADE
In *AMERICA*:

SHEWING,

That our Loss, by being beat out of all the Foreign Markets for *Sugar* and *Indigo* by the F···ʰ, has been owing to the Neglect of our *African Trade*, which only, can supply our Colonies with *Negroes*, for the making of Sugars, and all other Plantation Produce:

That the Support and Security of the *Negroe-Trade* depends wholly on the due and effectual Support of the *Royal African Company of England*, which has hitherto preserved this invaluable Trade to these Kingdoms·

That the Difficulties and Discouragements which the said Company labours under, threaten the absolute Loss of the Negroe Trade to this Nation; and consequently the total Ruin of all the *British* Plantations in *America*.

And also, What the *Royal African Company* have a natural Right to hope for *this Session of Parliament* from their Country, in order to enable them to support and maintain the *British* Interest, Rights and Privileges in *Africa* against the *French*, and all other Rivals in the same most valuable Trade

In a LETTER to the Right Honourable ***********

Every one knows, that our African Company *is now in a Manner dissolved to the great Joy both of the* Dutch *and* French, *and it behoves us, if we are not infatuated, to put it speedily on a better Foot than formerly, and not to let such an important Branch of our Commerce be lop'd off, to the enriching our Neighbours, and our own Scandal———*

———The Negroe-Trade *alone is of a most prodigious Consequence, and capable to render our* African Company *the most flourishing of any in the Kingdom, and t must be confessed, that it is the most beneficial to this Island, of all the Companies that ever were formed by our Merchants,* &c ——— A Proposal for humbling Spain, &c 1742

LONDON

Printed for J ROBINSON, at the *Golden Lion* in *Ludgate-Street*, 1745.
[Price One Shilling]

[1]

THE
AFRICAN TRADE,
THE GREAT
PILLAR and SUPPORT
OF THE
British PLANTATION TRADE
in General, *&c.*

SIR,

IS *Majesty* having been graciously pleased, in Consequence of an Address from the Honourable House of Commons, the last Session of Parliament, to lay his Royal Commands on the *Lords Commissioners of Trade* to make their Representation of the State of the Commerce to *Africa* this Year to Parliament, I flatter

B   myself

[2]

myfelf I could not do my Country a more feafonable Service than by endeavouring to fet a Matter of this Momeut in its true Point of Light.

The Trade to *Africa* involves in it no lefs than the Confideration of our whole *Weft-India-Trade* in general ; a Trade of fuch effential and allowed Concernment to the Wealth and Naval Power of *Great Britain*, that it would be as impertinent to take up your Time in expatiating on that Subject as in declaiming on the common Benefits of Air and Sun-fhine in general.

Relative to the commercial Interefts of thefe Kingdoms, a Subject of more real Importance cannot come before the Houfe of Commons. It is hoped therefore, it will not be judged a Topick beneath the moft ferious Regard and Attention of the ableft Minifter. I am perfuaded, Sir, it will meet with all due Regard from you, who have nothing fo much at Heart as the true Intereft of your *Prince* and *Country*.

Every Man of any Obfervation at all, is now thoroughly fenfible of the furprizing and even rapid Progrefs of *France*, in raifing her *American Colonies* to the Height we have experienced them to be during the prefent War; aud in Confequence thereof, to have fo greatly advanced in NAVAL POWER. We feem however, to have been much at a Lofs to know by what kind of Policy it has come to pafs, that this Nation, of whom we had fo many Years the Start, fhould have been able to fupplant us in the *Sugar, Indigo, Coffee* and *Cocoa Trades*, &c. as they have apparently done: And · what is ftill more extraordinary, to have laid a fure Foundation to fupplant us even in our whole *American Commerce* in general ; for that, it is prefumed, will appear to be the Cafe before this Letter is concluded, unlefs fpee-

dy

[3]

dy and effectual Measures be taken to prevent so melan-
cholly a Cataftrophe in this most valuable Branch of our Trade
and Navigation.

It would be tedious to enumerate the Variety of *Caufes*
that have been conjectured to occasion this Profperity of the
French Sugar-Colonies, and the dangerous and precarious
State and Condition to which *Our own* are at this Time reduced.
According to the Judgment form'd of the Caufe, fuitable
Laws and Ecouragements have, from Time to Time,
been wifely adapted : But as those Laws have not hitherto effectually reftored our languifhing Trade, may we not
reafonably prefume there has been, and ftill continues to be,
fome *latent Caufe* which has proved greatly conducive to the
Aggrandizement of the *French Colonies*, while our Difre-
gard of *that Caufe*, has tended to the manifeft Injury and
Detriment of *Our own*.

When a Diftemper is got to a great Head before the primary Caufe is happily difcovered, we are pregnant in Sur-
mifes ; we are apt to multiply Caufes, when one alone
will often more naturally folve the Phænomena ; we too
frequently miftake the Effect for the Caufe : Thus, by
injudicioufly miftaking the true Source of the Malady, we
tamper with it by *Palliatives* only, till it grows more and
more obftinate, and at length becomes abfolutely incurable.

Had not too long Experience proved the contrary, one
would think it impoffible, that the obvious Connection
and Dependency fubfifting between our *Plantation* and
Guinea Trades fhould be fo notorioufly difregarded ; and remain as much unobferved as if there really were no fuch
Relation between thofe Branches of our Commerce. Yet
this has been the Cafe ; we have fuffered our *African Company*, the fole Guardians of our *Guinea Trade*, to moulder

B 2   and

[4]

and dwindle away almoft to Nothing; and then vainly have expected that our *Plantation Commerce*, not only firft founded on that Trade, but ftill daily upheld thereby, fhould ftand alone without its fundamental Prop and Support!

The Policy of our dangerous Rivals has been quite other-wife. *France* has long feen the effential Dependency between thofe Trades, and that the *one* cannot fubfift or profper without giving all due Encouragement to the *other*. Wherefore, while this Nation has unaccountably fuffered our *African Company* to labour under every Difficulty and Difcouragement, (as will appear) *France* has wifely cherifhed and encouraged *Theirs*; Is it to be wondered therefore, that our Enemies fhould raife a magnificent Superftructure of *American Commerce* and *Naval Power* on an *African Foundation*, while ours has been for many Years paft ———— neglected, and fuffered to decline?

That we may not miftake the Sentiments of the *French* upon this Matter, permit me, Sir, to lay before you a fmall Part only of a *Memorial*, prefented by the *Deputies of the Council of Trade in France, to the Royal Council in the Year* 1701, concerning the *Guinea Company*, the *Commerce of the French Colonies in America*, and the then State of the *Iflands* which the *French* poffefs there, *&c.*

This remarkable *Memorial* is introduced in fuch Terms as ought never to be forgot by any *Englifhman*; and, fuffer me to fay, Sir, deferves to be imprinted in indelible Characters upon the Mind of *every Minifter*, who has the Honour to ferve any *Prince* who wears the *Britifh* Crown.

The Words are as follows, *Viz.* " The Commerce of " *Guinea* has fuch Relation to that of the *French* Iflands in the " *Weft-Indies*, that the one cannot fubfift without the other.

" By

[5]

" By those Trades we have deprived our Competitors in
" Traffick of the great Profit which they drew from us,
" and may put ourselves into a Condition, by their Exam-
" ple, to draw Profit in our Turn from them, and ESPE-
" CIALLY FROM THE ENGLISH. We may encrease those
" Trades considerably, seeing that Nation in their Islands,
" with less Advantage than we, in Territories of less Ex-
" tent, and in much less Time, have found Means to em-
" ploy yearly above 500 Ships, while we do not without
" great Difficulty employ 100.

" Every Body is sensible of the Benefit of Navigation, and
" that the Happiness and Glory of a State very much de-
" pend upon it : There can be no Commerce without it ;
" it governs the Fortunes of the Merchants ; it maintains a
" great Number of Subjects, Seamen and Mechanicks.
" No one is ignorant that the Navigation of *France* owes
" all its *Encrease* and *Splendor* to the *Commerce* of *its*
" *Islands,* and that it cannot be kept up and enlarged other-
" wise than by *this Commerce.*

" It is beyond all Doubt, that this Commerce is more
" beneficial to the State than all others (of LONG VOYAGES)
" that are driven by the *French*; because it is carried on
" *without exporting any Money*", &c.

Thus we see how strong and express the Maxims of
France are with Respect to the necessary Connection and
Dependency between the *Plantation* and *African Trades,* and
that the one cannot subsist without the other. And have not
the *French* steadily reduced these their Maxims into Practice, to their great Profit, and our no small Injury ?

Whoever will take upon him to suggest that the same re-
ciprocal Connection, the same mutual Dependency does not
subsist in as essential a Manner between the *British Planta-*

[6]

tion and *British Guinea Trades*, as between these Trades belonging to *France*, let him difcriminate, and fhew wherein the Difference confifts.

But is it not notorious to the whole World, that the Bufinefs of *Planting* in our *British Colonies*, as well as in the *French*, is carried on by the Labour of *Negroes*, imported thither from *Africa* ? Are we not indebted to thofe valuable People, the *Africans*, for our *Sugars*, *Tobaccoes*, *Rice*, *Rum*, and all other *Plantation Produce* ? And the greater the Number of *Negroes* imported into our *Colonies*, from *Africa*, will not the Exportation of *British* Manufactures among the *Africans* be in Proportion; they being paid for in fuch Commodities only ? The more likewife our Plantations abound in *Negroes*, will not more Land become cultivated, and both *better* and greater *Variety* of *Plantation Commodities* be produced ? As thofe Trades are fubfervient to the Well Being and Profperity of each other ; fo the more either flourifhes or declines, the other muft be necefﬅarily affected, and the general Trade and Navigation of their *Mother Country*, will be proportionably benefited or injured. May we not therefore fay, with equal Truth, as the *French* do in their before cited *Memorial,* that the general NAVIGATION of *Great Britain* owes all its *Encreafe* and *Splendor* to the Commerce of its *American* and *African Colonies* ; and that it cannot be maintained and enlarged otherwife than from the conftant Profperity of both thofe Branches, *whofe Interefts are mutual and infeparable* ?

Whatever *other* Caufes may have confpired to enable the *French* to beat us out of all the Markets in *Europe* in the *Sugar* and *Indigo Trades*, &c. the great and extraordinary Care they have taken to cherifh and encourage their *African Company,*

[7]

Company, to the End that their *Plantations* might be cheaply and plentifully ftocked with Negroe Husbandmen, is amply fufficient of itfelf to account for the Effect, for this Policy, they wifely judged, would enable them to produce thofe Commodities cheaper than we, who have fuffered the *British* Intereft to decline in *Africa*, as that of the *French* has advanced, and when they could produce the Commodities cheaper, is it at all to be admired that they have underfold us at all the foreign Markets in *Europe*, and thereby got that moft beneficial Part of our Trade into their own Hands?

As their great Care and our great Neglect of the *African Trade*, has for many Years paft given *France* the Advantage over us in *Planting*, fo while the fame *Caufe* continues, Is it not impoffible, in the Nature of Things, that the *Effect* fhould ceafe, and our Trade return to its former flourifhing State? All other Meafures, as they hitherto have, fo always will prove only *temporary Expedients*, not *effectual Reftoratives*: They have none of them ftruck at the Root of the Evil; nor is it poffible to work a thorough Cure any other way, but by enabling the *African Company* effectually, to maintain and fupport the *British* Rights and Privileges on the Coaft of *Africa* againft the Encroachments of the *French*, and all other Rivals, and in Confequence thereof, by ftocking our own Plantations with greater Plenty of *Negroes*, and at *cheaper Rates* than our Rivals would, in fuch Cafe, be able to do.

That it has been many Years out of our Power to do this, is a Fact known to all well acquainted with thofe Trades, as they have been carried on by both Nations. By what Means this has come to pafs, doth not feem to be fo well underftood as could be wifhed I will therefore endeavour

farther

[8]

farther to clear this Matter up by an Induction of Particulars which will fpeak for themfelves.

And, though in drawing the Comparifon between the Encouragements and the Advantages the *French African* and *Plantation Trades* have received, to what ours have, for above thefe *Forty* paft, I fhall for Truth Sake be under the Neceffity of enumerating the peculiar *Privileges* and *Immunities* their *Guinea Trade* has received beyond what ours has done ; yet I would not be underftood to aim at the Adoption of the identical Meafures *France* has fallen into : Nothing more being intended than to exhibit the different States of the *African Trade*, as it has been long exercifed, and ftill continues to be, by both Nations , without which, it is apprehended, no right Judgment can be made of the Meafures requifite to be taken by this Nation to retrieve Our languifhing Trade, and reap thofe defirable Advantages which this valuable Commerce may be certainly made to afford us.

The *French Senegal Company*, who have *Forts* and *Settlements* in *Africa*, as well as our Company, to fecure their *Guinea Trade*, enjoy a Privilege of Trade to *Africa*, exclufive of all the other Subjects of *France* , which gives them a much greater Weight and Superiority of Intereft among the *Africans* than our *British* Company have had fince the Trade has been laid open to all his Majefty's Subjects : This not only enables the *French* to contract more advantageous Alliances with the *Negroe Princes*, and *Great Men*, whereby they enlarge and extend their Inland Trade for *Negroes* ; but, in Confequence of the Power derived from *this their fuperior Privilege*, they have many Years taken upon them to trade as freely within the Limits of the

British

[9]

Britifh Company's Charter as of their own; while our Company have for many Years lain under fuch Difcouragements, that they have not been able to repell their fhameful Encroachments. Nay, fo great is the Weight of Power the *French African Company* have obtained from their *Privileges*, that they will not fuffer any *Britifh* Veffel to come within many Leagues of their Settlements, without making Prize of them. So that, if we expect to carry on the Trade to *Africa* upon the Foot of a free and open Trade (which I hope it ever will be) to as great Advantage as *France* does, the Company muft have fome *Equivalent* for the Privilege they have parted with, and the *French* Company poffefs, to put it in their Power to fupport the *Britifh* Rights, Privileges, and Intereft, in fuch remote Parts, againft all other Nations, in their fulleft Extent.

By Virtue alfo of the Privilege the *French Company* enjoys, they, of Courfe, become the only Purchafers of *Negroes* within the Limits of their own *Charter*; and confequently, having no Bidders againft them, do, as it were, make their own Market. The Cafe is quite otherwife on thofe Parts of the Coaft where the *Britifh* Company have Settlements; for the *Britifh* Share in the Trade to *Africa*, being free and open to all his *Majefty*'s Subjects, naturally brings a great Concourfe of *feparate* Purchafers upon our Parts of the Coaft, who bid againft each other, as well as againft the Company. This naturally raifes the Price of *Negroes* to feparate *Englifh* Traders in general, while, as before obferved, the *French* fet their own Price, and are enabled thereby to fupply their *Colonies* above 50 *per Cent.* cheaper than we can do ours.

As the Demand of the *French* for *Negroes* in their Plantations has increafed, fo they have encroached, and traded

C   without

[10]

without Moleftation, as is before obferved, within the *Britifh*
Company's Rights and Privileges, and purchafed the choiceft
Negroes, within Sight of the Company's *Forts* and *Caftles*.
This ftill more and more contributes to enhance the Price
to *Britifh* Traders and Planters, by increafing the Number
of Purchafers beyond the Quantity brought to Market in
thofe Places. Yet this is no Difadvantage to the *French Company*; for what with the conftant low Price of *Negroes*
on thofe Parts of the Coaft which the *French* now ufurp,
to the entire Exclufion of the *Englifh*, together with a
Bounty, and feveral other Immunities which they allow upon all *Negroes* imported into the *French Colonies*, they
can well afford to raife the Price on our Coaft upon the
Britifh Purchafer, and confequently to the *Britifh Planter* in *America*; and yet very little enhance it to the
French Planter.

Still further to encourage the cheap and plentiful Importation of *Negroes* into the *French Colonies*, France has exempted their *African* Company from *one half of the Duty*
on all fuch Goods of the Produce of their *Sugar Colonies* as are
made in Return for *Negroes*, which is fo very *extraordinary*
and prodigious an *Encouragement* to induce to a cheap and
plentiful Supply of their Plantations, that it is not at all to
be admired they fhould, by fuch Policy, beat us out of the
Sugar and *Indigo Trades*, and lay a Foundation, by Dint of
Negroe-Labour, to beat us out of our whole Plantation
Trade in general.

The *French* likewife grant their Company an Exemption
from all Duties whatfoever on Goods imported into *France*,
and afterwards re-exported to *Africa*, wherewith to purchafe
Negroes,

[11]

Negroes to ftock their Plantations at a cheaper Rate than without fuch great Encouragements, they could poffibly do.

As thefe Advantages accrue from the Importation of *Negroes* into their Colonies, beyond what do into ours, they naturally draw with them *another* of no little Benefit to the *French Planter,* which the *Britifh* alfo are deprived of ; for fuch *Bounties, Immunities* and *Privileges,* attending the Negroe Trade, 'tis for the Intereft of the *French Company* never to let the *Planters* want a Supply of *Negroes* ——— This induces the Company to give large Credit to the *French Planters,* for the fake of the fubfequent Advantages that are infeparably annexed to the *Negroe Trade*; for fure thofe Advantages are very confiderable, tho' their Gain upon firft Importation fhould but be fmall, which is yet known to be otherwife.

That the *French* may want no Encouragement to beat all other Powers out of the *African Trade,* their Company is likewife allowed a *Bounty* of Eighty Livres for every *Mark Weight* of *Gold Duft* imported from *Africa* into *France,* which added to the other Profits of that Trade, we need not wonder to hear of the *French Guinea* Ships being fo rich in *Gold,* as feveral of them have *proved* during the prefent War.

So great, we fee, are the Advantages given by *France* to their *African* Trade, that this Confideration alone is fufficient to account for the furprizing Succefs of the *French Sugar Colonies,* without looking into any other Caufe that may have contributed thereto. For what is the natural Confequence of this greater Cheapnefs of *Negroes* ? Does it not occafion the *French* Plantations to be more plentifully ftocked than ours ? And has not this put them daily upon

C 2   cultivating

[12]

cultivating more and more Land, in order to accomplifh the End aimed at. They find by Experience, as all Nations ever may, that the general Culture of Land occafions a general Plenty of the *Neceffaries* and *Conveniences* of Life in their Colonies —— This general Plenty, of courfe, occafions a general Cheapnefs; and thus they are fenfible that they can maintain *Negroes* confiderably cheaper than the *Britifh Planters* can do, as well as purchafe them cheaper at firft Hand.

So confiderably dearer an Importation of *Negroes* into the *Britifh* Colonies, naturally occafions a proportionable Scarcity of them to what the *French* have; confequently, lefs Quantity of Land becomes cultivated, and therefore the common Neceffaries of Life dearer than in the *French Colonies*, the Intereft of Money higher, and the Maintainance of *white* Servants, as well as the *Blacks*, far more expenfive. For the Standard of the Charge of *Negroe-Labour*, as well as that of *white* Men, is the Price of the common Neceffaries of Life. Herein the *French* in their Colonies have an infinite Advantage over us, and all owing to the beforementioned great Encouragements of their *African Trade*.

By thefe fimple, yet profound and judicious Meafures, *France* foon experienced they could produce *Sugars* cheaper than we could do in the *Britifh Colonies*. This animated them to try the Experiment of fupplanting us at foreign Markets, and fairly, by Dint of Cheapnefs, and as good a Commodity, they gain'd their Point. From the fame Principles, they fucceeded alfo in the *Indigo* and *Coffee Trades*, and will doubtlefs, if not ftopt in their Career, be as fuccefsful in all other Plantation Produce; fo that in a few Years we muft expect to be reduced to the Neceffity of taking *Sugars*, *Tobacco*,

[13]

Tobacco, Rice, &c. as we now do *Indigo* of them, for our Home Confumption.

The *Dutch* alfo, whofe *American Colonies* bear little Proportion either to ours, or thofe of *France*, allow their *African Company* very great Encouragements to fupport their Interefts in *Africa*, by *Forts* and *Settlements*; and be-fides this, an exclufive Privilege of Trade alfo. They fet a due Value on the cheap Labour of *Negroes*, which they know will ever beat that of all *White Men* whatfoever, and that nothing can be done in *America* without thofe valuable *Africans*. And tho' their Colonies do not require any Thing like the Quantity of *Negroes* that ours, or thofe of *France* do ; yet they are not lefs follicitous to maintain their Intereft and Footing in *Africa*; and that for thefe plain Reafons : Firft, From the Advantages they reap from the direct Trade to *Africa*, by the Barter of their Merchandize for *Gold, Ivory, Gums, Dying Woods*, &c. Secondly, From Their Traffic in *Negroes*, to fell them to the *Spaniards*, and under that Pretext to introduce their Manufactures into the *Spanifh Indies* ; which is a Commerce of fuch Advantage alone, that the States of *Holland* will never part with their Settlements in *Africa*, or fuffer that Trade to lie under any Difcouragements, Thirdly, From a View they may natu-rally be prefumed to have, fome Time or other, to obtain an *Affiento* with *Spain* for *Negroes*.

As *Negroe Labour* hitherto has, fo that only can fupport our *Britifh* Colonies, as it has done thofe of other Nations. It is *that* alfo will keep them in a due Subferviency to the Intereft of their *Mother-Country* ; for while our Plantations depend only on Planting by *Negroes*, and that of fuch Pro-duce as interferes only with the Interefts of our Rivals, not

[14]

of their *Mother-Country*, our Colonies can never prove injurious to *British* Manufactures, never become independent of thefe Kingdoms, but remain a perpetual Support to our *European* Intereft, by preferving to us a Superiority of Trade and Naval Power.

But if the whole *Negroe Trade* be thrown into the Hands of our Rivals, and our Colonies are to depend on the Labour of the *White Men* to fupply their Place, they will either foon be undone, or fhake off their Dependency on the Crown of *England*. For *White Men* cannot be obtained near fo cheap, or the Labour of a fufficient Number be had for the Expence of their Maintenance only, as we have of the *Africans*. Has not long Experience alfo fhewn that *White* Men are not conftitutionally qualified to fuftain the Toil of Planting in the Climates of our *Ifland Colonies* like the Blacks?

Were it poffible however, for *White Men* to anfwer the End of *Negroes* in Planting, muft we not drain our own Country of *Husbandmen, Mechanicks*, and *Manufacturers* too? Might not the latter be the Caufe of our Colonies interfering with the Manufactures of thefe Kingdoms, as the *Palatines* attempted in *Penfilvania*? * In fuch Cafe indeed, we might have juft Reafon to dread the Profperity of our Colonies; but while we can be well fupplied with *Negroes*, we can be under no fuch Apprehenfions; their Labour will confine the Plantations to *Planting* only; which will render our *Colonies* more beneficial to thefe Kingdoms than the *Mines* of *Peru* and *Mexico* are to the *Spaniards*.

---

* *Vide* a Reprefentation of the Lords Commiffioners of Trade laid before the Houfe of Commons, 1732.

Doctor

[15]

Doctor Davenant tells us, that in the Time of King CHARLES II. our *Merchants*, interested in the *American Trade*, made a Representation to that King, setting forth, that by a just Medium, they made it appear, that the Labour of an hundred *Negroes* was, at that Time of Day, 1600 *l. per Annum* Profit to this Nation, deducting therefrom the Amount of the Value of what we consume in Plantation Produce. It was then estimated there were no more than 100,000 *Negroes* in *America*; but the most experienced Judges now do not rate them at less than 300,000: So that if we reckon them of no more Worth to *Great Britain* now than at that Time, and estimate the Value of our Home Consumption of Plantation Commodities at the highest Rate, the annual Gain of the Nation by *Negroe Labour* will fall little short of Three Millions *per Annum :* And it is to be hoped we shall not sacrifice such an Annuity rather than give all just and reasonable Encouragement for the due Support of our *African Company*, which has been the FOUNDATION of such Profit to these Kingdoms!

Such who have well considered how Plantations may be still rendered more beneficial to this Nation, have pointed out various Improvements that might easily be made therein by the Labour of *Negroes.*

It is certain that *Logwood* has been raised in the moist Lands of the *Bahama Islands*; and it might easily be propagated there (and probably in some other of our Colonies likewise) so as to raise not only sufficient Quantities to serve our own Exigencies, but also for Exportation to foreign Markets : And; certainly, such laudable Attempts are well worth our Encouragement ; more especially so, since this Trade has proved such a Bone of Contention between *Spain* and *Us*,

ard

[16]

and coft fo many *Britifh* Lives to obtain it in the Bays of .*Campeachy* and *Honduras*. As this Commodity is not only an effential Ingredient in the Dying of our Cloth, but is of fo bulky a Nature as to conduce much to the Encreafe of *Shipping*, it cannot be bad Policy fure to quicken the Genius of our *Planters*, by giving them all proper Encouragement to attempt an Experiment that appears rational and practicable, and fo manifeftly tends to the Improvement of our Commerce. And the principal Encouragement certainly will be, to put the *African Trade* on fuch an Eftablifhment that they may have *Negroes* as cheap, at leaft, as our Rivals.

It has been allowed alfo, that we might, with little Difficulty, extend the Planting of *Coffee, Cocoa, Indigo,* and *Cocheneal* fufficient, at leaft, to fupply ourfelves. The fowing of *Hemp* and *Flax*, making *Pot-afh, Pitch* and *Tar*, we know, may be carried almoft to what Height we pleafe in our Colonies. We have experienced the Danger and Difficulty of depending wholly on the *Eaft Countries* for *Naval Stores* *: And Negroes, certainly, may as eafily be bred to thofe Things as they ever were to *Sugar, Tobacco,* and *Rice Planting*; the Cheapnefs of their Labour will furmount all Difficulties in any kind of Planting, provided they can be purchafed cheap at the firft Hand.

While *France* fpares no Expence and Encouragement to bring their Settlements on the *Miffiffppi* to Perfection, for the Planting of *Tobacco*, and that upon the very back of

---

* *Vide* Doctor *Robinfon*'s Letter, the late Queen's Envoy at the Court of *Sweden*, on the Subject of Naval Stores, to Sir *Charles Hedges* Secretary of State, *Auguft* 4th, 1703.

our

[17]

our Colonies of *Carolina*, *Virginia* and *Maryland*, and down the River *St. Lawrence* to *Cape Breton*, and also at *Hispaniola*; while *France* is not content with having supplanted us in the *Sugar* and *Indigo Trades*, but are strenuously attempting to vye with us in the *Tobacco* and *Rice*, &c. and this wholly from the Dependence they make on the Labour of *Negroes*; certainly a *British* Legiflature will not think this a Time of Day to make our dangerous Rivals the Compliment of our *African Settlements*, to put it more and more into their Power to raise *new Colonies*, while we are rendered incapable of supporting our *old Ones*.

We feem to have forgot the Times wherein our Plantations were firft fettled. Had we a lively Idea of the Spirit, Refolution and indefatigable Endeavours of our induftrious Ancestors to eftablish them; did we confider how many Years they were arduoufly employed to accomplish fo great a Work; what immenfe Sums of Money were expended out of this Kingdom for clearing of Lands, erecting *Sugar Works*, and purchafing *Negroes* at their firft Eftablishment: Did we ferioufly weigh the invaluable Benefits *Britain* has received from her *American Colonies*, none but the greateft Enemy to his Country would fuffer them to labour under any Sort of Difcouragement whatever, confiftent with their Dependency on the Crown of *England*, much lefs to facrifice and give them up to Competitors. Yet this muft be their Fate, provided we are once deprived of the Labour of *Africans* to fupport them.

Our *African* Trade had its Being before we had any Plantations in the *Weft Indies*: From the Reign of *Queen Elizabeth* our Merchants feparately, or in joint Stocks, profecuted this Trade till the Commencement of the prefent Company.

D

[18]

ny. Nor have the Struggles, Difficulties, Hazards, and Expences of this prefent Corporation, firft to eftablifh their Trade on a good Footing, and fince, to preferve and maintain it to Pofterity, been any way inferior to the firft Adventurers in our *American Settlements :* But to put this Matter in its true Light, would take a Volume by itfelf.

There is no Reafon can be affigned for the Exiftence of any Trading Company in this Kingdom, but the fame will equally hold good with Regard to the Neceffity of fupporting that of our prefent *African Company* * ; with this Difference, in Favour of the latter, that our Plantation Trade not only owes its Rife to it, but its conftant Support and Prefervation to the prefent Time.

However important the *Eaft India Trade* may be judged to the Nation, yet it was never put in Competition with our *African* and *Plantation Trades.* The Manufactures of *England, Scotland* and *Ireland* will fupply all the Wants of the latter : but the *India* Company itfelf receives no inconfiderable Advantage from thofe *Trades* in general, by the large Quantities of *Eaft India* Commodities thefe Branches take off annually; And the *African Trade* alone, is capable of taking off *Ten Times* the Quantity it ever has done, was it once fettled upon a defirable Footing.

But, though the Benefits of Re-exportation of *India* Commodities, and the Advantages of Navigation arifing therefrom, are confiderable, yet are they not any way equal to thofe others we receive from the Confequences of

---

* *Vide* Sir *Jofiah Child.*

the

[19]

the Trade to *Africa*. A Cargo rightly forted for *A-frica*, confifts of about Seven-Eights *Britifh* Manufactures and Produce; and they return us no inconfiderable Profit; and that not only in *Gold, Ivory, Bees-Wax, Dying Woods, Gums,* &c. (none of which we can do without) but *Negroes,* whom we have experienced to be of more Value to this Nation than any Advantages that ever were, or ever can be prefumed to arife from the *Eaft India Company,* which exports our Silver, and imports many Things, which to be fure, we might well do without.

With Refpect to the Advantages derived from the *African* and *Indian* Trades, the *French* Memorial before cited, fhews the Difference in few Words, *Viz.* " The *Guinea* and *American Trades* are, beyond all doubt, " more beneficial to the State than all others of Long " Voyages that are driven, becaufe they are carried on " without exporting any *Money, &c.*"

However beneficial to the Nation the Exports of the *South-Sea Company* to the *Spanifh Weft Indies* may have proved, yet neither that Company, nor the Nation, could have received thofe Advantages, but by Virtue of introducing *Negroes* into *New Spain,* to work the *Mines* of *Peru* and *Mexico.* But how could this Company have ever had it in their Power to have complied with the *Affiento* for *Negroes,* had the *African* Company no Being to have preferved to us the *Negroe Trade?* That Company have experienced the Difficulties they have been reduced to, during the declining State of the *African Company,* to carry their Contract with the Crown of *Spain* into Execution. Should

D 2   the

[20]

the *African* Company therefore be diffolved, what Pretence could the *South-Sea* ever have to obtain the Re-eftablifhment of an *Affiento* again, when it could never be in their Power to comply with their Engagements?

Upon Suppofition of the Annihilation of our *African* Company, muft not the *Affiento* go into *French* or *Dutch* Hands, who are too wife to part with their Footing in *Africa*, or to let their *African* Companies labour under any Difcouragements; and will not they, of Courfe, receive the Benefits of the *Spanifh Weft India Trade* arifing therefrom, as *France* did before the Peace of *Utrecht ?* The *French* have not cherifhed their *Guinea Trade* with a View only to the Ruin of the *British Colonies*, but to exclude *Englifhmen*, for ever, from the next valuable Branch of Trade belonging to the *British* Empire. For if, by Vertue of another *Affiento* with *Spain, France* can fo effectually eftablifh their Manufactures in the *Spanifh Weft Indies*, that the *British* will become quite indifferent to them, have we any Reafon long to expect the leaft Share in the Trade of the *Galleons* and *Flotilla*; efpecially fince *France* has got two Thirds of that Trade into her Hands already? Our *Spanifh Merchants* have too much experienced the Succefs of that Nation in this Branch of Trade, not to be fenfibly affected, fhould the *Spanifh Affiento* revert again into their Hands.

Since the Nature of my Subject has naturally led me to touch upon the *Affiento*, it may not be amifs to take a little further Notice of it, fo far as it concerns the Intereft of our
African

[21]

African and *Plantation Trades* in general, as well as that of our *African* Corporation in particular.

In this Contract there are two Circumstances that seem to deserve our Attention; *Viz.* The Time when it was first obtained; and the Preamble to it.

The *Assiento* was signed by his Catholick Majesty at *Madrid*, upon the 26th Day of *March*, 1713, and is intitled, ASSIENTO, *a justado entre las dos Majestades Catholica, y Bretanica, sobre encargarse* LA COMPANIA DE INGLETERRA *de la Introducion de Esclavos Negros en la America Espannola*, &c. Or, The CONTRACT agreed upon between their *Britannick* and *Catholick* Majesties, for the ENGLISH COMPANY'S obliging themselves to supply the *Spanish West Indies* with black Slaves, &c.

With Regard to the Date, it should never be forgot that in the very preceding Year 1712, the Act which granted 10 *per Cent.* to the *African Company* on all Exports, &c. expired; and this without any Manner of Equivalent given to them, in Lieu of the Privileges and Immunities which induced them to lay out so large a Capital, in building Forts, and making Settlements in *Africa*.

This Company, thus left destitute of every Privilege and Encouragement, upon which they had been induced to sink an immense Property in *Africa*, by the Erection of *Forts, Castles*, and *Factories*, and thereby brought under the the Necessity either of abandoning their Property, or maintaining it at their sole Expence, for the public Benefit! — A Company thus circumstanced, and yet the great Support of the *Plantation Trade*, one would imagine, should have drawn the Eyes of our *Statesmen* at that Time of Day. Had they pointed out to her late Majesty, the proper Object on whom to have bestowed an *Assiento* for *Negroes*,

none

[22]

none, fure, could have been more naturally pitched upon than an *African Company*, to have fupplied the *Spaniards* with *Africans*; more efpecially fo, when the Nation, at that Point of Time, were under the ftrongeft Ties and O-bligations to have made the Company fome Compenfation for being deprived of thofe Privileges which firft induced the Adventurers to advance their Money. Had this been done, when all Circumftances concurred to it, it is not at all un-reafonable to prefume, that we might, by fuch Meafures, have prevented the *French* from gaining the Afcendant over us in the *Sugar* and *Indigo Trades*; and thereby have faved this Nation many Millions of Money.

The Advantages of this Contract would have enabled the Company fo to have fupported the *Britifh* Intereft in *Africa*, as to have prevented the *French* from drawing fuch great Currency of Trade, and, confequently, Quantity of *Negroes* to their Colonies.

This would alfo have prevented their overbearing En-croachments on our Parts of the *Gold-Coaft*, had the Com-pany remained in a Condition to have oppofed them. By Vertue of the Company's *Forts* and *Factories* in the *River Gambia*, they would alfo have drawn a geat Part of the *River Senegal* Trade to the *Britifh* Factories, and might eafily have united the Inland Parts of the *Gold Coaft Trade* with that of *Gambia River*; which, as it would have furnifhed an ample Supply of *Negroes*, both for our *Colonies* and the *Affiento*, fo nothing could have been a greater Check to the *French Negroe Trade* in general.

This would have had the defirable Effect, as before fhewn, to have produced a univerfal Plenty, and confe-quently,

[23]

quently, Cheapnefs of all the Neceffaries of Life in our Plantations; as, on the contrary, Want of Hands would have raifed
them in the *French* Colonies. May we not therefore very
reafonably believe, that had the Company continued in a
flourifhing State, by Vertue of this *Affiento*, we might eafily have ftopped the Career of the *French*, from carrying
their *Sugar* and *Indigo Trades* to greater Lengths than the
Supply of their own Confumption? And is it not high Time
to retrieve, and make amends for former Errors, by all
Means in our Power?

After the Number of *Negroes*, ftipulated by the *Affiento*, fo introduced into *New-Spain*, the fixth Article of that
Contract, tolerating alfo the Importation of as many more
there, for the Service of his *Catholick Majefty*, 'and whatever more his Subjects fhould require, we might, very probably, have doubled our Importation into *Spanifh America*,
had we been capable of fo doing, inftead of not complying
on our Part with the Contract; for the Wants of the *Spaniards* have been always very confiderably more than we
have fupplied. This would have proved a great additional
Advantage to the Nation; efpecially, as the Duty on the
Importation of any *furplus Negroes* would have been only
$16\frac{2}{3}$ Pieces of Eight *per* Head, inftead of $33\frac{1}{3}$, as in the
Conditions of the other Part of the *Affiento*. And fince all *Negroes* are moftly paid for in *Africa* with *Britifh* Manufactures,
this would have proportionably augmented our *Exports*
thither. So that the Advantage the Nation would have obtained by this Contract having been given to our *African
Company*, is eafier conceived than reprefented.

And

[24]

And indeed, by the Preamble to the *Affiento*, it is not impoffible but the *Spaniards* meant and intended *no other Company*, however they might be duped by an After-Explication; for it is expreffly called, The Contract agreed upon between their *Britannick* and *Catholick Majefties*, for the ENGLISH COMPANY obliging itfelf to fupply the *Spanifh Weft Indies* with Black Slaves, &c.

Now, what *Englifh Company* could be fuppofed to be meant by the *Court* of *Spain*, but that *Englifh Company*, which dealt in *Negroes*? that *Englifh Company* who were eftablifhed in *Africa*, as the *French* and *Portuguefe African Companies* were, with whom the *Spaniards* had before made the like *Affientos*? Such a Company only, the *Spaniards* doubtlefs imagined could fupply them much cheaper, and carry the Contract into Execution more effectually, than any other Company that fhould be under the Neceffity of purchafing *Negroes* either of the *Englifh African Company*, or of *Englifh* private Traders.

As the Connection between this Branch of the *Spanifh Weft India Trade* and that of *Africa*, is honeftly reprefented in a late Tract, not long fince publifhed, * I beg Leave, Sir, to tranfcribe a Paffage extremely pertinent to the prefent Occafion.

" I think, fays the judicious Propofer, it is very obvious
" to every common Eye, that if we can fettle ourfelves at
" *Buenos Ayres*, the *Spaniards* will lie under an abfolute
" Neceffity to open a Trade with us; Nay, it is not in

---

* A Propofal for humbling *Spain*, by a Perfon of Diftinction, printed for *Roberts*, 1742.

" our

[25]

" our Power to impose what Terms we please upon them ;
" but if we had no other Way to obtain it than the af-
" fording our Goods as cheap again, as they can furnish
" themselves with the other Way, even that, with a little
" Patience, would infallibly produce it. But without
" trusting to that, we should have them in a Manner at
" our Mercy, by having the Herb of *Paragua* * in our
" Hands.

" But we have still another Lure for the *Spaniards*, as
" powerful and as proper to produce the desired Effect,
" as any yet mentioned ; which is, the supplying them
" with *Negroes* in sufficient Numbers, and cheaper than
" formerly. This is the great Inconveniency which the
" *Spaniards* have laboured under this last Age ; for having
" in a Manner utterly destroy'd the natural Inhabitants,
" they are obliged now to perform the Work by *Ne-
" groes*, of which they could never get the Number they
" wanted ; and it is certain, if they were fully supplied,
" they would get yearly above twice the Quantity of Silver
" they now do. It must be confessed, they used all Means
" imaginable to obtain them. The *Genoese* undertook to
" supply them at a concerted Price betwixt them, for
" which End they formed a Company called the *Assiento*,
" who had their *Factors* at *Jamaica*, *Curasoa*, and *Brazil*,
" and pray consider what a prodigious Tour they made be-
" fore they got to the *Mines*, first from *Guinea* to *Jamaica*,
" from thence to *Porto Bello*, and then to *Panama*, where

---

* This Herb is a sovereign Remedy for the Diseases incident to the
Negroes in working the *Spanish Silver Mines*, without which, it is said,
they never could be work'd at all.

E

" they

[26]

" they are re-ſhip'd on board the Fleet when returning
" to *Callao*; which is a Voyage of four Months at leaſt,
" for they have the Wind in their Teeth every League of
" this Voyage.　After ſtaying ſome little Time at this
" mentioned Port, they are put on Ship-board again, and
" ſent to *Arica*, which is a Voyage of a Month, or there-
" abouts; and when landed they cannot have leſs than 150
" Miles to the *Mines* · From whence, I think, it is plain,
" that not above one *Negroe* in Three arrives at *Potoſi*, or
" the adjacent *Mines*, of thoſe that were originally bought
" by their Factors for that End.　Whereas the *Negroes*
" that might be ſent from *Buenos Ayres*, would be liable
" to none of the Inconveniencies, that the other poor
" Wretches ſuffered, as paſſing thro' ſo many unhealthy
" Climates, and ſo many tedious Voyages by Sea, enough
" to wear out Bodies of Steel, eſpecially, conſidering how
" they are accommodated all the Time both with Lodging
" and Diet: But this Way I propoſe they would have One
" ſhort Voyage by Sea; for from the Coaſt of *Guinea* to
" *Buenos Ayres* they would ſail four Parts in five of the
" Voyage before the Wind, and when landed, paſs thro'
" one of the moſt plentiful and healthieſt Countries in the
" World, even in a Manner to the *Mine's* Mouth; ſo that
" one may venture to affirm, that with careful Manage-
" ment they would not loſe One in Ten.　This Article
" alone is of a more prodigious Conſequence, and capable
" to render our *African Company the moſt flouriſhing of any*
" *in the Kingdom; and it muſt be confeſſed, that it is the*
" *moſt beneficial to this Iſland of all the Companies that ever*
" *was formed by our Merchants*　For a Cargo rightly ſorted
" for *Guinea*, conſiſts of fourſcore different Commodities

　　　　　　　　　　　　　　　　　　　　　　　　" at

[27]

" at leaſt, of which Seventy are of the Manufacture and
" Product of this Country ; and they return us *Gold, Slaves,*
" *Ivory,* and *Woods* for Dying, whereas other Companies
" export our *Silver,* and import us Things we might better
" be without.

" Every one knows, that our *African Company* is now
" in a Manner diſſolved, to the great Joy both of the
" *Dutch* and *French*, and it behoves us, if we are not in-
" fatuated, to put it ſpeedily on a better Footing than for-
" merly, and not to let ſuch an important Branch of our
" Commerce to be lopped off, to the enriching our Neigh-
" bours, and our own Scandal." So far our Author.

The firſt Attempts to make *Foreign Settlements* among
uncivilized Nations cannot be undertaken, but at conſiderable Expence and Hazard ; and the firſt Adventurers in all
Trading Countries have always received Encouragements
ſuitable to the Riſque and Contingency of their Engagements. This firſt gave Birth to *exclusive Grants* and *Privi-*
leges, and the Incorporation of Trading Societies, who in
a Body, with a *Joint-Stock,* were induced to engage in
ſuch commercial Enterprizes, as no private Traders would
ever attempt.

But when States have judged it eligible for the Intereſt of the Publick in general, to take away the *original*
Privileges and *Immunities,* that induced firſt Adventurers to
hazard their Properties, they have ever thought it juſt and
equitable to give them ample Compenſation · And this certainly will ever be judged conſiſtent with the common Laws
of national Juſtice.

E 2   Would

[28]

Would not the Proprietors of *Maryland*, *Penſilvania*, &c. think it the greateſt Grievance, the greateſt Hardſhip and Oppreſſion, if when their Anceſtors had, at an immenſe Expence and Hazard, eſtabliſh'd remote Colonies, and brought them to a flouriſhing Condition, that they ſhould have been arbitrarily deprived of their Patrimony without receiving an equitable Equivalent ? Wherein conſiſts the Difference between *Them* and *African Adventurers* ? Were not the latter the original Parent of the *African* Branch of Commerce, as the former were of our *American* Colonies?

How the Company has laboured to ſupport this Trade for the Intereſt of the Nation is now apparent. The Honourable Houſe of Commons were pleaſed, the laſt Seſſion, to appoint a Committee to inquire into the State of the Trade to *Africa*; and if I am rightly informed, of which You Your Self *Sir* are the beſt Judge, the ſaid Committee, after the ſtricteſt Inquiry, made a very particular Report, by which it appears, that the ſaid Company had expended on the Preſervation of the Trade upwards of 100,000 *l.* in 14 Years preceding *December* 31, 1743, above what they had received for that Service.

This *Hundred Thouſand Pounds* is not all the Company have diſburſed for the Service of the Nation, on Account of maintaining their Forts and Settlements for the Publick Intereſt: I am alſo informed, *Sir*, that their Expences for that Service, from the Year 1712 to 1736, have not amounted to ſo little as 300,000.*l.* more; for in this long Period, they advanced the whole Money for their Support. But, as I am not ſo clearly ſatisfied, whether the Company may, or may not, have an Equitable Right to ſome Compenſation from the Publick for this 300,000 *l.* for the

Maintenance

[29]

Maintenance and Support of their *Forts* and *Settlements* fince 1712.

The Company fuffered enough by the Trade being laid open to all His Majefty's Subjects without receiving an Equivalent; but for them to bear the Expence of their Settlements to ferve the Publick, and ruin themfelves, is what can never be expected of any Perfon or Corporation; and what the Laws of national Juftice are diametrically oppofite to. Wherefore, when their Cafe comes to be duely confidered by Parliament, doubtlefs the Wifdom and Equity of the Legiflature will grant the Company fuch effectual Relief, as the Juftice of their Caufe requires.

It will eafily be admitted, that any parliamentary Allowance granted them, from Year to Year, fufficient only for the due Support of their Settlements for the publick Benefit, can be no Kind of Relief to *African Proprietors* for the Money they have already advanced upon this Occafion. That is no more than conftituting the Company to be *Truftees* for fuch future parliamentary Allowance, annually accountable for the fame, and is no Redrefs of their Grievances.

Should it be faid, that the primary Motive to the Company to bear the Expences of the *Forts* and *Settlements* was the Prefervation of their own Property from falling into foreign Hands; yet, as this was for the National Intereft, and has hitherto fav'd to us the Being of the Trade, and the Company's Property is of no more Worth to the Proprietors than from the Advantages they could make of it by Virtue of their Trade; and fince alfo they have by thofe Expences been almoft difabled from Trading, fure that will not authorize their being ftripped of their Capital too.

[30]

too! This would favour fo barefacedly of the Tyranny and Oppreffion of the moft flavifh Countries, that no true *Englifhman*, I am perfuaded, can countenance any fuch Kind of Meafures.

I would fuppofe for a Moment, that the *Eaft-India Company* were deprived of their exclufive Privilege of Trade, as the *African Company* have been ; and that this Corporation were under the Neceffity, either of giving up their *Forts* and *Settlements* to the *Dutch*, or the *French*, or to preferve them, were obliged to maintain them at their own Expence for the Profit and Safety of *every Briton*, who fhould pleafe to take the Benefit thereof; would not this Company, in few Years, bury their whole Trading Capital, and the Profits of their Trade too, in *India*, from the great Expence of their Forts, and Diminution of their Trade, in Confequence of its being laid open ? Would not the Proprietors of *India Stock* juftly think it the greateft Hardfhip and Oppreffion, that after they had advanced their Money in the Service of the Publick, they fhould receive no Juftice from them ?

African Stockholders advanced their Money to erect *Forts* and *Settlements* to carry on their Trade with Security, upon the fame Motives that *India Stockholders* have theirs. As the Nation therefore has thought fit to take away the Privilege that induced People to hazard their Property, does not the good Faith and Juftice of the Nation ftand obliged to make them Amends in fome Shape or other to prevent their being totally ruined ?

If the Subjects of *Great-Britain* advanced their Money upon the Appropriation of any effectual *Fund* in the *Revenue* for the due Payment of *Intereft*, till the Redemption

of

ι [31]

of the *Principal Debt*; and if such *appropriated Fund*, was; before the Repayment of the Principal, either annihilated, or otherwise alienated, without the Consent of the *Publick Creditors*, would not this be a great Injustice to the Proprietors ? Wherein is the Difference between *African Stockholders*, who advanced their Money first upon an *exclusive Privilege*, and those who should advance it upon an *appropriated national Fund* ? If they should be both alike deprived of their Security, would not the one as much discourage Adventurers from hazarding their Money upon any Exigency of State, as the other will discourage Adventurers from hazarding their Property in any Foreign Undertaking, in Order to open New Branches of Trade upon such *temporary* and *precarious Privileges* ?

But when such a Body of Traders have advanced their Money, if they are then deprived of their peculiar Privilege, and have supported so beneficial a Trade for the general Interest of the Kingdom, have they not at least a Right to be reimbursed *that Money*; especially when, as I apprehend, They might doubt of their Power to dispose of their Property to any Foreign Nation ? May not *African Stockholders* therefore be justly considered in the Light of *Publick Creditors* ? They have ever depended on National Justice, and what else have other Publick Creditors to depend on ? If they have hazarded their Property for the Publick Interest, without any other Security than an absolute Dependence upon the Justice of the Nation, have they ever the less Right to Justice ? Does the Confidence they have reposed in the Publick render them the less meritorious ?

The Services their Money has done to the Nation are real and substantial ; the Company, we have seen, have been

[32]

been the Guardians and Preservers of the moſt valuable Trade belonging to theſe Kingdoms ; and the Amends they deſerve ought to be the utmoſt publick Encouragement that the Nature of their Caſe requires, conſiſtent with that general Freedom and Liberty of Trade, which all his Majeſty's Subjects now enjoy.

How, and in what Manner, the Trade in General, and the Company in Particular, may be juſtly provided for, in a Manner the leaſt burthenſome to the Nation, muſt be humbly ſubmitted to the Wiſdom of the Legiſlature. However, Sir, ſince It is the peculiar Privilege of a *Britiſh* Subject to be indulged in offering his Sentiments with Decency to Perſons in Authority, I would beg Leave, with Submiſſion, to ſuggeſt a few plain Propoſitions, agreeable to the Nature of the Caſe ; and which ſeem to me to be the leaſt that ought to be done, conſiſtently with Juſtice and good Policy.

But I will firſt premiſe, that although the Company paid out of their own Pockets ſo large a Sum as 300,000 *l.* in 18 Years, from 1712 to 1730, for the Uſe of the Publick, as is before mentioned, and for which they very well deſerve all Manner of Favour, Encouragement, and even an adequate Recompence, yet, as They have not, ſo far as I know, produced any liquidated Account thereof, nor poſſibly made any proper Claim for the ſame : I apprehend they muſt ſit down by their Loſs, and I ſhall not now offer any Thing on that Head, nor any other, farther back than the laſt 14 Years.

In the firſt Place I hope it will be always declared, That the Trade to *Africa* ought always to remain free and open to all His Majeſty's Subjects : and That no Duty, or other

Diſcouragement

[33]

Difcouragement whatfoever, fhould ever be laid on that Part of our Foreign Trade.

Secondly. That whatever Sum or Sums of Money have been made appear to have been expended by the Company in the laft 14 Years, from the Year 1730, more than They have received of the Publick Money, be provided for, this Seffion of Parliament.

Thirdly. That the future parliamentary Allowance, which fhall be granted for the Support of the Company's Forts and Settlements, be fufficient to uphold and maintain the *Britifh* Intereft in *Africa*, and effectually to fecure this valuable Trade to all his Majefty's Subjects.

Fourthly. That fuch parliamentary Allowance, as fhall be fo granted for the Purpofes aforefaid, be fecured to the Company for *a Term of Years*, by fuch an effectual appropriated Fund, as the Legiflature fhall judge proper for the due Payment of fuch Annuity.

Fifthly. That the Company fhall be yearly accountable for the fame, in fuch Manner as fhall be directed by Parliament.

It will never be faid, fure, that the Nation cannot afford to do this Company Juftice; or that the Calls for Moneys other Ways are fo extraordinary, that Juftice to the Company, and for the due Support and Prefervation of fo important and valuable a Trade, muft be ftill longer and longer poftponed! Can any Affair come under Confideration more worthy of immediate Care? So great have been the Hardfhips, Difficulties and Difcouragements *They* have already laboured under, that it is but of their Power to bear up under them any longer: But if *Gentlemen*, who have the Honour to ferve the Crown, will not believe

F

thi

[34]

this untill they fee the fatal Cataftrophe, the Company cannot be blamed; they have done their Duty, and if they
are to lofe their Property, the Meafures they have taken
to fecure this invaluable Commerce to thefe Kingdoms
hitherto, will prevent their *lofing their Reputations with
Pofterity.*

But does not the publick Revenue depend on Trade?
As fo very confiderable a Part of our Commerce abfolutely depends on the Well-Being of this Company, can he
be a true Friend to his Country, who will oppofe the giving
juft Relief to fo National a Corporation? If we have no
Negroes, we can have no *Sugars, Tobaccoes, Rice, Rum,*
&c. nor further Improvements in Plantation Commodities;
confequently, the *Publick Revenue,* arifing from the Importation of *Plantation-Produce,* muft be annihilated: And
will not this turn many hundred Thoufands of *Britifh
Manufacturers* a Begging, as well as Numbers of our
Publick Creditors, whofe Securities depend upon the Appropriation of thofe very Revenues, if our *African* and
American Trades are undone?

While the Company enjoy'd the fole Trade to *Africa,*
as the *India Company,* at prefent, does that to *Afia,* They
purchafed, built, and maintained their *Forts* and *Settlements* at their own Expence. But when publick Authority interpofed, and thought proper to lay the Trade open,
fure every reafonable Man will fay, They were, in common Juftice, rather entitled to fome publick Equivalent,
inftead of being reduced to the hard Neceffity of bearing the future Burthen of their Forts and Settlements for
the Publick Advantage. To deny them due Recompence,
and

[35]

and future Affistance, would be fo contrary, fo diametrically oppofite to the fovereign and immutable Laws of
Juftice and Equity, that it can never be apprehended,
that a *Parliament* of *Great-Britain* will encourage fuch
an unparalleled Inftance of Oppreffion. On the contrary, they have ever teftified the moft tender Regard to
publick Sufferers, and, fince the Nation has received fuch
Benefits from the *Sufferings* of this Trading Corporation,
I cannot but confidently perfuade myfelf, they will experience that Juftice and Redrefs, that the Peculiarity of
their Cafe fo manifeftly requires. Should this be the Cafe,
we are likely to reap ftill much greater Advantages by the
African Trade than hitherto we ever have done.

For if the Trade to the *Spanifh Indies* and the *Brazils*
is fo inviting, it is equally certain, that the *Inland Trade*,
duely extended upon the Continent of *Africa* (which can
only be effectuated by Means of the Company's Forts
and Settlements) may be rendered little inferior to either,
if not equal to the united Advantages of them both ---
The Continent of *Africa* is of great Extent, the Country
extremely populous, and this Commerce, by Reafon of its
Difcouragements hitherto, but yet in its Infancy.--- The
Trade to the Coaft of *Africa* is now well known, eafy,
and not hazardous. And if the Company are enabled by
publick Encouragement to extend the *Inland Trade*, the
Coaft Trade muft increafe in the like Proportion ; and all
the Subjects of *England* will partake of the Advantages,
as the Company fhall become profperous in propagating
Britifh Manufactures into the Heart of *Africa* --- As the
Trade is free and open to all *Britifh* Subjects, the Inte-

reft

[36]

reft of private Traders, and that of the Company, will go
Hand in Hand. We fhall experience the Truth of a
Propofition that this Nation has never yet been truly fenfible
of, *viz. That the Intereft of a Corporation, and that of feparate Traders is fo far from being incompatible, that they may
be made mutually fubfervient to each other.*

How impoffible it is for private *British* Traders to reap
any Advantage by this Trade, without the Company is
duely fupported, will more fully appear from the following Confiderations.

The *French*, by Virtue of their Settlements in the *River
Senegal*, and on the Ifland of *Goree*, claim to themfelves
the fole Trade of thofe Parts for near 300 Leagues; and
have ever taken and condemned fuch *British* Ships as
they find trading on any Part of that Coaft, or within
many Leagues of the fame: Whereas they have of late
Years encroached upon the Trade of our Company, and all
private *British* Traders, with Impunity, to the great Injury
of our *British Planters* and *Weft-India Merchants*, by the
exorbitant Rife in the Price of *Negroes*.

The *Dutch* alfo pretend, by Virtue of Conqueft from
the *Portuguefe*, and feveral old Grants and Donations from
the Kings of the Country, to an abfolute Right and Property, not only to the *Gold Coaft*, where our Company's Forts
and Settlements are chiefly fituated; but likewife to all
other Parts from *Cape Palmas* to *Cape Lopez*.

The *Portuguefe* too have feveral ftrong Settlements at
and near *Loango St. Paul's* on the Coaft of *Angola*, and
alfo claim a Right to the fole Trade of all that Part of
Africa to the Southward of *Cape Lopez*.

Nothing

[37]

Nothing therefore, Sir, can appear more evident, than that it has been owing to the *Royal African Company*, and the great Expence and Charge they have been at in erecting and supporting a Fort on *James Island* in the *River Gambia*, that the *French* have not long since wholly engrossed the Trade of that River to Themselves, as well as that of all the several Parts and Countries to the Northward of the same.

It is likewise as unquestionably owing to the Royal *African* Company's Forts and Settlements on the *Gold Coast*, that the *Dutch* have not got Possession of all the Coast and Parts adjacent , and that they have not long before now excluded the *English*, as well as all other Nations, from any Share in that Trade, as much as from the *Spice Islands* in the *East-Indies* And it is beyond all Doubt, that some, or all the Nations, who have Forts and Settlements on the *African* Coast, will finally and totally exclude the *British* Nation from every Part thereof, whether in actual Possession of those Nations or not, if ever that fatal Time should come, that the *British* Power and Interest should sink there, and their Forts and Settlements be abandoned or lost.

'Tis exceedingly surprising therefore, that any Person, who pretends to the least Knowledge in this Trade, should not easily discern the indispensible Necessity of effectually supporting the Forts and Settlements of the *African* Company, for the Security and Benefit of this Trade to all the Subjects of *Great-Britain* , since it has always been the well known Sense and Practice of all such Foreign Nations, as carry on any Trade to these Parts , is confirmed by all the Reasons

[38]

fons and Motives of many fucceffive *Britiſh* Princes; and
confiftent with the declaratory Part of an exprefs Act of
Parliament, as well as with all fubfequent Votes and Refolutions of the Reprefentative Body of this Kingdom.

Such appears to be the Nature and uncommon Circumftances of this Trade and Company, the Danger and Inconveniencies they are expofed to from foreign Nations, and
the Natives of thefe Countries; fuch is the Hazard the
Britiſh Trade would be ever liable to, fhould the Company's Forts be either loft, or not duely fupported, that
not only the *abfolute Loſs of this Branch* muft enfue; but
the *inevitable Ruin and Deſtruction of our Plantation Trade*
muſt be the neceſſary and unavoidable Conſequence.

Without this Trade therefore, Sir, is duely fupported
by a *Conſtitutional Security*, it can never be preferved at
all to thefe Kingdoms; nor can the great Advantages it pro-
mifes, beyond what it ever has done, be reaped. What
private Traders will profecute this Trade, when the Company's Forts and Settlements are in Foreign Hands, and
they every Moment liable to become a Sacrifice to our Rivals, and perfecuted and imprifoned in Dungeons, as was
the Cafe before this Company was eftablifhed ? Who will
become Proprietors in this Company to raife fuch a Joint
Trading Stock, as the Extent of this Commerce, we fee,
will eafily admit of; and this only upon the precarious
Security of an Allowance from the Publick from Year to
Year only ? To fettle this Company therefore upon a defirable Footing, fo as to raife and preferve its Credit with
the Publick in future, the annual Allowance granted by
Parliament muft, in my humble Opinion, not only be am-

ply

[39]

ply adequate to the Purposes for which it is granted; but must be secured for a certain Term upon Parliamentary Faith. Nothing less can transmit this Trade safe to Posterity, nor be a satisfactory Encouragement to future Adventurers to carry on this Trade to the Extent it is capable of.

If the Wisdom of Parliament should not judge the Merit of this Company to deserve future Encouragement, sure they have not only a Right to be paid for the past *Hire* and *Use* of their *Forts* and *Settlements*, but to have the Liberty of disposing of them to such Foreign Nations who will give the Company the most for them; for if the Forts and Settlements are no longer of any Worth to this Nation, and the Company can no longer maintain them upon the small Encouragement they have hitherto received, doubtless they will be allowed to sell what they can no longer keep, and what is no longer judged useful. It is not at all to be doubted, but the Company will find Purchasers enough, who would think they were worth an immense Sum to them, tho' they should be thought worth nothing to us. But the Consequences of such Reflections are of so melancholy a Nature to every Man who has the least Regard to the Interest of his *Prince* and *Country*, that we will drop these gloomy Apprehensions, and rather please ourselves with the agreeable Idea of seeing such a glorious Spirit appear in a *British* Parliament for the Support of this most important Commerce and Navigation, as will transmit our *African* and *Plantation Trades* with Security to latest Posterity

In

[40]

In what Manner foever fome may be pleafed to think of and receive thofe Propofitions, which have been made, in order to fettle this Company upon a lafting Foundation; yet, as they appear to the Propofer to be founded on the plain Principles of National Juftice, Intereft, and Honour, it is to be hoped an honeft Zeal to ferve a Caufe, wherein the Profperity of the Nation is fo nearly concerned, will be judged of with Candour.

The Profperity of this Company, Sir, muft terminate in that of our *Britifh Planters* and *Weft-India Merchants* in general, for, as the Company fhall be enabled to enlarge and extend the *Inland Parts* of the *African Trade*, which can no Way interfere with the Intereft of private Traders, the greater Plenty of *Negroes, Gold, Ivory*, and all *African Productions*, will be brought down to the Coaft for private Traders to take their Choice of; and confequently, in Proportion to the Plenty beyond the Demand, the Price of *Negroes, Gold, Ivory*, and every Thing elfe, will neceffarily fall.

When the Company are in a Condition to put a Stop to the Encroachments of our Rivals on the *African* Coaft, this will prevent the Encreafe of Buyers, and confequently have a natural Tendency ftill to fall the Price: And if a perpetual Union, Harmony, and good Underftanding be cemented between feparate Traders and the Company, which I heartily wifh may always be the Cafe, they will foon curb the over-bearing Encroachments of the *French*, and not only effectually ftop their Progrefs, but fap the very Foundation of their *Guinea* and *Plantation Trades*.--- Thus we fhall naturally reduce the Price of *Negroes*, and con-

fequently

[41]

fequently encreafe their Importation into our own Colonies, while we diminifh that of the *French* into theirs. —— This will enable us to make *Sugars* and *Indigo*, &c. cheaper than the *French* ; and not only to retrieve our languifhing Trade, but to put it in the Power of our *Britifh Planters* to make all fuch Improvements in Planting in general, by the Labour of *Negroes*, as the Soil will admit of: And as this will tend to the Encreafe and Profperity of the *Britifh* Intereft in *America*, fo *that*, in its Turn, will, of Courfe, become a greater Bulwark to our Intereft in *Europe*, by extending the general TRADE and NAVIGATION of thefe Kingdoms.

As the Company likewife extend their *Inland Trade* upon the Continent, fo, in Proportion, will the Exportation of our *Britifh* Manufactures Increafe ; and the Price of *Gold*, and all *other Produce* of *Africa*, as well as *Negroes*, become cheaper as they become more plentiful, by finding out and eftablifhing *New Inland Channels* of Commerce, with thefe populous and wealthy People. And fince they certainly ftand in as great need of *European Commodities*, as we do of their *Negroes*, their *Gold*, their *Ivory*, *Gums*, *Dying Woods*, *Bees-Wax*, &c. it certainly is our own Fault, if we do not render the *African Trade* as valuable to *Great Britain*, as the *Mines* of *Peru*, *Mexico*, and the *Brazils* are to the *Spaniards* and *Portuguefe* : And this too, with far greater Certainty and Security to this Nation, than any of thofe are to their refpective Nations, or any *Europeans* who are interefted in thofe Branches of foreign Trade.

G   Upon

[42]

Upon the happy Settlement of this Company, Sir, there will be no Comparison in Point of Profit to the *British Nation*, between the *Spanish Weſt India* or *Brazil Trades*, and that to *Africa*. The former undergo the weighty Incumbrance of *Indultoes*, both on the *Outſet* and *Returns*, and are liable to ſuch Interruptions from the Crowns of *Spain* and *Portugal*, as have rendered this Nation too much dependent on the Friendſhip of thoſe Kingdoms ; whereas the *African Settlements*, being duly ſupported at the Publick Expence, and the Company enabled to extend the *Inland Trade*, will be liable to no Manner of Incumbrance, Inſecurity, or Stagnation whatſoever. The *Spaniſh Weſt-India* and the *Brazil Trades*, are not only liable to great Hazards, but are ſo tedious in their *Returns*, that Traders of moderate Capitals cannot, with Prudence, engage in them , nor thoſe of conſiderable Ones, with any *Security*, like what our *Plantation* and *African* Trades will afford them, if duely cheriſhed, to the Extent they appear capable of being carried. But the *African Trade* alone, when eſtabliſhed upon a deſirable Foundation, can be liable to no Hazard any way comparable to the others ; every Trader in the Kingdom will have it in his Power to engage in it, ſuch Part of his Fortune as he ſhall chuſe to employ therein, either as a *Member* of the *African Corporation*, or as a *Separate Trader* : And this without the Precariouſneſs of ſuch *long Voyages* and *tedious Returns* as have ruined many in the *Spaniſh Weſt-India* and *Brazil Trades*.

Though *all other Branches* of our foreign Trade ſhould *fail* us, or the *Ballance* go againſt us, and thereby impoveriſh inſtead of enriching us ; yet while we ſhall encourage and extend our *Plantation* and *African Trades*, to the Pitch they

[43]

they are manifestly capable of being carried, we shall not, perhaps, experience any great Diminution in NAVAL Power. However, as other Branches of foreign Commerce depend upon the Humour and Caprice of other *Nations*, and therefore liable to such sudden Changes and Alterations, as have proved not only ruinous to private Adventurers, but diminutive of the *National Revenue*, it is certainly the best Policy to cherish and support, to the utmost of our Power, the *African* and *Plantation Trades*, which may be properly called *Our Own Foreign Trades*, as being absolutely under our own Steerage and Controul; as much under the Government and Direction of *Great Britain*, as the Trades of *Ireland* and *Scotland* are; *and consequently their Prosperity depends upon* OURSELVES.

And of what Advantage our *American Colonies* may be rendered to these Kingdoms, by the Labour of *Negroes*, has been set in a clear Light, by the *Lords Commissioners of Trade and Plantations* * ; and it is not to be doubted, but as they have had *all necessary Information* in Relation to the Nature and Importance of the *African Trade*, their *Report*, which is expected to be laid before the *House of Commons*, will *most fully and particularly* set forth the indispensable Necessity of effectually enabling the Company to support the Trade, which they have themselves, heretofore, represented to be the great Support of our Plantation Trade in general

But, if this Company are, any longer, to labour under the unparrallel'd Hardships and Difficulties they at present do, and no effectual Relief be given them, their Forts and Settlements must be abandoned to the Mercy of our Rivals and

* *Vide* the Representation of the Lords Commissioners of Trade and Plantations to the Right Honourable the Lords Spiritual and Temporal, in Parliament assembled *January* 14th, 1734-5.

G 2

Enemies.

[44]

Enemies : The *French* will engross our Share in the Trade to *Africa*, and more vigorously pursue the Prosperity of their *American Colonies*, while ours will become wretched and contemptible.——— They will hereby encrease in *Seamen* and *Naval Power*, while we shall be daily declining in both.——— They will obtain another *Assiento* with *Spain*, and introduce their Manufactures all over the *Spanish West-Indies*, while *British Subjects* will be *for ever excluded* from that Branch of our foreign Trade. The *African* and *Plantation Trades* will prove an inexhaustible Source of Treasure to *France*, to carry on their destructive Schemes of *universal Empire in Trade*, and thereby *in Power*. And what will then avail drawing the Sword against a Nation, who will have the Riches of *Africa* and *America*, to support their *mighty* ARMIES and their NAVAL POWER?

To conclude, Sir, I think it is not in my Power to propose any Thing more likely to conduce to Your true Honour and Glory, than to become the Patron and Promoter of such Measures as may secure and preserve the *African* Trade from being swallowed up by the *French* and other Nations So that the *Company*, the *Plantations*, *Your Country* may have Reason ever to celebrate Your Care, Vigilance, Honour and Justice in procuring such farther effectual Provision for the Support and Preservation of this most essential Branch of our Trade, as the Nature and Importance thereof manifestly requires

   I am

     With the most profound Veneration,
      S I R,
       Your most Humble,
  LONDON,   *And most Obedient Servant,*
Decemb. 11, 1744.
       A BRITISH MERCHANT.

THE CASE OF THE IMPORTATION OF
BAR-IRON

The Case of the Importation of Bar-Iron from our own Colonies of North America; Humbly Recommended to the Consideration of the Present Parliament, by the Iron Manufacturers of Great Britain (London: Thomas Trye, 1756). British Library, shelf-mark 1029.e.15.(5.).

This pamphlet was published anonymously on behalf of 'Iron Manufacturers of Great Britain' in order to influence the proceedings of parliament. The exact circumstances are clearly spelled out in the text. It speaks strongly in favour of a certain application which was made to parliament in 1751 (no doubt also written on behalf of the iron manufacturers) in order to free the importation of bar iron from the American colonies from custom duties. The author suggests that cheap imports of bar iron may save the English iron industries from Swedish and Russian competition, mainly because charcoal was much more cheaply produced in America than anywhere else.

THE

CASE

OF THE

IMPORTATION

OF

BAR-IRON,

FROM OUR OWN

Colonies of *North America*;

Humbly recommended to the Confideration of the prefent Parliament, by the IRON MANUFACTURERS of *Great Britain*.

LONDON

Printed for THOMAS TRYE, near *Grays-Inn Gate, Holborn.*

MDCCLVI.

[Price Six-pence.]

Preliminary Propofitions

I. **T**HERE cannot be a clearer Propofition concerning Trade, than, That it is the Intereft of every Manufacturing Country to get as great a *Choice* and *Variety* of *raw* Materials, and upon as *cheap Terms*, as can poffibly be procured. For an Error in this Refpect, is fundamental, and hardly to be corrected by any fubfequent Care or Diligence. Therefore the Legiflature hath wifely ordained, That though Wool, for Inftance, grows in greater Plenty in *England* than perhaps in any other Country, yet the Wools of all Nations fhall be admitted into *England Duty-free*; juftly confidering, That We can never have *too great* a Choice and Plenty of that neceffary Material of extenfive and profitable Induftry, or upon *too cheap* Terms.

II. A fecond Propofition, not inferior either in Evidence or Importance, is, That unlefs fome Commodities are taken from other Countries by Way of *Barter* in the Courfe of Trade, You can have but a fmall Vent for your own Manufactures, it being im-

A 2 poffible

4   *Preliminary Propofitions.*

poffible, for any Nation to make *all* their Payments
in Gold and Silver, even if they abounded with the
richeft Mines of thofe Metals — Nay, though it
were poffible, it may be greatly queftioned, Whether
it is not more for the *Intereft* of a *Manufacturing* Nation to import *fometimes* raw Materials by Way of
providing for the *future* Induftry of their People,
than to be *always* importing Gold and Silver;
which, when they come to be unconnected with
Labour and Induftry, (as in this Cafe they would foon
be) have no other Effect, than to introduce Lazinefs,
Vanity and Extravagance. —— And in the End
Poverty.

III. A third Propofition, by way of Preliminary,
is this, That *Cheapnefs* in regard to *Price*, and *Goodnefs* in regard to *Quality*, are the Support and Prop of
all Manufactures And that it is impoffible, in the
Nature of Things, for a Nation to preferve any Manufacture, if they ftrike off, or fuffer to be ftruck
off thefe two grand Pillars, Cheapnefs and Goodnefs.
They may indeed tamper for a while; and feem to
do fomething, not unlike a Quack, in Phyfic, towards botching up a broken Conftitution; but it will
foon appear, that all they have been doing, was
only to make bad worfe.

Thefe three *Preliminary* Propofitions being duly
weighed, every real Lover of his Country will be
fully qualified to judge of the Truth and Importance
of what is to follow.

I. IN

The C A S E *of the Importation,* &c. 5

I. **I**N the Year 1751, Application was made to Parliament for the Admission of Bar-Iron *Duty-free* from our own Colonies. And after various Struggles, as is always the Case, between Self-Interest and the Public Good, the contending Parties seemed to compromise the Difference,—By passing a Law for importing Bar-Iron *Duty-free* into the Port of *London only*, continuing the Restraint against all the other Ports of the Kingdom The only Indulgence, which could be obtained at that Juncture, was a Permission to Import *Pig-Iron* Duty-free into other Places Of which more shall be said in the Sequel

Now, when this Law was passed, those Persons who contended for the *Exclusion* of other Ports, rejoiced almost as much as if they had obtained a complete Victory : — And indeed, every Thing considered, the Termination of the Dispute in this manner, was little less. For, as to the Pig-Iron imported, that was to come of course into *their* Hands, in order to make it into Bars So that they were as much at Liberty to engross the Commodity, and to set their own Price upon it, as ever they were. And in regard to the Bar-Iron admitted into the Port of *London* Duty-free, this could give them no great Disturbance, because the *Dearness of Coals*, on Account of the heavy Duties paid in that *particular* Port, would effectually prevent any Manufacture from being set up in *London*, or its Neighbourhood : And the Expence of Land-Carriage from *London* to the manufacturing Parts of the Kingdom, would rather be too great for such a ponderous, low-priced Commodity

6   *The* C A S E *of the*

Commodity to fupport.   But left the induftrious
Artificers of *Birmingham, Walfall,* &c. fhould avail
themfelves even of this Circumftance, and get the
Waggons which carry their Manufactures to *London,*
to return Home with Bar-Iron, a Claufe was inferted, to prohibit the Carriage of *American* Bar-Iron
beyond ten Miles from the City : By which means,
the City of *London* itfelf enjoys no kind of Advantage from the Exclufion of the other Ports. In fhort,
as the Cafe ftands at prefent, this Iron *cannot* be ufed
in and about *London*, and it *fhall not* be permitted
to be carried to thofe Places where it may be ufed.

However, the Advocates for a *free Trade* were
glad of getting even *fo far* towards the Accomplifh-
ment of their good Defign ; hoping, that when the
prefent Clamours had fubfided, and Mens Minds
became more opened and enlarged by Length of
Time, and the natural Progrefs of Truth, a convenient Seafon might be found for making this particular Indulgence to the City of *London,* become a general Benefit to the whole Kingdom ——Thus ftood
the Cafe on both Sides in the Year 1751. It remains
now to fhew, What Turn Things have taken, and
whether the Reafons for applying to Parliament have
ceafed, or increafed fince that time.

But previous to this, it may be proper to obferve,
for the fake of thofe who are not converfant in Things
of this Nature, that the Perfons concerned in the
Iron Trade are generally ranged into two Claffes,
The *Iron* MASTERS, and the *Iron* MANUFACTURERS ;
And the forming a right Judgment on the Merits of
the prefent Difpute, will greatly depend on a juft
Diftinction between thefe two Bodies of Men.

                                                                As

Importation of B A R - I R O N.   7

As to the Iron Masters; You will pleafe to obferve, That the firft Procefs is to refine the Iron
from the Ore, by running the Metal into fhort pieces,
like Billet-Wood, called Pig-Iron; and the Proprietor of this Work is termed the *Furnace-Mafter.*
But Note, The only Fuel proper for this Operation
is *Wood-Charcoal.* The next Procefs is to meliorate
the Iron, ftill by means of a *Charcoal* Fire, to render it malleable, and draw it out into Bars by the
Strokes of the Great Hammer, The Owner of which
Work is ftiled the *Forge-Mafter.* But, generally
fpeaking, the fame Perfon, or Perfons, united in a
Company, are the Proprietors of both Works. And
perhaps of Slitting and Rowling Mills befides; whofe
common Appellation is therefore, That of *Iron-*
Mafters. Now, from the very Stating of this Cafe,
it plainly appears, That thefe Men, though few in
Number, muft be Men of great Subftance, great
Capitals in Trade, and capable of exerting a very
dangerous Influence, when they find it their Intereft
fo to do, over Men of needy Circumftances, and
fmall Capitals, dependent upon them.

We come therefore in the next Place, to the *Iron-*
Manufacturers. Thefe Men receive the Material for
their Workmanfhip from the *Iron Mafters* either in
Bars, Rods, or Plates, and work it up into all the
various Implements, for which *England* is now become fo famous over all the World   But pleafe to
obferve, for it is an important Article, That when
the Iron comes into the Hands of the Manufacturers,
the Ufe of *Wood-Charcoal* is from thence-forward entirely laid afide, and that they perform all their Operations with *Pit-coal.* Now, thefe Men, generally
fpeaking,

8 *The* C A S E *of the*

speaking, and by Way of Comparison with the former, are but of middling Fortunes : And the Nail-
ers in particular may be ranked among the lower, or
the lowest Class of Life But nevertheless, should
You add the whole of their Fortunes together, and
consider the immense Yearly Value or Produce of
their Labour——And should You make an Estimate
of their Usefulness to the *Landed Interest* of the Kingdom, to the several Branches of the Revenue, to all
Parts of Commerce internal and external, to Shipping and Navigation, to our Colonies abroad as well
as Ourselves at home,——There is no Sort of Comparison, in a *National* View, between the Importance
of the one, and that of the other. And yet the whole
Contest in this Affair lies between these two Sets of
Men, The *Iron-Masters* on one Side, and the *Iron-
Manufacturers* on the other : Whereas besides all other
Considerations, the Iron-Manufacturers are to the Iron-
Masters in Number, at least as Two .Thousand to
One.

This being premised, We now return to the Point
in hand ; And shall divide all that need be said on this
Subject, into *Facts*, — *Reasons*, — and *Answers* to
Objections.

F A C T S.

I
T is a *Fact*, that the Iron-Manufacture in *England* is increasing every Day ; So that the Demand for raw Materials is growing greater and
greater. And though the Rise of this Manufacture
is but of late Date, compared with some others, yet
it hath exceeded them all in its Extent and-National
Advantage,

Importation of B A R - I R O N. 9

Advantage, the *Woollen* only excepted. So that it
may juftly now be' reckoned the SECOND Manufacture
in the Kingdom.

II. It is a *Fact*, That the Price of all Bar-Iron
whatfoever is greatly encreafed fince the laft Application to Parliament. And if it fhould go on for any
confiderable Time longer, enhancing in proportion
to what it hath done of late Years, the whole Manufacture will be in Danger of being ruined in *England*,
and of removing to fome other Country.

III. It is a *Fact*, That the moft neceffary and ufeful
Part of the *Swedifh* Iron imported into this Kingdom,
called *Orgroons*, is by means of *Pre-contracts*, and
other Ways of fecret Management both at home and
abroad, monopolized into a few, a *very* few Hands.
And it is much to be feared, That the *Ruffia* Iron will
fhortly undergo, if it hath not already undergone,
the fame Fate. Not to mention, That both *Swedifh*
and *Ruffia* Iron, being Subject to the Controll of their
refpective Governments before Exportation, may be
ftopped at Pleafure, (and from the prefent Appearance of public Affairs we know not how foon)
or may have additional Duties laid upon them, in
proportion as thofe Governments fhall take a Difguft
to, or perceive, that the *Britifh* Nation cannot do
without their Iron, —— I fay *additional* Duties, for
there are fome Duties laid on already, and more are
threatened; which will make thofe Commodities
come ftill Dearer to the *Englifh* Manufacturers. The
Swedifh Duties were long ago as high as three Pound
twelve Shillings and Sixpence *Sterling* per Ton,

B   according

10   *The CASE of the*

according to the Account of one of our Adverfaries. [See a Pamphlet, intitled, *The Intereft of* Great Britain *in fupplying herfelf with Iron*] And We have too good Grounds for apprehending, that when the prefent Contract for *Orgroon* Iron is expired, the *Swedifh* Government will come to fome farther Refolutions, by no means favourable to the Manufactures of *Great Britain*.

As to the manner of vending our own *Englifh* Iron, no Man can be fo blind, but muft plainly fee, That a few rich Men, linked together in a *common Intereft*, are much likelier to combine with one another to keep up the Price againft the poor, numerous, and unconnected Manufacturers, than the Manufacturers can againft them.

IV. It is a *Fact*, That both the *Swedifh* and *Ruffian* Governments have of late *circumfcribed* and *ftinted* the making of Bar-Iron within their refpective Dominions: The *Swedes*, by limiting the annual Quantity to be made, and the Emprefs of *Ruffia*, by forbidding the Erection of any Works within fuch and fuch Limits, under the fevereft Penalties. The Confequence of which Reftraints will be doubly prejudicial to the Interefts of the *Britifh* Manufacturers; firft, becaufe the Quantity imported will not anfwer the Demand of an *increafing* and *growing* Manufacture; and yet, fecondly, the Price will be enhanced in Proportion to the Demand. Thus the Evil will be multiplied upon us both Ways.

V. It is a *Fact*, That the Price of Cord-Wood in *England*, *neceffary* for making Charcoal, is *more than doubled*

Importation of B A R - I R O N 11

doubled of late Years ; and that the Commodity itfelf begins to be extremely fcarce

VI. It is a *Fact*, That the *American* Bar-Iron has
fome Qualities in it, peculiarly ufeful in feveral of our
capital Manufactures, *viz.* There is one Sort, called
Beft Principio, as good as any in the World for making Fire-Arms. And there are but few Forges
here in *England* which produce an Iron proper for that
Purpofe. There is alfo another Sort of *American*
Iron, of a tough, wirey Nature, fit, not only for
making Wire, *which requires fome of the beft of Iron*,
but alfo for making excellent long Nails.

VII. It is a *Fact*, That when the *American* Pig-
Iron is brought over here, it not only undergoes the
Expence of Carriage and Re-carriage into diftant
Parts of the Country, where the Forges are fituated,
in order to be made into Bars, (by which means the
Price of the Commodity is ftill enhanced) but it alfo
hath not Juftice done it, when it is put into our
Englifh Forges : That is to fay, the Price of Charcoal being fo dear here in *England*, and the Demand
for *any Sort* of Bar-Iron being great, the Iron-Maf-
ters will not allow a Sufficiency of Charcoal to meliorate and purify the Metal, and bring it to its due
Confiftence and Perfection Hence it is, that the
Credit and Reputation of the Iron Manufacture,
unlefs fpeedily remedied, will greatly fuffer,— and
fuffei in every View, *viz* both by being made in a
lefs workman-like Manner by the Manufacturer, in
order to make himfelf Amends for the exceffive
Dearnefs of the raw Material ; and alfo, bec..ufe it

B 2   is

is impoffible for him, were he ever fo defirous, to
make good Goods out of bad Materials

VIII It is a *Fact*, That the Excife, the Poft-Office, the Stamp-Duties, and all other Branches of
the Revenue, (taking in a Courfe of Years) rife, or
fink in Proportion to the Number of Perfons induftrioufly imployed, who are the Confumers of Excifeable Commodities, and the Caufes of ufing Stamp-
Paper, and of the Circulation of Multitudes of Letters.   The Revenues of the Excife and Poft-Office,
in particular, have been doubled, trebled, quadrupled, and even fextupled, in the Counties of *Stafford* and *Warwick*, fince the firft fettling of the Iron
Manufactures in thofe Provinces.

N O W, as thefe are all *Matters of Fact*, the Truth
of which We muft infift upon, and do moft humbly
recommend to the mature Attention of the Legiflature, and of every real Patriot and Lover of his
Country; We fhall, in the next Place, beg Leave
to give our *Reafons* for this prefent Application to
Parliament.

R E A S O N S.

I. **B**Ecaufe it hath already been made to appear,
That every Motive for the Admiffion of
American Bar-Iron, which fubfifted before the Year
1751, is now grown ftronger, and calls the more
urgently for public Attention.   And the prefent
alarming Connection of *Ruffia* with *France*, fhould
roufe us the more to turn our Thoughts towards
                                                      our

Importation of B A R - I R O N.   13

our own Colonies for Supplies of Iron ; — agreeably
to what was done formerly in regard to Pitch and
Tar; when *Sweden,* under the Influence of the same
constant Enemy, endeavoured to distress us in the
Use of those necessary, important Articles   May
the Success attending that Affair, be an Encouragement to do the like in this.

II. Because the Importation of Bar, instead of Pig
Iron, would be a considerable Saving to the Importers, and consequently to the Manufacturers, in
the Price of Freight : That is to say, As *four* Tons
of Pig-Iron are generally the Quantity allowed for
making *three* Tons of Bar, it therefore follows, that
one fourth Part of the Freight, or 25 ℔ *Cent.* would
be saved by importing Bars rather than Pigs. Bars
likewise are a more commodious Stowage in the
Hold than Pigs. — Not to mention, that by opening
a new Market, the Iron-Masters would have it less
in their Power to fix their own Price upon the Commodity than they have at present, because the *American* Iron *would not then pass through their Hands*;
and that the necessary Expences of Carriage from
the Port to the Forge, and from the Forge to the
Manufacturer, would thereby be superseded : Also,
that the Material itself would, most probably, be
better made in *America*, where Charcoal is cheap,
than in *England*, where it is excessive dear, and consequently, not a Sufficiency allowed.

III. Because both *England* the Mother Country,
and her Colonies, will be equally benefited by this
Proposal; — and benefited without any Expence,
Loss

14 *The* C A S E *of the*

Loſs or Hazard. No Squadrons are to be fitted out to bring this Point to bear; no Forces to embark, no Troops to march, and no foreign Enemy to contend with.— All that is neceſſary, is, Only to *untie* the Hands of Induſtry, and to let honeſt Labour have its free and natural Courſe among our own People.

IV. Becauſe the Admiſſion of Bar-Iron from our Colonies *Duty-free*, would conſiderably advance many other Articles of *American* Commerce, which now in a manner lie neglected, or untouch'd. As for Example, Iron being ponderous, and taking up little Room, and other Goods light, and taking up a great deal, a proper Cargo might be made up, at all Times, by joining both together; and by this means, not only the former Articles of Trade might be brought Home upon better Terms than uſual, but alſo many new ones might be introduced, which perhaps are at preſent little thought of. The Country on both ſides of the *Mohawk* River, which comes down to *Albany*, and thence to *New York*, is the fitteſt in the World, according to the judicious Mr *Colden's* Account, in his *Hiſtory of the Five Indian Nations*, for raiſing of Hemp. But, the Importation of this Article, as likewiſe of Flax from *North America*, hath not hitherto ſucceeded to the Degree it was expected; which is ſolely owing to this Circumſtance, That Hemp and Flax taking up much Room, and yet being of little Weight, were not able of themſelves to ſupport the *whole* Charges of Freight and Inſurance. Now the Admiſſion of Bar-Iron tends to remedy this Inconvenience, becauſe 20, 30 or

Importation of B A R-I R O N. 15

ot 40 Tons may be put into the Bottom of a Ship, by way of Ballaſt, and yet no Room be loſt for the Stowage of Hemp or Flax. Thus therefore, by the mutual Aſſiſtance of the *Heavy* and the *Light*, a compleat Cargo of excellent *raw Materials* might be brought from the Colonies to the Mother Country, giving Imployment and Bread to Thouſands both there and here.

V. A fifth Reaſon, and the moſt intereſting to *Great Britain*, ariſes from the following Circum-ſtance; *viz.* That the Manufactures of *Great Britain* cannot be vended in ſuch Quantities in our North-ern Colonies, as the *Americans* themſelves demand, for want of proper Returns, by way of Barter or Payment.— But, were the *Americans* allowed to ſend us *more* raw Materials, (Materials which we muſt purchaſe with ready Money from other Countries, in Alliance with the *French*, our natural Enemies) the *Engliſh* Manufacturers would give them more wrought Goods in Exchange. A moſt advantage-ous Commerce on both Parts; or there is no ſuch Thing in Nature! And this likewiſe is the proper Method of promoting the Intereſt of the Colonies, and of the Mother Country at the ſame Time: This would multiply our Shipping and Navigation, would increaſe his Majeſty's Revenue, and do every thing that is neceſſary to make a Nation great and pow-erful; — without involving us in any Diſputes with *France* or any other Power, or bringing on any Ex-pence or Inconvenience whatſoever.

VI. The laſt Reaſon we ſhall aſſign, is, Becauſe it appears very clear, that the *American* Bar-Iron is

capable

16   *The* C`A S E *of the*

capable of great Improvements, as to the *Quality,*
or Nature of it — We' do not pretend to foretel,
what different Sorts of Ore may yet be difcovered,
when more Works fhall be erected, more Experience acquired, and new Veins fhall be tried: (Tho'
furely we might be allowed to fuppofe, that what,
happens in all other Cafes will happen in this, *viz.*
That new Experiments will bring on new Difcove-
ries and greater Perfection.) But We do affert, That
in regard to the *American* Ore already difcovered,
great Improvements can be made in the Fluxing and
Refining of it. And the Manufacturers, who may
be allowed to be the beft Judges, have Reafon to
fuppofe, that certain Sorts of it may be brought near
to the Quality of the *Swedifh Orgroon,* if made into
Bars in fuch a woody Country as *America,* where
there is no Need of ftinting the Expence of Charcoal.

Such therefore being the Reafons for this humble
Application, We now proceed to our ANSWERS
to fuch Objections as are, or can be brought againft
us.

Objection " **I** F the *Americans* are permitted and
    I.   " taught the Way to make Bar-Iron,
" they will not ftop there, but will proceed to ma-
" nufacture it in all its Branches: To which. End
" their Slaves will be of infinite Ufe, becaufe they
" are obliged to work much cheaper than any Free-
" men will, or can: And fo, from becoming our
" ufeful Cuftomers, they will foon commence our
" moft dangerous Rivals."

General

Importation of BAR-IRON. 17

General Remark.

This Objection comes a little ungracefully out of the Mouth of an *Iron-Master* ; and such a Zeal in *Him* doth not carry the proper Marks of Sincerity along with it. — Were the Case as the Objector represents, the *Iron Manufacturers* would be the first Persons to take the Alarm, and to oppose such a Measure. But they know better, and desire every Reader to suspend his Judgment for the present, till he has heard what can be said on the other Side.

Answer 1st, This Objection, against permitting or teaching the *Americans* to make Bar-Iron, comes too late : For they are both permitted and taught already. Nor will they now be perswaded to leave off, and to break up their numerous Works, merely to please the Iron-Masters of *England*.

Answer 2d, If there is any Danger to be apprehended, That the *Americans* will in time commence Iron Manufacturers, it can arise only from the *absolute* Necessity that we shall put them under, to act in this Manner, by not allowing them the Means of purchasing our Manufactures. Which Necessity has been the Cause of their setting up so many Works already of different kinds. Take away therefore this Necessity and Compulsion ; and then You are sure of their Custom, because the *English* can sell the Goods to them much cheaper than they can manufacture them. Therefore we now proceed to a

C

Answer

18   *The* C A S E *of the*

Answer 3d, *viz* That as far as concerns the Iron-Manufacture, this supposed *Rivalship* between the Colonies and Us, is *impossible*, provided we do not compel them by *Necessity*. For the Price of Labour is at least *Cent. per Cent.* cheaper in the Counties of *Warwick* and *Stafford*, than it is in any Part of the *British* Plantations. And as to the Labour of Slaves, We could make it appear, were this the proper Place, That Slaves do not *now*, *never* yet did, and never will perform their Work either so *cheap*, or so *well*, as hath been done by Persons, who are spurred on by Rivalship and Emulation, and the Hopes of Gain. For indeed all Mankind will exert that provident Fore-cast, that Industry, and those Abilities out of *Choice*, and for the Sake of their *own Interest*, to which no Power on Earth can force or compel them. Moreover, as to Pit-Coal, that most necessary Article in the Iron Manufacture, the *Americans* on the Sea Coast, and on this Side the *Apalatean* Mountains, have it not among them. And while that is the Case, neither they, nor *any other Nation* will be able to make any Figure in the Iron Manufacture, unless it be our own Fault, by permitting them to have our Coals at an easy Rate. The *Swedes*, for Example, are the greatest *Iron-Masters* in the World. They are likewise a free People, and work for excessive low Wages, They have Plenty of Charcoal, and very cheap, were Charcoal the proper Fuel for this Purpose. Moreover they have turned their Thoughts for many Years past wholly to Commerce, and they understand Metallurgy as well as any People whatever. Why therefore, with *all these* Advantages, are they *so far* behind the *English*

in

Importation of B A R - I R O N. 19

in the Iron-Manufacture? The Reason is plain, They want Pit-Coals, and they cannot procure them, but at such a Price, as muft neceffarily turn the Balance in our Favour   Judge now of the Weight and Strength of this formidable Objection.   Is it not like every other Spectre, terrible at a Diftance; but upon nearer Approach, vanifhes into — *Nothing?*

Objection II. " As foreign Iron pays a Duty to the
" Government of 2*l.* 8*s* 6*d* ℔ Ton, the Importation
" of *American* Iron, *Duty-free*, would ftop the Con-
" fumption of the other, and by that Means preju-
" dice the Revenue, which at this critical Juncture
" can bear no Lofs, nor Defalcation."

Anfwer 1ft, The Difference of the Diftances between *England* and the *Baltic*, and *England* and
North America, together with the Nature of the refpective Voyages, will ftill preponderate on the Side
of *Sweden* and *Ruffia*, unlefs thefe Powers fhould
lay on higher Duties and Difcouragements than they
do at prefent : So that the Foreign Materials will
ftill be confidered by the Manufacturers as the *chief*
Articles of their Confumption   This appears the
ftronger, if you confider, That it is impoffible to
import Iron from North *America* in any other
Shape than as *Ballaft* to other Freights; becaufe, if You was to freight a Ship *wholly* with Iron,
the Carriage could not be afforded for lefs than 25*s.*
or 30*s.* ℔ Ton, which is fuch an Expence as the
Material could not bear.   But, when it comes only
by Way of Ballaft, taking up no Room that was
wanted for other Purpofes, it may be brought home

for

20   *The* C A S E *of the*

for 6*s.* or 8*s.* per Ton. This being the Cafe, it evidently follows, That an Importation of Iron by Way
of Ballaft need not raife any great Alarms, either in
regard to *British*, or Foreign Iron, becaufe it never can
amount to very great Quantities: Perhaps in a long
Procefs of Time, it may rife up to 8, or 10,000 Tons
℔ Year. However, if this Method fhould tend to
diffolve the prefent Monopolies of *Swedish* and *Ruffian*
Iron, and confequently lower the Price of them,
(which is one great Point to be wifhed, and aimed
at) it would be fo far from leffening the Revenue,
that it would greatly increafe it, becaufe, in that
Cafe, greater Quantities of Foreign Iron would ftill
be imported For, We muft beg Leave again to
remark, that the Iron Manufacture is not in a declining, but in an increafing State.

Anfwer 2d, Granting even, That the Quantities of
Foreign Iron would be leffened by a few Tons, or
perhaps Scores of Tons, if *American* Iron was admitted Duty-free, (though the contrary Suppofition
is much more probable) Yet, as this could never
happen, but by a very great Increafe of the Manufacture, and confequently by a much larger Confumption than ufual, of every Excifeable Commodity,
by raifing the Revenue of the Cuftoms, the Poft, and
Stamp Offices, the Lofs one Way would be compenfated more than *fourfold* another Way. Nay, if *one*
additional Ton of *American* Iron fhould be made into
Birmingham-Toys, it would more than make Amends
to the Government for the Non-payment of *ten* Tons,
i e. of 24*l* 5*s.* 9*d.* Duty of *Swedish* Iron, at the
Cuftomhoufe.

Anfwer

Importation of BAR-IRON. 21

Answer 3d, This tender Regard for the Revenue is a *New* Topic, and only taken up to serve the present Turn. At other Times, it used to be objected by the Iron-Masters, That the Importation of *American* Iron would not at all diminish the Consumption of the Foreign, and consequently, not prejudice the Revenue. And the Reason *then* assigned was, That the *American* Iron being exactly of the same Quality with the *English*, it would wholly supplant the Use of our own Iron, but not that of Foreigners. This was their former Plea, when they had a different Point to serve : But the Truth is, That as *America* is a very large Country, And as there are great Varieties of Ore already discovered, the Iron coming from thence hath various Qualities, some similar to the *English*, some to the *Swedish*, and others to the *Russian*. But, as to stopping the Consumption of either *English*, *Swedish*, or *Russian*, in any *considerable* Degree, it is all Flourish and Declamation. And we can hardly perswade Ourselves, That the Persons are in Earnest who make the Objection. Indeed the present Scheme may lower the exorbitant Price, and Monopoly of all three. And this is the *true* Foundation of the Opposition made to it.

" *Objection* III   If the *Americans* are suffered
" to import their Iron *Duty-free*, all the *English*
" Furnaces and Forges must stand still : Because
' We cannot pretend to sell as cheap as they can :
" Our Woods likewise must be grubbed up, for it
" will not be worth the while to preserve them. And
" the Country, which is already too bare of Timber,
" will still be barer "

Answer

Answer 1st, That the making of *English* Iron is a most profitable Branch of Business, may be inferred, without farther Proof, from the immense Estates got in that Trade : And, that the *English* Iron-Masters may sell as cheap as the *Americans*, if they please, and cheaper too, all Circumstances considered, is a certain Fact ; Because though the *Americans* have one Advantage over the *English*, namely, Cheapness of Charcoal, the *English* have *many* over them, namely, Cheapness of Labour, Exemptions from the Expence of Freight, Commissions, Port-Charges, Warehouses, the Consumption of Rust, &c &c. Not to mention, that they have likewise the Advantage of Works already built, a long Establishment, Correspondencies formed and settled, and a *commanding* Influence over many of the *poorer* Manufacturers, which hath appeared on many Occasions.

Answer 2d, As to the Destroying of Woods, We know the Fact to be quite the Reverse to what is set forth in the Objection : We know, that Furnaces and Forges are the very *worst Nurses* that could be thought of for rearing up young Woods and Coppices. And We appeal to all the World, whether it is not a notorious Truth, that for one Acre which they have been the cause of planting and preserving, they have been the Means of grubbing up and destroying Thousands. In short, the proper Term for them is *Wood-Devourers*, instead of *Wood-Preservers*. — Besides, We must insist, that the shrowding or cropping of Oak for Charcoal, (which is too common a Practice) is so far from being a Means of making

making the Trees to grow fit for Timber, that it absolutely spoils them for that Use.

Answer 3d, Experience, which is the surest Guide, hath plainly shewn, that Self-Interest is a very unfit Judge of future Effects, and of the Consequences of Things of this Nature.—— The present Cry is, " That " if Bar-Iron from *America* was to be admitted *Du-* " *ty-free*, the Country would still grow barer of " Timber, because it would not be worth while for " the Land-Owners to suffer the Trees to grow."—— Suppose therefore that instead of Bar-Iron you had said *Wool*, and that an Out-cry was to be raised against the free Importation of Wool . — " For, if " Wool shall be admitted to come from other " Countries, especially from *Ireland*, *Duty-free*, Alack- " a-day, what will become of Us? — Our Sheep- " Walks must all be destroyed, not a Flock, not a " single Sheep will be left , because it will not an- " swer to rear or keep them   The Tenants must all " break ; the Landlords lose their Rents; and the " Government its Taxes.   These will be the Con- " sequences of admitting the Importation of Wool " *Duty free*." Now, You must allow, that this Plea, were it made (and most probably it *was* made) at the Time, when it was debated, Whether it was right to admit foreign Wools *Duty-free* .—I say, that this Plea is at least as good and as reasonable as Yours.   You must acknowledge likewise, that the Proprietors of Sheep Lands, and the Growers of Wool, are, in every Sense, a much more considerable Body of Men than the Iron-Masters, and the Proprietors of a few Wood-Lands   And you must

confess

24   *The* C A S E *of the*

confeſs, becauſe it is in vain to deny it, that there is
a much greater Plauſibility in the Argument for oppoſing the Importation of Wool from our *Neighbours*
in *Flanders*, *Germany*, and *Poland*, eſpecially from our
next-door Neighbours, the *Iriſh*, (in all which Countries Land and Labour are *much cheaper* than in *Eng-*
land)— than it would be to oppoſe the Admiſſion
of Bar-Iron coming from ſo diſtant a Country as
North America, where, if Land and Charcoal are
cheaper, Labour (the *principal* Concern) is infinitely dearer.   Yet, notwithſtanding the Plauſibility of
the Objection, ſure and long Experience hath made
it to appear, that the Admiſſion of foreign Wool
Duty-free, hath been ſo far from preventing the
Growth of *Engliſh* Wool, that we have at this Day
more Sheep and more Wool, the Product of *Great*
Britain, than ever we had in former Times.   And
if you are deſirous of knowing the *Reaſon* of this
Fact, it is plainly this,—The free Admiſſion of Materials is the Cauſe of Labour; Labour is the Cauſe
of Populouſneſs , and a populous Country will always produce more Commodities, and have a readier
Market for them, than if it had been thinner peopled.

Objection IV. " Granting that raw Materials ought
" to be admitted *Duty-free*, yet, as Bar-Iron is ra-
" ther a *Manufacture* than a *raw Material*, it there-
" fore follows, that the Arguments in favour of
" raw Materials, ſhould conclude *againſt* Bar-Iron."

Anſwer. This Objection is a mere Play upon
Words; and therefore deſerves the leſs Regard —
By

Importation of B A R - I R O N. 25

By raw Materials, in a Commercial Senfe, is to be underftood that State or Condition of the Material, which is fitteft for Carriage from Place to Place, and *moft acceptable to the great Body of the Manufacturers.* For in Cafes of this Nature, the general Good of the Whole, or more properly, *the Good of the Majority,* ought to take place of every private Confideration. And therefore, if the Importation of Iron in *Bars,* rather than in *Pigs,* is of moft Service to the *general National Manufacture,* We conceive ourfelves fully authorifed, by the Ufe and Cuftom of all Commercial Authors, to call Bar-Iron a *raw Material.* In fhort, a Commodity may be a *Manufacture* regarding one Thing, and yet a *raw Material* refpecting another. But, as We are contending for *Things,* not for *Words,* if you can give us a properer Term, we will willingly adopt it, provided it fhall appear, that You and We mean the fame Thing. — Hemp and Flax are always called *raw Materials;* and yet Hemp and Flax, and even Wool, undergo feveral Operations before they are imported.— Nay, woollen and linnen Yarn are imported *Duty-free,* becaufe they are confidered as raw Materials

Objection V. " The Arguments here made ufe of
" for admitting raw Materials *Duty-free,* either prove
" nothing, or prove too much. For, if they are
" valid and conclufive, they tend to prove, that
" *Swedifh* and *Ruffian* Iron ought to be admitted *Du-*
" *ty-free,* as well as *American* "

Anfwer 1ft, In all Cafes whatever, where raw Materials will come the cheaper to the Manufacturer by
D   being

26   *The* C A S E *of the*

being admitted *Duty-free*, there We readily allow, the Rule for the free Importation of them ought *always* to prevail. Nor is it of any Use to plead, that our present System of Laws have, in some Cases, determined otherwise, unless You could prove at the same Time, that all the Laws now in being in regard to Commerce, are so good, that they cannot be made better; which, We conceive, would prove a very arduous Attempt. But in respect to *Swedish* and *Russian* Iron, it doth not appear to us, that the Importation of them Duty-free would lower the Price to the *English* Manufacturer : Because the Governments of *Sweden* and *Russia* would be the only Gainers, by laying on *additional* Duties, in Proportion to what was taken off in *England* Now this is a Circumstance in which our Colonies in *North America* widely differ from *Sweden* and *Russia:* For these Provinces, those especially which are immediately under the Jurisdiction of the Crown, can lay no Duties whatsoever, without the Consent of the Government at Home

Answer 2d, In Cases of Competition, our Colonies ought to have the Preference, because they take *English* Manufactures in return, neither *prohibiting* nor *taxing* them But *Sweden* prohibits almost all our Manufactures · And we know not how soon *Russia* may do the like, and give the Preference to the Manufactures of *France* However that may prove, one Thing is certain , namely, That what are not prohibited, are considerably taxed both by *Russia* and *Sweden* This therefore is another Circumstance, which demonstrates, that the Cases are

not

Importation of B A R - I R O N. 27

not parallel; and confequently, that the Objection is very ill founded, and of no Weight.

UPON the Whole, We are now willing to believe, that every difinterefted Perfon, every impartial Man in the Kingdom, will readily agree, That Bar-Iron ought to be imported from our Colonies *Duty-free,* both for their fakes and ours. As to thofe who are blinded by Prejudice, or warped by miftaken Notions of Self-Intereft, We do not pretend to work Miracles for their Cure: But as far as inconteftible Facts may be allowed to fpeak, as far as Reafons for the public Good can influence or perfwade, as far as folid Anfwers can preponderate over weak, frivolous and captious Objections; — fo far We humbly hope We have maintained our Caufe; and, relying on the Goodnefs of it, may truft the Event to the proper Guardians of our Trade and Liberties, THE PARLIAMENT OF GREAT BRITAIN. If We afk any Thing for Ourfelves, that is either incompatible with the Public Good, or with the Intereft of His Majefty's Revenue, We defire not to fucceed: But if the propofed Benefit is general, and our Interefts mutual, We cannot help flattering Ourfelves, that Thofe of the *beft Hearts,* and *beft Abilities,* both in the Senate and out of it, will efpoufe the Caufe, and become the Patrons of fo large and numerous a Body of Men, and fo neceffary to the Commerce of thefe Kingdoms, as

Their Obliged Humble Servants,

THE IRON MANUFACTURERS

OF GREAT BRITAIN.

[28]

POSTSCRIPT.

IF the Objection drawn from the *supposed* Loss of the Revenue (Pages 18, 19.) should make any Impression at this *critical* Juncture, We have a Proposal in Readiness, which would not only remove that Difficulty, but also greatly increase the public Revenue, at the same Time that it would contribute not a little to the further Progress of the Iron Manufacture: It is this, *To lay a double Duty upon the Exportation of Coal and Culm to foreign Parts.* For it is well known that Coal is a *raw Material* in the most proper and extensive Sense of that Word; It is also certain, That the *French*, the *Dutch*, and other Competitors in Trade, fetch immense Quantities of Coals from this Kingdom, paying for them in Spirituous Liquors, Teas, and other smuggled Goods: And that these Coals are, for the most Part, used in the Manufacture of such Articles as are intended to prevent the Sale of *English* Merchandise: It is moreover an indisputable Fact, that *Germany*, *Holland*, *Flanders*, *France*, and *Spain*, cannot be supplied from any other Collieries but from those of *Great Britain*, because there are none others which have the Quantities sufficient to supply them with. Why then are these raw Materials permitted to be exported, *in a manner*, Duty-free? I say, Duty-free;

for·

POSTSCRIPT. 29

for as to the prefent Duty, it is fo trifling and inconfiderable, that little Care is taken in the Collection
of it: Whereas, were the Duty doubled, the very
Increafe of the Sum would make it important, and
infure its Collection. It is therefore a great Supine-
nefs, to fay no worfe, not to avail ourfelves of a
Circumftance fo favourable to our Trade, fo totally
in our own Power: And thofe Perfons would be hard
put to it, to affign any Reafon, why the Manufacturers of *Germany*, *Holland*, *Flanders*, or *France*,
fhould be fuffered to buy *English* Coals at a cheaper
Rate (which they now do) than the Manufacturers
of the City of *London*, the Metropolis of the whole
Kingdom. — Were the Duty doubled, thefe Foreigners would be obliged to pay near 30,000 *l* a
Year more than they now do · And this Sum would
go a confiderable Way towards fupplying the Expences of the prefent War, at the fame Time that it
would promote our own Manufactures.

F I N I S

WILLIAM KNOX, THE INTEREST OF THE MERCHANTS

William Knox, *The Interest of the Merchants and Manufacturers of Great-Britain, in the Present Contest with the Colonies, Stated and Considered* (Cork: Mary Edwards, 1775). National Library of Ireland, shelfmark Cork 1775(2).

William Knox (1732–1810), a government official and pamphleteer, was Irish by birth. In 1756 he was appointed Provost Marshal in the colony of Georgia. During the five years he spent there, besides serving the empire, he became a lavishly rich rice farmer and a slave owner. He returned to London in 1762, officially as Georgia's colonial agent, but his first-hand expertise of the plantation system was also used in many different contexts. Increasingly, however, Knox became unpopular in Georgia because of his defence of British dominance and in particular for his defence of the Stamp Act of 1765. In the same year he was dismissed by the Georgian Assembly as a typical British usurper and an enemy of the rights of the colonists.

In order to show just how important colonies were to Britain, Knox published a number of tracts, of which *The Present State of the Nation* (London: J. Almon, 1768) is perhaps the best known. In that text he presents the orthodox view of the role of plantations for the mother country as well as providing a vision of an even greater British empire. According to Knox, plantations were beneficial both to the mother country and the colony. However, only a year after this he published another tract, *The Controversy between Great Britain and her Colonies Reviewed* (London: J. Almon, 1769), which is much more negative in tone towards the plantation system. It highlights at an early point the upcoming conflict between Britain and her American colonies, which would some years later explode into bloody fighting. In this pamphlet he argues for reforms and reconciliation. Appointed as under-secretary in the American department he obviously sat on two chairs; on the one hand fighting rebellious Americans and on the other hand promoting reform (and defending his possessions in Georgia). But it was all too late and as a consequence of the War of Independence his estates in Georgia were confiscated.[1]

This text has been rekeyed due to the rarity and poor preservation of the original. The original page breaks are indicated by forward slashes.

---

1   For further information on Knox, see his entry in *Oxford Dictionary of National Biography* (Oxford: Oxford University Press, 2004), written by Leland J. Bellot.

THE

INTEREST

OF THE

Merchants and Manufacturers

OF

GREAT–BRITAIN,

IN THE

PRESENT CONTEST

WITH THE

COLONIES,

STATED AND CONSIDERED.

C O R K:

Printed for MARY EDWARDS, Bookseller and Stationer, in Castle-street; by DENNIS DONNOGHUE, Broad-lane.

M,DCC, LXXV. /

THE contest between Great-Britain and her Colonies, being now arrived at a height that calls for some speedy decision, and this contest having been represented as only a dispute between the administration and the colonies, the following short state of the case is submitted to the consideration of every candid Englishman; from which it will appear, how far the merchants and traders in this country are interested in it, and on which side they ought to wish the decision to fall.

IT is admitted on the part of Great-Britain, that the Colonies are part of the dominions of the Crown, that the inhabitants are the subjects of the Crown, and intitled, by birth, to all the right and franchises of Englishmen, born within the island of Great-Britain; and in consequence every native of the Colonies is eligible to, and man of them actually enjoy offices and employment in the state, and seats in parliament, and may be the King's chief ministers in Great-Britain. In all foreign countries, they have the same protection with the King's English subjects, and enjoy the same advantages of treaties and alliances. Their persons and properties are equally protected by the laws of England, and they may, equally with the natives of Great-Britain, become Proprietors, by purchase or inheritance, of any land within the island of Great-Britain. /

The possessions of the Crown in America are immensely extensive, and the island of Great-Britain, compared with them, appears very inconsiderable. No art or power can enlarge Great-Britain, but there is abundant scope in America for making Additions, still more extensive, to what the Crown already possesses there.

THIS most important difference in the circumstances of the two territories requires a different plan of policy to be adopted in respect to the culture and improvement of each. But still the personal rights of the inhabitants ought to continue the same, and the prosperity and happiness of the subjects in the Colonies ought to be equally attended to, and promoted by government, as that of the subjects in England, for they are equally the King's subjects and Englishmen.

THE lands in America have been granted by the Crown on very cheap terms to the occupiers; and where a country is so very extensive, and the inhabitants few, the lands must continue cheap for many ages, in comparison of the price of lands in Great-Britain. Should then the occupier of the American lands cultivate the same products as are cultivated in Great-Britain, and have equally liberty to carry them to the same market, they must presently destroy the commerce and culture of Great-Britain, by selling at a less price – Now nothing could argue greater folly and wickedness, any government, than the suffering the people of the ancient dominions to be destroyed, for the sake of raising a new Empire, and new subjects in / another part of the world – Wisdom, justice and policy, therefore, required that the means to be used to forward the prosperity of the new dominions, should be such as not to injure the old; and that, where all parts cannot have the same advantages, compensation should be made, for what is with-held in one way, by the grant of superior advantages in another.

THE right to the soil of America is allowed to have been in the Crown of England, antecedent to the settlement of any English subjects there for the first, and all future adventurers carried with them grants from the Crown, of the lands on which they settled; and all the lands in the Colonies are at this day held by their occupiers, under titles derived from the Crown. The Crown had, therefore, a right to prescribe conditions to those who obtained those grants; and the grantees were bound, in law and equity, to a performance of those conditions. Moreover, the adventures in this new country stood in need of the assistance and succour of their fellow subjects in England. They were unable to subsist, much less to protect themselves. The bounty, the confidence, and humanity of individuals in England were freely exercised towards them; and the power of the state, raised and maintained at the sole expence of the people of England, was fully exerted in their behalf. The people of England have, therefore, a right to reap advantage from the success of the adventurers. /

UNDER these two titles, of a right to the soil in the Crown, and a right to compensation in the people of England, let us view the conduct of the Legislature (which comprehends both) towards the Colonies. In respect to the persons of the natives of the Colonies, no distinction or difference has ever been made. There is not a single Act of Parliament, from the first establishment of the Colonies to this day, which makes a distinction between a man born in England, and a man born in America. The original equality has been inviolably adhered to. The same law and rights are for a native of America in England, as for an Englishman. And an Englishman is, in America, subject to the same law, and claims no other rights than a native there.

THE most violent partizan of the Colonies can here then have no ground of complaint; for neither the Crown or the people of England have here made any claim, or sought compensation.

THE lands of America, and their products, have alone been the objects upon which they have made any demands; and whether they have asserted their claims in an arbitrary, cruel, and unjust manner, as the Colonies say they have, we shall soon see.

THE people of England and the American adventurers being so differently circumstanced, it required no great sagacity to discover that, as there were many commodities which America could supply on better terms than they could be raised in England, so must it be much more for the / Colonies advantage to take others from England, than attempt to make them themselves. The American lands were cheap, covered with woods, and abounded with native commodities. The first attention of the settlers was necessarily engaged in cutting down the timber, and clearing the ground for culture for before they had supplied themselves with provisions, and had hands to spare from agriculture, it was impossible they could set about manufacturing. England, therefore, undertook to supply them with manufactures, and either purchased herself, or found markets for the timber the Colonies cut down upon their lands, or the fish they caught upon their coasts. It was soon discovered that the tobacco plant was a native of, and flourished in Virginia. It had been also planted in England, and was found to delight in the soil. The Legislature, however, wisely and equitably considering that England had variety of products, and Virginia had no other to buy her necessaries with, passed an act prohibiting the people of England from planting tobacco, and thereby giving the monopoly of that plant to the Colonies. As the inhabitants increased, and the lands became more cultivated, further and new advantages were thrown in the way of the American Colonies. All foreign markets, as well as Great-Britain, were open for their timber and provisions, and the British West India Islands were prohibited from purchasing those commodities from any other than them. And since England has found itself in danger of wanting a supply of timber, and it has / been judged necessary to confine the export from America to Great Britain and Ireland, full and ample indemnity has been given to the Colonies for the loss of a choice of markets in Europe, by very large bounties paid out of the revenue of Great-Britain, upon the importation of American timber. And as a further encouragement and reward to them for clearing their lands, bounties are given upon the tar and pitch, which are made from their decayed and useless trees; and the very ashes of their lops and branches, are made of value by the late bounty on American pot-ashes. The soil and climate of the Northern Colonies having been found well adapted to the culture of flax and hemp, bounties equal to half the first cost of those commodities have been granted by Parliament, payable out of the British revenue, upon their importation into Great-Britain. The growth of rice in the Southern Colonies has been greatly encouraged, by prohibiting the importation of that grain into the British dominions from other parts, and allowing it to be transported from the Colonies to the foreign territories in America, and even to the Southern parts of Europe. Indigo has been nurtured in those Colonies by great parliamentary bounties, which have been long paid upon the importation into Great-Britain; and of late are allowed to remain, even when it is carried out again to foreign markets. Silk and wine have also been objects of parliamentary munificence and will one day probably become considerable American products under that encouragement. /

IN which of these instances, it may be demanded has the Legislature shewn itself partial to the people of England and unjust to the Colonies? or wherein have the Colonies been injured? We hear much of the restraints under which the trade of the Colonies is laid by Acts of Parliament, for the advantage of Great-Britain, but the restraints under which the people of Great-Britain are laid by Acts of Parliament for the advantage of the Colonies, are carefully kept out of sight; and yet upon a comparison, the one will be found full as grievous as the other. For, is it a greater hardship on the Colonies, to be confined in some instances to the markets of Great-Britain for the sale of their commodities, than it is on the people of Great-Britain to be obliged to buy those commodities from them only? If the island Colonies are obliged to give the people of Great-Britain the pre-emption of their sugar and coffee, is it not a greater hardship on the people of Great-Britain to be restrained from purchasing sugar and Coffee from other countries, where they could get those commodities much cheaper than the Colonies make them pay for them? Could not our manufacturers have Indigo much better and cheaper from France and Spain than from Carolina? and yet is there not a duty imposed by Acts of Parliament on French and Spanish Indigo, that it may come to our manufacturers at a dearer rate than Carolina Indigo, though a bounty is also given out of *the money* of the people of England to the Carolina Planter, to / enable him to sell his Indigo upon a *par* with the French and Spanish? But the instance which has already been taken notice of, the Act which prohibits the culture of the tobacco plant in Great-Britain or Ireland, is still more in point, and a more striking proof of the justice and impartiality of the supreme Legislature; for what restraints, let me ask, are the Colonies laid under, which bear so strong marks of hardship, as the prohibiting the farmers in Great-Britain and Ireland from raising, upon their own lands, a product which is become almost a necessary of life to them and their families? And this most extraordinary restraint is laid upon them, for the avowed and sole purpose of giving Virginia and Maryland a monopoly of that commodity, and obliging the people of Great-Britain and Ireland to buy all the tobacco they consume from them, at the prices they think fit to sell it for. The annals of no country that ever planted Colonies, can produce such an instance as this of regard and kindness to their Colonies, and of restraint upon the inhabitants of the Mother Country for their advantage. Nor is there any restraint laid upon the inhabitants of the Colonies in return, which carries with it so great appearance of hardship, although the people of Great-Britain and Ireland have, from their regard and affection to the Colonies, submitted to it without a murumr for near a Century.

IT is true the Legislature, in this as well as in other instances, has had a view to divert the Colonists from manufacturing; but has not that / object been pursued by means the most generous and just? Ought the Colonists to complain that they are *diverted* from working up their flax and hemp, by getting a better price for it rough, that they could hope to obtain by manufacturing it? Or is it blameable in the Legislature to excite them to the culture of commodities which yield a better profit from their cheap lands, than they could have by employing their labour in manufacturing? But why do they not manufacture? They are not hindered from making any commodity they might think fit for their own use, erecting any machine for the purpose, except mills for slitting iron. The only reason is, that they find it more their interest to cultivate the lands, and attend the fishery, than to manufacture. Their interest it is alone which restrains them, and such is the wisdom, the equity, the bounty the government, they are so impatient of, as employ no other means to *divert* them from manufactures, than by giving them greater profits for their labour in other things. This is a point which cannot be too much inculcated, for it ought to be universally known and considered, especially by the trading part of this kingdom. I therefore repeat it, that the only means employed by the Legislature, for *diverting* the Colonies from manufacturing, is the giving them better prices for their labour in other things: And the Colonies well know this to be the case, and they conduct themselves according to that knowledge,; for in every instance where they think they can employ their labour profitably in manufactures, they do / it. This the people of England do not know; but they ought to be made acquainted with it: they imagine the inhabitants in the Colonies are prohibited from making any thing for themselves, much more from trading in their own manufactures: Whereas the fact is, they are prohibited from making no one thing for their own use, or from exporting any one of their own manufactures, except hats, wool, and woolen goods. And they do make many things, and export several manufactures, to the exclusion of English manufactures of the same kinds. The New-England people import from the foreign and the British islands, very large quantities of cotton, which they spin and work up with a linen yarn into a stuff, like that made in Manchester, with which they clothe themselves and their neighbours. Hats are manufactured in Carolina, Pennsylvania, and in other Colonies. Soap and candles, and all kinds of wood-work, are made in the Northern Colonies, and exported to the Southern. Coaches, chariots, chaises, and chairs, are also made in the Northern Colonies, and sent down to the Southern. Coach-harness, and many other kinds of leather manufactures, are likewise made in the Northern Colonies, and sent down to the Southern; and large quantities of shoes have lately been exported from thence to the West-India Islands. Linens are made to a great amount in Pennsylvania; and cordage and other hemp manufactures are carried on in many places with great success: and foundery ware, axes, and other iron tools and utensils, are also become / articles of commerce, with which the Southern Colonies are supplied from the Northern. Thus while the Legislature is paying the money of the people of England in bounties to one part of the American subjects, another is employed on rivalling the people of England in several of their most valuable manufactures.

THUS far, at least, the conduct of Great-Britain towards the Colonies cannot justly be taxed with oppression, nor the comparative situation of America deemed unequal and disadvantageous: But we are told by the advocates for American claims that the profit of all their labours centers here and that the inhabitants of America are condemned to work for the people of England; let us therefore examine the truth of these two propositions. – If it be true that the inhabitants of America are condemned to work for the people of England, is it not equally true that the people of England are condemned to work for the people in the Colonies? Nay, not for their fellow-subjects there only, but for the slaves of their fellow subjects! If a planter in Virginia raises tobacco for the English merchant, does not the English manufacturer make him clothing for himself and his Negroes in return; and wherein can the one be said to work for the other's advantage, more than the other does for his? Do any of the Colonies send their products to England for nothing or do they take any thing from England in payment which they do not want? Does England fix prices upon their products, and say, You shall sell them to us for so much; or does she insist upon / their buying her commodities at higher prices than her own natives pay, or than she sells them for to other countries? Nothing of all this is pretended to be the case; then pray in what sense is it that the people of the Colonies can be said to work for the people of England, other than that in which the people of England work for them? The thresher may be said, it is true, to work for the miller; but does not the miller work also for the thresher? But the profit of all the labour of the Colonies centers in England. If this be true, the consequence will plainly shew it; for no state or society of men was ever known to thrive by unprofitable labour. Whence then arises the present wealth and greatness of America (of which we hear so much upon other occasions) if England has reaped the fruit of all the labour of the Colonies? The settlers, we all know, did not carry great riches with them, and whence could they have acquired them, but from the profits of their labour? But the trade of England, say they, has been greatly augmented by the Colonies. It is by no means clear that the same increase would not have happened if the Colonies had never existed; for England had many avenues open for her commercial industry. But, without pursuing that consideration, from what source did the Colonies derive the ability, and the means of trading with England? Who paid for the axe and the saw with which they cut down the tree, and made it into boards, to cover their huts at their first landing? Or through whose credit have they since built towns, improved their farms, and erected for / themselves stately houses? Is it not to the English merchants they are indebted for all their opulence? We see a recent instance of this in the Ceded Islands; whilst the English merchants gave them credit, the adventures were making large strides to wealth and grandeur. The value of lands was every day raising, plantations were settling, and towns springing out of the woods; but the instant that credit was with-held, the bubble burst, and the airy scene vanished like a dream; distress and calamity succeeded to opulence and parade, and the highest estimated lands can no longer find purchasers at any a price: Now, had the English merchants continued to give credit, and make advances for these adventurers, there is no doubt their projects would at length have succeeded; they would have raised products, and, by industry and good management acquired fortunes. What then should we have thought of them, or what ought we to have thought of them, if, when they came to make remittances to the English merchants, they should have complained, that it was hard they should be condemned to work for the people of England; that England reaped all the fruits of their labour and industry, and that it was the highest cruelty and injustice to oblige them to send their products to England, that the English merchants might gain a commission on the sale of them.

THE Northern Colonies, it is true, have not had such ample credit with the English merchants as the Islands, but the circumstances under which the plant-ers in both made their settlements, are / not so dissimilar as to render what has been stated respecting the one, inapplicable to the other. The great amount of their debt to the English merchants, is a full proof that it was upon the stock of the people of England they have hitherto subsisted.

THE merchants in the Colonies, no more than the planters in the continent, are wealthy men. They buy their goods in England upon nine months credit at least; the planter is supplied by them, throughout the year, upon the credit of his crop at the end of it. The planter has his house to build, or improvements to make, or new land to clear and take in, all which requires ready money, and therefore, when his first crop comes, he must sell it for cash, and cannot pay the merchant any thing towards the reduction of his debt that year. The acquisition of the next year's crop requires a fresh advance; hence the planter becomes indebted to the merchant for two year's supply before he makes him any payment; and as it very seldom happens that at the end of the second year he pays the expense of one, he goes on increasing his debt, but at the same time increasing his estate in a much greater proportion; and all this time the English merchant, who supports the whole, is without any returns.

THUS it is that England reaps the advantage of all the toil and labour of the Colonies. She pays for the purchase of the land, for the labour employed in clear-ing it, for the maintaining the stock necessary for its cultivation; her return is a commission upon the sale of the produce, with a / moderate interest, not very well paid, upon the capital advanced, while all the benefit of the increase value belongs solely to the Americans.

THE truth of what has been advanced will be still more evident from a com-parison of the state of the Colonies of other nations with our own. We have seen the slow progress the French made in Canada the many years they had it; and the large strides it is making to wealth and importance since it became a British Colony. Grenade too has flourished in a still greater degree, and the same cause has wrought the happy change in the circumstances of both, which is no other than the superior credit given to the planters by the English merchants, to what they had from the French merchants. Now if we inquire into the cause of this unbounded confidence and credit given by the English merchants to the Colonies, from which the Colonies have reaped so great advantage, it will come out to be *the security which they have for their property by the operation of the law of England in the Colonies;* they give no such credit to the subjects of other states, either in Europe or America: And yet there are countries in which they might lay out their money to greater profit than in the British Colonies; but in foreign countries they cannot be certain of a legal security for their property, or a fair and effectual means of recovering it; whereas in the British Colonies they know the laws of England follow their property, and secures it for them in the deepest recesses of the woods. Take from them that security, and there is an end of their confidence, and consequently an effectual check to the / prosperity of the Colonies. And indeed good reason it should be so, for there is no want of evidence to shew how willing the Colonies are to avail themselves of Acts of their own Assemblies to injure their British creditors; witness the attempts in Jamaica and Virginia to make the lands and negroes freehold, and not liable to the payment of book debts; so that a planter might buy land and negroes on English credit, and leave them to his children, without paying a shilling to the English merchant, with whose money he bought them; and witness also a late act of the assembly of Grenade, postponing the payments due to their English Creditors for Eighteen Months. These and such like practices in the Colonies, gave occasion to the Act of Parliament the 5th of George the Second, for subjecting lands and negroes in the Colonies to the payment of English book debts, which may truly be called the *palladium* of Colony credit, and the English merchants grand security; and yet this Act of Parliament is one of those which are now complained of by the Colonies, and the British merchants are modestly desired to apply to Parliament for its repeal, and thus ruin their trade and fortunes with their own hands.* But / indeed a repeal of this or any other Act, would not be necessary to destroy their

---

* The following petition of several merchants of London to the King in the year 1732, and the report of the Lords of Trade thereupon, will shew the necessity of the interference of Parliament in the British merchants behalf, and the great ground there was for passing the Act of that year, for the merchants' security, which the Colonies now want / to set side.

'Sheweth,

That the merchants trading to the said Colonies and Plantations have great sums of money due to them from the inhabitants, and, as the laws now stand in some of the Colonies and Plantations, your Majesty's subjects residing in Great-Britain are left without any remedy for the recovery of their just debts, or have such remedy only as is very partial and precarious; whereby they are like to be considerable sufferers in their property, and are *greatly discouraged in their trade to America:*

security, if the / Colonies attain their avowed and main object, the setting aside the authority of Parliament; for if it be once admitted, that Parliament has no authority to make laws to bind the Colonies, all its acts instantly become waste-paper, and the merchants can no longer apply to parliament to give them redress against any unjust proceedings of an American Assembly. Whoever, therefore, goes about to overthrow the authority of Acts of Parliament in the Colonies, ought to be considered as the assassins of the British merchants' security, and, by destroying their confidence in the Colonies, force them to with-hold their credit, and thereby do the greatest injury to the Colonies themselves. /

THE right of the Parliament to impose taxes, or the expediency of exercising it over the Colonies, is now no longer the subject of dispute. All the late declarations of the Colonies deny, in express terms, the authority of the Legislature to bind them in any case whatsoever. This is the avowed purpose of their opposition to the execution of Acts of Parliament, and of their obstruction of the commerce of the people of England.

I ACQUIT them of any intention of separating from Great-Britain; for I believe them too wise to renounce all the advantages of being treated as Englishmen in Great-Britain and throughout the world; of enjoying the protection of her fleet and armies equally with the people of England; and at the same time, neither contributing revenue to their support, or dealing with her for any thing which they can buy cheaper, or sell dearer elsewhere. They would no doubt like to continue to have the monopoly of supplying the British West-India Islands with lumber and provisions; to have the monopoly of supplying Great-Britain

---

That in several of the said Colonies and Plantations greater and higher duties and impositions are laid on the ships and goods belonging to your Petitioners, and other persons residing in this kindom, than are laid on the goods and ships of persons inhabiting the said Colonies and plantations to the great discouragement of Great-Britain.

> Wherefore your Petitioners most humbly beseech your Majesty, that your Majesty will be graciously pleased to take the premises into your royal consideration, and give your Petitioner such relief as to your Majesty, in your great wisdom, shall seem meet.'

This petition having been referred to the Lords of Trade, their Lordships, in their report thereon, take notice,

'That the difficulty attending the execution of the law, after a verdict hath been obtained in favour of the plaintiff, / consists in *a privilege claimed by some of the Colonies* particularly that of Jamaica, *to exempt their houses, lands, and tenements, and in some places, their negroes also, from being extended for debt*; but we conceive it to be highly reasonable, that all lands, tenements, hereditaments, and negroes, throughout the several Colonies and plantations, should be made liable to the payment of just debts and demands.

These two (alluding to another matter mentioned by their Lordships also) last mentioned grievances have been more than once recommended to the Governors of Virginia and Jamaica for redress. But *the assemblies of those Colonies could never be induced to divest themselves of these privileges by any act of their own*; and therefore, in our humble opinion, those points may be very proper objects for a Parliament's consideration in Great-Britain, as they are of importance to your Majesty's subjects trading to America.' /

and Ireland with tobacco; to receive large bounties upon other of their products out of the revenue of England; to have the advantage of fishing on the English fishing-banks of New-foundland; and in the gulph and river of the English conquered Colony of Quebec, provided they continued to pay no revenue, were subject to no restraints upon their trade, but might carry their commodities wherever they thought fit, import all forts of goods from all countries, and lay / out their money wherever they found they could buy cheapest. This is all very natural, and no one can blame the Colonies for seeking what is so evidently for their own interest; but that they should expect the people of England, the trading part especially, to countenance them in their pursuits of a plan so manifestly ruinous to them, is indeed such a proof of their contempt for our understandings, as no people ever gave before. They plainly tell the British merchants, 'Gentlemen, we have now made fortunes out of your capital, and we find that the people in England pay such heavy taxes for the payment of the interest of a debt, which they contracted in our defence; and for the maintenance of a military force, of which we enjoy the protection; that some of their manufactures come higher charged to us, than we can get the like for from Holland or France: We also find, that from the same cause they cannot afford to give as high prices for some of our Commodities, as we can sell them for in other countries. Now there are certain Acts of Parliament, which oblige us to come to you for what we want; and to carry to you many of our commodities in payment, we desire therefore that you will assist us in our endeavours to set aside the authority of these laws, that we may trade where we will; and come no more to you but when we cannot do so well elsewhere. There is another thing too, which we want you to join us in; we are prevented by an Act of Parliament from entailing our estates to the / prejudice of our English creditors; we now owe them about four millions, and if this Act was out of our way, we could make all our families rich at once, by purchasing lands, and building houses, with this money, and settling them upon our children, instead of paying our English creditors: but as we are afraid the Parliament might perceive our drift, in applying for repeals of these laws, or if they even repealed them *now*, they might hereafter re-enact them, or others of a like nature, which would defeat our purpose of rising upon the runs of England; we have taken up a resolution of getting rid of all these Acts at once, and at the same time making ourselves secure against all future Acts that might be made to our prejudice, or for your benefit. This resolution is no other than to deny the authority of the Legislature to make any Acts whatever to bind us. In this our grand purpose, we hope you will do all you can by petitioning, instructing, and remonstrating in our behalf; for if you do not join us in destroying yourselves, we tell you once for all, that we will neither buy goods of you, nor pay you for those we have already bought, for we are determined to carry our point by one means or another.'

I APPEAL to the understandings of my countrymen whether this is an exaggerated representation of the Colony claims, as set forth and stated in their several pamphlets, and the resolutions of their public assemblies. And I think I need not use any further arguments to convince the / merchants and manufacturers of Great-Britain, how fatal to their interests the success of the Colonies in their designs must be. The continuance of their trade to the Colonies, clearly and entirely depends upon the laws of England having authority there. It is their operation which binds the commerce of the Colonies to this country. It is their operation which gives security to the property of the trader sent thither. Give up the authority of Parliament and there is an end to your trade, and a total loss of your property. But if that authority is supported and maintained, the trade of the Colonies must remain to Great-Britain, and the property you intrust them with will remain secure, protected by Acts of Parliament made in your behalf.

FINIS.

JOSIAH CHILD ET AL., SELECT DISSERTATIONS ON COLONIES

Josiah Child, Charles Davenant and William Wood, *Select Dissertations on Colonies and Plantations* (London: W. Hay, 1775). British Library, shelfmark 103.c.6.

This entry comprises three different texts by three different authors, of which Josiah Child and Charles Davenant are well-known economic authors while we know very little of the third, William Wood. The texts were written at very different times – in 1669 (Child), 1698 (Davenant) and 1718 (Wood) – and only later compiled into a book (1775). For late eighteenth-century writers such as Adam Smith and David Hume these three texts must have been regarded as presenting the orthodox views on colonies and plantations, and as such they were targets for critic of the 'mercantile' system. Although the exact purpose of compliling these texts is unknown, it is clear that the future of the American colonies (and to some extent the colonial system) was a highly-debated topic at this time. This compilation was published in the year the War of Independence broke out, and one year before the Declaration of Independence was written (as well as one year before Adam Smith's *Wealth of Nations* was published).

Josiah Child (1630–99) was the well-known Director and later Chairman of the East India Company. He started out as a Whig, but with wealth and fortune – he died one of wealthiest men in England – his sympathies changed towards the Tories. Especially during the short reign of Charles II he and the East India Company had great success. After 1688, the Company's fortunes changed for the worse, but Child himself seems not to have been finacially affected by the Company's increasing problems. As an economic writer Child was able to reach a great audience. His first published tract, *Brief Observations concerning Trade and Interest of Money* (London: E. Calvert and H. Mortlock, 1668), was written order to advocate an 'abatement' of interest by law to 4 per cent. He wrote the tract mainly for practical political reasons during his work for the Council of Trade. In 1693 he published *A New Discourse of Trade* (London: John Everingham), in which he dealt with topics such as the role of merchant companies, the Navigation Acts, the employment of the poor, overseas plantations and 'the Ballance of trade'. His main object with this text, however, was to explain why the Dutch had been able to achieve such a wonderful increase in their foreign trade and shipping. For this purpose he presented a list of fifteen reasons, including that the Dutch had lower interest rates, they were more experienced merchants, they had established a great fishing industry in the Nordic Sea, they encouraged (and enumerated) new inventors, and they had established an outstanding ship-building industry.

However, beyond these particularities he was searching for some general principles which could make a commmonwealth rich and powerful. According to Child, national wealth is mainly a result of production and manufactures; he was by no means a follower of the favourable balance of trade dogma. If well organized (i.e. if it encouraged production at home and served the principle of import substitution), foreign trade would support production and enable employment to grow at a fast rate. He also believed that an orderly colonial or plantation system could do much to encourage domestic production, most importantly by delivering raw materials to be worked up in the motherland's factories (see further the Introduction to this volume).

Charles Davenant (1656–1714) was a political and economic writer as well as a government official who, being committed to the rule of James II, lost all his positions after 1688. He was on the pay-roll of the East India Company during the 1690s. It was also during this decade that he began to write and publish economic tracts. In 1695 his first major work appeared, *An Essay Upon the Ways and Means of Supplying the War* (London: Jacob Tonson, 1695), which gained him some reputation. Another tract in defence of the East India Company followed in 1696, entitled *An Essay on the East India Trade* (London: n.p., 1696). After the succession of Queen Anne in 1702 he was back in public service again, and he was made Inspector General of Exports and Imports.

As an economist Davenant must on the whole be 'classed as an adherent of the mercantile theory'.[1] However, he was by no means a follower of the traditional favourable balance of trade doctrine. On the contrary, he explicitly critized the idea that a great amount of money was equivalent to great wealth for a nation. Rather he was a protectionist, arguing for infant-industry tariffs, but of quite a liberal stance.[2]

Nothing is known of William Wood except that he published this pamphlet on plantations. He here puts forward the benefits of plantations in accordance with the views of others at this time. For further discussion of these arguments, see the Introduction to this volume.

---

1   *Palgrave's Dictionary of Political Economy*, ed. H. Higgs, 3 vols (London and New York: Macmillan, 1894), vol. 1, pp. 483–4.
2   W. J. Ashley, *Surveys: Historic and Economic* (London: Longman, 1900).

SELECT

DISSERTATIONS

O N

Colonies and Plantations.

B Y

Those CELEBRATED AUTHORS,

Sir JOSIAH CHILD,

CHARLES D'AVENANT, LL. D.

AND

Mr. WILLIAM WOOD.

WHEREIN

The NATURE of PLANTATIONS, and their CONSEQUENCES to GREAT BRITAIN, are seriously considered. And a PLAN proposed, which may settle the UNHAPPY DIFFERENCES between GREAT BRITAIN and AMERICA.

LONDON:

Printed and sold by W. HAY, at the Artists Academy, near Exeter Exchange, Strand.

M DCC LXXV.

(Price One Shilling and Sixpence)

INTRODUCTION.

THE Work here prefented to the Public, containing Diſſertations on Colonies and Plantations, feems, at this critical Conjuncture, to ftand in Need of little Apology or Introduction; fince the Thoughts of every Perfon, particularly thofe celebrated for their Knowledge in Trade, muft be acceptable to all *Englifh* Readers; and a Satisfaction to our Politicians to be informed of the Sentiments of thofe, who maturely confidered the Subject fo many Years ago. The bare Name of Sir JOSIAH CHILD, who wrote in 1669, ftamps a Credit upon every Thing that comes from his Pen: And, as obferved before, needs no Apology for the Extracts of his Works; nor for thofe of Dr. D'AVENANT, whofe Difcourfe upon the ·Plantation Trade was publifhed in 1698. This great Author had likewife a peculiar Advantage from the Poft he enjoyed, (of Infpector General of the Exports and Imports), which gave him an Opportunity of a thorough Information relative to every Thing which concerns the Trade of *Great Britain:* And as he laid the Plan which has been adopted, and carried on ever fince, under the Title of *the Plantation Office,* it is prefumed, the Obfervations contained in this Pamphlet for regulating the Bufinefs of the feveral Coiv **INTRODUCTION.**

lonies in *America*, will be acceptable to the Public.
He recommended that two Deputies should be
chosen, from each Province, to meet once a Year or
oftner; and that His Majesty should appoint a Commissioner, who should take the Chair, and preside in
the said Congress. That the Meeting should be held
at *New York*, as being near the Center; and that
the Governor thereof should be the King's High
Commissioner, during the Sessions, after the Manner of *Scotland.* Dr. *D'Avenant* likewise inserts the
Business proper for the Congress, and represents such
a Constitution to resemble the Court of the *Amphictiones*, being a Council where the general Affairs of *Greece* were debated; which, if they could
have preserved in its original Purity, and according
to it's first Design, that Country had not been so
early a Conquest to the *Romans.* The next Author
from whom the third Dissertation is taken, is Mr.
William Wood, a Person who has written very ably
upon the Subject of Trade, as appears by his
Work published in the Year 17?8.

His Writings are in a plain Style, which show
that he considered Matter more than Manner:
His Book is entitled a SURVEY OF TRADE, wherein is contained, likewise, *Considerations on Money and
Bullion.*

From the above Writers we may observe, that
Great Britain, as well as our Northern and Southern Colonies in *America*, are closely united together in Interest; and that a regular System
should be adopted, so as to render the three several
Estates one compact Body; nor would those, who
are Friends to the general System, wish that any
Thing should divide them; the unhappy Situation in which the *Massachuset's* and *New York* are
now brought, may, perhaps, require half a Century to recover; and if they should continue to
maintain a civil War in their Country, burning
their

INTRODUCTION. ❦

their Towns, and deſtroying their Lands, will
make them unfit for Trade whether with us or any
other Nation ; but as to the Part of *Great Britain,*
they may repair that Injury by *Canada,* and make
that Country and People rich; which Favour would
otherwiſe have been conferred on our preſent Colonies.   Theſe Obſervations are made chiefly with
a View of ſhowing the *Americans* the Stake they
riſque in the preſent Conteſt ; and in Hopes, even
yet, ſome Plan of Conciliation may be adopted;
and if any Thing can be ſuggeſted from this Publication, the Editor will think himſelf happy in
having promoted the mutual Welfare of *Great
Britain* and *America.*

E R R A T A.

Page 37. Line 6.   for 1788, read 1688.
—— 39. —— laſt but two. — *again* —— *a Gain of.*
—— 45. —— 9.   — *Principle* —— *Principal.*

SELECT

SELECT

DISSERTATIONS

O N

Colonies and Plantations.

DISSERTATION I.

The Nature of Plantations, and their Confequences to GREAT BRITAIN, *ferioufly confidered.*

By Sir JOSIAH CHILD.

THE Trade of our *Englifh* Plantations in *America,* being now of as great bulk, and employing as much Shipping, as moft of the Trades of this Kingdom, it feems not unneceffary to difcourfe more at large concerning the Nature of Plantations, and the good or evil confequences of them in relation to this and other Kingdoms; and the rather becaufe fome Gentlemen of no mean capacities are of opinion, that his Majeftie's Plantations abroad have very much prejudiced this Kingdom, by draining us of our People; for the confirmation of which Opinion, they urge the Example of Spain, which they fay is almoft ruined by the depopulation which the *Weft Indies* hath occafioned; to the End, therefore, a more particular Scrutiny may be made into this matter, I fhall humbly offer my Opinion in the following Propofitions, and then give thofe Reafons of Probability, which prefently occur to my Memory, in confirmation of each Propofition.

1. Firft I agree, *That Lands* (though excellent) *without Hands proportionable, will not enrich any Kingdom.*

A

3. *That*

(2)

2. *That whatever tends to the depopulating of a King-dom, tends to the Impoverifhment of it.*

3. *That moft Nations in the civilized Parts of the World are more or lefs rich or poor, proportionably to the Paucity or Plenty of their People, and not to the fterility or fruitfulnefs of their Lands.*

4. *I do not agree that our People in* England *are, in any confiderable Meafure, abated by Reafon of our Foreign Plantations, but propofe to prove the Contrary.*

5. *I am of Opinion, that we had, immediately before the late Plague, many more People in* England, *than we had before the inhabiting of* Virginia, New England, *Barba-does, and the reft of our* American *Plantations.*

6. *That all Colonies or Plantations do endamage their Mother-kingdoms, whereof the Trades of fuch Plantations are not confined by fevere Laws, and good executions of thofe Laws, to the Mother-kingdom.*

7. *That the* Dutch *will reap the greateft advantage by all Colonies iffuing from any Kingdom of* Europe, *whereof the Trades are not fo ftriftly confined to the proper Mother-kingdoms.*

8. *That the* Dutch, (though they thrive fo exceed-ingly in Trade), *will in Probability never endamage this Kingdom, by the Growth of their Plantations.*

9. *That neither the* French, Spanifh, *nor* Portugueze, *are much to be feared on that account, nor for the fame, but for other caufes.*

10. *That it is more for the Advantage of* England, *that* Newfoundland *fhould remain unplanted, than that Colonies fhould be fent or permitted to go thither, to in-habit with a Governor, Laws, &c.*

11. *That* New England *is the moft prejudicial Planta-tion to the Kingdom of* England.

I. *That Lands, though in their Nature excellently good, without Hands proportionable, will not enrich any King-dom.*

This Firft Propofition, I fuppofe, will readily be af-fented to by all judicious Perfons, and therefore, for the Proof of it, I fhall only alledge Matter of Faft.

The Land of Palestine, *once the richeft Country in the Univerfe, fince it came under the* Turks *dominion, and confequently unpeopled, is now become the pooreft.*

Andalufia and *Granada*, formerly wonderfully rich, and full of good Towns; fince difpeopled by the

Spaniard,

(3)

Spaniard, by expulfion of the *Moors*, many of their Towns, and brave Country Houfes, are fallen into rubbifh, and their whole Country into miferable Poverty, though their Lands naturally are prodigioufly fertile.

An Hundred other Inftances of Fact might be given to the like Purpofe.

II. *Whatever tends to the populating a Kingdom, tends to the Improvement of it.*

The former Propofition being granted, I fuppofe, this will not be denied; and of the Means, (*viz.* good Laws), whereby any Kingdom may be populated, and confequently enriched, is in effect the Subftance and Defign of all my forgoing Difcourfe; to which, for avoiding Repetition, I muft pray the Reader's Retrofpection.

III. *That moft Nations, in the civilized Parts of the World, are more or lefs Rich or Poor, proportionably to the Paucity or Plenty of their People.*

This Third is a confequent of the Two former Propofitions, and the whole World is a Witnefs to the Truth of it: *The Seven United Provinces are certainly the moft populous Tract of Land in* Chriftendom, *and for their bignefs, undoubtedly the richeft.* England for its bignefs, except our Forefts, Waftes, and Commons, which, by our own Laws and Cuftoms, are barred from Improvement, I hope, is yet a more populous Country than *France*, and confequently richer; I fay, in proportion to its bignefs: *Italy* in like proportion more populous than *France*, and richer; and *France* more populous and richer than *Spain*, &c.

IV. *I do not agree that our People in* England *are in any confiderable Meafure abated, by reafon of our Foreign Plantations, but purpofe to prove the Contrary.*

This I know is a controverted Point, and do believe, that where there is one Man of my Mind, there may be a Thoufand of the Contrary; but I hope, when the following Grounds of my Opinion have been thoroughly examined, there will not be fo many Diffenters.

That very many People now go, and have gone from this Kingdom, almoft every Year for thefe fixty Years paft, and have and do fettle in our Foreign Plantations, is moft certain. But the Firft Queftion will be,

A 2　　　　　　　　　　　　　　　*Whether*

(4)

Whether if England *had no foreign Plantations for thofe* People *to be tranfported unto, they could or would have* ftayed *and lived at Home with us?*

I am of Opinion, they neither would nor could.

To refolve this Queftion, we muft confider what kind of People they were, and are, that have and do tranfport themfelves to our Foreign Plantations.

New England, (as every one knows), *was originally inhabited, and hath fince fucceffively been replenifhed by a* Sort of People *called* Puritans, which could not conform to the *Ecclefiaftical Laws of* England, but being wearied with *Church Cenfures and Perfecutions*, were forced to quit their Fathers Land, to find out New Habitations, as many of them did in *Germany* and *Holland*, as well as at *New England;* and had there not been a *New* England found for fome of them, *Germany* and *Holland* probably had received the reft: But *Old England to be* fure *had loft them all.*

Virginia *and* Barbadoes *were firft peopled by a · loofe* fort of *vagrant People*, vicious and deftitute of Means to live at Home, (being either unfit for Labour, or fuch as could find none to employ themfelves about, or had fo mifbehaved themfelves by Whoring, Thieving, or other Debauchery, that none would fet them on Work), which Merchants, and Mafters of Ships by their Agents, (or Spirits as they were called), gathered up about the Streets of *London*, and other Places, cloathed and tranfported, to be employed upon Plantations; and thefe I fay were fuch, as had there been no *Englifh* Foreign Plantation in the World, could probably never have lived at Home to do Service for their Country, but muft have come to be hanged or ftarved, or died untimely of fome of thofe miferable Difeafes that proceed from Want, and Vice; or elfe have fold themfelves for Soldiers, to be knockt on the Head, or ftarved in the Quarrels of our Neighbours, as many Thoufands of brave *Englifhmen* were in the Low Countries, as alfo in the Wars of *Germany*, *France*, and *Sweden*, &c. or elfe (if they could, by begging, or otherwife, arrive to the Stock of Two Shillings and Sixpence, to waft them over to *Holland*,) become Servants to the *Dutch*, who refufe none.

But the principal Growth and Increafe of the aforefaid Plantations of *Virginia* and *Barbadoes* happened
in,

(5)

in, or immediately after, our late Civil Wars, when the worsted Party by the fate of War, being deprived of their Estates, and some of them having never been bred to Labour, and others made unfit for it by the lazy habit of a Soldier's Life, there wanting Means to maintain them all abroad with his Majesty, many of them betook themselves to the aforesaid Plantations, and great Numbers of *Scotch* Soldiers of his Majesty's Army, after *Worcester* Fight, were by the then prevailing Powers voluntarily sent thither.

Another great swarm, or accession of new Inhabitants to the aforesaid Plantations, as also to *New England*, *Jamaica*, and all other His Majesty's Plantations in the *West Indies*, ensued upon his Majesty's Restoration, when the former prevailing Party being by a Divine Hand of Providence brought under, the Army disbanded, many Officers displaced, and all the new Purchasers of publick Titles dispossessed of their pretended Lands, Estates, &c. many became impoverished, destitute of Employment; and therefore, such as could find no way of living at Home, *and some which feared the re-establishment of the Ecclesiastical Laws, under which they could not live*, were forced to transport themselves, or sell themselves for a few Years, to be transported by others, to the Foreign English Plantations. The constant supply that the said Plantations have since had, hath been such vagrant loose People, as I have before mentioned, picked up especially about the Streets and Suburbs of *London* and *Westminster*, and by Malefactors condemned for Crimes, for which by the Law they deserved to die, and some of those People called *Quakers, banished for meeting on Pretence of Religious Worship.*

Now, if from the Premises it be duly considered, what kind of Persons those have been, by which our Plantations have at all Times been replenished, I suppose it will appear, that such they have been, and under such Circumstances, that if his Majesty had had no foreign Plantations, to which they might have resorted, *England*, however, must have lost them.

To illustrate the Truth whereof a little further, let us consider what Captain *Grant*, the ingenious Author of the *Observations upon the Bills of Mortality*, saith, (page 76.) and in other Places of his Book, concerning

A 3   the

(6)

the City of *London*, and it is not only faid, but unde-
niably proved, *viz. That the City of* London, *let the
Mortality be what it will, by Plague, or otherwife, repairs
its Inhabitants once in Two Years.* And (page 101.)
again, If there be Encouragement for an Hundred Perfons in *London*, (that is, a way how an hundred may
live better than in the Country), the evacuating of a
Third or Fourth Part of that Number, muft foon be fupplied out of the Country, who, in a fhort Time remove
themfelves from thence hither, fo long, until the City,
for want of Receipt and Encouragement, regurgitates
and fends them back.

1. What he hath proved concerning *London*, I fay
of *England* in general, and the fame may be faid of
any Kingdom or Country in the World.

*Such as our Employment is for People, fo many will our
People be;* and if we fhould imagine we have in *England* Employment for One hundred People, and we
have born and bred amongft us One hundred and
Fifty People; I fay, the Fifty muft go away from us or
ftarve, or be hanged to prevent it, whether we had any
Foreign Plantations or not.

2. If by Reafon of the Accommodation of living in
our Foreign Plantations, we have evacuated more of
our People, than we fhould have done, if we had no
fuch Plantations, I fay, with the aforefaid Author in
the cafe of *London*; and if that Evacuation be grown to
an excefs, (which I believe it never did, barely on the
account of the Plantations), that Decreafe would procure its own Remedy; for much want of People
would procure greater Wages, and greater Wages, if
our Laws gave Encouragement, would procure us a
fupply of People, without the Charge of breeding them,
as the *Dutch* are, and always have been fupplied in
their greateft Extremities.

Objection, But it may be faid, Is not the Facility of
being tranfported into the Plantations, together with
the enticeing Methods, cuftomarily ufed to perfuade
People to go thither, and the Encouragement of living there with a People that fpeak our own Language,
ftrong Motives to draw our Peopie from us; and do
they not draw more from us, than otherwife would
leave us, to go into Foreign Countries, where they underftand not the Language?

I anfwer;

(7)

I anfwer; 1*ft.* It is not much more difficult to get a Paffage to *Holland*, than it is to our Plantations.

2*dly*, Many of thofe that go to our Plantations, if they could not go thither, would and muft go into Foreign Countries, though it were Ten Times more diffi-cult to get thither than it is; or elfe, which is worfe, (as it hath been faid), would adventure to be hanged, to prevent begging or ftarving, as too many have done.

3. I do acknowledge, that the facility of getting to the Plantations may caufe fome more to leave us, than would do, if they had none but foreign Countries for Refuge : But then if it be confidered, that our Plantations fpending moftly our *Englifh* Manufactures, and thofe of all Sorts almoft imaginable in egregious Quantities, and employing near Two-thirds of all our *Englifh Shipping, do therein give a conftant Suftenance to it, and may be two hundred thoufand Perfons here at home;* then I muft needs conclude upon the whole Matter, that *we have not the fewer, but the more People in* England, *by Reafon of our* Englifh *Plantations in* America.

Object. 2. But it may be faid, Is not this inferring and arguing againft Senfe and Experience? Doth not all the World fee, that the many noble Kingdoms of *Spain* in *Europe* are almoft depopulated and ruinated, by Reafon of their Peoples flocking over to the *Weft Indies?* And do not all other Nations diminifh in People, after they become poffeffed of foreign Plantations.

Anf. 1. I anfwer, With fubmiffion to better Judgements, that, in my Opinion, *contending for uniformity in Religion, hath contributed Ten Times more to the depopulating of* Spain, *than all the* American *Plantations :* What was it but that, which caufed the Expulfion of fo many Thoufand *Moors*, who had built and inhabited moft of the chief Cities and Towns of *Andalufia*, *Granada*, *Arragon*, and other Parts ? What was it but that and the *Inquifition*, that hath and doth daily expel fuch vaft Numbers of rich *Jews* with their Families and Eftates into *Germany, Italy, Turky, Holland,* and *England?* What was it but that, which caufed thofe vaft and long Wars between that King and the Low Countries, and the effufion of fo much *Spanifh* Blood and Treafure, and the final Lofs of the *Seven Provinces*,

A 4

which

(8)

which we now fee fo prodigioufly rich, and full of
People, while *Spain* is empty and poor, and *Flanders*
thin and weak, in continual fear of being made a prey
to their Neighbours.

Anfw. 2. I anfwer; We muft warily diftinguifh between
Country and Country; for though Plantations may have
drained *Spain* of People, it does not follow; that they
have or will drain *England* or *Holland*; becaufe, where
Liberty and Property are not fo well preferved, and where
Intereft of Money is permitted to go at 12 *per Cent.*
there can be no confiderable Manufacturing, and nomore
of Tillage and Grazing, than as we proverbially fay,
will keep Life and Soul together; and where there is
little Manufacture, and as little Hufbandry of Lands,
the Profit of Plantations, *viz.* The greateft Part thereof, will not redound to the Mother-kingdom, but to
other Countries wherein there are more Manufactures
and more Productions from the Earth; from hence it
follows, Plantations thus managed prove Drains of the
People from their Mother-kingdom; whereas Plantations belonging to Mother-kingdoms, or Countries,
where Liberty and Property is better preferved, and
Intereft of Money reftrained to a low Rate, the Confequence is, that every Perfon fent abroad with the
Negroes and Utenfils he is conftrained to employ, or
that are employed with him; it being cuftomary in
our Iflands in *America*, upon every Plantation, to employ Eight or Ten Blacks for One White Servant; I
fay, in this Cafe, we may reckon, that for Provifions,
Clothes, and Houfehold Goods, Seamen, and all
others employed about Materials for Building, Fitting,
and Victualling of Ships, *Every* Englifhman *in* Barbadoes *or* Jamaica *creates Employment for Four Men at
Home.*

3*dly*, I anfwer, That *Holland* now fends as many, and
more People yearly, to refide in their Plantations, Fortreffes, and Ships in the *Eaft Indies*, (befides many into
the *Weft Indies*) than *Spain*, and yet is fo far from declining in the Number of their People at Home, that
it is evident they do monftroufly encreafe: And fo I
hope, under the next Head, to prove that *England* hath
conftantly encreafed in People at Home, fince our Settlement upon Plantations in *America*, although not in
fo great a Proportion as the *Dutch*.

V. I

(9)

V. *I am of Opinion that we had immediately, before the late Plague, more People in* England, *than we had before the inhabiting of* New England, Virginia, Barbadoes, &c.

The Proof of this at beſt I know can but be conjectural; but. in Confirmation of my Opinion, I have, I think of my Mind the moſt induſtrious *Engliſh* Calculator this Age hath produced in publick, *viz.* Captain *Grant*, in the forementioned Treatiſe, Page 88. His Words are, " Upon the whole Matter we may there-
" fore conclude, that the People of the whole Nation
" do encreaſe, and conſequently the Decreaſe of *Win-*
" *cheſter, Lincoln,* and other like Places, muſt be attri-
" buted to other Reaſons than that of refurniſhing
" *London* only."

2. It is manifeſt by the aforeſaid worthy Author's Calculations, that the Inhabitants of *London,* and Parts adjacent, have encreaſed to almoſt Double within theſe ſixty Years, and that City hath been uſually taken for an Index of the whole.

I know it will be ſaid, that although *London* have ſo encreaſed, other Parts have as much diminiſhed, where-of ſome are named before; but if to anſwer the Diminution of Inhabitants in ſome particular Places, it be conſidered how others are encreaſed, *viz. Yarmouth, Hull, Scarborough,* and other Ports in the *North;* as alſo *Liverpoole, Weſtcheſter,* and *Briſtol; Portſmouth, Lime,* and *Plymouth*; and withal if it be conſidered what great Improvements have been made this laſt ſixty Years upon breaking up and encloſing of Waſtes, Forreſts, and Parks, and draining of the Fens, and all thoſe Places inhabited and furniſhed with Huſbandry; &c. then I think it will appear probable that we have in *England* now, at leaſt had before the late Plague, more People than we had before we firſt entered upon Foreign Plantations, notwithſtanding likewiſe the great Numbers of Men which have iſſued from us into *Ireland*; which Country, as our Laws now are, I reckon not among the Number of Plantations profitable to *England,* nor within the Limits of this Diſcourſe, al-though, peradventure, ſomething may be pickt out of theſe Papers, which may deſerve conſideration in rela-tion to that Country.

But

(10)

But it may be said, If we have more People now than in former Ages, how came it to pass, that in the Times of the Kings *Henry* IV. & V. and other Times formerly, we could raise such great Armies, and employ them in foreign Wars, and yet retain a sufficient number to defend the Kingdom, and cultivate our Lands at Home?

I Answer; *First,* The bigness of Armies is not always a certain Indication of the numerousness of a Nation, but sometimes rather of the Nature of the Government, and Distribution of the Lands; as for Instance, Where the Prince and Lords are Owners of the whole Territory, although the People be thin, the Armies upon Occasion may be very great, as in *East India,* *Turkey,* and the Kingdoms of *Fez* and *Morocco,* where *Taffelet* was said to have an army of One hundred and fifty, or Two hundred thousand men, although every Body knows that Country hath as great a scarcity of People, as any in the World. But since Freeholders are so much encreased in *England,* and the servile Tenures altered, doubtless it is more difficult, as well as more chargeable to draw great numbers of men into foreign Wars.

2. Since the Introduction of the new Artillery of Powder, Shot, and Fire-arms into the World, all War is become as much rather an Expence of Money as Men, and Success attends those that can most and longest spend Money rather than Men; and consequently *Princes Armies in* Europe *are become more proportionable to their Purses, than to the Numbers of their People.*

VI. *That all Colonies and foreign Plantations do endamage their Mother-kingdoms, whereof the Trades of such Plantations are not confined to their said Mother-kingdoms, by good Laws, and severe Execution of those Laws.*

1. *The practice of all the Governments of* Europe, *witness to the Truth of this Proposition.* The *Danes* keep the Trade of *Iceland* to themselves; the *Dutch Surinam,* and all their Settlements in *East India;* the *French St. Christophers,* and their other Plantations in the *West Indies;* the *Portuguese Brazil,* and all the Coasts thereof; the *Spaniards,* all their vast Territories upon the Main in the *West Indies,* and many Islands there; and our own Laws seem to design the like,

(11)

as to all our Plantations in *New England*, *Virginia*, *Barbadoes*, &c. although we have not yet arrived to a compleat and effectual Execution of those Laws.

2. Plantations being at first furnished, and afterwards successively supplied with People from their Mother Kingdoms, and People being Riches, that Loss of People to the Mother Kingdoms, be it more or less, is certainly a Damage, except the Employment of those People abroad, do cause the Employment of so many more at Home in their Mother Kingdoms, and that can never be, except the Trade be restrained to their Mother Kingdom, which will not be doubted by any that understands the next Proposition, *viz.*

VII. *That the* Dutch *will reap the greatest Advantage by all Colonies, issuing from any Kingdom in* Europe, *whereof the Trades are not so strictly confined to their proper Mother Kingdoms.*

This Proposition will readily be assented unto by any that understand the Nature of low Interest and low Customs: Where the Market is free, they shall be sure to have the Trade that can sell the best Penny-worths, that buy dearest and sell cheapest, which (Nationally speaking) none can do but those that have Money at the lowest Rate of Interest, and pay the least Customs, which are the *Dutch;* and this is the true Cause why, before the Act of Navigation, there went Ten *Dutch* Ships to *Barbadoes* for one *English.*

VIII. That the *Dutch*, (though they thrive so exceedingly in Trade) *will in probability never endamage this Kingdom by the Growth of their Plantations.*

1. In Fact the *Dutch* never did much thrive in Planting, for I do remember, they had, about Twenty Years past, *Tobago*, a most fruitful Island in the *West Indies*, apt for Production of Sugars and all other Commodities that are propagated in *Barbadoes*, and as I have heard Planters affirm, better accommodated with Rivers for Water Mills, which are of great Use for grinding of the Canes; this Island is still in their Possession, and *Corasoa*, and some others; and about Sixteen or Seventeen Years past, they were so eager upon the Improvement of it, that besides what they did in *Holland*, they set up Bills upon the *Exchange* in *London*, proffering great Privileges to any that would transport themselves thither. Notwithstanding all which, to this

Day,

(12)

Day, that Ifland is not the tenth Part fo well improved as *Jamaica* hath been by the *Englifh* within thefe Five Years; neither have the *Dutch* at any other Time, or in any other Parts of the World, made any Improvement by Planting; what they do in the *Eaft Indies* being only by War, Trade, and Building of fortified Towns and Caftles upon the Sea Coafts, to fecure the fole Commerce of the Places, and with the People which they conquer; not by clearing, breaking up of the Ground, and Planting, as the *Englifh* have done.

This I take to be a ftrong Argument of Fact to my prefent Purpofe.

2. The fecond Argument to prove this Propofition, is from Reafon': I have before mentioned the feveral Accidents and Methods by which our foreign Plantations have from Time to Time come to be peopled and improved.

Now the *Dutch* being void of thofe Accidents, are deftitute of the Occafions to improve foreign Plantations, by digging and delving as the *Englifh* have done.

For 1ft. In *Holland*, their Intereft and Cuftom being low, together with their other Encouragements to Trade, mentioned in the former Parts of this Treatife, gives Employment to all their People born and bred amongft them, and alfo to multitudes of Foreigners.

2. *Their giving Liberty, or at leaft Connivance to all Religious, as well* Jews *and* Roman Catholicks, *as* Sectaries, gives Security to all their Inhabitants at Home, and expels none, nor puts a Neceffity upon any to banifh themfelves upon that Account.

3. Their careful and wonderful providing for and employing their Poor at Home, puts all their People utterly out of Danger of Starving, or Neceffity of Stealing, and confequently out of Fear of Hanging; I might add to this, that they have not for a long Time had any Civil War among them; and from the whole conclude, that the *Dutch* as they did never, fo they never can or will, thrive by Planting; and that our *Englifh* Plantations abroad are a good Effect, proceeding from many evil Caufes.

IX. *That neither the* French, Spainards, *or* Portugueze *are much to be feared on the Account of Planting, not for the fame, but for other Reafons.*

That

(13)

That the *French* have had Footing in the *Weſt Indies*, almoſt as long as the *Engliſh*, is certain, and that they have made no conſiderable Progreſs in Planting, is as certain, and finding it ſo in Faɛt, I have been often exerciſing my Thoughts about Enquiry into the Reaſon thereof, which I attribute eſpecially to two.

Firſt, Becauſe *France* being an abſolute Government, hath not, until very lately, given any Countenance or Encouragement to Navigation and Trade.

Seeondly, and principally, becauſe the *French* Settlements in the *Weſt Indies*, have not been upon Free-holders as the *Engliſh* are, but in Subjeɛtion to the *French Weſt India Company*; which Company, being under the *French King*, as *Lord Proprietor* of the Places they ſettle upon, and taxing the Inhabitants at Pleaſure, as the King doth them, it is not probable they ſhould make that ſucceſsful Progreſs in Planting; *Property, Freedom, and Inheritance being the moſt effeɛtual Spurs to Induſtry.*

2. Though ſome, (who have not looked far into this Matter,) may think the *Spaniards* have made great Progreſs in Planting, I am of Opinion, that the *Engliſh*, ſince the Time they ſet upon this Work, have cleared and improved fifty Plantations for One, and built as many Houſes, for one the *Spaniards* have built; this will not be very diffcult to imagine, if it be conſidered.

Firſt, That it is not above Fifty or Sixty Years ſince the *Engliſh* intended the propagating foreign Plantations.

Secondly, That the *Spaniards* were poſſeſſed of the *Weſt Indies*, about our King *Henry* the VII's. Time which is Two hundred Years paſt.

Thirdly, That what the *Spaniards* hath done in the *Weſt Indies*, hath been Ten Times more by Conqueſt, then by Planting.

Fourthly, That the *Spaniards* found, in the *Weſt Indies*, moſt of the Cities and Towns ready built and inhabited, and much of the Ground improved and cultivated before their coming thither.

Fifthly, That the Inhabitants which they found there, and ſubdued, were ſuch a people, with whom ſome of the *Spaniards* could and have mixed, from whence hath proceeded a Generation of People, which they call *Miſtiſes*; whereas the *Engliſh*, where they have ſet down and planted, either found none, or ſuch as were

mere

(14)

mere wild Heathens, with whom they could not, nor ever have been known to mix.

Sixthly, That now after such a long Series of Time, the *Spaniards* are scarce so populous in any Part of the *West Indies*, as to be able to bring an Army of Ten thousand Men together in a Month's Time.

From all which I conjecture;

First, *That His Majesty hath now more* English *Subjects in all his foreign Plantations, in Sixty Years, than the King of* Spain *hath* Spaniards *in all his, in Two hundred Years.*

Secondly, *That the* Spaniards *Progress in Planting bears no Proportion to the Encrease of the* English *Plantations.*

Thirdly, That seeing the *Spaniards*, in the Time of their greatest Prosperity, and under so many Advantages, have been such indifferent Planters, and have made so flow Progress in peopling those Parts of the *West Indies*, which they possess, *It is not much to be feared that ever the* English *will be mated by the* Spaniards *in their foreign Plantations, or Production of the native Commodities of those Parts.*

Now, the Reasons why the *Spaniards* are so thin of People in the *West Indies*, I take to be such as the following, *viz.*

First, and principally, *Because they exercise the same Policy and Governments, Civil and Ecclesiastical, in their Plantations, as they do in their Mother Kingdom*; from whence it follows, that their People are few and thin abroad, from the same Causes, as they are empty and void of People at Home; whereas, although *we in* England *vainly endeavour to arive at a Uniformity of Religion at Home, yet we allow an* Amsterdam *Liberty in our Plantations.*

It is true, *New England* being a more independant Government from this Kingdom, than any other of our Plantations, and the People that went thither, more One peculiar Sort or Sect, than those that went to the rest of our Plantations, they did for some Years past exercise some Severities against the *Quakers*; but of late, they have understood their true Interest better, insomuch as I have not heard of any Act of that Kind for these Five or Six Years last, notwithstanding am well informed, that there are now amongst them many
more

(15)

more *Quakers* and other *Diſſenters* from the Forms of religious Worſhip, then were at the Time of their greateſt Severity, which Severity hath no other Effect, but to encreaſe the *New England Non-conformiſts*.

Secondly, A Second Reaſon why the Productions of the *Spaniſh Weſt India* Commodities are ſo inconſiderable in reſpect to the *Engliſh*, and conſequently why their Progreſs in Planting hath been, and is like to be much leſs than the *Engliſh*, as alſo the Encreaſe of their People, I take to be the Dearneſs of the Freight of their Ships, which is Four Times more than our *Engliſh* Freight ; and if you would know how that comes to be ſo, Twelve *per cent*. Intereſt will go a great Way towards the Satisfying you, although there are other concomitant leſſer Cauſes, which, whoſoever underſtands *Spain*, or ſhall carefully read this Treatiſe, may find out themſelves.

Thirdly, A Third Reaſon I take to be the Greatneſs of the Cuſtoms in *Old Spain* ; for undoubtedly *high Cuſtoms do as well dwarf Plantations as Trade*.

Fourthly, The *Spaniards* intenſe and ſingular Induſtry in their Mines for Gold and Silver, the Working wherein deſtroys abundance of their People, at leaſt of their Slaves, doth cauſe them to neglect, in great Meaſure, Cultivating of the Earth, and producing Commodities from the Growth thereof, which might give Employment to a greater Navy, as well as Suſtenance to a far greater Number of People by Sea and Land.

Fifthly, Their Multitude of *Friars, Nuns, and other recluſe and eccleſiaſtical Perſons* which are prohibited from *Marriage*.

Thirdly, The Third Sort of People I am to diſcourſe of, are the *Portugueſe*, and them I muſt acknowledge to have been great Planters in the *Brazils* and other Places; but yet, if we preſerve our People and Plantations by Good Laws, I have Reaſon to believe, that the *Portugueſe*, (except they alter their Politicks, which is almoſt impoſſible for them to do,) can never bear up with us, much leſs prejudice our Plantations.

That hitherto they have not hurt us, but we them, is moſt apparent ; for in my Time, we have beat their *Muſcovado* and *Paneal Sugars* quite out of Uſe in *England*, and their *Whites* we have brought down in all theſe Parts of *Europe*, in Price, from Seven and Eight

Pounds

{ 16 }

Pounds *per Cent*. to Fifty Shillings and Three Pounds *per Cent*. and in quantity; whereas formerly, their *Brazil Fleets* confifted of One hundred, to One hundred and twenty thoufand Chefts of Sugar, they are now reduced to about Thirty thoufand Chefts, fince the great Increafe of *Barbadoes*.

The Reafon of this Decay of the Portuguefe *Productions in Brazils, is certainly the better Policy our* Englifh *Plantations are founded upon.*

That which principally dwarfs the *Portuguefe Plantations*, is the fame before-mentioned, which hinders the *Spaniards*, viz. *extraordinary high Cuftoms at Home, high Freights, high Intereft of Money, Ecclefiaftical Perfons,* &c.

From all that hath been faid concerning Plantations in general, I draw thefe Two principal Conclufions.

Firft, *That our* Englifh *Plantations may thrive beyond any other Plantations in the World, though the Trades of all of them were more feverely limited by Laws, and good Execution of thefe Laws to their Mother Kingdom of* England, *exclufive to* Ireland *and* New England.

Secondly, *That it is in His Majeftie's Power, and the Parliament's if they pleafe, by taking off all Charges from Sugar, to make it more entirely an* Englifh Commodity, *than White Herrings are a* Dutch Commodity, *and to draw more Profit to this Kingdom thereby, than the* Dutch *do by that: And that, in Confequence thereof, all Plantations of other Nations muft, in few Years, fink to little or nothing.*

X. *That it is more for the Advantage of* England, *that* Newfoundland *fhould remain unplanted, than that Colonies fhould be fent or permitted to go thither to inhabit under a Governour, Laws,* &c.

I have before difcourfed of Plantations in general, moft of the *Englifh* being in their Nature much alike, except this of *New Foundland*, and that of *New England*, which I intend next to fpeak of.

The Advantage *New Foundland* hath brought to this Kingdom, is only by the Fifhery there ; and of what vaft Concernment that is, is well known to moft Gentlemen and Merchants, efpecially thofe of the Weft Parts of *England*, from whence efpecially this Trade is driven.

It is well known, upon undeniable Proof, that in the Year 1605, the *Englifh* employed 250 Sail of

Ships

(17)

Ships fmall and great, in fifhing upon that Coaft; and it is now too apparent, that we do not fo employ, from all Parts, above eighty Sail of Ships.

It is likewife generally known and confeffed, that when we employed fo many Ships in that Trade, the current Price of our Fifh in that Country, was (*Communibus Annis*,) 17 Rials, which is 8 *s*. 6 *d*. per Quintal, and that fince, as we have leffened in that Trade, the *French* have encreafed in it, and that we have annually proceeded to raife our Fifh from 17 Rials to 24 Rials, or 12 *s*. (*Communibus Annis*) as it now fells in the Country.

This being the Cafe of *England* in Relation to this Trade, it is certainly worth the Enquiry,

1ft, *How we came to decay in that Trade.*

2dly, *What Means may be ufed to recover our antient Greatnefs in that Trade, or at leaft to prevent our further Diminution therein?*

The Decay of that Trade I attribute,

Firft, and principally, to the growing Liberty which is every Year more and more ufed in *Romifh* Countries, as well as others, of eating Flefh in *Lent* and on Fifhdays.

2. To a late Abufe crept into that Trade, (which hath much abated the Expence within thefe twenty Years of that Commodity,) of fending over private Boat-keepers, which hath much diminifhed the Number of the Fifhing-Ships.

3. To the great Increafe of the *French* Fifhery of *Placentia*, and other Ports on the Back-fide of *Newfoundland*.

4. To the feveral Wars we have had at Sea within thefe twenty Years, which have much empoverifhed the Merchants of our Weftern Parts, and reduced them to carry on a great Part of that Trade at Bottomry, *viz*. Money taken upon Adventure of the Ship at twenty *per* Cent. *per Annum*.

2dly, *What Means may be ufed to recover our antient Greatnefs in that Trade, or at leaft to prevent our farther Diminution therein.*

For this, two contrary Ways have been propounded.

1. To fend a Governor to refide there, and to encourage People to inhabit there, as well for Defence of the

B   Country

(18)

Country againft Invafion, as manage the Fifhery there by Inhabitants upon the Place; this hath often been propounded by the Planters and fome Merchants of *London.*

2. The fecond Way propounded, and which is directly contrary to the former is, by the *Weft Country* Merchants and Owners of the Fifhing-Ships, and that is to have no Governor nor Inhabitants permitted to refide at *Newfoundland,* nor any Paffengers, or private Boatkeepers fuffered to fifh at *Newfoundland.*

This latter Way propounded is moft agreeable to my Propofition, and if it could be effected, I am perfuaded would revive the decayed *Englifh* Fifhing-Trade at *Newfoundland,* and be otherwife greatly for the Advantage of this Kingdom; and that for thefe following Reafons,

1. Becaufe *moft of the Provifions the Planters which are fettled* at Newfoundland *do make ufe of,* viz. *Bread, Beef, Pork, Butter, Cheefe, Clothes, and* Irifh *Bandel Cloth, Linen, and Woollen,* Irifh *Stockings, as alfo Nets, Hooks, and Lines,* &c. *they are fupplied with from* New England *and* Ireland; *and with Wine, Oil, and Linen by the Salt Ships from* France *and* Spain, *in Confequence whereof the Labour, as well as the Feeding and Clothing of fo many Men is loft to* England.

2. The Planters fettled there, being moftly loofe vagrant People, and without Order and Government, do keep diffolute Houfes, which have debauched Seamen, and diverted them from their laborious and induftrious Calling; whereas, before there were Settlements there, the Seamen had no other Refort during the Fifhing Seafon, (being the Time of their Abode in that Country;) but to their Ships, which afforded them convenient Food and Repofe, without the Inconveniences of Excefs.

3. If it be the Intereft of all Trading Nations principally to encourage Navigation, and to promote efpecially thofe Trades which employ moft Shipping; (than which nothing is more true, and more regarded by the wife *Dutch:*) Then certainly it is the Intereft of *England* to difcountenance and abate the Number of Planters at *Newfoundland,* for if they fhould encreafe, it would in

a few

(19)

a few Years happen to us in Relation to that Country as it hath to the Fifhery at *New England*, which many Years fince was managed by *Englifh* Ships from the Weftern Ports; but as Plantations there encreafed, fell to be the fole Employment of the People fettled there, and nothing of that Trade left the poor old *Englifh* Men, but the Liberty of carrying now and then by Courtefy or Purchafe, a Ship-loading of Fifh to *Bilvoa*, when their own new *Englifh* Shipping are better employed, or not at Leizure to do it.

4. *It is manifeft that before there were Boat-keepers, or Planters* at Newfoundland, *Fifh was fold cheaper than now it is, by about forty* per Cent. and confequently more vended; the Reafon whereof I take to be this; the Boat-keepers and Planters, being generally at firft able Fifher-men, and being upon the Place, can doubtlefs afford their Fifh cheaper than the Fifhing Ships from *Old England*, fo doubtlefs they did at firft as well at *New England* as at *Newfoundland*, until they had beat the *Englifh* Ships out of the Trade; after which being freed from that Competition, they became lazy as to that laborious Employment, having Means otherwife to live and employ themfelves, and thereupon enhaunced the Price of their Fifh to fuch an Excefs, as in Effect proves the giving away of that Trade to the *French*, who by our aforefaid impolitick Management of that Trade, have of late Years been able to under-fell us at all Markets abroad; and moft certain it is, that thofe that can fell cheapeft will have the Trade.

5. *This Kingdom being an Ifland, it is our Intereft, as well for our Prefervation as our Profit, not only to have many Seamen, but to have them as much as may be within Call in a Time of Danger.* Now the Fifhing Ships going out in *March*, and returning Home for *England* in the Month of *September* yearly, and there being employed in that Trade two hundred and fifty Ships, which might carry about ten thoufand Seamen, Fifhermen, and Shoremen, as they ufually call the younger Perfons who were never before at Sea: I appeal to the Reader, whether fuch a yearly Return of Seamen, abiding at Home with us all the Winter, and fpending their Money here which they got in their Summer Fifhery, were not a great Accefs of Wealth and Power to this Kingdom, and a

B 2   ready

(20)

ready Supply for his Majefty's Navy upon all Emergencies,

6. *The Fifhing Ships yet are, and always have been, the Breeders of Seamen;* the Planters and Boatkeepers are generally fuch as were bred, and became expert at the Coft of the Owners of Fifhing Ships, which Planters and Boatkeepers enter very few new or green Men.

7. By the building, fitting, victualling, and repairing of fifhing Ships, Multitudes of *Englifh* Tradefmen and Artificers (befides the Owners and Seamen) gain their Subfiftance; whereas by the Boats which the Planters and Boat-keepers build, or ufe at *Newfoundland, England* gets nothing.

Object. But againft all that I have faid, thofe that contend for a Governor at *Newfoundland,* object,

1. That without a Governor and Government there, that Country will be always expofed to the Surprizal of the *French,* or any Foreigners that fhall pleafe to attack it.

2. That the Diforders of the Planters, which I complain of (and fome others, which for Brevity's Sake, I have not mentioned) cannot be remedied without a Governor.

To which I anfwer, Firft, that when we cannot preferve our Colonies by our Shipping, or fo awe our Neighbours by our Fleets and Ships of War, that they dare not attempt them, our Cafe will be fad, and our Property will be loft, or in imminent Danger, not only Abroad, but at Home likewife.

2*dly,* All the Fifh that is killed at *Newfoundland* in a Summer, is not fufficient to maintain Strength enough on Shore to defend two fifhing Harbours againft ten Men of War, whereas that Country hath more Harbours to defend, than are to be found in *Old England.*

3*dly,* If a Governor be eftablifhed, the next Confequence will be a Tax upon the Fifhing, and the leaft Tax will encreafe the Price of Fifh, and that unavoidably will give the Trade away wholly into the *French* Hands.

4*thly,* A Government there is already of antient Cuftom among the Mafters of the fifhing-Ships, to which the Fifhermen are inured, and that free from Oppreffion, and adapted to the Trade, infomuch that although a better might be wifhed, I never hope to fee it.

XI. *That* New England *is the moft prejudicial Plantation to this Kingdom.*

I am

(21)

I am now to write of a People, whose Frugality, Industry, and Temperance, and the Happiness of whose Laws and Institutions do promise to themselves long Life, with a wonderful Increase of People, Riches, and Power: And although Men ought to envy that Virtue and Wisdom in others, which themselves either can or will not practise, but rather to commend and admire it; yet I think it is the Duty of every good Man primarily to respect the Wellfare of his native Country; and therefore though I may offend some, whom I would not willingly displease, I cannot omit in the Progress of this Discourse, to take Notice of some Particulars, wherein Old England *suffers Diminution by the Growth of those Colonies settled in* New England, and how that Plantation differs from those more Southerly, with Respect to the Gain or Loss of this Kingdom, *viz.*

1. All our *American* Plantations, except that of *New England,* produce Commodities of different Natures from those of this Kingdom, as Sugar, Tobacco, Cocoa, Wool, Ginger, sundry Sorts of dying Wood, &c. Whereas *New England* produces generally the same we have here, *viz.* Corn and Cattle; some Quantity of Fish they do likewise kill, but that is taken and saved altogether by their own Inhabitants, which prejudiceth our *Newfoundland* Trade, where, as hath been said, very few are, or ought, according to Prudence, to be employed in those Fisheries, but the Inhabitants of *Old England.*

The other Commodities we have from them, are some few great Masts, Furs, and Train-Oil, whereof the yearly Value amounts to very little, the much greater Value of Returns from thence being made in Sugar, Cotton, Wool, Tobacco, and such like Commodities, which they first receive from some other of his Majesty's Plantations, in Barter for dry Cod-Fish, Salt, Mackarel, Beef, Pork, Bread, Beer, Flour, Pease, &c. which they supply *Barbadoes, Jamaica,* &c. with, to the Diminution of the Vent of those Commodities from this Kingdom; the great Experience whereof in our *West-India* Plantations would soon be found in the Advantage of the Value of our Lands in *England,* were it not for the vast and almost incredible Supplies those Colonies have from *New England.*

B 3   2. The

(22)

2. The People of *New England*, by Virtue of their primitive Charters, being so strictly tied to the Observations of the Laws of this Kingdom, do sometimes assume a Liberty of Trading, contrary to the *Act of Navigation*, by Reason whereof many of our *American* Commodities, especially Tobacco and Sugar, are transported in *New English* Shipping, directly into *Spain*, and other foreign Countries, without being landed in *England*, or paying any Duty to his Majesty, which is not only Loss to the King, and a Prejudice to the Navigation of *Old England*, but also a total Exclusion of the *Old English* Merchant from the Vent of those Commodities in those Ports, where the *New English* Vessels trade; because, there being no Custom paid on those Commodities in *New England*, and a great Custom paid upon them in *Old England*, it must necessarily follow that the *New English* Merchant will be able to afford his Commodity much cheaper at the Market, than the *Old English* Merchant: And those that can sell cheapest, will infallibly engross the whole Trade sooner or later.

3. Of all the *American* Plantations, his Majesty hath none so apt for the Building of Shipping as *New England*, nor none so comparably qualified for breeding of Seamen, not only by Reason of the natural Industry of that People, but principally by Reason of their Cod and Mackerel Fisheries: And, in my poor Opinion, here is nothing more prejudicial, and in Prospect more dangerous to any Mother Kingdom, than the Increase of Shipping in their Colonies, Plantations, or Provinces.

4. The People that evacuate from us to *Barbadoes* and the other *West India* Plantations, as was before hinted, do commonly work one *English* Man to ten or eight Blacks; and if we keep the Trade of our said Plantations entirely to *England*, *England* would have no less Inhabitants, but rather an Increase of People by such Evacuation, because that one *English* Man, with the ten Blacks that work with him, accounting what they eat, use, and wear, would make Employment for four Men in *England*, as was said before; whereas, peradventure, of ten Men that issue from us to *New England* and *Ireland*, what we send to, or receive from them, doth not employ one Man in *England*.

To

(23)

To conclude this Chapter, and to do Right to that moſt induſtrious *Engliſh* Colony, I muſt confeſs that though we loofe by their unlimited Trade with our foreign Plantations, yet we are very great Gainers, by their direct Trade to and from *Old England.* Our yearly Exportations of *Engliſh* Manufactures, Malt, and other Goods from hence thither, amounting in my Opinion to ten Times the Value of what is imported from thence, which Calculation I do not make at Random, but upon mature Confideration, and, peradventure, upon as much Experience in this Trade, as any other perſon will pretend to ; and, therefore, when ever a Reformation of our Correſpondency in Trade with that People ſhall be thought on, it will in my poor Judgement require great Tenderneſs and very ſerious Circumſpection.

B 4   THE

DISSERTATION II.

ON

Colonies and Plantations.

By

CHARLES D'AVENANT, LL. D.

INSPECTOR of the Exports and Imports.

DISSERTATION II.

on

Colonies and Plantations.

By

CHARLES D'AVENANT, LL.D.

Inspector of the Exports and Imports.

(**27**)

SELECT

DISSERTATIONS

ON

Colonies and Plantations.

DISSERTATION II.

On the Plantation Trade.

By CHARLES D'AVENANT, LL. D.

HE that Writes in order to recommend any Matter to the Public Care, muſt begin with removing the Objeċtions to the Thing itſelf; for it will be unneceſſary to propoſe Methods whereby the Plantations in *America* may be ſecured and improved, unleſs it can be firſt made appear that they are beneficial to the Kingdom.

All Trades have their Rivals and Concurrents in Profit, who conſequently are Enemies; they have likewiſe their Friends and Supporters; but the Diligence of one Enemy is more prevailing and aċtive, than the Kindneſs of many Friends: There is alſo a Third Party, who, having not well conſidered and ſtudied the Concerns of Foreign Traffic, are Neuters, being indeed not quite certain in their own Opinion, whether it be good for *England* or not, and ſo become indifferent in any Deliberations relating to it.

And the Deſign of theſe Papers being to incite the Young Gentlemen to bend their Thoughts to Matters of this Nature, in the Branches of Trade, which ſhall be here treated of, we ſhall endeavour to remove former Prejudices; they who are Adverſaries to any particular

(28)

ticular Traffic, for Reafons refpecting themfelves, will not be altered; but we fhall do our beft to confirm the Friends to Trade in general; we fhall try to bring over the Neuter Side; and to engage thofe who are the Flying Squadron in all fuch Debates, by fhewing them that their Land-intereft depends more on Foreign Commerce than is commonly imagined.

The moft material Objections to our Colonies in *America* are,

1ft, That they drain this Kingdom of People, the moft important Strength of any Nation.

2dly, That they are a Retreat to Men of Notions oppofite to the Religion of their Country, and to Perfons difaffected to the Government.

As to the Firft Head, it is evident that fince we had thefe Plantations, *England* has rather encreafed than diminifhed in People.

In the Firft Difcourfe we have fufficiently made it appear, that fince the Year 1600, the Wealth of this Kingdom is all Manner of Ways augmented; that our general Rental is more; that the Purchafe of Land is come from 12 to 18, and in fome Countries 24, 25, and 26; and that our Stock of all Kinds is greatly multiplied, as alfo the Species of Money. Now this Acceffion of Riches can have noways proceeded but from our Encreafing in the Number of Inhabitants,

For the Collective Body of a Nation has but Two Courfes of acquiring Wealth, either by Inroads and Depredations upon its Neighbours, or by the Trade, Labour, Arts and Manufactures of its People; and when it is not grown Rich one Way, we may prefume that the Hands are encreafed which have multiplied its Riches.

There are almoft undeniable Reafons to be drawn from Political Arithmetic, fhewing that fince the Year 1600, we are encreafed in Number of Inhabitants about 900,000, which could not be, if the Plantations were fuch a Drain of the People as is injurious to the Commonwealth.

We admit (over and above the Acceffion of Foreigners to us, and not reckoning what the *Weft-Indies* fend to us again) that for 80 Years laft paft, they may have carried away, *communibus Annis*, about 1000 Perfons, and that is the moft; but then it is generally of fuch

Sort

(29)

Sort of People, as their Crimes and Debaucheries would quickly deftroy at Home, or whom their Wants would confine in Prifons or force to beg, and fo render them ufelefs, and confequently a Burthen to the Public.

If the Majority of thofe who are thus tranfported, or tranfport themfelves, confifts of fuch as would perifh here or beg, it muft certainly be advifeable to tranfplant them to Places, where they may be of more Ufe, or grow better by Removal.

Virginia and *Barbadoes* were at firft peopled by fuch a Race; it is true (as Sir *Jofiah Child* has obferved) that afterwards they came to have another Sort of Inhabitants, when the Miferies of the Civil War had reduced many good Families of the King's Party to change Climate.

And again, thofe two Plantations, *Jamaica* and other Parts of *America*, had a new Acceffion of People, when the Reftoration of King *Charles* II. had brought many Perfons difcontented either in Religious or State Matters, to feek Refuge in a diftant Country.

New-England had its original Rife and Planting from the Perfecutions on account of Confcience, fet afoot by the warm Churchmen in the Reigns of King *James* and King *Charles* I.

So that, in a Manner, feveral Nations which in Time may grow confiderable, have been formed out of what was here thought an Excrefcence in the Body Politic.

And it may not be unfeafonable in this Place, to offer to Public Confideration, whether it would not be more religious to tranfport many of thofe miferable Wretches, who are frequently executed in this Kingdom for fmall Tranfgreffions of the Law? it being per-adventure one of the Faults of our Conftitution, that it makes fo little Difference between Crimes; for Experience tells us, that many Malefactors have, by after Induftry and a Reformation in Manners, juftified their Wifdom, whofe Clemency fent them Abroad.

It muft undoubtedly be for the common Good to pre-ferve thofe Abroad, whom their Vice or Neceffities would deftroy at Home; but it may be a Queftion, whether or no it is confiftent with the Welfare of a Country, to allow to the Malcontents in Religious or State Affairs, a Retreat, and fuch a one, in which they may acquire both Power and Riches. The Examination
of

(30)

of this Point will lead us to anfwer the Objections made upon the fecond Hand.

From the very beginning of the Reformation, there have been Differences in this Kingdom, not truly in the Effential, but Ceremonial Parts of Religion; but the Enemy of Man (working on our Ambition, Pride, Avarice, Thirft of Rule, and other our Natural Defects) has fo improved thofe Quarrels, as to make us contend, from Time to Time, about Matters indifferent, as hotly as if the entire Glory and Power of God had been in Queftion.

And to ftate Things fairly, almoft every Religious Faction that has chanced to get the Sway, has thrown off the Meeknefs that was firft pretended, each fhewing in its Turn a perfecuting Spirit, which Spirit is not of God.

Such therefore as found themfelves difturbed and uneafy at Home, if they could have found no other Retreat, muft have gone to the *Hans Towns, Switzerland, Denmark, Sweden,* or *Holland,* (as many did before the Plantations flourifhed, to our great detriment) and they who had thus retired to the European Countries, muft have been for ever loft to England.

But Providence, which contrives better for us than we can do for ourfelves, has offered in the New World a Place of Refuge for thefe, peradventure, miftaken and mifled People, where (as fhall be fhewn by and by) their Labour and Induftry is more ufeful to their Mother Kingdom, than if they had continued among us.

And as to Malcontents in the State, perhaps it is for the Public Safety, that there fhould always be fuch an Outlet or Iffue for the Ill-humours which from Time to Time are engendered in the Body Politic. And the *Romans,* by fuch Kind of Colonies, did continually difcharge their City of thofe turbulent Spirits who difturbed their Country's Peace; and the Senate thereby appeafed the Tumults which did fo frequently arife about the Agrarian Law.

Defire of having more, and not the Fear of lofing what they poffefs, lies at the Bottom of moft difaffections to Government; it is therefore fafeft to let fuch unquiet Minds remove to Places where their Appetite after Riches may be better fatisfied.

Hardly

{ 31 }

Hardly any Government can be so evenly managed, as to content all Sorts of Men; and the Ministers are often a Weight to some who reverence and love the Prince's Person, and to such a Retreat is convenient, in which they may shun the private Animosities and Oppression of Persons, perhaps too powerful to be complained of.

One of the worst Circumstances in universal Monarchy, is, that the Tyranny it introduces is no where to be avoided; so that he who was oppressed by a *Roman* Emperor, could retire no where but into the Arms of Death, and this made so many great Men kill themselves; whereas now, such as cannot be easy in one Country, may remove and be at Quiet in another.

In all likelihood, it would be very much for the Good of Human Kind, and add extremely to the Wealth and Greatness of *England*, by new Encouragements, wholesome Laws, and a more easy Naturalization, to make this Kingdom the Asylum for all oppressed and afflicted Persons, who desire to shun that despotic Power, which the neighbouring Princes are every where setting up; and if we are made the general Asylum, our own Malcontents may retire without any Prejudice; for the Recruits of People such a Course might produce, would answer the annual Evacuation occasioned by our *West-India* Colonies.

Their Plantations have, indeed, ruined the *Spaniards*; but it is because there are many Things amiss in their present Conduct. Their Monasteries hinder Marriage, the Inquisition frights away Strangers, and, in general, there is no Provision at all made to repair what their Colonies carry out. But the *Hollanders*, who send out greater Numbers every Year than *Spain*, are not dispeopled by it, their Constitution inviting more over to them than they send Abroad.

Upon which Account we cannot but wonder at their Policy who were the first Promoters of that Law in 1695, which puts a Difficulty upon, and restrains the Sale of any Plantation or Parcel of Land in *America* to Foreigners; whereas, indeed, we should invite and encourage Aliens to plant in the *West-Indies*, whereby the Crown gains Subjects, and the Nation gets Wealth by the Labour of others. This Statute does, peradventure, want revising.

And

{ 32 }

And Countries that take no Care to encourage an Accession of Strangers, in a Course of Time, will find Plantations of pernicious Consequence. It may be computed, that there have gone from *England* to the *West-Indies*, for many Years, by a Medium, about 1800 Persons annually; but then there is Reason to think, that, for some Time, the Persecutions Abroad have brought over to us, by a Medium, about 500 Foreigners every Year; and there are Grounds to believe, that, for these last 20 Years, the *West-Indies* have sent us back, annually, about 300 Persons of their Offspring, with this Advantage, that the Fathers went out poor, and the Children came home rich.

But if such Measures should hereafter be taken as will hinder the Accession of Strangers, or discourage the Planters from returning back, then these Colonies would drain us every Year of 1800 Persons.

However, this can be no Damage to the State, if they consist of Men turbulent and unquiet at Home, unless it can be made out, that they acquire Abroad such Riches, Power, and Dominion, as may render them, in Process of Time, formidable to their Mother Country.

As the Case now stands, we shall shew that they are a Spring of Wealth to this Nation, that they work for us, that their Treasure centers all here, and that the Laws have tied them fast enough to us; so that it must be through our own Fault and Misgovernment, if they become independent of *England*.

It is true, if a Breach of the Navigation Act be connived at, even our own Plantations may become more profitable to our Neighbours than to us. Corrupt Governors, by oppressing the Inhabitants, may hereafter provoke them to withdraw their Obedience, and by supine Negligence, or upon mistaken Measures, we may let let them grow (more especially *New England*) in naval Strength and Power, which, if suffered, we cannot expect to hold them long in our Subjection. If, as some have proposed, we should think to build Ships of War there, we may teach them an Art which will cost us some Blows to make them forget. Some such Courses may indeed drive them, or put it into their Heads to erect themselves into independent Commonwealths.

But while we keep a strict Eye upon their Conduct, and chiefly watch their Growth in Shipping of Strength
and

(33)

and for War, whatever other Increase they make, either in Wealth, or in Number of Inhabitants, cannot be turned against us, and can never be detrimental to this Nation.

While we are strong, and they weak at Sea, they may be compelled to obey the Laws of *England*, and not to trade directly, and upon their own Account, with other Countries, and they may be easily brought under, if evil-minded Persons should think at any Time to seduce them from their Allegiance.

Of all the *American* Plantations, *New England* (as Sir *Josiah Child* has observed) is the most proper for building Ships, and breeding Seamen, and their Soil affords plenty of Cattle; besides which, they have good Fisheries, so that if we should go to cultivate among them the Art of Navigation, and teach them to have a naval Force, they may set up for themselves, and make the greatest Part of our *West-India* Trade precarious. With their native Product they can furnish *Jamaica*, *Barbadoes*, and other Parts, with most Sort of Provision, by which they may draw from thence Sugar, Tobacco, and Cotton; and if they have a Strength of Ships, to countenance the Breach of their original Charter, by which they are tied to observe the Laws of *England*, they may carry the Growth of our Plantations to foreign Countries, and in Exchange bring from thence such Commodities and Manufactures as they want, to the great Hurt of the King's Customs, and to the Damage of the general Trade of *England*.

From all which it appears, how much they may be mistaken in their Politics, who, because we lose by the *Baltic* Trade, propose to the Government to build Ships of War in this Colony of *America*, not computing and weighing how prejudicial such a Project may be upon other Accounts; for, besides many other Evils encouraging them to do so, it would carry from hence a great Number of Artificers, which, in Case of a War, would be wanting in *England*.

Colonies are a Strength to their Mother Kingdom, while they are under good Discipline, while they are strictly made to observe the fundamental Laws of their original Country, and while they are kept dependent on it. But otherwise, they are worse than Members lopped from the Body politic, being indeed like offensive Arms

C   wrested

(34)

wrefted from a Nation to be turned againft it as Occafion fhall ferve.

Not that we think the Greatnefs thefe Colonies may arrive in a natural Courfe, and in the Progrefs of Time, can be dangerous to *England*. To build Ships in the Way of Trade, or for their own Defence, can adminfter no true Caufe of Jealoufy. There is much Difference between letting them be in a Condition to defend themfelves, and rendering them a kind of Staple for naval Stores, which can be hardly Politic, and perhaps very bad Hufbandry; but to prove this laft Affertion, would launch us out into an Argument too tedious for this Difcourfe.

Wife Countries never teach their Colonies the Art of War; if they need it not to oppofe their Neighbours, it is better they fhould be without it; and if it be neceffary to them, they will learn it of themfelves. When Colonies are near, it is beft they fhould be protected by the Force and Arms of their Mother Country; but when they are very remote, they may be allowed Arms and Shipping for their own Protection.

And, generally fpeaking, our Colonies while they have *Englifh* Blood in their Veins, and have Relations in *England*, and while they can get by trading with us, the ftronger and greater they grow, the more this Crown and Kingdom will get by them; and nothing but fuch an arbitrary Power as fhall make them defperate, can bring them to rebel.

Having examined what is objected to Plantations in general, we fhall proceed to fhow the Advantages and Gain they brought to *England* when they were in a profperous Condition.

In the Effay on the *Eaft-India* Trade * we did compute, that in the yearly Increafe of the Nation's general Stock, amounting to two Millions, in the whole 900,000 *l.* was to be allowed for the annual Profits made by our *Weft-India* Traffic, and there fhall be by and by fhown the Grounds we went upon in that Computation, and tho' there may be fome Miftake in the Repartition we then made, yet, whoever confiders the Matter carefully, will find we were right in the main Account.

But here Mr. *Pollexfen* will object, that there is no national Gain but where there is a Return made in Gold

* D'Avenant's Works, Vol. I. p. 94.

or

(35)

or Silver, which he thinks is the only Balance whereby we can guefs at Lofs and Profit. He infinuates, that no Importation of Commodities for Home Confumption is to be efteemed a Gain, fo that, by his Way of arguing, the Returns for what is exported to foreign Parts, is only to be called Profit, and that not unlefs it come in Bullion.

Whoever follows him in this Notion, will never judge rightly in any Matter concerning Trade, and though no Merchant, from the Light of common Senfe merely, we think ourfelves able to make it appear he is miftaken.

We fhall endeavour to fhow, that, generally fpeaking, by whatever the Returns are more worth than the Commodity exported, the Nation is by fo much a Gainer, let the Goods imported be perifhable or not.

But to underftand this Point clearly, we muft look a little backwards into the Manners and Nature of our own People.

About forty Years after we had tafted the Benefits of foreign Traffic, we began to be infected with foreign Luxury : In the Beginning a Stop might have been put to the Progrefs of the Evil, but there are Grounds to apprehend it has now taken Root too deeply, and is grown above the Correction of Wifdom and the Laws.

Befides, for thefe thirty-feven Years laft paft, the Duties on imported Goods have been fuch a main Branch of the Crown - Revenue, that, upon this Score, perhaps, our Vanities were not fo difcountenanced as the Public Welfare might require.

But the People are not fo accuftomed to the Ufe of foreign Materials, that they can hardly fubfift without them. However, this Excefs becomes lefs dangerous, when we can purchafe them with the Product of diftant Countries under our Dominion, or with whom we deal, than if we were to buy them with Money, or with Things merely of our own Growth.

For there is a limited Stock of our own Product to carry out, beyond which there is no paffing : As for Example, there is fuch a Quantity of Woollen Manufacture, Lead, Tin, &c. which, over and above our own Confumption, we can export abroad, and our Soil, as it is now peopled, will not yield much more; and there is likewife a limited Quantity of thefe Goods, which fo-

C 2   reign

(36)

reign Confumption will not exceed: Now, if our Expence of foreign Materials be above this, and more than
our own Product will fetch, for the Overplus we fhould
be forced to go to Market with Money, which would
quickly drain us, if we did not help ourfelves other
Ways, which are either by exchanging our Plantation
Goods for their Materials, or by bartering one foreign
Vanity for another ; and this we are enabled to do with
the Affiftance of our *Eaft-India* Traffic. It is true, Induftry and Frugality may encreafe our Exports, and fo
more of them will be confumed by Foreigners.

The *Weft* and *Eaft India* Trades have fo enlarged our
Stock, as to fet the general Balance for many Years on
our Side, notwithftanding all our Luxuries, which our
Home Product could not fo have anfwered, as to let the
Nation gather at the fame Time fuch a Mafs of Wealth
as the War has expended.

It is allowed that our Home Product, with the Profit
we made by the *Newfoundland* Fifhery, might fetch
from the *European* Markets, Wine, Oil, Fruits, wrought
Silks, raw Silk, Linen, &c. and befides, bring a Superlucration to this Kingdom of about 500,000 *l. per
Annum*. But having confidered more maturely this
Point than we could do when the Effay on the *Eaft-India*
Trade was written, we are therefore to think that the
Profit arifing from our *European* Trade was about
600,000 *l. per Annum*, added to the national Stock,
which, in thirty Years, is 18 Millions.

But 18 Millions could by no Means be a fufficient Sum
to anfwer the extraordinary Expences, Loffes, and Accidents, by Plague, Fire, and War, which did happen
before the Year 1688, and may be juftly computed at
30 Millions; and our Confumption all the while confidered, we muft have been impoverifhed to the laft Degree, but for the formentioned Helps.

The *Weft* and *Eaft-India* Commodities coming from diftant Parts, we make *Europe* pay us good Freight, which
is clear Gain, and by their Means we beat down the
Price of feveral Wares, as wrought Silks, raw Silk,
Linen, Sugar, &c. and by Goods and Drugs brought
from thence, we dye and manufacture feveral of our own
Commodities at a cheaper Rate; all which makes Trade
in general more beneficial to us.

In

(37)

In handling Matters of this Nature, fomething fhould be laid down to form an Idea upon; whether it is quite Right or no the Reader may judge, but if it comes near the Fact, it will hold in Proportion.

We have faid in the Effay on the *Eaft-India* Trade, * that about *Anno* 1788, the Increafe or Addition to the general Stock of *England* arifing from foreign Tade and home Manufactures, was at leaft 2 Millions yearly, and we made our Repartition thus:

	l.
From our Manufactures and home Product fent to the Plantations, and from the Returns thereof, exported to foreign Parts, — — — —	900,000
From our Woollen Manufacture, Lead, Tin, Leather, and our other native Product fent to *France, Spain, Italy, Germany,* &c. — — —	500,000
From the neat Profit accruing by the *Eaft-India* Trade, — — —	600,000
Total, £.	2,000,000

Whoever examines the Cuftom-houfe Books for fix Years, and rightly computes the Drawbacks and Exports, will find the firft Article not much miftaken; and we hope to prove the Computation relating to the *Eaft-India* Trade, in the next Difcourfe; but having granted that the Returns for thefe Goods are partly made to us in perifhable Commodities, we are to fhow, that, notwithftanding this, thefe Traffics did add to our national Stock a very large Sum.

To explain this, we muft lay down, that according to the beft Enquiry we can poffibly make, the Imports and Exports together in Times of Peace did make the Bulk of this Nation's Trade amount to about 10,000,000*l. per Annum.*

To gain yearly 2 Millions, there muft be 20 *per Cent.* Profit by Trade in general, whereas the Merchants think themfelves happy, with a clear and conftant Gain of 12 *per Cent.* But then we are to confider, that as in fome Cafes the Nation may lofe where the Merchant gets, fo in the whole, the Nation may well get 20, where the Merchant gets but 12 *per Cent.* and this Diftinction will lead us to comprehend the whole Matter.

* D'Avenant's, Works Vol. I. p. 94.

C 3

As

(38)

As for Example: A Parcel of Goods sent from hence to *Virginia* may fetch 10 Hogsheads of Tobacco, in which the Merchant may gain at the Rate only of 10 *per Cent.* but when this Tobacco is shipped again for *Amsterdam*, in the Freight backward and forward, and outward again, and in the Manufactory of the Goods sent, when the last Return comes to be made, all Parties concerned will be found to have got among them 20 *per Cent.* and much more, reckoning from the Prime Value of the Commodity exported.

And the Case of *England* seems to stand thus: We have Variety of Traffics, in some we doubled, in some trebled, and in some quadrupled the first Cost; we had likewise Dealings by which we gained 5, 8, 10, and 15 *per Cent.* and by some Trades we lost; but throwing all together by a general Medium, if, for some Years past, we had not made 20 *per Cent.* Profit by the whole Bulk of Trade, and so laid up a great Stock, we must probably have sunk under the Burthen of this last War.

Nor could we have subsisted if this Gain had not been over and above the perishable Commodities; that is to say, our own Product, joined with our Business, did not only supply our present Luxuries, but enabled us to lay up such a Stock; however, merely with the Help of our own Product we should have encreased, but not in the same Proportion; and the Wealth thereby acquired could not have maintained the War so long.

To come at the right Knowledge of what a People get by Trade, it must examined to what Value they can naturally export of their own Product, and to what Value they can carry to Market of the Product of other Parts; it must afterwards be computed what their own Consumption is of foreign Materials, by balancing this together; if there be an Overplus, that Overplus a Nation may be said to get by Traffic.

Nor is such a Balance needful, as Merchants make up every Year, to know whether a Country gets or loses by Trade, for as we have said in the first of these Discourses, it will appear by many Circumstances.

The Arguments in the first Discourse have perhaps sufficiently proved, that the Nation's general Stock towards the Year 1688, did begin to encrease annually about two Millions.

We

(39)

We have an Account from such as have formerly per-
used the Custom-house Books with great Care, that
from 1682 exclusive, to 1688 inclusive, the Value of our
Exports to *America* in Provisions of all Kinds, Apparel
and Household Furniture, might be, by a Medium of
six Years, about 350,000 *l. per Annum.*

That the Value of our Imports from the Southward
and Northward Parts of that Country, for the same
Term of Time, in Tobacco, Sugars, Ginger, Cotton-
Wool, Fustic-Wood, Indico, Cocoa, Fish, Pipe-staves,
Masts, Furs, &c. and Fish from *Newfoundland,* which
is in the Nature of a Plantation, might be about 950,000 *l.*
per Annum.

	l.
Returns, — — — — —	950,000
Prime Cost, ——— — — —	350,000
Gained,	600,000

We take it, that the Imports from the Plantations
might be about 950,000 *l.* in Times of Peace, whereof
350,000 *l.* being consumed at Home, is about equal to
our Exports thither, and the Remainder, *viz.* 600,000 *l.*
being re-exported, is the national Gain by that Trade.

To prove this Comptutation yet farther, the Writer
of these Papers has seen a Representation to King *Charles* II. from the Merchants interested in the *American*
Colonies, setting forth, that by a just Medium, the Labour of 100 Negroes is 1600 *l. per Annum,* Profit to this
Kingdom ; and we have Reasons to conclude, that there
are in *America* 100,000 Negroes, and if so, the *American* Colonies produce to *England* 1,600,000 *l. per Ann.*
but in all our Calculations we chuse rather to keep within a moderate Compass.

We agree so far with Mr. *Pollexfen,* that when we
speak of Trade in general, the Gain is so much only as
the Nation does not consume of the Imports ; but either
lays up in Commodities, in specie, or converts into Money, or some such adequate Treasure.

And the 600,000 *l.* so re-exported to the *European*
Markets, producing, in all Probability, 720,000 *l.* leaves
again 120,000 *l.* to the Trade of *Europe.*

And upon a better View of the *East-India* Trade than
we were able to make, when the Essay was written, we

C 4   find

(40)

find that the Exports to *India* in Bullion and Wares, might be about 500,000 *l. per Annum*, of which the Return might be about 1,800,000 *l.* whereof might be confumed at Home to the Value of 1,300,000 *l.* when it comes into the 2d, 3d, and 5th Hand, as fhall be explained hereafter, and re-exported to *Europe*, at leaft 500,000 *l.* which 500,000 *l.* may be ftated as the clear Gain by that Trade: and the faid 500,000*l.* exported to *Europe*, producing 680,000*l.* leaves a Gain of 180,000 *l.* to the Trade of *Europe*.

So that to make up the two Millions national Profit by Trade,

	£.
The Plantation Trade may bring in — —	600,000
The *Eaft-India* Trade may bring in ———	500,000
The *European*, *African*, and *Levant* Trade, by our own Product, may bring in — — —	600,000
Ditto, by Re-exports of Plantation Goods, — — — — —	120,000
Ditto, by Re-exports of *Eaft-India* Goods, — — — — —	180,000
In all,	2,000,000

And according to the beft Enquiry we are able to make, and from a general View of the Numbers of the People, the Stock of all Kinds that was in this Nation, and the Confumption both of our own Product and of foreign Materials, we have many Reafons to believe that this was the genuine State and true Pofture of Trade in 1688.

And as we have laid down in the firft Difcourfe, we take it that thefe two Millions did every Year turn into national Stock of different Kinds, which was vifible in the Increafe of the Species of Money, of Shipping, in the Improvements of Land, in our magnificent Buildings, in our Quantity of Plate, Jewels, fumptuous Apparel, and rich Furniture, and in the vaft Stores that were lying by us, both of our home Product and foreign Commodities, which were our principal Strength and Support while the War lafted.

Befides the 2 Millions Encreafe by Trade, if it imported our prefent Matter, we could fhow that there was a
great

(41)

great Increaſe every Year by the Inland Buſineſs of the Nation ; and theſe Additions to the Kingdom's Stock has enabled us to manage a Nine Years War, and to ſet out ſuch Fleets and Armies as were never heard of among our Anceſtors.

But we are very far from dogmatiſing upon this Sub-ject, for as we have ſaid ; * " Whoever will categorically " pronounce in Points ſo difficult, muſt look into a great " many Things."

The Writer never pretended any more than to ſhow probable Conjectures for other Perſons to reaſon upon. His firſt Account of our general Trade, publiſhed in the Eſſay on the Eaſt India Trade, Vol. I. p. 94. may have ſome Error in the Repartition of it ; and the Scheme now offered may be liable to Exception, but it is framed from the beſt Enquiry he is able to make, and hereafter he will be very willing to correct any Miſtake or ill-grounded Notion, upon better Lights and farther Information.

The Novelty of theſe Calculations will make them at firſt be much diſputed by many Perſons ; but if we had Leiſure to ſhew the Medium we go by in every Par-ticular, (which would require much a larger Volume than is here intended) moſt People would agree we come very near the Truth, and that it is as much as can be expected in ſo dark and intricate a Subject, and in an Art ſo little cultivated, as that of Reaſoning upon Things by Figures.

If the Profit from the Plantations be ſuch as are here taken Notice of, or ſomething near it, we have not any Reaſon to complain of wanting theſe Inhabitants, be-cauſe the Superlucration from the Labour of the ſame Number of Men, over and above their own Nouriſh-ment, could no Manner of Ways have been ſo beneficial to the Kingdom.

For admit the American Colonies to contain not quite 200,000 Perſons of *Engliſh* Parentage, which perhaps is pretty near the Truth, the Labour of ſuch a Number of Men reckoned in the Maſs, could by no Means bring to the Nation 720,000*l. per Ann.* clear Profit.

But in the Southward Parts, cultivating a plentiful Soil productive of Commodities not to be had elſewhere, and every Head in the Iſlands employing peradventure, Six others of Negroe Slaves and European Strangers,

D'Avenant's Works, Vol. I. p. 388.

they

(42)

they bring it to pafs, that One Head there is as profitable as Seven Heads would be in *England*.

For though the Labour in fome whole Manufactures may bring a Superlucration to the Public of above 1 *l.* yearly *per* Head, yet the Mafs of Mankind reckoned together, it is fufficient Profit, and will very much enrich a Country, if One Head with another brings to the Public 6*s.* and 8*d. per Ann.* or 7*s.* Gain, over and above his Nourifhment; whereas thofe Planters, as the foregoing Account fhews, bring much a larger Profit to this Nation.

But here it may be objected, that the Northward Parts have drained us moft of People, and yet yield Commodities of little Value; the Fact is fo, but, if it were otherwife, the Plantation Trade could not perhaps be carried on.

For thofe Soils which produce the Richer Goods, are not proper to cultivate for the Nourifhment of Life, and to yield Corn, Beef, Pork, Peafe, Flour, &c. fo that the Southern Parts, efpecially in a Time of War, would be deftitute of Neceffaries, were it not for the Induftry of the more Northern Climates.

It is true, thefe Provifions might be furnifhed from *England*, but at fuch a Rate as would peradventure much difcourage the Southern Planters. And the Northern Planters, *viz.* the People of *New-England*, *Maryland*, *Penfylvania*, *Carolina*, &c. though they furnifh the Product of the Earth to the Southern Colonies, yet they fetch from this Kingdom Variety of Manufactures, all Sorts of Clothes and Houfehold Furniture, much oftener renewed and thrice as Good, as the fame Number of People could afford to have at Home; fo that the Queftion whether the Northern Colonies are good for *England* or no, will depend upon making a right Balance between the Commodities we fend thither, and the Provifions we might fend to the Southward Plantations, if they were not fupplied from *New-England*, &c. but we are inclined to think the prefent Courfe moft advantageous to this Kingdom; and for this Reafon the Provifions we might fend to *Barbadoes*, *Jamaica*, &c. would be the unimproved Product of the Earth, as Grain of all Kind, or fuch Product where there is little got by the Improvement, as Malt, Salt Beef, and Pork. Indeed the Exportation of Salt Fifh thither would be more advantageous;

(43)

geous; but the Goods which we fend to the Northern Colonies are fuch whofe Improvements may be juftly faid, one with another, to be near Four-fifths of the Value of the whole Commodity, as Apparel, Houfehold Furniture, and many other Things.

It is true, if in *New-England,* or in other Parts there, they fhould pretend to fet up Manufactures, and to clothe, as well as feed their Neighbours, their Nearnefs and low Price would give fuch Advantages over this Nation, as might prove of pernicious Confequence; but this Fear feems very remote, becaufe New Inhabitants, efpecially in a large Extent of Country, find their Account better in rearing Cattle, Tilling the Earth, clearing it of Woods, making Fences, and by erecting necef-fary Buildings, than in fetting up Manufactures, which is the laft Work of a People fettled 300 or 400 Years, growing numerous, and wanting Territory.

And as the Cafe ftands, it feems reafonable to think, that the Northern Colonies are a Help to the Southward Planters, as their Frugality and Temperance of Living is a Counterpoife to the Excefs and Luxury with which a Rich Soil, eafy Acquifition of Wealth, and a warm Climate, has infected the Southern Inhabitants.

Though every *Englifh* Head in the Southward Plantations, when they flourifhed, did employ about Six others, yet, reckoning the whole Colonies together, our People could not be but about double the Number of the Negroes and European Strangers; fo that our Dominions there might contain about 300,000 Perfons.

And it is Matter of great admiration, how in the Space of fo few Years, fuch a Number of Men fhould be got together in a Country for the moft Part fo wild and uncultivated.

There are very near One-fixth as many People there, as in all likelihood *England* did contain at the Time of the *Norman* Conqueft.

And fuch a large Encreafe, with fo fwift a Progrefs, is no where to be met with but among the *Ifraelites* and the *Turks*; in the *Turkifh* Dominions, where *Ertrogul,* a Prince of the *Oguzian* Tribe, planting himfelf with 400 Families at the Village *Saguta,* by the Mountain *Tmolus,* about the Year 1235, laid the Foundation of the *Ottoman* Empire, which in 215 Years after, came to

subdue

(44)

fubdue a great Part of *Afia*, and to get a confiderable Footing in *Europe*.

It is true, they more enlarged their Dominions by Conqueft than by any Arts of Peace; however, thofe Numbers which their Wars continually wafted, could never have been fupplied, if they had not been a fober and temporate People, whereby they became long-lived, and fitter for Propagation.

And to the Sobriety and temperate Way of Living, practifed by the Diffenters retired to *America*, we may juftly attribute the Encreafe they have made there of Inhabitants, which is beyond the ufual Proportion to be any where elfe obferved.

The Supplies from hence do by no Means anfwer their prefent Numbers; it muft then follow that their Thrift, and regular Manner of Living, inclines them more to marry, and makes them more healthful for Generation, and affords them better Means of having the Neceffaries to fuftain Life, as wholefome Food, and Cleanly Dwelling, and Apparel, the want of which, in other Countries, is a high Article in the Burials of the Common People.

We do not pretend here to excufe the heterodox Opinions thefe Diffenters from our Church may have conceived about Religious Matters, nor to juftify their 'Schifm; but it muft be owned that the Sobriety, which at leaft they profefs outwardly, is beneficial both in Practice and Example.

For where Riot and Luxeries are not difcountenanced, the Inferior Rank of Men become prefently infected, and grow Lazy, effeminate, impatient of Labour, and expenfive, and confequently cannot thrive by Trade and Tillage; fo that when we contemplate the great Increafe and Improvements which have been made in *New-England*, *Carolina* and *Penfylvania*, we cannot but think it Injuftice not to fay, that a large Share of this general Good to thofe Parts is owing to the Education of their Planters, which, if not entirely virtuous, has a Show of Virtue; and if this were only an Appearance, it is yet better for a People that are to fubfift in a new Country by Traffic and Induftry, than the open Profef-fion and Practice of Lewdnefs, which is always attended with National Decay and Poverty.

By what has been faid in this Difcourfe, we hope it is fufficiently proved that the Plantations are advantageous

to

(45)

to *England*, and that the Southward and Northward Colonies, having such a mutual Dependence upon each other, all Circumstances considered, are almost equally important.

And to make these distant Colonies a lasting Benefit to this Nation, must take its Rise from the Wisdom which shall be shown from Time to Time in their general Conduct and Government.

The principle Care will always be to keep them dependent upon their Mother Country, and not to suffer those Laws, upon any Account, to be loosened, whereby they are tied to it; for otherwise they will become more Profitable to our Neighbours than to us.

The late ill Order in our Affairs, which perhaps was unavoidable in so big a War, does sufficiently evince what a mutual Dependence the Southern and Northern Colonies have one upon another; for so little Care was taken for the Convoys that were to protect the Supplies of Provisions for our Islands, that though all Necessaries might have been as well (though not quite so cheap) sent from *Ireland*, as from the Northern Plantations, yet it is apparent that many Times the Southern Parts must have perished for Want, if they had not been supplied by the Northern Colonies.

But however useful they may have been to his Majesty's Islands during the late War, yet perhaps it will concern the Public to look a little into the Posture of Affairs upon the Continent.

And there are some general Points, which peradventure may deserve Consideration, when it shall be thought convenient to put our Business in *America* under such a Form and Settlement as may be safe and lasting; and they are as follows:

1st, Without doubt the Negligence of former Times has suffered a greater Number of Plantations upon the Continent, than do well consist with the Navigation and other interests of their Mother Country.

2dly, It cannot be for the Public Good of a Kingdom to furnish Colonies out of it with People, when the Product of such Colonies is the same with the Kingdom's, and so rivals the Kingdom both in its Navigation and its Product, at the Markets where such Product is vended.

3dly, It can hardly be the Interest of a Country to suffer its People to make Settlements of several Plantations,

(46)

tations, that yield One and the same Commodity. For Inhabitants thus difperfed, are neither fo ufeful to each other in Time of Peace, not ftrong enough to defend themfelves in Times of War: So that their Mother Kingdom is ufually at a great Charge for their Defence; whereas, if they lay in a more compaCt and lefs extended Territory, they could be more ready to give each other mutual Help, and not be expofed, as they are, to every little Strength and infult of an Invader.

4thly, As many Empires have been ruined by too much enlarging their Dominions, and by grafping at too great an extent of Territory, fo our Intereft in America may decay, by aiming at more Provinces, and a greater TraCt of Land than we can either cultivate or defend. Upon which Account, it may perhaps be fome Time or other worth the Confideration of the State, whether a Way might not be propofed of collecting within a narrower Compafs the fcattered Inhabitants of the Continent, by inviting fome to cultivate the Iflands where their Labour is moft profitable to this Kingdom, and by drawing the reft, if poffible, to Four or Five of the Provinces beft fituate and moft productive of Commodities not to be had in *Europe*. But this is to be done with great Deliberation, with a due Regard to Property, by Degrees, and by good Encouragement.

5thly, Former Times have not only been faulty in fuffering too many Provinces to be erected; but in the Repartition of the Land taken in, there are Corruptions connived at very prejudicial to the Plantation Trade, and the King's Cuftoms from thence arifing. As for Example, it is much wondered at, that *Virginia*, the firft *Englifh* Settlement upon the Continent, made about 80 Years ago, fhould have thriven no better; fome attribute it to the Badnefs of the Climate, but other Reafons may be plainly affigned for its ill Succefs, which perhaps are as follow:

The Planters and Inhabitants have been, and at this Time are difcouraged from Planting Tobacco in that Colony, and Servants are not fo willing to go thither as formerly, becaufe the Members of the Council, and others, who make Intereft in the Government there, have, from Time to Time, procured Grants of very large TraCts of Land, fo that there has not, for many
Years,

(47)

Years, béen any wafte Grounds left for to be culti-
vatɛd by thofe who bring with them Servants, or by
fuch Servants as have ferved their Time faithfully with
their Mafters, it being all taken up and engroffed be-
fore-hand; whereby they are forced to pay a Yearly
Rent for this Ground, or to go the utmoft bounds of
Colony for Land to improve, by which Means they are
expofed to Danger, and this often furnifhes Matter for
War or Quarrels with the *Indians*.

The Manner of taking up Land in *Virginia* is thus:
Every Adventurer or Planter has, upon his Arrival, a
right to 50 Acres of Land in the Colony: If he intends
to take up any, he is firft to make Oath before the
Governor or Council, or at a County Court, of the
Number of Perfons he defigns to import, and they of
courfe grant him a Certificate thereupon, which is entered in the Secretary's Office, and is then produced
by him to the Surveyor of the County where the Land
lies wafte, who makes a Survey, allowing 50 Acres,
according to the Number of his rights, i. e. Perfons Imported, which, with the rights, is carried to the Secretary's Office, on which a Patent is made out, and figned
by the Governor in Council, who caufes the Seal of the
Colony to be affixed to it, which gives the Claimer an
Eftate in Fee-fimple; but upon the following Conditions: 1ft, To pay the King 1*s.* *per Annum* Quit-rent
for every 50 Acres. 2dly, To Seat fuch Land within
Three Years (otherwife it is prefumed to be deferted).
By Seating Land is meant that they build a Houfe, and
put fome Stock of Cattle upon it. 3dly, To keep Four
able Men armed upon the new Plantation, if it lie far
up in the Country.

Thefe are the Terms upon which the Land is granted,
but they are feldom obferved. The Quit-rent is rarely
paid. Inftead of Building and Stocking, they fell a few
Trees, and throw up a little Hut covered with Bark,
and put three or four Hogs into the Woods: No
Servants are left to defend or Cultivate the Ground,
but in this fallacious Way they are fuffered to keep up
their Claim, and to maintain Poffeffion.

And thefe Grants being procured upon fuch eafy
Terms, and very often upon wrong Suggeftions and falfe
Certificates, it comes to pafs, that many hold 20 or
30,000 Acres of Land a-piece, and that largely furveyed;

(48)

ed ; fome Patents including double the Quantity of Land that was intended to be graated : And from hence it proceeds that many Hundred thoufand Acres are, as they call it, taken up, but not planted, which Practice drives away the Inhabitants and Servants bred up only to Planting, and forces them into Colonies where their Labour is not fo profitable either to the Crown or to the People of this Kingdom, as it would be in a Province not producing Commodities that are of *Englifh* Growth. And thefe practices are, without doubt, a chief Caufe that our Colony in *Virginia* has had no better Succefs.

We have dwelt the longer in reprefenting this Matter of Fact, concerning which we have certain Information, only to fhow of what ill Confequence it is to grafp at an extended but a barren Dominion. And this Confideration, perhaps, will lead the Public fome Time or other to make Provifion :

1ft, Hereafter to hinder any new Plantation, efpecially on a Soil producing what may be had from the Soil of *England* or *Ireland*.

. 2dly, To endeavour the rendering this Territory lefs extenfive, but better peopled, and confequently in a readier Condition to improve and defend itfelf.

3dly, To eftablifh fomething like an Agrarian Law, by which we would not be underftood to propofe a levelling the Property and rightful Poffeffion of the Inhabitants, but only to reftrain fuch a fradulent taking up of Land (to ufe their own Term) as is a Bar to the Induftry of others.

Our Intereft in *America*, generally fpeaking, may bring an immenfe Profit to this Kingdom, if it was well looked after by the Government here, but otherwife in all. likliehood it will either decline or come to be a Strength that may be turned againft us.

If fuch a Sheme of a Council of Trade as we have propofed in the Second Difcourfe, be not thought advifeable, it is fubmitted to Public Confideration, whether the Plantations are not of importance enough to deferve a particular Council to be eftablifhed by the King, for the Infpection of Affairs thereunto relating, in the following, or fome fuch like Method.

1ft, That the Care of *America* be made the Province of a felect Number of Lords and Gentlemen of Reputation,

{ 49 }

tation, both for Parts and Fortune, and in such a Number as will admit of Two Committees, that so Business may be better dispatched.

2dly, That they be authorized under the Great Seal of *England*, by the Name and Stile of Lords Commissioners for the *English* Plantations in *America*, to consider and inspect all Affairs relating to the Government, Trade, Revenues, Plantations, and further Improvement of those Countries.

3dly, And no Business being well done in this Kingdom, where Attendance is not recompensed with some Advantage, that every Commissioner have a Salary of 1000 *l. per Ann.*

4thly, That the respective Colonies be required to send a true State of their Case to these Lords; as for Example, of their Situation, Extent of Territory, Numbers of People, Produce, Revenue, Civil Policy, with Proposals which Way to improve every Country, to their own and their Nation's Profit; and all to be registered in the Plantation Office.

This, compared with what Enquiries the Lords may themselves make, and Informations they may receive at Home, may give them such an Idea and Knowledge of all Affairs in *America*, as it will not be difficult for them to put Things into a Form and Order of Government that shall always preserve those Countries in their Obedience to the Crown, and Dependence upon this Kingdom; and probably, if they are thus made the peculiar Care of some Body of Men, they will be a lasting Revenue to the King, an inexhaustible Mine of Treasure to *England* in general, and a great Means to multiply Seamen and encrease our Navigation.

Such a Constitution will be something like what we call the Council of the *Indies* in *Spain*; but here it may be objected, that the *Spaniards* are not very good Patterns to follow in any Model or Scheme of Government; to which it may be answered, that whoever considers the Laws, and Politic Institutions of *Spain*, will find them as well formed, and contrived with as much Skill and Wisdom, as in any Country perhaps in the World: So that the Errors *that* People is observed to commit from Time to Time, do not proceed from a wrong and ill Projection, but from the negligent, loose, and unsteady Executions of their Councils.

D *Xenophon,*

(50)

Xenophon, in that Tract which is published at the End of the First Part of these Discourses, says, " That Governments refemble their Governors." This Maxim of his is certainly right; and from thence it follows, that the Welfare of the *American* Colonies will very much depend upon the Conduct and Behaviour of such as are sent to recide and govern there by the King's Authority.

In former Times, this Part of Policy has without Doubt been very much neglected, there having generally been put at the Head of these Affairs Abroad, indigent, ignorant, or extravagant Persons, of which one Sort made a Prey, and the others, by their Examples, corrupted the Manners of the People.

A good General, by the very March and Demeanor of a Regiment, can make a near Guess at the Understanding and Abilities of the Colonel, if he be unskilful and without Discipline, every private Centinel shall carry the Marks of it about him.

The same holds, and much more strongly, in the Government of higher Matters : It must therefore be of great Importance to the State, that he who is to command a Country containing many thousand Families, should be a Man of Abilities, Experience, Dexterity, Courage, Temper, and Virtue ; he ought to be endowed with such a general Knowledge as may comprehend the Nature of the Soil where he is, what Improvements it is capable of, and what Trades will be most advantageous to it. He should be able likewise to look into the Genius of the People he is to govern : he should be a Man of Discipline, Sobriety, and Justice, for he that is not so in his own Person, can never expect Order, nor compel others to obey the Laws. A People to whom Riches and Plenty furnish Matter for Vice and Luxury, should be governed by a strict and skilful Hand, which may reform their Manners, and at the same Time both promote and direct their Industry.

In all Appearance, hardly any Thing would more conduce to the good Government of these Places, than to follow one Course, which the King of *France* strictly observes in his Plantations, and it is to give very large Appointments to the Governors out of his own Coffers, not allowing them any Perquisites, or to draw any Advantages or Profit from the Inhabitants.

And

(51)

And as care fhould be taken to keep them obedient to the Laws of *England*, and dependent upon their Mother Country, fo thofe Conditions, Privileges, Terms, and Charters, fhould be kept facred and inviolate, by which they were firft encouraged at their great Expence, and with the Hazard of their Lives, to difcover, cultivate, and plant remote Places, where in truth they labour as well for us as for themfelves, for here at laft their Treafure centers.

The Northern Colonies are not upon the fame Foot as thofe of the South; and having a worfe Soil to improve, they muft find their Recompence fome other Way, which only can be in Property, and Dominion : Upon which Score, any Innovations in the Form of Government there, fhould be cautioufly examined, for fear of entering upon Meafures by which the Induftry of the Inhabitants may be quite difcouraged.

It is always unfortunate for a People, either by Confent or upon Compulfion, to depart from their primitive Inftitutions, and thofe Fundamentals by which they were firft united together : Liberty, choice of their own Chief Magiftrates and Officers, was the Part conftituent of principal Societies that have fucceeded fo well in the Northward Regions ; to appoint them Governors from hence, will certainly be for the Good of the Courtiers here, but whether this Courfe in the Event will be advantageous for thofe Plantations, is not fo eafy to determine.

But, without Doubt, it muft be very prejudicial both to the Southward and Northern Colonies, that many Offices and Places of Truft there fhould be granted by Patent to Perfons in *England*, with Liberty to execute fuch Employments by Deputies, by which Means they are generally farmed out to indigent Perfons, who grind and fleece the People : So that the Inhabitants, though many of them are rich, fober, and judicious Men, yet they are excluded from Offices of Truft, except fuch as are chargeable in the Execution, which is inconfiftent with all the Rules of well governing a Country.

They who have vifited the North Tract of *America*, and who have obferved the feveral Ways and Degrees of Cultivation, with refpect to the Quality and Quantity of their Produce, the Oeconomy of the People, and the Adminiftration of the refpective Governments, cannot better exprefs the Difproportion throughout, between

D 2

Place

(52)

Place and Place, than by comparing them with the many Principalities and States of *Germany*, where the Proteſtant Countries are, for the moſt Part, better peopled, and their Towns better kept, than thoſe under Catholic Governments: And ſo it fares with the Hans or Free Towns, as they are called, above thoſe under abſolute and arbitrary Princes: Where the Conſtitution is freer, and the Magiſtracy more ſober, the People are more induſtrious, and the Country improves in proportion.

And had it not been for Provinces begun and carried on by People of Sobriety, the *Engliſh* Empire abroad would be much weaker than it is at preſent; it having been the Unhappineſs of ſome to take their Original from another Race of Planters, vicious, needy, or criminal, who, though a Profit to the Kingdom by being there, yet by no Means in proportion with the other Sort. And as Licentiouſneſs breaks out much more apparently in ſuch Places, ſo that it is not all, for Governors (as is ſaid) are too apt to make their Advantages of it, who, by indulging ſuch Extravagancies, find their own Accounts the better; it being plain that the common People are but too ready to exchange their Liberties for Licentiouſneſs, and to wink at thoſe who will connive at them.

If ever any Thing great or good be done for our *Engliſh* Colonies, Induſtry muſt have its due Recompence, and that cannot be without Encouragement to it, which, perhaps, is only to be brought about by confirming their Liberties, and eſtabliſhing good Diſcipline among them: That, as they ſee they are a free People in Point of Government, ſo they may, by Diſcipline, be kept free of the Miſchiefs that follow Vice and Idleneſs.

And as great Care ſhould be taken in this Reſpect, ſo, without Doubt, it is adviſable, that no little Emulations or private Intereſts of neighbour Governors, nor that the Petitions of hungry Courtiers at Home, ſhould prevail to diſcourage thoſe particular Colonies, who, in a few Years, have raiſed themſelves by their own Charge. Prudence, and Induſtry, to the Wealth and Greatneſs they are now arrived at, without Expence to the Crown: Upon which Account any Innovations or Breach of their original Charters (beſides that it ſeems a Breach of the Public Faith) may, peradventure, not tend to the King's Profit.

In thoſe Colonies, which, by Charter, are not governed from hence, as to all Dues belonging to the Crown Revenue,

(53)

Revenue, the King has an immediate Influence, by having an Officer of his own upon the Spot, as in other Places.

And the Dues of the Crown arifing from the Improvements of the Soil, it feems more probable that fuch Improvement fhould be made by thofe who have an Intereft and Property in the Country, and who work for themfelves, than by Governors fent from hence, whofe moft common Aim is to grow rich by fleecing the Inhabitants; and this Property is, without Doubt, the beft Caution and Pledge for their good Behaviour, both to the King and to his Subjects in thofe remote Parts, who, as it is faid, in former Times, have been feverely handled by tranfient Governors.

The Welfare of all Countries whatfoever depends upon good Government; and, without Doubt, thefe Colonies will flourifh, if they are intrufted to honeft, difcreet, and fkilful Hands, who will let them perceive they enjoy the Rights and Liberties of *Englifhmen*, though not in *England*.

Induftry has its firft Foundation in Liberty: They who either are Slaves, or who believe their Freedoms precarious, can neither fucceed in Trade nor meliorate a Country. We fhall not pretend to determine whether the People in the Plantations have a Right to all the Privileges of *Englifh* Subjects; but the contrary Notion is perhaps too much entertained and practifed in Places which happen to be diftant from St. *Stephen*'s Chapel. Upon which Account it will peradventure be a great Security and Encouragement to thefe induftrious People, if a declaratory Law were made that *Englifhmen* have Right to all the Laws of *England*, while they remain in Countries fubject to the Dominion of this Kingdom. But as the arbitrary Proceedings and Mal-adminiftration of Governors fhould be feverely animadverted upon, fo frivolous and wrong Complaints fhould be as much difcouraged.

And in this Place we think ourfelves obliged to take Notice, that Public Enquiry ought to be made into the oppreffive and fcandalous Behaviour of fome Merchants towards the Sugar and Tobacco Planters.

When the Matters of *America* fhall come under fuch a Confideration, as may produce a Settlement, the Parties concerned in Trade, Property, and Intereft, will be able to Inftance many particular Regulations that may

D 3   improve

(54)

improve the Country and render the Traffic more profitable. In the mean while we have offered what has oc-
cured to our Obfervation, to which we fhall add fome
few Remarks relating to the Trade, Government, and
Civil Policy of thofe Countries; which are,

1ft, That no Province fhould obftruct or clog the
Paffage of any Ship, or Goods coming from *England*
through it, with any Cuftom or Duty; for that it plainly
incommodes and difcourages the King's Subjects, and
puts them upon making Shift without the Ufe of thofe
Goods, and fo far hinders the Confumption of our *Englifh* Product and Manufacture, and thereby hurts Trade
and Navigation; befides, it is unwarrantable by the
Laws of *England*.

2dly, That where the Navigation Act forbids it not,
a Coaft Trade from Province to Province fhould be
allowed there, as it is here from County to County; by
which Means Sloth will be punifhed with Want, as it
fhould always be, and Induftry will receive its juft
Reward.

3dly, That one Province fhould not protect the Fugi-
tives of another for Crimes or Debts, but that Juftice
fhould be done according to the Conftitution of the feveral Provinces.

4thly, It feems neceffary to put *Newfoundland*, now
growing confiderable, under fome Government or other
Regulation as the Plantations are.

5thly, It may be worth the Confideration of the State,
whether this prefent Peace may not be a proper Seafon
to build Forts and Citadels for Security of the Principal Iflands, in Cafe of a future War.

6thly, Care fhould undoubtedly be taken, not to lay
fuch heavy Duties upon the *Weft-India* Commodities,
as may difcourage Induftry, difpeople the Iflands, and,
in Procefs of Time, perhaps make the Planters defperate. And here it may not be improper to take Notice
particularly of the high Impofition laid upon refined
Sugars, imported hither upon a wrong Notion of advancing our Manufactures; whereas, in truth, it only
turns to the Account of about 50 Families, (for the Re-
finers of *England* are no more) and is greatly prejudicial,
and a Bar to the Induftry of at leaft 14,000 Perfons,
which are about the Number of thofe who inhabit our
Iflands producing Sugar.

7thly,

(55)

7thly, It would very much conduce to the Support and Prosperity of the Sugar and Tobacco Plantations, to put the *African* Trade into some better Order. So great a Part of. our Foreign Business arising from these Colonies, they ought undoubtedly to have all due Encouragement, and to be plentifully supplied, and at reasonable Rates, with Negroes, to meliorate and cultivate the Land. The Labour of these Slaves is the principal Foundation of our Riches there ; upon which Account, we should take all probable Measures to bring them to us at easy Terms.

There are Three Ways of managing the *African* Trade; by a Joint Stock, by an open Traffic, or by a regulated Company ; which of these will be the best is not very easy to determine : but in Matters of this Nature, Experience is the surest Guide we can have to follow.

And Experience has taught us, that this Trade has not been governed with good Success, by a Company with a Joint Stock. For it is alledged that they have not supplied the Planters with such a Plenty of Negroes as was requisite ; that they forced them to accept of such a Sort as they thought fit to bring ; that the usual and fair Rate should be, One Head with another, from 16 *l.* to 20 *l. per* Head, which by ill supplying the Market, they brought to 40 *l.* and 45 *l. per* Head. That in their Dealings, they took Bond and Judgment of the Planters, with an Interest of 10 *l. per Cent.* executing their Securities upon Non-payment, by seizing the Plantations with the utmost Rigour. And that these Courses have almost depopulated the Southern Islands.

It must certainly be prudent in any Trade, Manufacture or Business, to render the first Material as cheap as possible. Slaves are the first and most necessary Material for Planting ; from whence follows that all Measures should be taken that may produce such a Plenty of them, as may be an Encouragement to the Industrious Planter.

For these Reasons, it is submitted to better Judgements, whether it may not be for the Interest of *England* to manage the *African* Trade, as that to *Turkey* is carried on by a regulated Company. By which we mean, that it should be free for any Merchant to deal to *Africa*, and from thence to the Islands, and from the Islands to the other Colonies, paying so much *per* Pound, as may

D 4   be

(56)

be thought needful to bear the common Expences of the Trade, and to maintain Forts and Garrifons upon the Coaft, if they are thought neceffary.

In the Regulations of our Foreign Traffic, the Nature of the Trade itfelf, and the Manners of the People with whom we deal, are to be confidered; but Experience is chiefly to be confulted.

The Courfe of many Years, and the Practice of all our Neighbours, feem to approve of a Joint Stock, as the beft Courfe of managing the *Eaft-India* Trade; and we fhall endeavour to fhew in the next Difcourfe, that it is not well to be fupported any other Way.

But we are inclined to think, that to lay the *African* Trade a little more open, and to put it under a regulated Company, is more confiftent with the Intereft of our Plantations.

The Circumftances of the *African* and *Eaft-India* Trade differ extremely: In the *Indies* we have powerful Concurrents, who, in Procefs of Time, may be able to fupplant us, againft whom united Wifdom, Stock and Councils, are of abfolute Neceffity; but we are not under Apprehenfions of Rivals upon the Coaft of *Afric*.

The Stock of the *Eaft-India* Trade was 1,574,608 *l.* and the Trade will bear a Stock of two Millions, which is too great a Sum, and too confiderable a National Concern, to be trufted to the diforderly Meafures of an unfkilful Number of Traders; whereas experienced Planters will be the chief Dealers to *Africa*; and the Stock needful (as far as is yet known) for the *African* Trade does not exceed 200,000 *l.* and the Stock employed by the late Company, as we are informed, did not amount to above 75,000 *l.*

The Writer of thefe Papers has feen a Scheme for the general Government of the Northward Plantations, which feems contrived with very good Judgement; upon which Account, he thought it not unfeafonable to offer the Heads of it here to Public Confideration.

1. That the Colonies of *Bofton, Connecticut, Rhode Ifland, New York,* both the *New Jerfeys, Penfylvania, Maryland, Virginia,* and *Carolina,* may be authorifed to meet once a Year, and oftener if Need require, by their ftated and appointed Deputies, to debate and refolve of fuch Meafures as fhall be moft advifable, at any Time, to take for their Public Tranquility and Safety.

2. That

(57)

2. That in Order to it, Two Perfons well qualified for Underftanding, Sobriety and Subftance, be appointed by each Province, as their Reprefentatives or Deputies, which, in the whole, will make the Congrefs to confift of Twenty Perfons.

3. That the King's Commiffioner for that Purpofe efpecially to be appointed, fhould have the Chair, and prefide in the faid Congrefs.

4. That they fhould meet as near as conveniently may be to the moft central Colony, for the Eafe of the Deputies.

5. Since that may, in all Probability, be in *New York*, both becaufe it is near the Centre of the Colonies, and for that it is a Frontier, and the Governor in the King's Nomination; that Governor to be likewife the King's High Commiffioner during the Seffion, after the Manner of *Scotland*.

6. That their Bufinefs fhould be to hear and adjuft all Matters of Complaint or Difference between Province and Province: As 1ft, Where Perfons quit their own Province and go to another, that they may avoid their juft Debts, though able to pay them. 2dly, Where Offenders fly Juftice, or Juftice cannot well be had upon fuch Offenders in the Provinces that entertain them: 3dly, To prevent or redrefs Injuries in Point of Commerce. 4thly, To Confider of Ways and Means to fupport the Union and Safety of thefe Provinces, againft their common Enemies: In which Congrefs, the Quotas of Men and Charges will be much eafier and more equally allotted and Proportioned, than it is poffible for any Eftablifhment made here to do; for the Provinces knowing their own Condition and one another's, can debate that Matter with more Freedom and Satisfaction, and better adjuft and Balance their Affairs in all refpects for their Common Safety.

That in Times of War the King's High Commiffioner fhould be General or chief Commander of the feveral Quotas, upon Service againft the Common Enemy, as fhall be thought advifeable for the Good and Benefit of the whole.

This Conftitution has fome Refemblance with the Court of the *Amphictiones*, which was a Kind of Council where the general Affairs of *Greece* were debated; which if they could have preferved in its original Purity,

and

{ 58 }

and to the firſt Deſign of it, that Country had not been
ſo eaſy a Conqueſt to the *Romans.*

The Welfare of all Countries in the World depends
upon the Morals of their People.

For though a Nation may gather Riches by Trade,
Thrift, Induſtry, and from the Benefit of its Soil and
Situation; and though a People may attain to great
Wealth and Power, either by Force of Arms, or by the
Sagacity of their Councils; yet, when their Manners
are depraved, they will decline inſenſibly, and at laſt
come to utter Deſtruction.

When a Country is grown vicious, Induſtry decays,
the People become effeminate and unfit for Labour.
To maintain Luxury, the great Ones muſt oppreſs the
meaner Sort; and to avoid this Oppreſſion, the meaner
Sort are often compelled to ſeditious Tumults, or open
Rebellion.

Such therefore who have modelled Governments for
any Duration have endeavoured to propoſe Methods by
which the Riotous Appetites, the Luſts, Avarice, Re-
venge, Ambition, and other diſorderly Paſſions of the
People, might be bounded.

And to preſerve Societies of Men from that perpetual
War with which the State of Nature muſt be attended,
and to reſtrain that Diſcord which muſt for ever embroil thoſe who only follow the wild Dictates of ungo-
verned Nature, the Founders of Cities, States, and Empires, have ſet a-foot Forms of religious Worſhip to awe
their Minds, and deviſed wholeſome Laws to keep within Bounds the Perſons of the People.

It has been ſet forth in the Series of this Diſcourſe, of
what Profit the *American* Plantations have been to *England*; and it may not be improper before we conclude,
to add ſomething concerning their future Polity and
Government, and to ſhew what methods, in all Likelihood may preſerve their Being in that remote Region,
give them Stability and a firm Exiſtence, and ſo render
them a laſting Mine of Riches, and a perpetual Advantage to this Kingdom.

And as a Foundation, we think it neceſſary to lay
down, that thoſe Countries cannot ſubſiſt long in a
flouriſhing Condition, and in their Obedience to this
Crown, unleſs Care be taken to cultivate Morality and
Virtue among them, to promote Religion, and to eſtabliſh

(59)

tablish found Laws, by which they may be well and wifely governed.

But here it may be objected, 1st, What Form of Religion shall be set up among a People, who, many of them, have left their Native Soil, chiefly to enjoy a more ample Liberty in religious Matters ? 2dly, How can virtuous Principles be instilled into Men, the Bad-nefs of whose Lives and Manners have compelled most of them to feek another Habitation ?

To the First Objection we answer, That the same Liberty of Confcience ought to be permitted there as here ; but that the Governors and Magistrates should take Care to keep the People to the Obfervation of fome Religion or other ; and now more efpecially, fince the Laws have in a Manner allowed every Man to chufe which Sect he pleafes.

To the Second Objection we fay, That the *Roman* Nation was first compofed of Thieves, Vagabonds, fu-gitive Slaves, indebted Perfons, and Outlaws; and yet, by a good Conftitution and wholefome Laws, they be-came and continued for fome Ages, the moft virtuous People that was ever known ; fo that as loofe Adminif-tration corrupts any Society of Men, fo a wife, fteady, and ftrict Government, will in Time reform a Country, let its Manners have been never fo depraved.

And the fame good Government would undoubtedly reclaim thofe Vices which fome of our *American* Planters may have carried thither.

Whenever a Country lofes that Reverence that is due to Religion and the Laws, we may fafely Pro-nounce, that its Ruin is not very Diftant.

And as Contempt of Religion and the Laws, is a fure Mark of a declining Nation ; fo new Colonies and Societies of Men muft foon fall to Pieces, and dwindle to nothing, unlefs their Governors and Magistrates in-terpofe, to feafon betimes the Minds of fuch a new People, with a Senfe of Religion, and with good and virtuous Principles.

Themiftocles did once fay, that of a fmall City he could make a great People. This he fpake from the right Senfe he had of his own Abilities and Skill. Go-vernors and Magistrates that are the Reverfe of him, and who rule weakly, can render a potent Country in a fhort Time poor, defpifed, and Miferable.

Such

(60)

Such to whom the Government of thefe Colonies is intrufted, fhould endeavour to hinder the growth of all Kind of Vices, as Intemperance and Luxury; for Luxury is the Parent of Want, and Want begets in the Minds of Men Difobedience and Defire of Change.

To fee that Impiety be not countenanced, nor Books expofed to the Vulgar, which tend to the Overthrow or weakening of the general Notions of Religion, fhould be no lefs their Care.

It is no lefs their Duty to promote Virtue, and to encourage Merit of any Kind, and to give it their helping Hand: Such as have been counted great and able Statefmen in all Countries, have fo done; and judged that to propagate what was good, and to fupprefs Vice, was the moft material Part of Government.

They fhould difcountenance Immoralities of all Sorts; they fhould fee them expofed in Public; they fhould caufe the Pulpits to declaim againft them; they fhould make them a Bar to Preferment, and the Laws fhould be all pointed againft them.

Such a Conduct, with Encouragements to Learning and learned Men, a careful Education of their Prime Youth, in feafoning of them betimes with the Senfe of Honour, and a Love to their Mother Country, will go very far towards correcting the Manners of thefe new-planted and licentious People.

They will reap this Fruit by cultivating Letters and Learning, that the wife Precepts and great Examples which are to be met with in ancient Hiftories, will inflame the Minds of their Young Men with a Defire of the Renown and Glory with which good Actions are attended; and from thence they will learn to fubdue thofe Paffions and Appetites that otherwife may lead them into warm, foolifh, and deftructive Counfels.

But this is not a Diet for the Vulgar; Philofophy and Moral Rules will prevail very little with the Common People, and but few Underftandings are capable of the Benefits which may be received from thence: Wife Lawgivers have therefore endeavoured to keep the inferior Rank of Men within Bounds, by a Senfe of Religion, and a Fear of offending that Power by which they were created.

And becaufe the Capacities of Men were at firft very grofs, requiring grofs Objects, the Divine Rights

inftituted

(61)

inftituted in the Beginning had not their Foundation
in the Mind, but confifted in bodily Worfhip, Cere-
monies and Sacrifice: It is true, the wifer Sort had
generally One Religion for themfelves, and another for
the Vulgar.

However, they governed and kept the Common People in Awe with thefe Holy Myfteries, and that Kind
of Worfhip that was in Practice by the Laws and Cuftom of their Country, never difturbing them with any
nicer Speculations.

A few of the Sublimer underftandings might adore
God, becaufe he is the moft perfect Being ; love Virtue for its own fake ; and, upon the fame Score, revere
Juftice ; but thefe Principles were not fufficient to keep
a giddy Multitude in Order; therefore, in all Civilized Countries, a Form of Divine Worfhip has been
fettled.

And here we cannot help taking Notice, that if Philofophy will not fuffice to bind the Common People to
their Duty, what muft be faid of fome modern Politicians, who fhew no Defire of fetting up Morality, and
yet are pulling down revealed Religion.

Statefmen have been accufed of being uncertain themfelves in religious Points; but till lately they were never
feen to countenance in others fuch a Loofenefs, and
till of late Years, it was never known a Recommenda-
tion to Preferment.

Would it any Thing avail the Public to have the fettled Opinions concerning Divine Matters quite altered
by the Law ? If not, Why do fuch as propofe Innovations in revealed Religion, find fo many open Advocates,
and thofe of the higheft Rank ? On the contrary, muft it
not much diftract the State, to fet the Minds of Men once
more afloat in thefe myfterious Points, which are now believed, and cannot perhaps be examined with any Safety to
the Public ? How comes it to pafs that the Majority fuffer
themfelves to be guided, and often with hard Reins, by
by a fmall Number ? Can it be imagined this is brought
about by a right Difpofition of Power, whereby the
weak come to hold the ftrong in their Dominion ? Or
can it be thought that Laws are fufficient to Subject the
Bodies of Men to Government, unlefs fomething elfe
did conftrain their Confcience and their Minds ?

It

(62)

It is hardly to be doubted, but that if the Common People are once induced to lay afide Religion, they will quickly caft off all fear of their Rulers. But fuch as object againft the Revealed Religion, as it is now tranf-mitted to us, have they another Scheme ready? When they have pulled down the old Frame, can they fet up a better in its Room? Moft certainly by their own Lives either in private, or in Relation to the Public, they feem very unfit Apoftles to propagate a new Belief.

When the Common People all of a fudden become corrupt, and by quicker Steps than was ever known; when they do not revere the Laws; when there is no mutual Juftice among them; when they defraud the Prince; when they proftitute their Voices in Elections, it may be certainly concluded, that fuch a Country is by the Artifice of fome, and the Negligence of others, fet loofe in the Principles of Religion.

Nothing therefore can more conduce to correcting the Manners of a depraved People, than a due Care of religious Matters; a right Devotion to God will beget Patience in national Calamities, fubmiffion to the Laws, obedience to the Prince, love to one another, and a Hatred to Faction; and it will produce in the Minds of all the different Ranks of Men, true Zeal and Affection to their Country's Welfare.

For thefe Reafons, if it fhould be thought conveni-ent to fettle a Council of Trade by Authority of Parlia-ment, as has been propofed in the Second of thefe Dif-courfes, or fuch a Council for the *Indies*, as is mentioned in this Tract, the Legiflative Power may, from Time to Time, recommend to either of thefe Eftablifhments the Care of infpecting the State of Religion in our *American* Colonies; and they may enjoin the Governors who fhall be fent to refide there.

1. To look into the Lives and Manners of the prefent Clergy.

2. To fee that no Doctrines are publifhed, deftructive to the very Fundamentals of Religion itfelf.

3. Not to enflame, but rather to reconcile thofe Dif-ferences, which of Neceffity muft arife among People of fuch different Perfuafions.

4. To cultivate into the Minds of the Inhabitants, fober Living, Friendfhip, general Obfervance of the De-votion each profeffes, Charity, Meeknefs and Piety, efpecially

(63)

especially among those who are trusted to guide the Consciences of others.

5. To Season betimes the young Men of better Rank and Fortune with a love to *England*, their original Country, that when they return hither with the riches the Industry of their Parents has acquired, they may become good Patriots here, and useful Members of the Commonwealth.

In order to Protection, they ought to believe *England* their native Soil; and in order to preserve them in their Obedience, we ought to imprint this Notion in their Minds as much as possible.

Few Crimes, either private or relating to the Public, can be committed by those whose Minds are early seasoned with the Principle of loving and promoting the Welfare of their native Country. For, generally speaking, all our Vices whatsoever turn to her Prejudice; and if we were convinced of this betimes, and if from our very Youth we were seasoned with this Notion, we should of Course be virtuous, and our Country would prosper and flourish, in Proportion to this Amendment of our Manners.

Wherever private Men can be brought to make all their Actions and Counsels, Thoughts and Designments, to center in the common Good, that Nation will soon gather such Strength as shall resist any home-bred Mischief or outward Accident.

No great Thing was ever done, but by such as have preferred the Love of their Country to all other Considerations; and wherever this Public Spirit reigns, and where this Zeal for the Common Good governs in the Minds of Men, that State will flourish and encrease in Riches and Power; and wherever it declines, or is set at nought, Weakness, Disorder, and Poverty, must be expected.

This Love to their Native Soil, where it has been deeply rooted, and where it could be preserved, has made little Cities famous and invincible, as *Sparta*, *Corinth*, *Thebes* and *Athens*, and from thence all the *Roman* Greatness took its Rise. But where they are wretchedly contriving their own Ends, without any Care of their Country's Profit, or trafficking its Wealth and Liberties for Rewards, Preferments and Titles; where every One is snatching all he can from the

Prince;

(64)

Prince; and where there is a general Neglect of national Interest, they grow luxurious, proud, falfe and effeminate; and a People fo depraved, is commonly the Prey of fome Neighbour feafoned with more Wife and better Principles.

In a Kingdom but too near us, we may fee all Sorts of Men labouring the Public Welfare, and every one as vigilant in his Poft, as if the Succefs of the whole Empire depended on his fingle Care and Diligence; fo that to the Shame of another Place, they feem more intent upon the Profperity and Honour of their Country, under a hard and oppreffive Tyranny, than they are in fome free Nations, where the People have an Intereft in the Laws, and are a Part of the Conftitution.

Homer in his two Poems feems to intend but two Morals. In the *Illiads* to fet out how fatal Difcord among the great Ones is to States and Armies. And in his *Odyffeys* to fhew, that the Love of our own Country ought to be ftronger than any other Paffion; for he makes *Ulyffes* quit the Nymph *Calypfo* with all her Pleafures, and the Immortality fhe had promifed him, to return to *Ithica*, a rocky and barren Ifland.

The Affairs of a Country relating either to Civil Government, War, the Revenues, or Trade, can never be well and profperoufly conducted, unlefs the Men of principal Rank and Figure diveft themfelves of their Paffions, Self-intereft, overweening Opinion of their own Merits, their Flattery, falfe Arts, mean Ambition, and irregular Appetites and Purfuits, after Wealth and Greatnefs.

No People did ever become famous and powerful but by Temperance, Fortitude, Juftice, Reverence to the Laws, and Piety to their Country; and when any Empire is deftined to be undone, or to lofe its Freedom, the Seeds of this Ruin are to be firft feen in the Corruption of its Manners. In vicious Governments all Care of the Public is laid afide, and every one is plundering for himfelf, as if the Commonwealth were adrift, or had fuffered Shipwreck; and where a People is thus depraved, their National Affemblies have the firft open Marks of the Infection upon them, from whence fpring all Diforders in the State whatfoever. For then, fuch as have moft Eloquence, Valour, Skill in Bufinefs, and moft Intereft in their Country, throw off the Mafk of Popularity which they had put on for a Time, and in
the

the Face of the World defire Wealth, Honours, and Greatnefs upon any Terms; and this Ambition leads them to corrupt others, that their own natural Vices may be the lefs obferved; fo that in a Conftitution ripe for Change, thofe who are beft efteemed and moft trufted begin to buy the People's Voices, and afterwards expofe to Sale their own Suffrages; which Practice is always attended with utter Deftruction, or the Lofs of Liberty.

This Error in the firft Concoction does prefently deprave the whole Mafs; for then the Dignities of the Commonwealth are made the Reward of Fraud and Vice, and not the Recompence of Merit. All is bought and fold, and the worft Men who can afford to bid higheft, are accepted; and where the Management is once got into fuch Hands, Factions are fuffered to grow, rafh Counfels are embraced, and wholefome Advices rejected; every one is bufy for himfelf, and carelefs of the Common Intereft; Treachery is winked at, and private Perfons are allowed to become wealthy by the public Spoils: All which is followed with the Lofs of Reputation Abroad, and Poverty at Home.

It is hoped the Reader will not think this fhort Digreffion about moral Virtue unfeafonable, when he confiders how much the Wealth and Profperity of thefe Colonies, whom we would here recommend to public Care, depend upon the Manners of their People.

Societies of Men are held together by the Bands of Religion and Laws; and having faid fomething upon the Firft of thefe Heads, we fhall now proceed to handle the Second.

It will, without Doubt, greatly conduce to the Welfare of the Plantations, if their Laws and Politic Inftitutions were revifed and confidered by difinterefted Perfons, who fhould have no Concern but to form them a Conftitution by which they may be well and wifely governed.

In order to this, it is fubmitted to better Judgements, Whether a Council of Trade, or a Council of the *Indies*, or fome fuch like Authority to be appointed efpecially for this Purpofe, fhould not infpect all the prefent Laws and Politic Inftitutions of thefe Countries, to the End that a true State of this Affair may, at a convenient Seafon, be laid before the Parliament of *England*.

E   And

(**66**)

And we are humbly of Opinion, that if such **Laws as** may be thought prejudicial to them, or hurtful to this Kingdom, were abrogated here; and if such of their old Laws as shall be judged sound and wholesome; and if such new Institutions as may be esteemed necessary for those Parts, did receive some Sanction from the Legislative Power of this Kingdom, it would make our whole Business in *America* more consistent, and fasten with surer Ties those Colonies to this Nation.

What we propose is thus: That their first Model of future Government should be framed here; that afterwards they may have Power to make for themselves such Laws as they shall think needful for their better Polity; and these Laws, thus enacted among them, not to be rescinded but by Authority of Parliament in *England*.

And this seems the more necessary, because, heretofore, many good Laws, formed there, have been abrobated here, upon the false and corrupt Suggestions of interested Persons; besides, nothing can be more pernicious to a People, than Levity in making and rescinding Laws.

A Model has been offered, in this Discourse, to public Consideration, for erecting the Ten Provinces or Places that lie Northward into one National Assembly, where all Things relating to their better Government may be transacted.

And it is submitted to better Judgements, Whether it would not greatly tend to the Welfare and Safety of those Places, that Laws, not contrary to the Law of *England*, enacted in such an Assembly, should remain in Force, till altered by the Legislative Power of this Kingdom.

Without Doubt, it would be a great Incitement to their Industry, and render them more pertinacious in their Defence, upon any Invasion which may happen, to find themselves a free People, and governed by Constitutions of their own making.

All Governments have lasted according to the Strength and Vigour of Mind with which they were at first begotten, and as their Founders have been skilful; and, as weak, crazy, and diseased Parents engender sickly, shortlived, and ricketty Children; so impotent Statesmen frame politic Institutions not durable, easily overthrown, and unable to resist Accidents.

But

(67)

But, peradventure, Governments are by no kind of Wisdom to be rendered immortal; at least those which, in Appearance, were formed with the greatest Skill, have been subject to frequent Changes, and are most of them buried in the Ruins of Time.

For, as we are said to bring with us into the World those Diseases by which our Decay and Death is to be wrought; so Governments, in their primitive Institutions, have within them the very Seeds of Destruction by which, at last, they are to be subverted.

In the framing of absolute Monarchies, that Power which is given to a single Person for the Safeguard of the People, does always turn to such Excess and Tyranny, as, in conclusion, proves destructive to the whole: In the forming of Commonwealths, that Division of Power which is made between the many and the few, gives rise to that Discord and those Civil Wars, which, in Process of Time, either destroy, or quite alter the Constitution.

Mixed Governments seem contrived for the longest Duration; but the Division of Power which is likewise in such Forms, and was intended for their Preservation, must, in Time, prove their Ruin, unless Faction can be avoided, which is the Bane of all politic Institutions; some Tyrants, indeed, are wise enough to make it now and then subservient to their Designs; but, in mixed Governments, it is equally pernicious to Prince and People.

For which Reasons, if it should be thought convenient to set afoot the National Assembly here proposed for the Northern Colonies, early Care must be taken to put a Stop to the Growth of Faction; for, if that be suffered to reign, it will, in Process of Time, render what was intended for their Good, a Burthen to the Country.

With good Government it is not improbable but that these Colonies may become, hereafter, great Nations; upon which Account it seems of Importance to give them, in their Infancy, such politic Institutions as may preserve them for many Ages in Wealth, Peace, and Safety; and in order to this, the nearer they are brought to the Model of the *English* Government, will, undoubtedly, be the better.

And if they have Governors from hence, or to be approved of here, or of their own electing, (according to their several Charters) and if they are allowed a National

E 2   Assembly,

(68)

Affembly, it would give them the perfect Enjoyment of our Liberties and Conftitution.

The original Inftitutions and Laws of moft Countries are found and good; but as Vice prevails, they become obfolete, and are forgotten; from whence grow thofe Difeafes in the Body Politic that require the ableft Phyficians.

But how much a Government fwerves from its firft Inftitution, by fo much it has a wrong Bent; it fhould, therefore, be the Care of thofe to whom the Rule and Direction of thefe Places is committed, to keep them, as much as poffible, to their original Inftitution.

In the Model here propofed, the Governors will, of Courfe, be vefted with all the Powers neceffary for the Safety and Protection of the whole; and thofe Affemblies may have certain Rights which will be as well an Eafe and Safeguard to the Governors, as beneficial to the People; but if either Part invades the other, it muft throw the Public into dangerous Convulfions.

That Government is happy where the Bounds between the chief Power and the People are fo wifely laid out and fixed, that no Encroachments can be eafily apprehended; for the Difputes and Quarrels concerning thefe Bounds and Limits have always been the chief Gain and Harveft of bad and defigning Men, and the Field in which they exercife thofe Wicked Arts that fo often embroil a Country.

To make this National Affembly a lafting Benefit to the Colonies, fuch as are fent to govern thofe Parts fhould take all poffible Care to eure the prefent Vices, and prevent the future Corruption of the People.

The Natural Steps to Ruin in Politic Inftitutions, that have a Mixture in them of Popular Government, feem to be in this Manner: 1ft, Extended Dominion, Power atchieved by Arms or Riches flowing in by Trade, beget Effeminacy, Pride, Ambition and Luxuries of all Kinds; thefe Vices, as they obtain Strength and Growth, produce quickly private Poverty, and then public Want; private Poverty puts ill Men upon wicked Arts to get Wealth, and public Want but too often makes thofe ill Men neceffary in a corrupted State.

Thus the *Roman* Gentry were fo debauched by their Luxuries, and preffed with their Wants, that they affifted *Cinna*, *Sylla*, *Marius*, *Cataline* and *Cæfar* to invade

(69)

vade the Commonwealth ; till, at laft, *Cæfar's* Tyranny became all the Refuge which the Public had in its Diforders and Calamities.

When the Gentry for fome Time have been fet loofe in their Principles, the Common People begin to lay afide their Worth and Integrity, and the whole Mafs of Blood in the Body Politic grows fo corrupted, as not to be capable of thofe Remedies which good Lawgivers and wife Statefmen would offer; fo *Auguftus* faw the *Romans*, in that Age, not fit for Freedom, which, probably, hindered him from reftoring Liberty, and made him chufe rather to continue the Empire in the Hands of a fingle Perfon, and tranfmit it to *Tiberius*.

Thefe National Affemblies, the Ufe of which are here recommended for our Northern Colonies, will be of little Benefit, unlefs the People, by whofe Voices they muft be chofen, can be kept from being corrupted in their Elections; for, otherwife, they will prove but a falfe Appearance of Freedom, which is the worft Kind of Slavery.

And, in fome Countries, we have formerly feen Liberty in Danger, from that Part of the Conftitution which fhould have been the Guardians of it; and this has happened when Princes (having either had Favourites to fupport, or Defigns to promote oppofite to the Welfare of their Subjects, or intending to grafp at more Power than was given them by the Laws) have fecretly enccuraged debauching the People in Elections, to make open Sale of their Voices.

In States where this is practifed, intriguing Perfons, full of wicked Arts, will get into Poffeffion of being conftantly elected, who, at firft, fhall feem the beft Patriots, and moft jealous of the Nation's Right; but this lafts no longer than till they can bring to a good Market that Credit and fair Repute they had gained before; when their Price is offered and agreed upon, they defert their Country's Caufe, and help on, or at leaft approve, of all that Mifgovernment which had been before the Object of their popular Speeches and venial Eloquence.

Nor could it be difficult for former Princes to corrupt both the Electors and the Elected; for, in moft Kingdoms, the Court has been a Shop with Wares in it to fit all Kind of Cuftomers; there is Hope for fome which feeds many at a fmall Expence; there are Titles for the

    Ambi-

(70)

Ambitious; Pleasures for the Young and Wanton; Places
for the Busy; and Bribes to be closely conveyed for such
as desire to maintain an Appearance of Honesty, and to
betray their Trust but now and then in important Matters.   With these Baits and Allurements Princes might
easily draw into their Nets the unthinking Gentry of their
Land, and thereby poison the Fountain Head of the Laws,
and sap the very Foundations of the Politic Institution.

·The Common People are the first to complain of Misgovernment, and the first who feel the bad Effects of it;
long Wars are carried on at the Expence of their Blood;
heavy Taxes pinch them most; Revenues are mismanag-
ed at their Cost; they soonest feel Decay of Trade and
the Nation's Poverty, and yet, generally, it is their Fault
if Things are ill-administered, or at least if they are suffered to continue long under an ill Administration; they
are the corrupted Matter for false and designing Statesmen to work upon; they fight the Quarrels of turbulent
and ambitious Spirits; they are the first that follow se-
ditious Orators.   In the *Roman* Commonwealth they first
debauched the State, by making Sale of their Voices in
Election of Magistrates, and in other Constitutions they
send up to National Assemblies the Men whose merce-.
nary Eloquence is so fatal to the Public.

When those who have a Right of Election in mixed
Governments shall have been in this Manner corrupted,
they will send up to their National Assemblies Persons
by whom, in all Senses, they shall be truly represented;
and when this happens to a People, they will soon be
rent asunder by Factions; public Zeal shall be made ri-
diculous, and often dangerous to its Professors; Treachery shall have a stated Price, and the Shame of doing it
shall be quite extinguished: And, in a Country where
the prime Youth have been thus bred in a vicious School,
and received early a bad Tincture, how can there be
found Hands with which the Duties and Offices of State
can be well and wisely guided?

And when it happens in such Forms of Government,
that the Spring Head shall be tainted, from whence are
to be drawn the Men of Experience, Action, and Coun-
sel; busy Persons, by different Arts, some by abject Flattery, others by perplexing Matters to be bought off, will
soon prevail to be let into many of the chief Offices and
Dignities of the State, which they will so pollute with
their

(71)

their foul Dealings, and weaken and make contempt'ble by their Ignorance, that cleaner and abler Hands It afterwards be hardly invited in to restore Things, and give them a better Complexion.

And, in such Times, the worst of Men, who insinuate best, and are ever the most active, will get into many Posts of Trust and Importance; and endeavour, if possible, to engross the whole Commonwealth to themselves, and invade all her Parts, where they will lie strongly intrenched, and watchful to oppress Virtue and Merit of any Kind, with which they are at open War; for, if Endowments of the Mind, Love to the Nation, Integrity, Experience, Conduct, and solid Wisdom, should once obtain, get Ground, and be taken Notice of, they who shine, and are recommended by no such Qualities, must quit their Holds, and withdraw, or remain the universal Contempt of that People, whose Affairs they are so little able to administer.

Princes well inclined and disposed to govern rightly, are very unfortunate when their Lot is to reign in a Country so corrupted. The Sun, though it be the Element of Light and Heat, cannot shine out to cheer and comfort Nature in Places where there are always rising from the Earth, Damps, Fogs, and unwholesome Vapours; in the same Manner, when ill Men are got into a Court, they hang like so many dark Clouds before the Throne, obscuring the Prince's Glory, hindering him from exerting Half his native Worth, and rendering his Warmth and good Influence less beneficial to the People.

And though such a Nation should have on the Regal Seat, a Prince formed after the Model of their own Wishes, brave in the Field, and wise in Council; those bad Men, whom bad and corrupted Times must of Necessity bring about him, will endeavour, as much as in them lies, to make all his noble Qualities and Virtues as useless to the World as possible; with their weak and pernicious Counsels casting a Mist before his Wisdom; and, by their ill Conduct of the Nation's Strength and Wealth, putting a Stop to the Progress of his Valour.

To preserve these Assemblies which are here proposed for the Northern Colonies, it will not only be necessary to take Care of the Manners of the People, but likewise to provide that the Assembly itself be not corrupted.

E 4   The

(72)

The ancient Custom in the mixed Governments form-ed in these Northern Countries (which will be the best Model for them to follow) was, that National Assemblies should be frequently called and sent Home, as soon as the Nation's Business was dispatched. The Wisdom of elder Times did never think it convenient, that one and the same Assembly should sit many Years brooding of Faction; for it is in those continued Sessions, where the Skill is learnt of guiding, and being guided where the Youth is depraved, and elder Sinners hardened; where those Parties are formed that give the cunning Speakers so much Weight and Value, and where they can bring their Subtilty and Eloquence to Market.

And, in former Reigns, the departing from a Princi-ple so essential in its Constitution, had like to have chang-ed the whole Face of the *English* Government; for Leeches and other blood-sucking Worms are ingendered in standing Pools, but flowing Waters do not corrupt or breed so many Insects; the keeping a National Assembly long sitting debauches the Gentry of a Kingdom, and opens a Way to Offices of Trust, not known among their Ancestors; but when such Assemblies are called together to consult upon the Difficulties of State, and are dissolv-ed as soon as the Public Business is dispatched, the Mea-sures of the false Politicians become presently quite al-tered: They who design to rise, must mount by other Steps than formerly; intriguing, heading Parties, running into Faction, and sudden changing of Sides, will avail the busy Men but little; a Year or two is not sufficient to mould and fashion an Assembly to their Designs; every new Sessions young Gentlemen are sent up, whom it is not so easy to corrupt; they can fix nothing where there is a perpetual Flux and Reflux of Matter, it is like build-ing on a Quicksand; when such as intend to advance themselves in the World see all this, and that those As-semblies are no more the Field in which they can exercise their wicked Arts with any Advantage, they naturally fall into other Methods, and are honest of Course, when it is no longer their Interest to be otherwise.

In such a Constitution there is no need to silence trou-blesome and perplexing Rhetorick with some good Office, nor to buy off and reconcile, at any Rate, Men of tur-bulent and ambitious Spirits; and, when it is not need-ful to hire People to save their own Country, how much
cheaper

(73)

cheaper and more eafy is Government rendered to Princes, who, then, have a free Choice among their Subjects to call whom they pleafe into the Service of the State? Whereas, otherwife, their Favours are confined to one narrow Place; and as thereby their Goodnefs is made more extenfive, fo the Stations requiring Abilities and Experience muft be better filled, when a Court has not the Neceffity upon it to find out Places for Men, rather than Men that are fit for the Places.

In Countries where this Poft, fo effential to Liberty, is thus preferved from Corruption, all Matters relating either to War or Peace, public Revenues or Trade, will go on profperoufly; and a National Affembly, fo conftituted, will always produce wholefome Laws, right Adminiftration, and a perpetual Race of honeft and able Minifters.

What has been here faid of great Empires, will, in fome Proportion, hold in the Direction of lefs Matters, and in the Rule of our Northern Colonies; but, if the Governors now there, or to be fent thither, find the chief Magiftrates and Officers in the Government, and the whole Mafs of the People already corrupted, they will be but ill received and liftened to, in their Endeavours to reform the general Vices and Immoralities of the Country; for Men, when they labour under any Difeafe, are fond of confulting Remedies; but it is not fo with Governments fickly and diftempered, it being then the Intereft of a great many, that the Malady fhould be rather nourifhed, than any Cure hearkened after, and, at fuch a Seafon, they who would promote Ethics, in all Likelihood will meet but with a cold Reception: For, if in the refpective Colonies wicked and ambitious Perfons are got into Power, they will find their Account better in having Flattery promoted than in hearing Truth, fince they would be undone, if the People fhould be wakened out of their prefent Lethargy; they will not defire to have Abufes corrected, as being their beft Foundation; they will be afraid of wholefome Precepts and Examples, as being fo many Reproaches to their Conduct; they will not dare to be brought to the Bar of right Senfe and Reafon, by which their Actings are never fquared; they will not defire to have Morality advanced, as prejudicial to their Defigns; they will dread Reformation of any Sort, as knowing they muft be laid afide with Scorn, and

return

(74)

return to their first Obscurity whenever things are capable of being mended.

And let the Governor be never so knowing and vigilant either by the Prevalency of their Faction, or by being able to give Opposition and to disturb his Business, or by having learnt the Ways of gaining such as are nearest his Person, or by affecting high Zeal to his Service, they will creep into Stations of the chiefest Trust and Importance, in which, when they are once planted, it will cost him more Care and anxious Thoughts to defend them than to protect his Country.

But they prevail most if he happens to be under any pressing Wants, because it recommends their Tricks and Arts, whereby this Want is to be supplied; and often they will entangle his Affairs, to render necessary their single Skill, which is, how to deceive the People. At his first Arrival they will never let him into a true Knowledge of Men, nor who are fittest for his Service; for they openly say, there is no more requisite to the Discharge of any Trust than an Interest to procure it; a right Maxim for them to establish, who are the Product of mere Favour. They imagine all Wisdom consists in found Flattery, and that he who approves the present does enough to secure the Future. Men of deep Reach they are afraid of, and with Reason, for such look quite through their Deeds, which bear no Enquiry. Men of Experience they count dangerous, and so they are to Magistrates that want it. All-sufficient in their own Thoughts and clothed with Presumption, they often take upon them to steer the Commonwealth, whose utter Ruin they madly venture every Moment, being so far unable to sit at Helm, that they are hardly fit to handle the very Sails; when it looks smooth above, they believe all safe at Bottom, never founding any Depths, as having no Plummet, and when the Ship goes right, it is Chance only that brings it into harbour.

In forming that National Assemby which is here proposed for the better Government of the Northern Colonies, the Principal Matter to be recommended to the Common People is to elect Men of Fortune, Integrity, Public Spirit, and Virtue; and above all Things, to avoid those Pests of Human Kind, fine Talkers and busy intriguing Speakers, whom they anciently called Orators.

It

(**75**)

It cannot indeed be properly faid that Eloquence is a Plant of our Soil, (for it really never grew any where but in a Commonwealth) however we may have fomething like it; and in modern Times there have been fome who could fpeak with a dangerous Degree of Force; and grave Actions, Prefidents, vehement Figures, and Popular Arguments, can prevail very much in Affemblies, where a great many are difpofed beforehand to be perfuaded.

This Age muft needs have fomething that at leaft refembles the former Eloquence; for as in *Greece* and in *Rome*, fo not long fince there have been feen great Speakers courted, and in the Pay of Foreign Kings and States, and bought up by their own Princes at any Price. Whether or no we have reached the ancient Strength of Speaking, fhall not be now decided; but this may be boldly pronunced, That, in former Reigns, there have appeared Men in this Kingdom as ready to betray the People, as turbulent and contriving, and who have made as bad Ufe of their Faculties, and who have fold their Words as dear, as any of the *Greek* or *Roman* Orators.

Whenever Liberty is fubverted, or a Conftitution changed, the Mifchief commonly proceeds from fuch Perfons as firft fpeak well to gain a good Opinion, and end well to get good Places; never any private Men, or collective Body of a People, are betrayed but by thofe in whom they put a Confidence: And hardly any have had the Power to do much hurt, but we lifted them up with our own Voices; they were firft the Nation's, and then the Prince's Favourites: And though Breach of the People's Truft was their original Rife, yet Princes have formerly been unfortunate enough to believe they could be well and faithfully ferved by Perfons fo loofely principled.

When we have heard Men affert boldly our civil Rights and the Country's caufe, and fpeak popularly, without fifting their Defigns or furveying their Ambition, without examining their Pretenfions or looking into their Difcontents, we have furrendered ourfelves blindly to their Conduct, and gone along with them in all Things, they have led and governed us; we have cried them up, extolled their Capacities, and augmented their Reputation; and all this has been but to make them

worth

(76)

worth the taking off, and but giving them something
to betray, which they did the firſt Opportunity; and in
the mean while many Princes have heretofore been un-
happily perſuaded by their Boſom Enemies, that theſe
popular Speakers were the only Perſons proper for their
Service.

It is true, in mixed Governments, whoever will be
conſiderable, muſt be well ſkilled in all Matters relating
to its National Aſſembly; he muſt be Maſter of its
Rules and Orders; he muſt have ſome general Knowledge in the Laws; he muſt know how to appeaſe and
allay a Heat, and be able to ſtir up and excite a little
Warmth upon Occaſions; and, to recommend what he
ſays, he muſt ſpeak well, which they commonly do who
think diſtinctly.

But many have been poſſeſſed to a high Degree of all
theſe Qualities, who yet have been utterly barren and
deſtitute of all other Worth and Virtues; ignorant in
Men, without any Knowledge of the true Nature of their
own Government; Strangers to paſt and preſent Hiſtory;
unknowing in the Poſture, Intereſt, and Power of Foreign States; quite unſkilful in the Condition, Strength,
Wealth, and Trade of their Native Country; and, which
is worſt of all, without any Public Spirit or right Zeal
for the Common Good.

Both Prince and People are very unfortunate, who
much depend upon thoſe whoſe chief Talent is the Art
of Speaking. *Oliver, Charles* Cardinal of *Lorrain, Pom-
pone de Believre*, Cardinal *Ximenes*, the Duke of *Sully*,
Woolſey, Sir *Thomas More*, the *Cecils*, Treaſurer *Buck-
hurſt*, Secretary *Walſingham*, the Cardinals *Richlieu* and
Mazarin, Secretary *Thurole*, *Cornelius de Wit*, and the
Treaſurer *Southampton*, with ſeveral others who may be
reckoned, were not recommended, and did not ſubſiſt
by this ſingle Gift and Faculty, but ſhined with many
Excellencies, and had Variety of Endowments, which enabled them to handle wiſely the Affairs of State in
their Times, and rendered their Miniſtry ſo ſucceſsful.

Eloquence is without doubt an Inſtrument very neceſ-
ſary in Popular States, and it has introduced and brought
upon the Stage of the World many good and famous
Men; ſuch as *Pericles, Epaminondas, Ariſtides, Cimon,
Xenophon, Thucidides, Æmilius Paulus, Cicero*, and the
Catos,

(77)

Catos, who performed great Things for the Honour and Advantage of their Commonwealths. But if it happens to light into Hands not entirely virtuous, it is a Tool with which great Mifchiefs may be wrought; for thereby *Sylla*, *Craffus*, *Pompey*, and *Cæfar*, crept firft into that Power, which overthrew the *Roman* Liberty.

The Art of fpeaking yields good Fruit to the Commonwealth, when it is joined with Courage and Vigilance for the State, as in *Pericles*, with Love to the Public not to be fhaken, as in the *Scipios*, and with Integrity and Juftice, as in *Arifides*; but it does more Hurt than Good, when it is accompanied with unlawful Ambition, as in *Cæfar*; with Vanity and Riots, as in *Alcibiades*; with Cowardice, as in *Demofthenes*; and with Corruption, as in *Demades*; for nothing can fooner haften the Ruin of a Country, than to have Men lifted high in the Opinions of the People, followed and trufted, in whom their Vices are much more prevailing than their Virtues.

Many have wondered how it came to pafs that the Model of a Commonwealth, which *Solon* recommended to the *Athenians*, had no longer duration. He was a Lawgiver reckoned inferior to none that ever pretended to guide a State, endowed with all noble Faculties of the Underftanding, and born in an Age when Mankind had attained to the fublimeft perfection of Virtue and Wifdom; yet he lived to fee his Scheme of a Democracy overthrown, to make Room for the Tyranny of *Pififtratus*; and though 40 Years after it was reftored and mended by many excellent Laws, that Form of Government was foon rent afunder, and in one Century quite abolifhed.

But though he had fortified his Conftitution with all poffible Forefight and human Prudence, yet there was fomething rooted in the very Nature of the *Athenians*, that muft eternally hinder them from remaining long under one Sort of Eftablifhment; which was, that in the moft important junctures, and in the niceft Bufinefs, they might at all Times be blown any Way by the Breath of Orators; and that in their Councils they might be guided, ruled, and managed by Eloquence: They feldom liked a Man fo much for doing well as for fpeaking finely, which is indeed the Vice of moft States whofe Affairs are chiefly governed

by

(78)

by popular Affemblies, and is, peradveñture, the Reafon
that Governments, purely democratical, are not durable
and perfect; for in mixed Conftitutions, fuch as was
that of *Sparta*, the Wifdom of a few, the Senate, and
the Authority of a fingle Perfon, the King, was fome
Counterpoife to that dangerous Intereft and Power
which bad Men will now and then obtain, by talking
magnificently to the People : Whereas, in democratical
Inftitutions, and principally in *Athens*, Orators have
carried all Things before them with a Sway unlimited ;
and being firft corrupted themfelves with Money, have
afterwards, with falfe Rhetoric, corrupted their Cities to
give unrighteous Judgements, to banifh and put to Death
their beft Citizens, and to make unfeafonable Leagues,
and enter into deftructive Wars, with other the like
Meafures, that were foon attended with Ruin to the
Public.

Whoever looks over with Care the Hiftory of thofe
Times, will plainly fee that the Liberty of *Athens* was
fubverted by their Orators; they were the firft Promoters
of thofe rafh Advices, that by Degrees undermined the
Conftitution; and they were the original Movers of
that War with *Antipater*, which ended in the *Athenians*
being forced to receive a Garrifon in the very Port of
Munichia, and at laft in the Slavery of all *Greece*; and
without feeking for other Reafons, we may fafely affirm,
that the Orators, with their Corruption, Violence, and
Fraud, pulled down and deftroyed the Democracy of
Solon.

When Men who have thus recommended themfelves,
by the Art of Speaking, to a good Opinion in the World,
have got into Power, their firft Bufinefs is either to
create or encourage Faction; they devife or revive
Names of Diftinction to keep up Difcord ; and from the
different Inclinations and Sentiments we naturally have,
as well in Politic as in Religious Affairs, they find Matter to raife and foment Divifions, till at laft they try to
range the Church, the People, and its National Affembly, as it were, under Two Banners.

The corrupt Part of thefe oppofite Sides, growing
quickly too ftrong for fuch as mean their Country well,
produce what we call *Parties*, which, in Procefs of
Time, muft be the Ruin of mixed Governments.

Rome,

(79)

Rome, though a large Empire, formed with great Wisdom, and supported all along by Men of the sublimest Virtue, was, notwithstanding, destroyed at last by Factions; much more then must they pull down Nations depraved, weak within, and surrounded abroad by powerful Enemies or false Friends.

But they are yet more dangerous to States where both Parties have had the chief Power committed to them, with this Effect only, that each Side in its Turn has shown how little fit they were to be trusted with it.

Who would give up his Name to a Faction, and devote himself entirely to it, that has known grave Republicans become supple Flatterers, and Old Flatterers grow zealous Patriots? And what Prince must not have a mean Opinion of such Parties, when he has seen neither of them at bottom better principled, than the other, and both Sides agreeing to rob him, to give up any Thing when fairly invited to it, and ready to enrich themselves with the Nation's Treasure?

In former Times, when by their fine Talking, and by the Strength of their Parties, bad Men had got into the Management of Public Business, they presently introduced Disorder, Decay of Trade, Private Misery, and National Want; they were an equal Weight upon King and People; by their Errors they first embroiled the Crown, and to maintain those Errors, the Crown was often put to Hazard. No Prince could have so much the Affection of his Subjects, but by their Conduct he was in a Way to loose it; the Kingdom had not Wealth enough for their Negligence and Profusion; they had neither Skill to recover a Misfortune, nor knew they how to make any right Use of an Advantage; giddy with Success, and frighted by Calamity, Wise after Danger, and distracted in it, they endeavoured to give the Court a distinct Interest from the People, and yet were always dividing among themselves, hating each other as much as good Men hate them; they were without Experience of their own, and yet despised the Knowledge of others: Arrogant and impatient of Contradiction, though always in the wrong; they were rash in resolving Points of the highest Nature, but slow in the Execution of the most trivial Matters; and though they first recommended themselves by finding Fault with former Ministers, yet they justified the worst of them

by

(80)

by their Proceedings; they were eager and active
enough, when the Nation was to be fleeced, but supine
and indifferent in what related to its Prefervation; growing rich, while their Country became poor, and as
carelefs of the Public Honour as of their own.

And it has been the general Unhappinefs of fuch corrupted Countries, that the bad Men are bold and enter-
prizing, forward and active; whereas fuch as keep their
Integrity are unactive, cold and lazy; contented with
the barren Praife of not being guilty themfelves, they
fuffer others to invade fo much Power as that they can
do hurt, and do it fafely; and in a Nation debauched
in Principles many Parts of the State may be filled
by Perfons of high Knowledge and Virtue, but their
Love and Zeal for the Public, and their Vigilance for its
Safety, their Prudence, Forefight and Caution, fhall be all
rendered ineffectual, by the over-ruling Madnefs of others.
The Side which would tread in the Path of Honefty
and Wifdom, fhall be overborn and fhoved out of the
Way, by the Crowd and ftrong Faction of thofe who
find their Account in promoting Diforder and Mifgovernment. Such as maintain their Underftanding in
this general Frenzy, fhall be admired, but not followed; efteemed, but not confulted; heard but not regarded.
Mend Things they cannot; if they will be quietly Wife
and fay nothing, they are endured; and if unactive, they
are fuffered; when their fuperior Skill is forgiven and
connived at; when fuch as have more than common
Endowments are allowed to fubfift and preferve themfelves, though they cannot fave their Country, it is
thought a fufficient Favour; but all the while they fhall
be made uneafy, purfued with malicious Whifpers black-
ened as difaffected, and made obnoxious to the People,
till at laft they are forced either to retire, or let
their Brethern of the State ruin and betray the Nation
in quiet.

When a Country thus generally depraved in its Manners, comes to have upon the Throne a virtuous Prince,
with what Difficulty muft he labour for the Public
Good, among a people fantaftical, conceited, greedy,
proud, defigning, ambitious and mercenary? Such a
King, when he contemplates in his high Wifdom all
their natural and acquired Vices, muft hardly think
them worth ruling.

Such

(81)

Such a Country may have a Hero come over to secure their Religion and Civil Rights, which were invaded, and to-arm them against an Enemy whose Power threatened to enslave *Europe*; yet he may meet with but few to imitate and assist his Virtues: And though his Ends were the same with those of *Dion*, who came from *Athens* to restore the *Sicilians* to their Freedom, yet, like *Dion*, he may find the leading Men buried in their Vices, fitter Instruments of a Tyranny than for the Sway of a good Prince, not thankful for his Benefits, nor capable of Liberty.

If such Men as are here described, and of this Stamp and Character, in former Ages, by fine Words, joined with wicked Arts, have crept into Stations of great Trust, where they rend and gnaw the very Bowels of the Commonwealth, there is Reason to Caution those who would form a Model for the better ordering of our *West-India* Colonies, to fortify their Constitution, as much as possible, against the Fraud and Corruption of these busy Talkers, which peradventure is to be brought about, if the Governors to be sent thither take Care to recommend to the People, to choose for the Assemblies here proposed, Persons in whom they shall always have observed Public Virtue, by which we mean a constant and perpetual Will to do their Country good.

Absolute Monarchies, corrupted in their Morals and Discipline, impaired in their Wealth, sunk in Credit, and weakened by inbred Disorders, do very rarely retrieve their Condition; but mixed Governments have an innate Vigour and strength of Constitution, which can throw off those Diseases that seem to affect them, and whereby they can be recovered from that Decay of Health to which they have at any Time been reduced by unskilful Statesmen.

Machiavel says, that to render a Commonwealth long-lived, it is necessary to correct it often, and reduce it towards its first Principles, which is to be done by Punishments and Examples. If the wild Proceedings of rash and giddy Ministers are now and then looked into, and animadverted upon, it creates Fear and a Reverence to the Laws; and in great Men strong Examples of Clean Hands, Self-denial, personal Temperance, and Care of the Public Treasure, do awaken the Virtue of others, and revive those Seeds of goodness which lie hid in

F

the

(82)

the Hearts of moſt People, and would ſpring out, but that they are choaked up for a Time by avarice and ambition.

And now (in a few Words, to recapitulate the whole Matter of this Diſcourſe) we have ſet forth of what Advantage the Plantations in *America* are to *England*; there has been propoſed a Model for their future Government, in which, to manage their Affairs by a National Aſſembly, is chiefly recommended; we have ſhown the Steps by which Vice is firſt inſinuated into a Country; we have laid down, that when a People is corrupted, its National Aſſembly grows ſoon debauched in Principles; that when the Vices of the Age are gathered to a Head, they produce a great Ulcer called Faction, which is a complication of bad Humours, ſuffered to grow in the Body Politic, through the Negligence and weakneſs of ill Stateſmen; we have ſet forth that corrupted Times embolden bad Men to thruſt themſelves into the Affairs of State, who are always the Authors of warm and bold Councils, which (as * Livy ſays) are pleaſant in their firſt Appearance, but difficult to manage, and fatal in their event.

And all theſe Points have been here handled, with a Deſign to ſhow that if it ſhould be thought expedient to regulate the Conſtitutions of the Northern Colonies, and to give them Power to govern their Affairs by a National Aſſembly; they who form a Model of this Kind, ſhould take Care to propoſe Methods of correcting the Manners of the People, the mending of which has at all Times, and in all free Countries, produced Wiſe and juſt National Aſſemblies, and in ſuch there have been always reared up able Miniſters; and from Stateſmen of that Kind there may continually be expected a ſteady and ſafe Adminiſtration, wherein Faction ſhall be rooted out; for the Progreſs of the Cure is by the ſame Steps as the Diſeaſe firſt grew upon the Body Politic.

To contrive for the Public, and to promote the Common Good, ought not only to be their Care to whom the Adminiſtration of Affairs is committed, but all private Perſons ſhould bend their Study the ſame Way; and

---

* Tit. Liv. Lib. 35. *Conſilia calida & audacia, prima ſpecie læta, tractatu dura, eventu triſtia ſunt.*

whoever

(83)

whoever has received Lights either from Nature, Education, or Experience is bound to Produce them for the Service of his Country.

As he who has gathered any useful Instructions by contemplating the Growth or Fall of many Monarchies and States, and by weighing the different events of Wise and foolish Councils, should communicate his Observations for the Benefit of others; so they, whose understandings move in a lower Sphere, and who have employed their chief Time and Thoughts in considering the Revenues, Trade, and Common Business of a Kingdom, if they have gained any Knowledge, either by Study or Practice, should offer it to the World, since thereby at least they may furnish Materials, and give some hints for abler Heads to Work upon, and improve for the Nation's Profit.

Many may imagine they owe no more to the Commonwealth than to Fight in its Defence, to pay the Prince his Dues, to be just to one another, and obedient to the Laws: It is true, these are Virtues with which, if a Majority of the People be not seasoned, the Government must run into immediate Confusion: But a great deal more than all this is necessary to make a Country flourish.

A Government cannot be maintained without a sufficient Fund of Revenue; and a Revenue is wildly given, where the People's Strength that must grant it is not duly understood; Taxes not contrived with Skill are a present Burthen, and yet answer so as to bring upon the Kingdom a great future Debt: When the Nature of the Commodities to be charged, and a true Consumption of them are not rightly considered, Funds given upon them prove defective, and such as destroy all Credit; where it is not known how to manage and collect Revenues, the People are disturbed and frightened with a Variety of new Impositions, and yet the Public is no Way eased nor relieved by what they bring in, but becomes still more and more necessitous.

But let the Taxes be never so well contrived and ordered, if a Nation be plunged in great Debts which require large Payments from the People, nothing can support such Expence but Foreign Trade; for all Countries have a certain Stock with which their Tillage, Labour, Arts, and Manufactures are carried on: And it is the

F 2   radical

(84)

radical Moifture of the Commonwealth, and if it be
quite drawn away, the Body Politic becomes Confump-
tive, Hectical, and dies at laft (being Subject to Difeafes and Death itfelf, like human Frames) ; and as human Bodies are not to be kept alive but by receiving in
of Nourifhment, to Repair the Hourly decays which
Time produces, fo Nations cannot fubfift long unlefs
they receive from Time to Time reliefs and refrefh-
ments from Abroad, which are no Way fo well to be
adminiftered as by the help of a well-governed and
extended Traffic.

The Confiderations have induced the Writer of thefe
Papers to communicate thefe Schemes, and his Notions
concerning Credit, his Obfervations relating to the Public Revenues and the Trade of this Kingdom, and in
this Tract to give a fhort View of Practical Ethicks;
which, perhaps, may be thought needlefs at prefent,
and rather ufeful to Pofterity.

The Morals here advanced are directed to, and intended for our Colonies Abroad : But in fucceeding
Times our Manners may come to be depraved, and
when this happens, all Sort of Miferies will invade us,
the whole Wealth of the Kingdom will not be fufficient
for its Defence ; Trade will forfake our Shores, and go
to fome Nation where the Rules of Virtue are better
obferved.

The preventing Remedy againft fuch Diftempers is to
be had from the Precepts of Morality, which Writers
upon all Sort of Subjects fhould endeavour to incul-
cate ; for the Vices or Virtues of a Country influence very
much in all its Bufinefs ; fo that he who would propofe
Methods by which the Affairs of a Kingdom may be any
Way bettered, fhould at the fame Time, confider the
predominant Paffions, the Morals, Temper, and Inclinations of the People : And fo far as to the Plantation
Trade.

THE

THE GREAT

ADVANTAGES

OF OUR

Colonies *and* Plantations

TO

GREAT BRITAIN,

AND

Our Interest in preserving and encouraging them, and how they may be further improved.

By Mr. WILLIAM WOOD.

(87)

SELECT
DISSERTATIONS
ON
Colonies and Plantations.

DISSERTATION III.

The great Advantages of our Colonies and Plantations to Great Britain, &c.

By Mr. WILLIAM WOOD.

HAVING taken a View of our *Foreign Traffick* with the several Countries, to which we have the most general and beneficial *Commerce*, I shall now proceed to say something of our *Colonies* and *Plantations* in *America*; which, together with our *Newfoundland Fishery*, have been the chief Encrease of our Navigation and Seamen, and the greatest Encouragement to both. On which Account, as well as in regard to their Product, they are of the utmost Concern for us to preserve and encourage. And if we take care, to preserve them from foreign Insults and Invasions, they will, as they encrease in People, probably, consume much more of our Manufactures, than at present they do; though they now give Employment to many Thousands of Artificers here at Home, and take off great Quantities, especially of our inferior Manufactures; the Returns of which are made chiefly in Tobacco, Sugar, Indigo, Ginger, Cotton, Dying-woods, &c. by which we are not only supplied for our own, Consumption, but with a considerable Surplus, which is annually re-exported to *Holland*, *Hamborough*,

F 4   *Flanders,*

(88)

Flanders, the *Eaſt Country, Streights*, &c. which a-mounts annually to a very great Sum; and is of vaſt Advantage to us, in the general Balance of Trade. And as they produce Commodities indiſpenſably neceſſary to this Part of the World, they may, with Induſtry and Conduct, be made (if we do not ſuffer the *French* to encroach upon us, or rival us) an inexhauſtible Mine of Treaſure to their Mother-country.

I ſhall not here concern myſelf when, or how, any of our Colonies or Plantations were firſt ſettled, any farther, than that ſome of them had their Original, Riſe, and Planting, from the Perſecutions amongſt us, on account of Conſcience; ſet a-foot by the warm Churchmen, in the Reigns of King *Charles* the Firſt, and of his Son King *Charles* the Second, when ſuch as found themſelves diſturbed and uneaſy at Home, retired thither; who, if they had not had that Retreat, muſt have gone to the *Hans Towns, Switzerland, Sweden*, or *Holland*, (as many did, before the Plantations flouriſhed), to the Detriment of *England* in its Trade and Manufactures, and they who had thus retired to *European* Countries, muſt have been for ever loſt to *England*.

But Providence, which contrives better for us, than we can do for ourſelves, offered in the New World, a Place of Refuge for thoſe People, where (I ſhall herein ſhow,) their Labour and Induſtry is more uſeful to their Mother Kingdom, than if they had continued amongſt us.

It is Matter of Queſtion with ſome, whether our Colonies and Plantations in *America* are not prejudicial to *Great Britain*; and a minute Point with others, whether any Advantage to it. To which I ſhall only ſay, it muſt be allowed, that a Country, which takes no Care to encourage an Acceſſion of Strangers, in a Courſe of Time, will find Plantations of pernicious Conſequence. As for Example; the Colonies in *America* have ruined the *Spaniards*; but this can be no Argument againſt our having them; for there are many Things amiſs in the *Spaniards* conduct; their Monaſteries hinder Marriages; the Inquiſition frightens away Strangers; and in general, there is no Proviſion at all, to repair, what their Colonies carry out. Whereas the

(89)

the *Hollanders*, who fend out greater Numbers every Year than the *Spaniards*, are not difpeopled by it ; their Conftitution inviting more over to them than they fend abroad, and in our Colonies and Plantations, all Foreigners may be made *Denizons*, for an inconfiderable Charge ; whereby many of all Nations are invited, and encouraged to fettle and plant in our *Indies*: And the Crown gains *Subjects in them. and their Children*; and tho Nation gets Wealth by their Labour and Induftry. There is alfo Reafon to think, that for fome Years the Plantations have fent of their Offspring, and the Perfecutions abroad have brought over to His Majefty's Dominions, as many Perfons every Year, as have went to them. Therefore I may fafely advance, that our Trade and Navigation are greatly encreafed by our Colonies and Plantations, and that they are a Spring of Wealth to this Nation, fince they work for us, and their Treafure centres all here: And as the Laws have tied them faft to us, it muft be through our own Fault and Mifgovernment, if they do not ever continue to enrich *Great Britain*; or any, or all of them, become independant of it.

It is indeed true, if a Breach of the Navigation Act fhould be connived at, even our own Plantations may become more profitable to other Nations than to this Kingdom; but while the Governors, and the feveral Officers under the Crown, whofe Bufinefs it is to take care hereof, do their Duty ; while they are not fuffered to carry the Growth of their own, or other our Colonies to foreign *European* Countries ; and in Exchange, bring from thence the Commodities of fuch *European* Countries, or foreign Colonies, to be confumed amongft them ; we can never be in Danger of this, nor can they ever be detrimental to this Nation.

But by infifting, that no Breach in the Navigation Act be connived at, I would not have it inferred, that I am againft permitting the Inhabitants of our Colonies and Plantations to trade with, or fell their Product one with another ; or that they fhould be prohibited to trade to the Colonies or Plantations of any Foreign Nations, with the Goods and Merchandize of the Growth and Manufacture of *Europe*, which have been fent from hence ; or the Provifions of our Northern Colonies, although in return they fhould not bring Gold and Sil-

ver,

(90)

ver, but the Product of that Country they fhall trade
to ; and although fuch Product interfere with, or be of
the fame Species with any of our Colonies or Plantations Produce.

This may not perhaps be relifhed by our Planters;
but if they will not allow it to be for their Intereft in
particular, I am fure they cannot difpute its being for
the Intereft of *Great Britain* in general. For by this
Means we render Foreign Colonies and Plantations, to
be in effect the Colonies and Plantations of *Great
Britain*. And this brings me to fay, That all Laws in
our *Southern* Plantations, which lay great Duties on Sugar,
Indico, Ginger, and other *Weft India* Commodities, imported into them, will be found, when fully and im-
partially confidered, not only prejudicial to them, but
to the Trade and Navigation of this Kingdom ; and
that it is our Intereft, and fhould be our care, that no
Laws, laying fuch high Duties, remain in Force, or be
paffed for the future, in any of our Plantations.

Fo th e Inhabitants, by carrying on a Trade with
their foreign Neighbours, do not only occafion a greater Quantity of the Goods and Merchandize of *Europe*
being fent from hence to them, and a greater Quantity
of the Product of *America*, to be fent from them hither,
which would otherwife be carried from, and brought to
Europe by Foreigners; but an Encreafe of the Seafaring
Men, and Navigation in thofe Parts; which is of great
Strength and Security, as well as of great Benefit and
Advantage, to our Colonies and Plantations.

The Commodities they bring from the Countries traded with by them, whether Sugar, Indico, Cochineal,
Logwood, Cotton-wool, Sarfaparilla, and other Drugs,
are fuch, as are either exported from *Great Britain*,
or ufeful to us, in working up Manufactures, or fuch
as we fhould want, and muft fend for, at a much dearer
Price from the Mother-countries of thofe People, with
whom ours may trade in *America*.

And though fome of our Colonies are not only for
preventing the Importation of all Goods of the fame
Species they produce, but fuffer particular Planters to
keep great Runs of Land in their Poffeffion uncultivated, on purpofe to prevent New Settlements; whereby they apprehend the Prizes of their Commodities may
be affected ; yet if it be confidered, that the Marlets

in

(91)

in *Great Britain*, depend on the Markets of all *Europe* in general; and that the *European* Markets in general depend on the Proportion, between the annual Confumption, and the whole *Quantity of each Species annually produced by all Nations;* it muft then follow, that whether We or Foreigners are the Producers, Carriers, Importers, and Exporters of *American* Goods, yet their refpective Prices in each particular Colony (the Difference of Freights, Cuftoms, and Importations confidered) will always bear Proportion to the general Confumption of the whole Quantity of each Sort, produced in all Colonies, and in all Parts; allowing only for the ufual Accidents, that Trade and Commerce, Agriculture and Manufactures are fubject to in all Countries; fuch as a particular Colony being under or over traded to; and under or over fupplied with Goods and Shipping from other Places; having greater or fmaller Crops, and demanding more or lefs Supplies of Shipping one Year than another.

If this be admitted, then it muft certainly be the true Intereft of our Colonies, as well as of their Mother Kingdom, to enlarge their Settlements, and to fuffer the Produce of Foreign Plantations in *English* Shipping to be freely imported and exported again to *Great Britain;* for narrow-limited Notions in Trade and Planting are only advanced by, and can only be of ufe to particular Perfons; but are always injurious to the Publick; in preventing the Employment of our own People, and giving our Competitors the Opportunity of employing greater Numbers of theirs, producing greater Quantities of Goods, and under-felling us at Foreign Markets.

If a Trade fhould be carried on, by which the Product of our Colonies (except Liquors and Provifions) fhould be fold to Foreigners; and our People in any of our Colonies and Plantations, in return, receive the Goods and Merchandize of any foreign Country in *Europe*, for Confumption among them, it would, indeed, be greatly prejudicial to the Trade and Navigation of *Great Britain;* but this is fufficiently provided againft, by the *Act of Navigation.*

Having premifed this, of the Plantation Trade and Product in general, I fhall now confider them apart, in thefe Refpects; and in order to that, fhall not mention the Countries, as they range on the Continent, or lie in Latitude, but rank thofe that produce Commodities of a
different

·(92)

different Nature to this Kingdom, under one Head, and those that produce Commodities of the same Nature, under another.

'Those under the First Head, are *Virginia, Maryland, Barbadoes, Antigua, Montserrat, Nevis, St. Christopher's,* and *Jamaica,* whose Product is Tobacco, Sugar, Indico, Cotton, Ginger, and sundry Sorts of Drugs and Dying Woods.

Those under the Second Head, are *New-England, New-York, Carolina, Pennsylvania, &c.* whose Product is Beef, Pork, Bread, Beer, Pease, Rice, *&c.* Cod-fish, Maccarel, *&c.* Masts, Boards, Staves, *&c.* Furs, Pitch, Tar, Turpentine, Train Oil, *&c.*

The Product of the First are of a different Nature from what is produced from the Lands of *Great Britain;* and of the Quantities thereof imported, such a Part has been annually re-exported, as has been one great Means of the Balance we have had in our Trades Abroad, particularly with *Holland* and *Hamborough.*

The Produce of the other is not of a different Nature, unless Rice, Train Oil, *&c.* and might be sent to our Sugar Plantations, from *Great Britain.*

But, however the Countries, under the Second Head, may interfere with the Product of this Kingdom, or may produce Commodities of little Value, annually, (as it must be owned) different from what *Great Britain* produceth; I shall think, until I hear better Reasons, than I have hitherto met with, (even those advanced by Sir *Josiah Child* against them) and while the *French* are forming such Schemes, and settling such Provinces, on the Continent of *America,* whereon Sir *Josiah* owns such Materials are to be had for building of Ships, (which shall be considered) that it is highly incumbent upon, and greatly the Interest of *Great Britain,* to preserve, and encrease, maintain, and encourage its Colonies on the Continent of *America.*

But, to the First Head or Division, it is computed the Value of Tobacco, of *Virginia* and *Maryland,* annually imported from thence, exclusive of the Customs, is 600,000 *l.* Two Thirds of which is re-exported; and that the like Value of the Sugars, Indico, Ginger, Cotton, *&c.* annually imported from *Jamaica, Barbadoes, Antigua, Montserrat, Nevis,* and *St. Christopher's,* is 1,300,000 *l.* One Third of which is also re-exported.

And

(93)

And it is computed, that there is exported from *Great Britain*, and *Ireland*, to the several Colonies, and Plantations, belonging to the Crown in *America*, to the Value of 850,000 *l.* and that the Importations from them all, including Silver and Gold, &c. are to the Value of 2,600,000 *l.* So that over and above what we send to our Colonies and Plantations, in our Manufactures, native Product, and foreign Commodities, we have a Balance in Return thereof, to the Value of 1,750,000 *l.* which centres and remains among us; and is not like such a Balance in foreign Trade, as must be carried out again in Money directly, or in Goods, or Bills of Exchange, to any other Part of the World.

It will probably be objected, that as the Colonies, under the Second Head, make us not any Return of themselves, in Proportion to what they take annually from us, or yield Commodities of little Value, so they have drained us most of People: The Fact is so; but if it were otherwise, the Affairs of other Plantations could not, perhaps, be so well carried on; for those Soils which produce the richer Goods, are not so proper to cultivate for the Nourishment of Life, and to yield Corn, Beef, Pork, Pease, &c. (which if they were, the Hands in them are much more advantagiously employed, for the Interest of themselves, and their Mother Kingdom;) so that the Southern Plantations, especially in Time of War, would be destitute of many Necessaries, or put upon employing their Hands in planting Provisions, were it not for the Nearness and Industry of the Northern Colonies.

'Tis true, these Provisions might be furnished from *Great Britain*, but at such a Rate, as would, peradventure much discourage the Southern Planters; for besides their being all considerably dearer, so some Kinds of them could neither be so good nor so fresh.

But though the People of *New York, New England, Pensylvania, Carolina,* &c. may furnish *Jamaica, Barbadoes, Antigua, Montserrat, Nevis,* and *St. Christopers,* with what might be sent them from this Kingdom; yet they make it ample Amends, by fetching, or taking from it Variety of Manufactures, all Sorts of Cloaths and Houshold Furniture, much oftner renewed, and as good as the same Number of People could afford to have it at Home. So that the Question whether the

Northern

(94)

Northern Colonies are good for *Great Britain* or no, will depend upon making a right Balance, between the Commodities we send thither, and the Provisions we might send to the Southern Plantations, if they were not supplied by *New England*, &c. But I am inclined to think, the present Course most advantagious to this Kingdom, for this Reason, because the Provisions we might send to *Barbadoes*, &c. would be the unimproved Product of the Earth, as Grain of all Kind, or such Product where there is little got by the Improvement, as Salt Beef, Pork, &c. but the Goods we send to the Northern Colonies, are such whose Improvemeuts may be justly said, one with another, to be near four fifths of the Value of the whole Commodities, as Apparel, Houshold Furniture, and many other Things.

'Tis true, if in *New England*, or any other of our Northern Colonies in *America*, they should pretend to set up Manufactures, and so cloath, as well as feed their Neighbours ; their Nearness and low Price would give them such Advantage over this Nation, as might prove of pernicious Consequence : But this Fear seems very remote, unless they are discouraged in rearing Provisions, &c. (as were the People of *Virginia* and *Maryland*, in planting Tobacco, by the high Impositions laid upon it's Importations into this Kingdom, (who in several Counties in those two Colonies, made Shoes, Stockings, Hats, Linen, and Woollen, not only for their own, but the Use of their Neighbours,) which they have been lately in some Sort, eased in,) because new Inhabitants, especially in a large Extent of Country, find their Account better, (as the People in *Virginia* and *Maryland*, though Tobacco has such high Impositions, or Duties, upon it's Importations into *Great Britain*,) in rearing Cattle, Tilling the Earth, clearing it of Woods, making Fences, and by erecting necessary Buildings ; than in setting up Mannfactures ; which is the last Work of a People settled three or four hundred Years, growing numerous, and wanting Territory.

As the Colonies and Plantations belonging to *Great Britain*, are of very great Advantage, and highly beneficial to it ; so as the Case stands at present, it seems reasonable to think, that the Northern Colonies are a Help to the Southern Planters ; as they are chiefly dependent on our Southern Plantations to take off their
Product

(95)

Product, and without it, not, now, having wherewithal to anfwer the Value, fent to them annually in all Kinds of Manufactures from *Great Britain*. And as the Northern Colonies now anfwer their Returns for them, by Means chiefly of our SUGAR ISLANDS, it fhews plainly how much it behoves us, to fecure and preferve, encreafe and encourage them; for without our Southern Plantations, our Northern Colonies can be of no real Advantage to us; fince what they are at prefent, muft ceafe on the Decay or Lofs of the SUGAR ISLANDS, from whence their Value to *Great Britain* chiefly arifes, and for Want of WHICH they would be otherwife prejudicial Colonies to their Mother Country.

But the Northern Colonies might be made more advantagious to their Mother Country than they have hitherto been, or otherwife can be, if all neceffary Encouragement were given by this Kingdom for their fupplying us with Naval Stores, which they may be made capable of doing in very great Quantities: Whether the prefent Encouragement is equal to the Concern it may be to us, I fhall not pretend to fay; only that we ought not to regard the Expence of any prefent Encouragement at firft, when we confider the future Advantages and Security, not only of our Trade and Navigation, but of all his Majefty's Dominions: And, 'tis moft certain, whatever fhall be paid the Northern Colonies as a Bounty at firft, to enter heartily and chearfully upon the doing of this, will not be loft to the Nation, but ftill remain with us; which can't be faid of what we pay to the Eaft Country, (over and above what they take from us in Manufactures,) which I have obferved in my fecond Divifion, amounts to 200,000*l.* a Year, and would be fo much faved to the Nation, could we have the fame from our own People.

For though our Naval Stores from the Northern Colonies would be at firft dearer to the Public than at prefent from the Eaft Country, yet the enhanced Price would be gain to the *Product of our own Lands, to the Labour of our own People, and to the Freight of our own Ships*, and would centre among ourfelves, which is now paid to the Eaft Country, and never returns to us.

The Encouragements likewife at firft neceffary, need not be continued long; for the People, induced by thefe Encouragements at firft, to turn their Lands to the raifing of Hemp, &c. and to the making of Tar, &c. in
Lieu

(96)

Lieu of fowing Corn, &c. would fall into this Method; and their Gain would turn to fo much better Account, they would not leave it, after once entered into it; and the Improvement this would be to our Northern Colonies, would employ a greater Number of Hands, and to a much greater Advantage than at prefent they do; which would confequently occafion their greater Demand and Confumption of the Manufactures and Goods of *Great Britain* of all Sorts.

Nor is it out of the Way to obferve, that our Shipping being our Security, and our Naval Stores fo effentially neceffary; our being obliged to fetch them from the Eaft Country, may, fome Time or other, be of pernicious Confequence to the Kingdom, fhould the Balance of Power in the *Baltic* come fo to alter, that a Prince, an Enemy to *Great Britain*, fhould be poffeffed of it; efpecially fhould we be fo negligent (*as we have fometimes been*,) to have no Stores of that Kind by us at fuch a Time. This is not fo remote a Fear, or *Chimera*, as fome may imagine: Whereas, when our Naval Stores fhall be fo encouraged in our Northern Colonies, that they may fully fupply us; we fhall be in a much fafer Condition, even as to this Kingdom; and although the Public may at firft pay dearer for thofe Stores from thence, than from the Eaft Country, I have above fhown, that even the whole Price will be paid to our own People, and centre among ourfelves, a Saving of 200,000 *l. per Annum*, Money, to *Great Britain*, an Increafe of the Confumption of our Manufactures, and confequently the Employment of Hands here at Home; the great Improvement of our Northern Colonies, the Increafe of our Seamen and Navigation, and a general Security and Advantage to his Majefty's Dominions.

This I thought fit to offer to the Confideration of thofe, whofe Power it lies in to give thefe Encouragements, and to whom, perhaps, the Advantages we might reap from our Northern Colonies by thefe Means have not occurred.

No Trades deferve fo much our Care to procure and preferve, and Encouragement to profecute, as thofe that employ the moft Shipping; although the Commodities carried be of fmall Value in themfelves, as a great Part of the Commodities from our Colonies are. For befides the Gain accruing by the Goods, the Freight in fuch Trades, often more than the Value of the Goods,

is

(97)

is all Profit to the Nation ; and they likewife bring with them great Accefs of Power by the Increafe of Ships and Seamen, the proper Strength and Security of this Kingdom.

COLONIES and PLANTATIONS are both Strength and Riches to their MOTHER COUNTRY, while they are ftrictly made to obferve the Laws of it ; and while ours have *Britifh* Blood, in their Veins, and Relations in *Great Britain,* and can get by Trading with us, the ftronger and greater they grow, the more the Crown and this Kingdom will get by them ; and nothing but our arbitrary Treatment of them, and our Mifgovernment, can make them otherwife than beneficial and advantageous to us.

As there is not any Thing more certain, than that our *Weft India* Trade has greatly enlarged our STOCK, and encreafed our Navigation, and fet the general Balance of Trade with fome Countries for many Years on our Side ; fo, notwithftanding all our Luxuries, which our Home Product would not fo well have anfwered, it has enabled the Nation to gather at the fame Time fuch *a Mafs of Wealth* as our Wars have expended.

And if the Benefit or Profit from the Plantations be fuch as is here taken Notice of, or fomething near it ; it cannot be any longer a Matter of Queftion with fome, whether our Colonies, and Plantations in *America,* are not prejudicial to *Great Britain,* or a Mute Point with others, whether any Advantage to it ; nor can we have any Reafon to complain of wanting the Inhabitants, they may, in the Courfe of their Settling have taken from us ; becaufe the Superlucration from the fame Number of Men, over and above their own Nourifhment, could no Manner of Ways have been fo beneficial to the Kingdom ; for to admit that the Number of white People, of *Britifh* Parentage in them, are 250,000—which, perhaps, is pretty near the Truth, the Labour of fuch a Number of Men reckoned in the Mafs, could by no Means bring to the Nation One Million Seven Hundred and fifty thoufand Pounds *per Annum* clear Profit ; for though the Labour in fome whole Manufactures, may bring a Superlucration to the Public, of above one Pound yearly *per* Head, yet the Mafs of Mankind reckoned together, 'tis fufficient, and will very much enrich a Country, if one Head with another brings to the Public Six Shillings

G   and

(98)

and eight Pence, or feven Shillings *per Annum* Gain, (over and above his Nourifhment, &c.) whereas thefe Planters, or his Majefty's Subjects in *America*, as the foregoing Account fhews, bring a much larger Profit to the Nation, at leaft 7 l. 4 s. a Head *per Annum*, befides the Employment they give to the great Number of Ships thither, which amounts to above 100,000 Tons.

I have reckoned the whole People of his Majefty's Dominions in *America* together, as unwilling, for Reafons not fo proper to mention in fo publick a Manner, to affign each Colony and Plantation it's Proportion; and can't help declaring that it is a Matter of great Admiration to me, how in the Space of fo few Years, fuch a Number of Men fhould be got together in Countries, for the moft Part, fo wild, and uncultivated; but we may juftly attribute the Increafe they have made of Inhabitants, to the Sobriety and temperate Way of living practifed by the Diffenters, who retired to them.

As the Supplies from hence do by no Means anfwer the prefent Numbers, it muft then follow that their Thrift and regular Way of living inclines them more to marry, and makes them more healthful for Generation, and affords them better Means to have the Neceffaries of Life, as wholefome Food, and cleanly Dwelling and Apparel; the Want of which in other Countries, is a high Article in the Burials of the common People.

In all our Colonies and Plantations there is an univerfal Tolleration allowed, and in none of them any Difference arifing among the Inhabitants concerning Religion, every Man worfhipping GOD, according to his Confcience; and however uncharitable and indifcreet the Inhabitants of *New England* might formerly be, They are now become to underftand the Gofpel of JESUS, and the Intereft of their Province, much better than they did.

I would not be thought to be either excufing the Opinions, or juftifying the Separations of any of the Diffenters from our eftablifhed Church, when I advance that the Sobriety they all generally profefs, is both beneficial in Practice and Example.

But the Truth of the Matter is, that where Riot and Luxuries are not difcountenanced, the inferior Rank of Men become prefently infected and grow lazy, effeminate, impatient of Labour, aud expenfive, and confequently

(99)

fequently cannot thrive by Trade, Tillage, and Planting; fo that when we contemplate the Increafe and Improvements, which have been made in our Colonies and Plantations, particularly *New England* and *Penfilvania*, we cannot but think it Injuftice, not to fay that a large Share of this general Good to thefe Parts is owing to the Education of their Inhabitants, which, if not entirely virtuous, has a Show of Virtue; and if this was only an Appearance, 'tis yet better for a People, that are to fubfift in a new Country by Traffick and Induftry, than the open Profeffion and Practice of Lewdnefs and Debauchery, which is always attended with national Decay and Poverty.

Having before proved the Benefit and Advantage, the Plantations and the Trade thereof are to us, it brings me to confider, what Improvement may be made in either, or what Difficulties and Difcouragements affecting the fame may be removed. In former Times, the Governors, or Perfons entrufted with the chief Command or Power in our Colonies and Plantations, have granted fuch large Tracts of Land, as well to themfelves, as other Perfons, that many Planters have been, and are at prefent prevented from enlarging their Plantations, or having more Settlements, and many Inhabitants from becoming Settlers; which we may probably conclude, as well prevents Servants from going to them as willingly as formerly, as ftaying there, when they have ferved the Time they indented for; and it is really become Matter of fad Complaint, that there is not in any of our Colonies or Plantations, though in moft of them fuch vaft Quantities uncultivated, any Land left near any Settlement, or of any Value, that is unpatented, or not granted to fome particular Perfon, which deferves immediate Confideration; whether we confider the Lofs that has already enfued, or muft enfue to this Kingdom, by fuch large Tracts of Land being uncultivated, or what very great Advantages the Cultivation of them would be to this Nation in general, and the Strength and Security to themfelves in particular.

As I know my own Heart, I can truly fay, I have as great a Regard to the Liberty and Property of all *Britons*, and defire the Continuance of thefe invaluable Bleffings we enjoy by our limited Conftitution, as much as any Subject in any Part of his Majefty's Dominions;

G 2   but

(100)

but I am an Enemy to the fine-fpun Notions, fome Men do, in Regard to their Intereft only, advance concerning them.

And being aware I may difoblige fome Perfons in faying what I intend on this Head, who have, either themfelves or their Predeceffors for them, patenteed and ran out great Tracts of Land, which they cannot or will not fettle or plant in their own Times, if ever their Children do in theirs; and will not fell on any Confideration, or but on moft exorbitant Terms: It may not be improper to defire fuch to read the Chapter of *Property* in Mr. *Locke's Effays concerning the true Original, Extent, and End of Civil Government.*

This Gentleman fays, " That when God gave the " World in common; when he gave the Earth to the " Ufe of the Induftrious, and Rational; it cannot be " fuppofed it fhould remain common, and uncultivated:" And, I muft fay, fo neither can it be fuppofed, that *the Crown* when it gave Leave for *Grants of Land* to be made to any of its Subjects, in any of its Colonies or Plantations, either expected or intended that fuch Grants, in Whole or in Part, fhould remain uncultivated.

Number of Men are to be preferred to the Largenefs of Dominion, and it is certain that the Encreafe of Hands, and the right Employment of them, is the great Art of Government; and that that Prince who fhall be to wife, and godlike, as by eftablifhing Laws of Liberty, fo fecure Protection and Encouragement to the honeft Induftry of Mankind, againft the Oppreffion of Power, and Narrownefs of Party, will confequently be more potent than his Neighbours.

I hope when this Matter is confidered, we fhall not have any Man, who wifhes the Security and Prefervation of his own Fortune, if wholly in *America;* the Encreafe and Encouragement of People and Settlements in our Colonies and Plantations; the Happinefs and Profperity, Strength and Greatnefs of *Great Britain;* that will look upon it as any Invafion on the Liberty or Property of a *Britifh* Subject, that Perfons who have great Tracts or Runs of Land in our Colonies and Plantations in *America,* and will not fettle, nor fell on any Confideration, or but on the moft exorbitant Terms, may be obliged to do the one or the other; whereby the Planters who have a Mind to enlarge their Plantations, may
be

(101)

be enabled to do it, as alfo Perfons who have acquired any Money by Trade, Labour, or Servitude; or are induftrious Men, and can be credited, may be encouraged to become *Settlers and fixed Inhabitants*.

The Grants of fuch great Tracts of Land have been generally procured on very eafy Terms, and very often upon wrong Suggeftions; many Perfons hold fome Thoufands of Acres a-piece, and largely furveyed; and fome Patents I have heard include on Survey, double the Quantity of Land mentioned or intended to be granted; and from hence proceeds that fo many Thoufand Acres are, as they call it, taken up, but not planted; which is what I am recommending to publick Notice, as being a Practice which drives away the Inhabitants, and Servants bred up only to Planting, as well as others, into Parts where their Labour is not fo profitable, either to the Crown, or to the People of this Kingdom; as it would in our Colonies and Plantations not producing Commodities that are of *Britifh* Growth; befides, fuch Practices are, without doubt, a chief Caufe that fome of them have had no better Succefs, or made no greater Progrefs in Settlements.

Therefore how little foever I approve any of the Maxims of the *French* Government, I cannot help applauding the Encouragement given by it, to encreafe and fettle their Colonies and Plantations in *America;* particularly, *Obliging every Ship or Veffel, bound to any of them, to carry fuch a Number, or fo many Perfons, in proportion to its Tunnage, Freight, or Paffage, free; not permitting any Perfon to take up more Land than he fhall plant or manure, in a limited Time, or is neceffary for him in his Planting; and furnifhing Perfons, who will become Settlers, with Negroes, and all Materials and Requifites, wanting in making Settlements, and only obliging them to repay the Publick, out of the Produce, One Third of what is produced, till thereby the Sum advanced be fully repaid.*

The want of our falling into Meafures fomewhat adequate to thefe, together with the falfe and narrow Notions entertained by too many of our Planters, is highly prejudicial, and may, in Time, be ruinous of our Intereft in *America;* where befides their Encreafe in new Settlements, and Acquifitions of Country, the Power of the *French* is already very great and formidable.

G 3

The

(102)

The general Good of the Community is ever to take place of that of any particular Perfons; and therefore if the large Tracts of Land in the Hands of any of his Majefty's Subjects, uncultivated, were but fettled, great and infinite would be the Benefit and Advantage to *Great Britain;* for it would not only be an Encouragement to our People to go to our Colonies and Plantations, but encreafe our Seamen and Navigation, and add to the Strength and Riches of this Kingdom.

It could not fail, together with a Law, that no Negroes hereafter fhould be brought up to any Trades, as *Coopers, Carpenters, Bricklayers, Smiths,* and other Artificers; of removing the Caufe, which makes not only Servants, for any Term of Years, but other Perfons, with their Families, fo much more unwilling to go than formerly to our Colonies and Plantations, as, indeed, fo much more chargeable to fend to them.

Befides what I have been recommending, concerning the great Tracts of Land uncultivated, and for the better Peopling our Colonies and Plantations; it is certainly highly incumbent upon the Inhabitants of our *Sugar Iflands* to incite their Legiflatures, (if they defire to preferve and fecure their Eftates, in them either from Invafions or Infurrections) to take their prefent State and Condition into Confideration, and to do every Thing that may be wanting or neceffary to be done, for the Security and Prefervation of themfelves; particularly, as I hinted before, that not any Negro be hereafter brought up to any Trade, or permitted to work in any Cannoe or Wherry : That particular Encouragement be given to all Perfons that fhall go and fettle in them; That every Owner of Negroes be obliged to keep a White Man or Woman, in proportion to a certain Number of Negroes, or pay a certain Sum Weekly, Deficiency; and that Fortreffes wanted be forthwith erected, and thofe already erected be kept in good Repair, and well provided with Arms, and all kind of Ammunition.

As there will probably be a confiderable Sum of Money arifing by the *Deficiency Law,* it may be applied to the better Subfiftance of the Soldiers in Garrifon; to the paying the Paffages of Tradefmen, and other People, that may come to the *Sugar Iflands,* and have not wherewithal to do it themfelves; and to fuch other Ufes as may be thought neceffary; and it may not be amifs that

it

(103)

itmay be provided, that if any PLANTER keep any more White Men or Women than in proportion to his certain Number of Negroes, he shall be allowed for such Number as he keeps more a Premium according to the Deficiency, and be paid for the same by the Receiver and Collector of such Money.

Perhaps it may be safely advanced, that the Charge of keeping a White Man in proportion to a certain Number of Negroes, whether it were Ten or more, would be sufficiently made good to the Planter, in the advanced Price of the Produce of his Plantation, or the Freight of it to *England;* if it were not considered, that the Negroes who are Tradesmen (all Things allowed) would answer to the Planter near as much by working in the Field with the Hoe, as the Charge of the White Tradesman; as also that greater Number of White People would consume a greater Quantity of all kinds of Goods imported, and occasion an Encrease of Settlements, which consequently would lessen the Publick Taxes on the present Inhabitants; which, in some of our Colonies and Plantations, have not only been thought burthensome, but grievous.

Though some of these Things may deserve the Notice of some of our Plantations in their publick Councils; yet it may, perhaps, be objected, that others of them may not be wanted, nor equally necessary in others of them; but, in such Case, the Situation, Largeness of Territory, Number of White People capable to bear Arms, as other Things, are severally to be considered; and even those Plantations which are small should regard their Fortresses being kept in good Repair, and that they have such a Number of White Men in them, capable to bear Arms, as may be able, as well to prevent an Invasion, as repel an Insurrection; which, in my poor Opinion, they cannot well have, whilst there is Liberty allowed for Negroes to be brought up to Trades of all kind, and no *Deficiency-Law* in Force.

I am sensible that what is here represented, will be treated by some of our Planters as romantick; and by others as not possible to be entered upon; and I shall be told, they will cause such a Charge and Expence, that few, if any Plantations, can be able to bear: I shall only say, that as Trade, all manner of Ways, occasions Consumption, bringing in a Resort of Strangers, and an Encreafe

(104)

creafe of People to all Countries where it flourifhes, and
is encouraged; fo, as much as the Number of People
are more in any of our Colonies and Plantations, by fo
much is there expended (if not of its own Growth) of
the Goods and Merchandize of *Great Britain*, and the
greater Quantity of our Woollen and Linen Manufactures, Goods, and Merchandize, Provifions, &c. that
is expended by them, is amply compenfated to them in
the Price and Quicknefs of a Market, or in the Freight
of their Product for *Great Britain*.

Now, as Numbers of People muft necefsarily occafion
a greater Confumption of all kind of Manufactures and
Provifions, fo the greater any Country's Demand for
them is, the greater will be its Trade; and confequently
the greater Number of Merchants who exercife Commerce to it, will render Goods much cheaper than in
Countries where there is not fo great a Confumption,
and always occafion an Encreafe of Shipping, which is
ever attended with the Product of any Country's, being
more in Demand, and felling at a much higher Price,
which muft be the Cafe whilft the Product of it is ven-
dible in any other Countries; but this is fo obvious, and
fo well known, that I need not dwell longer upon it.

I hope that the Time is now come, that the Planters
and Inhabitants of our Colonies and Plantations do perceive and will own, that the Prefervation of their Eftates
therein does moftly depend upon their doing what is fo
necefsary to be done; or fo much wanted for the putting
them on a better Footing, and in a better Condition than
it is feared any of them are upon, or in at this Time;
as well in regard to their Security, as in regard to their
Intereft.

As likewife that they will lay afide the falfe and narrow Notions and Schemes, entertained by too many of
them; fuch as that the Produce of their Plantations will
fell the better, the fewer the Settlements, which induces
them to engrofs great Tracts of Land; or that the laying Duties equal to Prohibitions on all Commodities of
the fame Species with their own Product, is the Way to
fecure a Vent for them; and that the raifing of Money
for the Support of the Government by Taxes on Trade,
or imported Commodities, will eafe their Landed Eftates.

Would they lay afide fuch Notions and Schemes as
thefe, which are all pernicious; and fall upon doing
                                                    fomething

(105)

something among themfelves, *for the Encreafe of People, and better Settlement of their Countries*, not only their own Interefts in them would be the better fecured, but the Intereft of their Mother Country greatly promoted.

In what I have been faying, I have had my Thoughts more particularly at *Jamaica*, the moft valuable Plantation belonging to the Crown, (its Situation confidered) and an Ifland, if fully fettled, that would produce three times the Quantity of *Sugar, Indico, Ginger, Cotton*, &c. it has hitherto done ; and which, if we fhould be difpoffeffed of, we muft never afterwards expect to be formidable by our Naval Force in that Part of the World, as we have been for many Years paft, by Means of that Ifland ; and the Lofs of *Jamaica* will, probably, be followed with the Ruin of our Intereft in *America*.

I hope, in any Thing I have faid, I fhall not be underftood as propofing to level the Property, or rightful Poffeffions of any Perfons, interefted in any of Our Colonies or Plantations, but only to reftrain fuch Methods as have been formerly practifed, of taking up large Tracts of Land, and to oblige the Perfons who have taken them up, or are in Poffeffion of them, by virtue of old Grants, either to fettle or fell them ; fo that it may not be any longer a Bar to the Induftry of others, and that our Colonies and Plantations may be a lafting Revenue to the Crown, an inexhauftible Mine of Treafure to *Great Britain*, and a great Means to multiply Seamen, and increafe our Navigation.

As it is the Bufinefs of the Planters, and Inhabitants of our Colonies and Plantations, to provide againft Invafions and Infurrections, and to regard the Security and Prefervation of their Fortunes in them ; it muft likewife be the Concern and Care of all entrufted with the Adminiftration of the Affairs of this Kingdom, that the Perfons who may be fent to reprefent the Crown be Men of Abilities, Experience, Courage, Temper, and Virtue ; They ought to be endowed with fuch a general Knowledge, as may comprehend the Nature of the Soil where they are ; what Improvements it is capable of, and what Trades will be moft advantageous to it : They fhould be able likewife to look into the Genius of the People they are to govern : They fhould be Men of Difcipline, Sobriety, and Juftice ; for they who are not fo

in

(106)

in their own Perſons, can expect no Order, nor compel others to obey the Laws; a People to whom Riches and Plenty furniſh Matter for Vice and Luxury, ſhould be governed by a ſtrict and ſkilful Hand; which may reform their Manners, and, at the ſame Time, both promote and direct their Induſtry.

The Welfare of our Colonies and Plantations will very much depend upon the Conduct and Behaviour of ſuch as are ſent to reſide and govern there by the King's Authority: And as that, of all Countries whatſoever, depends upon good Government; ſo, without Doubt, our Colonies and Plantations will flouriſh, if the Inhabitants do all that may be wanting and neceſſary on their Parts towards it; and if they are intruſted to honeſt, diſcreet, and ſkilful Hands, who will let them perceive they enjoy all the Rights and Liberties of *Britains*, though not in *Great Britain*.

It is an allowed Maxim, *That Induſtry has its firſt Foundation in Liberty;* and it is certain, that they who either are Slaves, or perceive their Freedom precarious, can neither ſucceed in Trade, nor meliorate a Country. I will not pretend to determine for or againſt the Opinions I have ſeen of our great Lawyers, whether the People in our Colonies and Plantations have a Right to all the Privileges of *Britiſh Subjects*: But the contrary Notion is too much encouraged, upon which Account it will, peradventure, be a great Security and Encouragement to the induſtrious People in that Part of the World, if a *declaratory Law* were made, that *Britons* have a Right to *all the Laws* of Great Britain, *for the Security of the Subject, while they remain in the Countries under the Dominion of this Kingdom.*

It is abſolutely neceſſary, that the Perſons to whom the Government of the Colonies and Plantations are entruſted, ſhould endeavour to hinder the Growth of all Sort of Vice, as Intemperance and Luxury; for theſe are the Parent of Want; and Want begets in the Minds of Men, Diſobedience and Deſire of Change: They ſhould think it their Duty to promote Virtue, and to encourage Merit of any Kind, and to give it their helping Hand: They ſhould diſcountenance Immoralities of all Sorts, and make them a Bar to any Preferments or Honours: They ſhould look into the Lives of the Clergy, and ſee that no Doctrines are preached, nor Principles advanced,

(107)

advanced, that are deſtructive to the very Fundamentals
of Religion itſelf, the Rights and Liberties of *Engliſh-
men*, and the Settlement of the Crown in the illuſtrious
Houſe of *Hanover*.

They ſhould not enflame, but rather reconcile thoſe
Differences which perhaps may ariſe among People of
ſuch different Perſuaſions, as may be under their Government ; and cultivate in the Minds of the Inhabitants
ſober Living, ſincere Friendſhip, general Obſervance of
the Devotion each profeſſes, Charity, Meekneſs, and
Piety, eſpecially among thoſe who are truſted to guide
the Conſciences of others; in fine, they ſhould endeavour, that the young Men of better Rank and Fortune,
be early ſeaſoned with a Love of *Great Britain*, their
Mother Country ; that when they return hither with
the Riches, the Induſtry of their Parents has acquired,
they may become good Patriots here, and uſeful Members
of the Commonwealth.

Having thus pointed at ſome Things deſerving the Conſideration as well as the Public Councils, in our Colonies
and Plantations, as of the Government here ; and not only
ſhowed what an immenſe Profit they are to this Kingdom,
but endeavoured at ſhowing how much more profitable
they might be to it, I think it incumbent upon me, as
the Labour of Negroes is the principal Foundation of
our Riches from the Plantations, to ſpeak here of our
Trade to *Africa;* which is a Trade of the greateſt Value
to this Kingdom, if we conſider the Number of Ships annually employed in it, the great Export of our Manufactures, and other Goods to that Coaſt, and the Value
of the Product of our Plantations, annually ſent to
Great Britain.

It is ſuch a Trade as requires our greateſt Care, and
tendereſt Regard, how it may be moſt effectually ſecured and preſerved to this Kingdom ; and for my own
Part, I ſhould be glad to ſee a Scheme from that Body
of Men, who have laboured to exclude all his Majeſty's
Subjects but themſelves, from trading to *Africa*, how
THEY propoſe to exclude or prevent the Subjects of
any other Nation.

For is not the Coaſt of *Africa* of very large Extent, at
leaſt a thouſand Leagues, and the Company's Settlements
as other Nations, but on a ſmaller Part of it ? Is the
Trade in general, any Ways dependant on the Settlements ?

(108)

ments? Or have not the *Turkey* Company the same Reafon to claim the Property of all the Lands of the *Grand Seignior*, becaufe they have Factories and Houfes in *Turkey*, as the *African* Company to claim a Property of all the Lands of the Princes in *Africa*, to whom they pay Rent for the Ground whereupon their Factories ftand? If the Company have a Property to the fole Trade of *Africa*, why do all other Nations trade to the *Places, as well where their Factories are, as where they are not?*

As the REVOLUTION (brought about by the Hand of GOD, through his Inftrument, King *William* the Third, of *glorious and immortal Memory*,) delivered the People of *Great Britain* from Popery and Slavery; fo it gave them that which is infeparable to their being Free-men, a *Liberty of trading to any Part of the known World*; to which they were not prohibited, by their own Con-fent; that is, by the joint Act of King, Lords, and Commons, in Parliament affembled.

For notwithftanding before the REVOLUTION, *Englifhmen* were not prohibited trading to any Part of the World; as they now ftand to the *Eaft Indies*, and *South Seas*, by Act of Parliament, yet they were terri-fied, and molefted in their Trade, both to the *Eaft Indies*, and *Africa*; and durft not trade fo freely, as it had been for the Intereft of the Nation they fhould have done, for Fear of having their Ships and Effects feized by, and confifcated to the Ufe of Perfons, who had ob-tained Grants from the Crown of thefe Trades folely to themfelves; who were not only affifted in doing this by our own Princes, in their lending them their Ships of War to cruize for Interlopers, (as they were called) but by our Judges in *Weftminfter-Hall*: But fince the hap-py Revolution, they were neither affifted by King *William* in making of Seizures, nor did they find they had any Power by Law, to confifcate any Interlopers Ships and Effects to their own Ufes; when the Courts of Juftice came to be placed in the Hands of Men of Integrity and Uprightnefs, thefe Men paid dear for any Confifcation they made.

. Thereupon both Companies applied themfelves to the Crown and Parliament; and the *African* Company, with whom I have here only to do, petitioned the Houfe of Commons, and endeavoured to obtain an *Act of Par-,* liament

(109)

liament, to exclude all other Perfons from trading to *Africa;* at laſt, after a Diſpute of ſome Years, between the Royal *African* Company, and the Merchants trading to our Colonies and Plantations. a Law paſſed, the ninth and tenth *Guhelmi tertii.* Entitled, *An Act to ſettle the Trade to* Africa; which was to have Countinuance for thirteen Years, and from thence to the End of the next *Seſſion of Parliament,* whereby, it was enacted, *That it ſhould and might be lawful to and for any of the Subjects of his Majeſty's Realms of* England, *as well as the ſaid Company, to trade from* England, *or any of his Majeſty's Plantations and Colonies in* America, *to the Coaſt of* Africa, *between Cape* Blanco *and Cape* Mount, *'ṫṫ anſwering and paying a* ' *Duty of* 10 per Cent. *&c.* ' That all Perfons trading ' to the Coaſt of *Afric,* as aforeſaid, and paying the ' Duties by this Act impoſed, ſhall have the ſame Pro- ' tection, Security, and Defence, for their Perfons, ' Ships, and Goods, by, from, and in all the ſaid Forts ' and Caſtles, and the like Freedom and Security for ' their Negotiation and Trade, to all Intents and Pur- ' poſes whatſoever, as the ſaid Companies, their ' Agents, Factors, and Aſſigns, and their Ships and ' Goods have, may, or ſhall have.

' And that all and every Perfon and Perfons trading ' to *Africa,* and paying the Duties as aforeſaid, may, ' and are hereby impowered, at their own Charge to ' ſettle Factories on any Part of *Africa,* within the Li- ' mits aforeſaid, according as they ſhall judge neceſſary, ' and covenient for the carrying on their Trade, without ' any Lets, Hindrance, or Moleſtation from the ſaid ' Company, their Agents, Factors, or Aſſigns. And ' that all Perfons not Members of the ſaid Company ſo ' trading and paying the Duties as aforeſaid, ſhall, to- ' gether with their Ships and Goods, be free from all Mo- ' leſtation, Hindrances, Reſtraints, Arreſts, Seizures, ' Penalties, or other Impoſitions whatſoever from the, ' ſaid Company, their Agents, Factors or Aſſigns, for ' or by Reaſon of their ſo trading, any Uſage or Cuſtom ' to the contrary in any wiſe notwithſtanding.'

Note, by this Act the Company as well as other Per- ſons were obliged to pay the Duty of 10 *per Cent.* on all Goods exported to *Africa,* which was applied to main- tain, ſupport, and defend all ſuch Forts and Caſtles as

were

(110)

were erected for the Prefervation, Improvement, and well carrying on that Trade.

In the Year 1708, the *African* Company applied again to the Crown and Parliament, though the Act mentioned was in Force till *July* 1713, and pray for an exclufive Trade to *Africa*. That Seffions the Houfe of Commons took the Difpute between them and the fepa-rate Traders, (as then called,) into Confideration; and it appeared to the Houfe, upon Examination, that the *African* Company under an exclufive Trade in the Time of Peace, between 1680 and 1689, employed Two hun-dred and fifty-nine Ships, being about twenty-eight Ships *per Annum*: and delivered into the Plantations, 46,396 Negroes, being 5155 *per Annum*.

That the Negroes imported after the Trade was laid open, into *Jamaica, Barbadoes,* and *Antegua*, only amount-ed to 42000 for three Years of Peace, which is near as many Negroes delivered to thofe three Iflands only in three Years under an open Trade, as there were in nine Years of Peace by the Company, into all the Plantations when exclufive.

That at the Time of the Examination, though we were in War, there were employed in this Trade above a hundred Ships capable of carrying 25,000 Negroes a Year into the Plantations belonging to the feparate Traders; which demonftrated that the Trade was above four Times as much encreafed as when it was exclufive, though that was a Time of Peace;—And that the Ex-port of the Manufactures, of Coarfe *perfects,* to that Coaft, had been encreafed from 4000 to 70,000 Pieces *per Annum*.

Thefe were fome of the Reafons that induced the Houfe of Commons to refolve, *That the Trade to* Africa *ought to be free and open to all her Majefty's Subjects of* Great Britain *and the Plantations*.

Notwithftanding this Refolution, the Company brought this Difpute into the Houfe feveral Seffions afterwards, and when under Confideration, it has been refolved as above, in different Houfes of Commons; and the laft Time it came before one, in Purfuance of the faid Re-folution, a Bill was paffed and fent to the Lords Houfe, where it was read twice, and committed, entitled, *A Bill for eftablifhing the Trade to* Africk *in a regulated Com-pany;* whereby it was intended to be enacted, ' That it
' fhould

(111)

' fhould and might be lawful to and for all and every
' the Subjects of *Great Britain*, and the Plantations
' thereunto belonging, to trade to any Part or Place of
' *Africa*, between *Cape Blanco* and the *Cape of Good*
' *Hope*, in fuch Goods and in fuch Quantities as he or
' they fhould think fit, paying fuch Duties as the Com-
' pany by that Act to be eftablifhed, fhould be impow-
' ered to lay on the faid Trade.

' That her Majefty by her Charter, might impower
' the faid regulated Company fo to be eftablifhed, to
' make By-Laws, Rules, and Ordinances, for the good
' Government of the faid Trade, and grant fuch other
' Powers as might be neceffary for carrying on and en-
' larging the faid Trade, and for laying and collecting a
' Duty for the Support thereof; but fo as fuch Corpo-
' ration fhall not be thereby impowered to trade in one
' joint Stock, exclufive of any of her Majefty's Subjects,
' or to oblige any of the Members of fuch Corporation,
' to trade in any other Manner than by the faid Act
' were impowered to do.

' That the Governor and Company hereby eftablifhed,
' may, by their By-Laws, appoint the Manner for the
' Payment of the faid Duties in fuch Time and Form as
' fhall be thought moft convenient, and as the Neceffity
' of the faid Company and the Benefit of the faid
' Trade fhall require, provided no fuch By-Laws, Or-
' dinances, or Rules, fhall any Way extend to the li-
' miting what Sort or Quantity of Goods any Perfon
' who is free of the faid Company fhall export to *Africa*,
' or what he fhall bring from thence, nor of whom or
' for what he fhall buy or fell the fame; it being the
' Intent of this Act; that every Member of the faid
' Company fhall be left free in thofe Matters, that a
' Monopoly may be avoided, and the Exportation of the
' Woollen, and other Manufactures of this Kingdom
' may be encreafed.'

Thefe are the Steps that have been taken in Relation
to the Trade to *Africa*, fo very advantageous to *Great
Britain*, by conducing fo much to the Support of our
Tobacco Colonies, and Sugar Plantations; and fince fo
great a Part of our foreign Trade arifeth from them,
they ought undoubtedly to have all due Encouragement,
and to be fupplied at the moft eafy and reafonable Rates
with Negroes.

Experience,

(112)

Experience, the fureſt Guide we can follow in Matter of Trade, has demonſtrably taught us, that this
Trade has not been carried on moſt to the Advantagè
of this Kingdom by a Company with a joint Stock. But
that ſince it has been free and open, it has greatly encreaſed; the Plantations have been much better ſupplied
with Negroes, aud the Advantages to the Kingdom have
been infinitely greater.

'Tis undoubtedly true, that when the Company had
the ſole Trade almoſt to themſelves, that they did not
ſupply the Plantations with ſuch a Plenty of Negroes as
was requiſite; and that as they forced them to accept
of ſuch a Sort as they thought fit to bring; ſo they put
their own Price upon the Product of the Plantations.
If it ſhall be alledged, that the *African* Company, when
excluſive, at any Time ſold choice Negroes, from 14 to
18 *l. per* Head, it may be remembered, that as they ſet their
own Price on the Product of the Plantations, ſo Sugar did
not ſell in any of them for half the Price, it has done for many
Years paſt, or ſince the Trade to *Africa* was laid open.

It muſt certainly be prudent, in any Trade, Manufacture, or Buſineſs, to render the firſt Materials as
cheap as poſſible; Negroes are the firſt and moſt neceſſary Materials for planting; from whence it follows, that
all Meaſures ſhould be taken that may produce ſuch a
Plenty of them, as may be an Encouragement to the
induſtrious Planter.

Every People, the more they are innured to Trade,
and encreaſed in it, the better they come to an Under-
ſtanding of their Intereſt in their Dealings; and therefore it cannot well be a Wonder, if Negroes ſhould be
dearer than ſome Years before the Trade was laid open.

But that Negroes have been of late Years, both
ſcarcer and dearer to us than formerly, may be accounted
for, as well from our own Demand of them, to ſupply
the Plantations, and the Demand of the *Spaniards,*
French, and *Portugueſe,* the two laſt much greater for
ten Years paſt, than ever before, as from laying the
Trade to *Africa* open; and all Things, both in Reſpect
to the Merchant and Planter conſidered, Negroes are
not near ſo dear on the Coaſt of *Africa*, as has been ſuggeſted by the Patrons of an excluſive Company, nay, not
much dearer, than when we had one eſtabliſhed, tho'
only by Virtue of the Prerogative Royal.

Neither

(113)

Neither we, nor any other Nation of *Europe*, are Owners of any Soil on the Coast of *Africa*; and such as have Forts and Castles thereon, dare not stir beyond the Reach of their Guns; and as we are enabled by our Manufactures and Goods of all Kind to trade the cheapest and most advantageously to *Africa*, and have a superior Strength to any Nation to protect our Trade on that Coast and elsewhere; I am in no Manner of Fear that any of our Neighbours can either rival us in it, or beat us out of it; but, on the contrary, am of Opinion, that we shall ever have the Advantage of all Nations in Trade to the Coast of *Africa*, if we do not confine it to an exclusive Company.

In treating of our Colonies and Plantations, their Product and Trade, I have discoursed on the *African* Trade, by Reason it is the Spring and Parent whence the others flow, and are dependent, and therefore properly fell in this Division, the Connexion being such as would not have been so clear in a separate Discourse.

I have not in these Considerations on our Plantation Trade, taken any Notice of *Bermudas* and *Providence*, or the *Bahama Islands*, as they are of little or no Consideration for their Produce, or otherwise useful to us, or necessary to be maintained by us, than as they may become dangerous to our Trade and Navigation in an Enemy's Hand, or as they may be a Receptacle for our Ships, and a Service to us, in annoying and interrupting the Trade of either the *French* or *Spaniards*, in that Part of the World.

Nor have I considered *Newfoundland* under this Head, the Fishery whereof is of very great Concern to us, both to preserve and encourage; and in which we had, about a hundred Years ago, upwards of 200 Sail of Ships annually employed, when we furnished all *Europe* with Fish, how few Ships soever we may now employ in this Trade.

F I N I S.

EDITORIAL NOTES

[Richard Eburne], A Plaine Path-Way to Plantations (1624)

p. 8, ll. 35–6: The Magold and the Sun: untraced.

p. 9, l. 9: *D. Keckerman*: Bartholomeus Keckerman (1571–1609), Calvinist theologian, polymath systematizer and author of numerous books on theology, politics and natural sciences. See J. S. Freedman, 'The Career and Writings of Bartholomew Keckermann (d. 1609)', *Proceedings of the American Philosophical Society*, 141:3 (September, 1997), pp. 305–64.

p. 20, ll. 5–6: Indigena ... Terrigene: indigena (Latin), meaning native peoples, or terrigena (Latin), meaning earth-born creature.

p. 38, l. 9: Henrie *the sixth*: Henry VI (1421–71), King of England and France from 1422 to 1461 and 1470 to 1471. In 1450 his troops lost the provinces of Normandy and Aquitaine, leaving Calais as the only English-held territory in France.

Balthasar Gerbier, A Sommary Description (1660)

p. 46, l. 31: *Charibdiens*: probably Caribbeans. The original Indian inhabitants were the Arawaks and Caribs.

p. 47, l. 8: *Texell*: Texel is the largest and most populated of the Friesian Islands in the Netherlands.

p. 47, l. 14: *Sir Balthazar Gerber*: see the headnote to this text, pp. 43–4 above.

p. 47, l. 26: *el Dorado* ... Manua: El Dorado, 'the gilded one' in Spanish, is a legendary city of gold that was sought by many early explorers of the Americas. The Manua islands are located in the south-western Pacific Ocean, forming part of American Samoa.

p. 47, l. 28: *Otto Keye*: Otto Keye, Dutch writer, traveller and author of *Onderscheyt Tusschen Koude en Warme Landen* (1659).

p. 48, l. 24: *Don Diego d'Ordas*, Captayn to *Cortez*: Diego de Ordás (1480–1532), Spanish conquistador who took part in the conquest of Mexico in the company of Hernàn Cortés (1485–1587).

p. 48, l. 26: *Gaspar de Sylva*, and *Jean Gonzales*: Gaspar de Sylva left Teneriffe with his two brothers and 200 men to aid Diego de Ordás. They ended their explorations in Trinidad, where they all died. Juan Gonsalves set sail from Trinidad to discover Guiana.

p. 48, ll. 27–9: *Philip d'Uren* ... *Pedro d'Ossima*: Geronimo d'Ortal was lieutentant to Deigo de Ordas and Govenor of Puerto Rico 1537–45. Ximenes may be Ximenes de Cisneros

(1436–1517), Spanish priest, statesman, regent and grand inquisitor. All these men were conquistadors and explorers mostly looking for El Dorado.

p. 48, l. 31: Duke of Buckingham: George Villiers, first Duke of Buckingham (1592–1628), courtier and favourite of James I. In 1623 Buckingham accompanied Charles I, when he was the Prince of Wales, to Madrid to negotiate a marriage to the Infanta Maria. Negotiations failed and Buckingham subsequently led an unsuccessful ambush on the Spanish silver fleet from Mexico.

p. 52, l. 14: *Hamack*: i.e. hammock.

p. 52, ll. 37–8: *Jean Claasen Langendijck ... Cajana*: Cajana is in Surinam. The first Europeans to reach Surinam were Dutch traders, and the first attempts to settle there occurred in the 1630s.

p. 55, l. 38: *St. Vincent*: St Vincent, a volcanic island in the Caribbean, is the largest island in the Grenadines chain. The island was claimed by both the English and the French.

p. 64, l. 37: *Cap Orannie*: probably referring to Orania in present-day Algeria.

p. 64, l. 38: *River Wiapoca*: a river in present day Brazil, colonized first by the Dutch in the early seventeenth century.

An Answer of the Company of Royal Adventurers of England Trading into Africa (1667)

p. 71, ll. 15–16: *Sir* Paul Painter ... *and* Thomas Knights: Sir Ferdinando Gorges (1565–1647) was an early English colonial entrepreneur in North America and founder of the Province of Maine in 1622. Gorges and Benjamin Skutt are recorded as Trustees of the New Royal African Company in 1672.

p. 73, ll. 27–8: Company *of* Adventurers: the Company of Adventurers of London, also called the Guinea Company, trading to the ports of Africa. It was founded in 1618 and its main activity was slave trading with Guinea and Sierra Leone. Its thirty-one-year monopoly on West African imports to England was contested but was upheld by the King as the Company maintained the English forts in the region.

p. 77, l. 8: East India Company: the East India Company was based in London and received its Royal charter from Elizabeth I in 1600. Initially it was called the Governor and Company of Merchants of London Trading into the East Indies.

p. 80, ll. 11–12: *Surrender of* St Christophers: St Kitts, formerly known as St Christophers, is an island in the West Indies. The first permanent European settlement was an English colony in 1623, followed by a French colony in 1625. The British and French briefly united to massacre the indigenous Indians, who were in turn planning to massacre them. The island was then partitioned, with the English in the middle and the French on either end. Over the following century the island fluctuated between English and French control. The island originally produced tobacco, but changed to sugar cane after 1640 due to competition from the colony of Virgina. The English had to surrender St Christophers and Surinam after a Dutch attack in 1667.

p. 81, l. 6: Dutch West-India Company: The Dutch West India Company operated between 1621 and 1793. It had trading posts on the Gold Coast and Angola, shipping African slaves to the Antilles and Surinam.

p. 85, l. 36: Guiney *Company*: see note to p. 73, ll. 27–8, above.

p. 87, l. 1: *L.* Willoughby: Francis, Lord Willoughby (1613–66). Following the establishment of the Commonwealth in England, Willoughby sailed for Barbados, arriving in

May 1650. Charles II had appointed him Governor and Willoughby attempted to get the settlers to accept the authority of the King. However, in 1651 a Commonwealth fleet commanded by Sir George Ayscue (*c.* 1616–72) arrived and persuaded the settlers to defect to parliament. After the Restoration Willoughby regained the governorship and remained there until his death.

News from New-England (1676)

p. 95, l. 10: Plymouth *Company*: the Virgina Company of Plymouth, which was given a charter by James I in 1608 and which was involved in the Massachusetts Bay colony. For an account of the native American attacks on the Massachusetts and Plymouth Bay settlements, see J. D. Drake, *King Philip's War in New England, 1675–1676* (Amherst, MA: University of Massachusetts Press, 1999).

p. 95, l. 14: Sachems: The Massachusetts tribes called their leaders 'sachems'. This is a reference to the Narrangasett tribe, which in 1675 allied itself with King Philip and the Wampanoag to fight the English colonists.

p. 98, l. 7: Coxcord: Concord on the banks of the Merrimack River in New Hampshire.

p. 99, l. 5: Northampton: Northampton in Massachusetts.

p. 99, l. 9: Warwick: Warwick in Massachusetts.

Arthur Dobbs, An Essay on the Trade and Improvement of Ireland (1729–31)

p. 107, ll. 10–11: Restoration *of King* Charles *the IId*: Charles II (1630–85), King of England, Scotland and Ireland. Following the execution of Charles I in 1649, Charles II remained in exile until the collapse of the Commonwealth following the death of Oliver Cromwell. He returned to England on 25 May 1660 and was crowned at Westminster Abbey on 23 April 1661.

p. 107, ll. 16–17: *the Reduction of* Ireland: Following the Glorious Revolution and the assumption of the throne by William III and Mary II, the majority of the Irish population sided with the deposed James II on religious grounds. This led to a series of uprisings and battles until William's defeat of James at the Battle of the Boyne in 1690. There then followed a period of land confiscations and reallocations to establish a Protestant ascendancy.

p. 108, l. 11: French Refugees: The Edict of Nantes was issued in 1598 by Henry IV of France to grant the Calvinist Protestants (Huguenots) substantial civil and church rights. Louis XIV revoked the edict in 1685, when Protestantism was made illegal. This led to an exodus, many of them skilled tradesmen, to the surrounding Protestant countries.

p. 108, l. 14: *Peace of* Reswyck: The Treaty of Ryswyck was signed by France, England, Spain, the Netherlands and the German principalities between 20 September and 30 October 1697.

p. 108, l. 33: Edict of *Nantz*: see note to p. 108, l. 11, above.

p. 113, l. 12: Sir *Josias Child*: Sir Josiah Child (1630–99), Governor of the East India Company. See the headnote to Josiah Child, Charles Davenant and William Wood, *Select Dissertations on Colonies and Plantations* (1775), pp. 253–4 above.

p. 117, l. 1: *Rakes, Sharpers, Gamesters*: referring to gamblers and other illicit people appearing in coffee houses at this time.

p. 125, l. 35: *Lady Day*: Lady Day is the Feast of the Annunciation and falls on 25 March. Until 1752 and the adoption of the Gregorian calendar it marked the start of the new year.

Representation of the Board of Trade Relating to ... his Majesty's Plantations in America (1733–4)

p. 141, ll. 18–19: *Accession of His late Majesty to the Throne*: George I (1660–1727), King of Great Britain and Ireland from 1714 until his death. He was succeeded by his son George II (1683–1760).

p. 146, l. 44: *Colonel* Vetch: William Vetch (1668–1732), Governor of Nova Scotia until 1715. Nova Scotia or Acadia, including New Brunswick, was conquered by the force under General Nicholson and Colonel Vetch (1668–1732) in 1710.

p. 147, ll. 4–5: *Colonel* Philipps: Richard Phillips (1661–1751) became Governor of Nova Scotia in 1717, and remained in post until 1749.

p. 147, l. 15: *Colonel* Shute: Samuel Shute (1662–1742), Governor of the Massachusetts Bay colony from 1716 until 1723.

p. 147, l. 18: *Mr* Belcher: Jonathan Belcher (1682–1757), Governor of Massachusetts and New Hampshire from 1730 until 1741 and Governor of New Jersey from 1746 until his death.

p. 148, l. 22: Falmouth *in* Casco Bay: situated in Maine in the present-day United States of America.

p. 148, l. 36: *Colonel* Dunbar: David Dunbar, Surveyor General for Nova Scotia.

p. 149, l. 25: *General* Hunter: Robert Hunter (1664–1734), Governor of New York and New Jersey from 1710 to 1720.

p. 149, l. 30: *Mr*. Rip van Dam: Rip Van Dam (*c.* 1662–1736), colonial Governor, born in Albany, New York. He became a prominent merchant in the West India trade, resisted Lord Bellomont's restrictions on commerce, and, as a consequence of the seizure of some of his vessels for supposed infraction of the custom laws, engaged in politics. He served on the council in New York from 1699 as its senior member and president and acted as Governor from the death of John Montgomery on 1 July 1731 until the arrival of his successor, William Cosby, on 1 August 1732.

p. 150, l. 1: *Colonel* Hart: John Hart served as Royal Governor for Maryland from 1714 to 1715 and continued as proprietary Governor from 1715 to 1720.

p. 150, l. 31: *Major* Gooch: Sir William Gooch, first Baronet (1681–1751), acted as Governor of Virginia from 1721 until 1749 although his official title was Royal Lieutenant Governor, as the nominal Governor remained in England.

p. 154, l. 17: *Royal* African *Company*: The Royal African Company was founded in 1672 and until 1698 enjoyed a monopoly on the African slave trade. The Company continued in the slave trade until 1731, when it switched its activities to ivory and gold dust. It was dissolved in 1752 to be succeeded by the African Company.

p. 154, ll. 28–9: *Treaty of Neutrality ... 1686*: the treaty of neutrality in America between England and France was concluded in November 1686 in London.

p. 156, ll. 28–32: *WESTMORELAND ... DOCMINIQUE*: Thomas Fane, sixth Earl of Westmorland (1683–1736), served as a commissioner on the Council of Trade and Plantations from 1719 until 1730. Martin Bladen (1680–1746) was an army officer and politician. Orlando Bridgeman is most likely Sir Orlando Bridgeman, second Baronet (*c.* 1670–

1738), who was nominated Governor of Barbados in 1737 but was found drowned in the Thames before leaving to take up his position. Sir Archer Croft, second Baronet (1684–1753). Paul Docminique was an MP who was listed as a commissioner on the Council of Trade and Plantations from 1714 until 1730.

[Malachy Postlethwayt], The African Trade, the Great Pillar and Support of the British Plantation Trade in America (1745)

p. 164, l. 19: Memorial: *Memorials presented, by the Deputies of the Council of Trade in France, to the Royal Council, in 1701 ... Concerning the Commerce of that Nation to their American Islands, Guinea, the Levant, Spain, England, Holland, and the North ... In French and English* (London, 1737).

p. 168, l. 19: *The* French Senegal Company: The Royal Company of Senegal was active from around 1680. It extended French influence far into the interior of Africa, increased the export of slaves, ivory and gum arabic, and encouraged with little success the cultivation of cotton and cacao. It was dismantled as the consequence of the Seven Years War (1756–63), when Great Britain captured all the French posts in Senegal. See A. Delcourt, *La France et Les Etablissements Français au Senegal entre 1713 et 1763* (Dakar: Mémoires Ifan, 1952).

p. 180, l. 3: Assiento: the famous monopoly on the sale of slaves to Spanish colonies, regulating the so-called triangular trade between Europe, the West Coast of Africa and the Americas.

p. 180, l. 11: *Peace of* Utrecht: A number of peace agreements were signed in Utrecht in 1713 between the major powers of Europe. In addition a commercial agreement was made between France and England which was later attacked, especially by proponents of the Whig party, who described it as too generous towards French trade interests.

p. 186, footnote, ll. 1–2: *A Proposal ... Roberts, 1742*: probably *The Profit and Loss of Great Britain in the Present War with Spain: from July 1739, to July 1741, in a Letter to a Friend* (London: J. Roberts, 1741).

p. 196, l. 12: *Island of* Goree: Île de Gorée is an island of Dakar, Senegal. It was one of the principal factories of the slave trade.

p. 196, l. 26: Cape Palmas *to* Cape Lopez: Cape Palmas is an island belonging to Liberia and Cap López is a peninsula on the coast of west-central Africa, in the country of Gabon. The Gulf of Guinea extends westward from Cap López, near the Equator, to Cape Palmas.

p. 196, l. 28: Loango: a slave port in present-day Congo.

The Case of the Importation of Bar-Iron from our own Colonies of North America (1756)

p. 211, ll. 7–8: *Law for importing Bar-Iron* Duty-free *into the Port of* London: 23 Geo. II. c. 29: *A Bill, intituled, An Act to encourage the importation of pig and bar iron from his Majesty's colonies in America; and to prevent the erection of any mill or other engine for slitting or rolling of iron ... or any furnace for making steel in any of the said colonies* (13 February 1750).

p. 215, l. 13: Orgroons: so-called 'Öregrund iron', shipped from Öregrund, a small harbour town in middle Sweden, and manufactured in the Bergslagen region of Sweden.

p. 226, l. 29: Birmingham-Toys: The term toy was used to refer to a vast range of small items both useful and decorative. Birmingham had developed into a centre for the manufacure of these goods, and its metal and smithery industry during the eighteenth and early nineteenth centuries was called the 'toy industry'. For a more detailed definition, see M. Berg, *The Age of Manufactures, 1700–1820: Industry, Innovation and Work in Britain* (London: Routledge, 1994), pp. 264–5.

William Knox, The Interest of the Merchants and Manufacturers of Great-Britain, in the Present Contest with the Colonies (1775)

p. 246, l. 38: *Ceded Islands*: At the end of the Seven Years War, in 1763, the Caribbean islands of Dominica, Grenada, St Vincent and Tobago were formally ceded from French to British control under General Robert Melville.

p. 248, l. 2: *Grenade*: i.e. Grenada.

Josiah Child, Charles Davenant and William Wood, Select Dissertations on Colonies and Plantations (1775)

p. 265, l. 9: Worcester *Fight*: The Battle of Worcester was the last decisive battle in the Civil War. On 3 September 1651 Oliver Cromwell defeated a Royalist army commanded by Charles II and primarily made up of Scottish forces.

p. 265, ll. 42–3: *Captain* Grant ... Observations upon the Bills of Mortality: John Graunt, *Natural and Political Observations mentioned in a following Index, and made upon the Bills of Mortality ... With reference to the Government, Religion, Trade, Growth, Ayre, and Diseases of the Said City* (London, 1662).

p. 267, ll. 34–5: *Expulsion of so many Thousand* Moors: The Moors were Muslims of Arabic descent who had settled in Spain from eighth century. However, their territories were challenged almost immediately and by 1492 the last Muslim ruler had surrendered to Ferdinand and Isabella of Castile and Aragon and the remaining Moors were driven out of Spain.

p. 270, l. 3: *King* Henry *IV. & V*: Henry IV (1367–1413), King of England and France from 1399 until 1413. He was succeded by his son Henry V (1387–1422), who ruled from 1413 until his death. Both reigns were marked by significant military operations: Henry IV experienced a military rebellion in England while Henry V mounted a number of expeditions in France.

p. 274, l. 40: *Severities against the* Quakers: There were a number of laws which enabled the arrest and persecution of Quakers, including The Blasphemy Act, The Conventicle Acts, The Five Mile Act and The Quaker Act.

p. 288, l. 18: *First Discourse*: Josiah Child, *A Discourse of Trade* (London, 1690).

p. 289, ll. 23–4: *Reigns of King* James *and King* Charles *I*: James I (1566–1625), King of England, and King of Scotland as James VI. His ascension to the English throne in 1603 united the two kingdoms. He was succeeded by his son Charles I (1600–49), who was executed by parliament.

p. 292, l. 29: *Breach of the Navigation Act*: The Navigation Acts were a series of laws beginning in 1651 that required all trade with the colonies to be shipped on British vessels. It was a contributory factor to the beginning of the American War of Indepencence.

p. 294, l. 42: *Mr.* Pollexfen: John Pollexfen (1636–1715) was a merchant and economist, author of *A Discourse on Trade and Coyn* (London, 1697). See Volume 4 of this collection, pp. 141–201.

p. 294, footnote, l. 1: *D'Avenant's Works*: Charles Davenant, *The Political and Commercial Works of that Celebrated Writer Charles D'Avevant*, 5 vols (London: R. Horsfield, 1771).

p. 307, l. 34: *Quit-rent*: a levy or land tax usually imposed by the government and used frequently in British colonies.

p. 309, l. 34: *Council of the* Indies *in* Spain: the council which controlled Spain's colonial empire on behalf of the king from 1524 until 1834, and was responsible for government, administration, justice, taxes, war and religious issues. It nominated governors and other high office-holders in the colonial administrations, and could also propose new laws.

p. 313, l. 27: *St.* Stephen's *Chapel*: St Stephen's Chapel in the Palace of Westminster had become the parliamentary debating chamber of the House of Commons. It was largely lost in the fire of 1834.

p. 317, l. 42: Amphictiones: religious and political federations in ancient Greece, the best known of which is the Amphictiones of Delphi.

p. 319, l. 39: Themistocles: Themistocles (*c.* 524–459 BC), leader of the Athenian democracy during the Persian Wars.

p. 324, l. 15: Homer: Homer is supposed to be the author of the ancient Greek poems the Iliad and the Odyssey.

p. 336, ll. 28–33: Oliver ... Treasurer Southampton: all notable statesmen of France, England, Holland and Spain.

p. 336, l. 30–p. 337, l. 1: Pericles ... Catos: ancient Greek and Roman statesmen.

p. 337, l. 5: Sylla ... Caesar: ancient Roman generals and politicians whose actions ended the Roman Republic in favour of a military empire.

p. 337, l. 10: Scipios: one of the ancient Roman families of political importance during the time of the Republic. Publius Cornelius Scipio (236–183 BC) was a general in the second Punic War and statesman of the Roman Republic. He is best known for defeating Hannibal of Carthage, a feat that earned him the agnomen Africanus.

p. 337, l. 11: Aristides: Athenian soldier and one of the ten commanders at the Battle of Marathon.

p. 337, l. 14: Alcibiades ... Demades: Alcibiades was a military commander and statesman who changed allegiances several times during the Peloponnesian War. Demosthenes was a prominent Athenian statesman and orator who led resistance to Macedonian expansion in the fourth century BC. When this proved impossible, Demosthenes bribed Demades (*c.* 380–318 BC), an Athenian orator and demagogue, to ask Philip of Macedon to save his life.

p. 337, l. 21: Solon: Solon was an Athenian statesman who is credited with founding Athenian democracy.

p. 337, l. 29: Pisistratus: Peisistratos or Peisistratus was a Greek statesman who became the tyrant of Athens after a coup and ruled intermittently between 561 and 528 BC. He gave his name to several Greek kings in the sixth and fifth centuries BC.

p. 338, ll. 24–6: Antipater ... *Port of* Munichia: Antipater was general to Philip of Macedon and Alexander the Great. Munichia is the ancient name for the port of Piraeus, the main port of Athens, known today as Kastella.

p. 341, l. 6: Dion: a Syracusan statesman and follower of Plato who went on to become the tyrant of Syracuse in Sicily. He led a popular rebellion against the tyrant Dionysus and subsequently replaced him.

p. 341, l. 35: Machiavel: Niccolò di Bernardo dei Machiavelli (1469–1527), Italian dipolmat and philosopher. His two most significant works, *The Prince* and *Discourse on the First Ten Books of Titus Livy*, celebrate real politics and the ideals of republicanism respectively.

p. 342, l. 20: Livy: Titus Livius, known as Livy, Roman historian and author of a monumental history of Rome, *Ab Urbe Condita*. Originally composed of 142 books, only 35 have survived.

p. 348, ll. 15–16: *King* Charles *the First ... the Second*: see note to p. 107, ll. 10–11, above.

p. 348, l. 19: *Hans Towns*: towns which were members of the Hanseatic League (from the German Hanse, 'association'), which was founded in the late medieval period by northern German towns and merchant communities to protect their trading interests. Over 150 towns were at some point included in the League.

p. 360, l. 12: *Mr* Locke's Essays: John Locke (1632–1704), philosopher and first of the English empiricists. His *Essay concerning the True Original, Extent and End of Civil Government* was published in 1694.

p. 369, ll. 5–6: Act to settle the Trade to *Africa*: see note to p. 154, l. 17, above.

For Product Safety Concerns and Information please contact our EU
representative GPSR@taylorandfrancis.com Taylor & Francis Verlag GmbH,
Kaufingerstraße 24, 80331 München, Germany

Printed and bound by CPI Group (UK) Ltd, Croydon, CR0 4YY

08/05/2025

01864492-0001